Arabian Romantic

Letter from the General Editor

The Library of Arabic Literature makes available Arabic editions and English translations of significant works of Arabic literature, with an emphasis on the seventh to nineteenth centuries. The Library of Arabic Literature thus includes texts from the pre-Islamic era to the cusp of the modern period, and encompasses a wide range of genres, including poetry, poetics, fiction, religion, philosophy, law, science, travel writing, history, and historiography.

Books in the series are edited and translated by internationally recognized scholars. They are published as hardcovers in parallel-text format with Arabic and English on facing pages, as English-only paperbacks, and as downloadable Arabic editions. For some texts, the series also publishes separate scholarly editions with full critical apparatus.

The Library encourages scholars to produce authoritative Arabic editions, accompanied by modern, lucid English translations, with the ultimate goal of introducing Arabic's rich literary heritage to a general audience of readers as well as to scholars and students.

The Library of Arabic Literature is supported by a grant from the New York University Abu Dhabi Institute and is published by NYU Press.

Philip F. Kennedy
General Editor, Library of Arabic Literature

ديوان

عبد الله بن سبيّل

LIBRARY OF
المكتبة
ARABIC
العربية
LITERATURE

Arabian Romantic

Poems on Bedouin Life and Love

ʿAbdallāh ibn Sbayyil

Edited and translated by
Marcel Kurpershoek

Reviewed by
Saad Sowayan

Volume editors
Clive Holes
Philip F. Kennedy

NEW YORK UNIVERSITY PRESS
New York

NEW YORK UNIVERSITY PRESS
New York

Library of Congress Cataloging-in-Publication Data

Names: Ibn Subayyil, ʿAbd Allāh, approximately 1853-1933, author. | Kurpershoek, P. M. editor translator. | Ibn Subayyil, ʿAbd Allāh, approximately 1853-d. 1933. Poems. Selections. English. | Ibn Subayyil, ʿAbd Allāh, approximately 1853-d. 1933. Poems. Selections.
Title: Arabian romantic : poems on bedouin life and love / ʿAbdallah ibn Sbayyil ; edited and translated by Marcel Kurpershoek.
Description: New York : New York University Press, 2018. | Includes bibliographical references and index.
Identifiers: LCCN 2018012635| ISBN 9781479837663 (hardcover : alk. paper) | ISBN 9781479845415 (e-book)
Classification: LCC PJ7836.S8 A2 2018 | DDC 892.7/16--dc23 LC record available at https://lccn.loc.gov/2018012635

New York University Press books are printed on acid-free paper, and their binding materials are chosen for strength and durability.

Series design by Titus Nemeth.

Typeset in Tasmeem, using DecoType Naskh and Emiri.

Typesetting and digitization by Stuart Brown.

Manufactured in the United States of America
c10 9 8 7 6 5 4 3 2 1

Table of Contents

To my daughters Danielle, Eline, and Sophie

Introduction

In Najd, the central part of Arabia, and adjacent areas, the name Ibn Sbayyil evokes images of Bedouin romance. As the headman of the small town of Nifī, he was enamored of the sight of Bedouin beauties who walked in the market street during the summer months, when their tribes were encamped at the wells just outside town. He marvels in verse at their stunning looks and casual demeanor as they chat with each other and with shopkeepers like himself. Unspoken, but implicit in his poetry, is the contrast with the village women who mostly stayed behind the walls of their adobe houses. They ventured out infrequently, wrapped head to toe in black and adhering strictly to a code that forbade them from speaking to men outside their group of relatives. This reflects the traditional difference in Najdī society between nomadic Bedouin (*baduw*) and sedentary parts of the population (*ḥaḍar*), or those who lived in "houses made of hair," i.e., tents made of cloth woven from goat hair, and those living in "houses made of mud." Though both types of housing have gone out of fashion in Saudi Arabia, the binary of Bedouin versus villager is a social archetype that even today remains firmly embedded in people's minds.

Ibn Sbayyil's work is defined by his physical and artistic position at the intersection of these two worlds that for centuries intermingled and lived side by side in economic, cultural, and social symbiosis, each sphere nevertheless also developing into opposing civilizational identities.[1] A villager himself, Ibn Sbayyil's fame rests to a large extent on his lively, detailed, and beautiful images of Bedouin life, and its seasonal cycles, as he observed it at close quarters: the Bedouin's arrival, mainly sections of the 'Utaybah tribe on whose traditional *dīrah* (tribal ranges) the townlet of Nifī was situated;[2] their stay of ninety days at Nifī's wells during the hot summer season, where their herds watered and grazed nearby; and their departure in early September westward to higher grounds.[3]

The poet compares the dark herds and people on the horizon to the appearance of rain clouds, calling this the springtime of his heart. Their packing up at the end of the hot season he describes as heralding his season of inner drought—with them depart the sentiments and fantasies the Bedouin girls inspired in him. Images from Bedouin life are amalgamated into intricate patterns of love poetry (ghazals). Exciting scenes of raiding, hazardous desert crossings, and the struggle to hoist water from deep wells turn into extended similes that reflect the poet's lovelorn state, all part of an interior monologue in which he relives the delights and torments of real or imagined affairs, and aspires to a mental balance that reconciles him with the impossibility of attaining his desire. Ibn Sbayyil pictures himself as a villager who cannot pretend to equal status with the "aristocratic" nomad lineages. For him, marrying a Bedouin belle is not in the cards.[4]

Ibn Sbayyil's work is thus informed by the antonymy between nomadic and sedentary elements of Najdī society: the moving and the fixed, the adventurous and the all too predictable, romance and humdrum domestic life, fantasy and everyday reality. Exasperated by the constraints imposed on him by his social status, the poet inveighs against those who stand in his way, against the shackles imposed by his condition, and against the iniquities of fate that put up insurmountable hurdles for true lovers. But more often than not, his bouts of rebelliousness give way to a more resigned mood and even a graceful acceptance of the world as it is. Poetry expresses his romantic longing for escape. Through his dreams in meter and rhyme, he achieves his desire in sublimated form, a harmony born from the conflicting currents in his soul.

Ibn Sbayyil and the "Romantic School" of High Najd

ʿAbdallah ibn Sbayyil (full name ʿAbdallah ibn Ḥmūd ibn Saʿd ibn Sbayyil) was approximately eighty years old when he died in Nifī in 1933.[5] Therefore, he may have been born around 1853. In the second half of the eighteenth century his ancestors, who belonged to the tribe of Bāhilah (pl. Bawāhil), left the town of al-Midhnab, in the southern part of al-Qaṣīm province, for the village of al-Athlah, together with their kinfolk of Āl ʿUwaywīd (hereafter al-ʿWēwīd) and a group of al-ʿAwāzim. From there a number of families, among them Ibn Sbayyil's ancestors, moved to Nifī.[6]

We know little about his life. As the headman of Nifī, he dealt with issues of a tribal nature and sometimes of political significance, as shown by his long ode in praise of Muḥammad ibn Rashīd (Poem 23),[7] the prince of Ḥā'il, under whose rule (1869–97) the Rashīdī House became the dominant power in Najd; and his later poem in support of ʿAbd al-ʿAzīz ibn ʿAbd al-Raḥmān, who reestablished the supremacy of the House of Saud (Poem 25).[8] Generally, tests of his leadership do not seem to have gone beyond dealing with the occasional robbery of livestock by marauding Bedouin.[9] There is no evidence in his poetry or elsewhere that he traveled anywhere outside Nifī. He may have visited friends with whom he was in poetic correspondence, but it is more likely that if he met them, he did so when they passed through Nifī. For a living, he probably tended date palms and perhaps sowed other crops. The crumbled walls of his shop in Nifī's market street are still visible. As a commercial supplier of the Bedouin and as the town's headman, whose duty it was to receive visitors to the town, he would have been known far and wide in that part of Najd. For many, his fame as a poet would have been an additional incentive to socialize and, for those with a taste for poetry, to engage in poetic correspondence with him.

Through his "poetic correspondence" we know of his friendships with men in positions of social standing, such as the tribal chiefs of two major confederations in the area, ʿUtaybah and Muṭayr, and also with his neighbor, Muṭawwaʿ Nifī. An unpublished manuscript that includes anecdotes and poems about the period shows Ibn Sbayyil in playful but robust altercations.[10] Even in his ghazals he is scarcely as Platonic as he is sometimes made out to be, and on occasion he shows himself as erotically aroused as any ardent lover.

He was influential in a group of poets whose geographical space was shared between sedentary colonies and Bedouin, whose seasonal rhythms were determined by their agricultural and nomadic occupations. They did so often in competition, occasionally in conflict, but largely on terms of mutual respect, with friendly relations, and in accordance with well-established rules. Most of the poets belonged to kin groups that had been sedentary for centuries, but they lived in the proximity of the Bedouin and constantly interacted with them.

Their view of the Bedouin was tinged with admiration for their energy, mobility, sociability, and prowess—an admiration that might have been rooted in a romantic longing for a more interesting life and that revolved around an image of young Bedouin women as the fulcrum of a powerful, yet unattainable, desire. None of the poets belonged to the more prominent Bedouin lineages or to the sedentary "aristocracy" of the principal Najdī towns. Some, like Ibn Sbayyil, were local notables and possessed the means to live a more or less stable life. Others, however, had to make a living as agricultural laborers who depended on seasonal, backbreaking work, and frequently suffered the hardship of poverty and pangs of hunger.[11] Yet this did not stop them from composing poetry so remarkable for its beauty that some of it has been preserved through oral transmission and jotted down until publication in recent years.

Admiration for Ibn Sbayyil's poetry and his playful, often tongue-in-cheek exchanges with other poets helped preserve a substantial part of his work. In this respect, he was more fortunate than many of his fellow poets from the area. Because of his stature, it is said that some of their work has been ascribed to him. Whether true or not, the assertion points to a shared sensibility among poets in the area where Nifī is situated, High Najd (ʿĀliyat Najd).[12] The style has been subsumed under the heading of "the romantic school" (*al-madrasah al-wijdāniyyah*).

Saad Sowayan has drawn attention to this group of Najdī poets who developed the amatory prologue (*nasīb*) and description of the beloved's departure and journey (*raḥīl*), as it is known in the early classical qasidas, into an independent subject. For him,

> they constitute a specific school in poetry that according to some might be called *al-madrasah al-wijdāniyyah*. The poetry of this school is notable for its "desert nostalgia" and its yearning for Bedouin life. The school acquired its characteristics through the creative brilliance of the poet ʿAbdallah ibn Sbayyil. Most of its poets are from High Najd, among whom Muṭawwaʿ Nifī, Fhēd ibn ʿWēwīd al-Mijmāj, and, among its later acolytes, Swēlim al-ʿAlī al-Suhalī acquired the greatest fame (*al-Ṣaḥrāʾ al-ʿarabiyyah*, 437).

I have translated it as "romantic school," rather than "sentimental" or "nostalgic," because the alternative descriptions carry connotations that might be misleading if applied to the cultural context in which Ibn Sbayyil and his fellows performed as poets.

The mixed Bedouin and sedentary background of Ibn Sbayyil and his fellow poets is evident in the themes and images of their work. Many, perhaps most, of them knew each other personally, and some were kin. The names of places mentioned in their verse reflect their distribution across a geographical area with distinct boundaries. Situated between the lava fields and mountains of the Hijaz in the west and the sands of al-Sirr in the east, it extends to al-Qaṣīm in the north and in the south to al-Shaʿrāʾ and al-Dawādimī—towns that play a role similar to that of Nifī as centers of supply and repair for the Bedouin. This area, High Najd, coincides for the major part with the tribal ranges of al-Rūqah, the northern half of the ʿUtaybah confederation. Other tribes mentioned in the poetry are

Barqā of ʿUtaybah to the south, Muṭayr to the east, Ḥarb to the northwest, and al-Buqūm and al-Shalāwā at the confines of the Hijaz.[13]

These thematic, geographical, and social features were reinforced by various degrees of kinship and personal relations among the poets. The ʿWēwīd family in al-Athlah, from where Ibn Sbayyil's kin and others settled in Nifī, also belongs to the tribe of Bāhilah. The poet ʿAbdallah ibn ʿAbd al-Hādī ibn ʿWēwīd[14] married his uncle's daughter, Ḥisnā, much to the chagrin of Fhēd al-Mijmāj, another young poet who was deeply in love with her. The mother of Fhēd was the sister of Ḥisnā's father, but her efforts on behalf of her son were unsuccessful. The other poet prevailed, primarily because male descent is given priority in the selection of one's daughter's marriage partner in a patrilineal system, a condition that accounts for a good deal of touching Arabic love poetry.

Fhēd, who is the more interesting poet of the two, is not of the Bāhilah tribe but from a branch of the Tamīm that left the town of al-Midhnab for al-Athlah, together with Ibn Sbayyil's family. There his grandfather married the sister of Ḥmūd al-ʿWēwīd, the grandfather of his rival. It compounded his disadvantage in the pursuit of Ḥisnā that he had to make his living as a hired agricultural hand. Like ʿAbdallah ibn ʿWēwīd, he was a contemporary of Ibn Sbayyil, and their work showed such a close resemblance that some of Fhēd's verse is said to have been attributed to the more famous Ibn Sbayyil.

A third poet is known by the sobriquet Muṭawwaʿ Nifī because he served as the imam of Nifī's mosque, taught elementary religion, and performed various religious functions. His real name was Saʿd ibn Nāṣir ibn Msāʿid, also called by the diminutive Sʿēdān or Sʿēdān al-Muṭawwaʿ.[15] He was born in al-Midhnab, the town of Ibn Sbayyil's forefathers, and after his religious education he settled in Nifī. He was the neighbor of Ibn Sbayyil, whose own house adjoined the mosque. Toward the end of his life he returned to al-Midhnab to live with his son and died in 1935, not long after Ibn Sbayyil. Though his literacy is not in doubt, the language of Muṭawwaʿ Nifī's poetry does not differ markedly from compositions by illiterate poets in the same tradition.[16] And the same holds true for Ibn Sbayyil.[17] Muṭawwaʿ Nifī's diwan consists mostly of short pieces. Among Najdī anthologists and cognoscenti he is especially appreciated for his poetic pranks and antics. With Ibn Sbayyil he engaged in brief, jocular exchanges—mostly to pull his leg, but occasionally their good-humored teasing degenerated into mudslinging.[18] In popular lore, the Muṭawwaʿ is associated with the mortar in which he pounded his coffee beans and herbs. This became a running gag that shows him steadfast in his refusal to sell it to the grandees who sought to acquire this allegedly priceless utensil. This is the theme of many of his boastful verses.[19]

Another characteristic of the Muṭawwaʿ's work, his penchant for composing amorous verse in the style of his neighbor, also attracted the curiosity of his contemporaries. For instance, his outbursts of passionate feeling for unnamed members of the other sex while carrying out his functions as the town's imam are shown as provoking indignation and outrage among his community and visitors. At the same time, it is made clear that these scenes are part of tongue-in-cheek, jocular play in a social game that explores the boundaries of the acceptable. And even if the friends and neighbors occasionally crossed these boundaries in their zest, it was not seriously held against them, and was excused with a smile of secret amusement.[20]

There was a relatively wide margin for this kind of teasing, innocent fun. Only later, once the movement of the rigidly Wahhābī *ikhwān* took control of Najd and beyond, did this come to be seen as inappropriate and somewhat scandalous. And only then did the word *muṭawwaʿ* become a synonym for intolerance of any deviation from severely enforced, religiously sanctioned norms and behavior. It also explains the occasional discrepancy between some of the content in surviving manuscripts of Nabaṭī poetry and what appeared in print over the past decades, and the even greater self-censorship in later republications compared to earlier published collections. Though firm dates are lacking, it is clear that Ibn Sbayyil by and large ceased composing poetry when the "brothers" and their austere Wahhābī culture took hold of Najd, that is, from some time in the early twentieth century till the end of his life.[21]

And yet, the trend set by Ibn Sbayyil and the other poets from High Najd persisted even as the *ikhwān* movement became pervasive in the country, mostly through oral tradition and in jotted notes kept in private custody due to the constraints on publishing these materials. The language, themes, and imagery proved influential in the entire area of Najd and assumed a dominant role in the tradition, such that it produced Swēlim al-ʿAlī al-Suhalī (1916–1985), a brilliant representative of the "romantic school" in the twentieth century.[22]

Many of the poems by ʿAbdallah al-Dindān, a more recent Bedouin poet of the Dawāsir tribe in southern Najd (d. 2004), elaborated on elements introduced by Ibn Sbayyil and his fellow poets in the second half of the nineteenth century.[23]

Al-Dindān was still composing poetry when he reached old age in the 1990s, and then as before he relied exclusively on the oral tradition since he was illiterate. By that time his style of poetry had probably run its course, one reason being that the imagery was no longer applicable in an oil-based economy and rentier state. Though dates of origin and expiry of forms of artistic expression are rarely precise, for this lyrical style of Bedouin-inspired poetry one might posit an approximate period from the second half of the nineteenth century, when Ibn Sbayyil flourished, to sometime between 1980 and 1990.

Geography, social and cultural patterns, kinship, and personal relations—these interconnected factors determined the environment these poets had in common and nurtured the emergence of the "romantic school." The main argument in favor of considering them as poets who orbited in a loosely coherent, not formally organized way of expressing themselves, are the distinctive features of the poetry itself. Clearly these are colored by the poets' environment, but the "literary" aspects represent an original development that drew on earlier examples and conventions to create something new and authentic.

First, Ibn Sbayyil and his circle invented a new language—fluent, expressive, emotionally charged, evocative, and readily understood—that harnessed rich imagery drawn from the Bedouin and sedentary environment to the inner world of the poet, his audience, and correspondents. This new poetic idiom differed markedly from the one that prevailed in the preceding era: one that to some extent came to rely on the use of rhetorical devices, hidden clues, and riddles, with the aim of impressing the audience. Though composed in the language of Nabaṭī poetry, it reflected an essentially literate culture.[24] In this sense, Ibn Sbayyil's poetry also marked a return to an idiom more naturally suited to the oral culture of the area.

Second, imagery and metaphors were developed into extended similes that at times grew into minitales with an autonomous existence within the overall structure of the poem.[25] Invariably, these similes are employed to lend greater poignancy to the suffering of the poet's lovestruck heart using graphic descriptions of scenes marked by as much stress and pain as the poet's imagination is capable of: tales of robbery and hot pursuit; perilous desert crossings with disastrous consequences; scenes of utter exhaustion and chaos when water is raised from deep wells under harsh conditions; the distress of wounded and worn-out animals on the brink of death; once-proud warriors who are at the mercy of their enemy on the field of battle; and other images that vividly illustrate scenes encountered by Burckhardt, Wallin, Musil, and other travelers in Arabia.

Also, this earlier poetry exhibits a palpable delight in vocabulary, phrasing, and imagery for their own sake. Sometimes this seems the overriding purpose of a poem, while the ultimate object—the vagaries of the loving heart in the throes of despair—seems to become an afterthought.

In Ibn Sbayyil's poetry this is never the case, however. It is a mark of his greatness that all facets of his compositions in this genre are integrated into an overarching structure: the frame for an inner dialogue in which the poet explores his soul's movements in the face of temptation and other challenges. Through it, the poet seeks to reconcile pressing reality with sentiment—a fundamental opposition that he bridges by substituting his dreams and fantasies for reality.

The Poetry

Ibn Sbayyil is unanimously praised as a master of the craft by Najdī critics.[26] The lyrical flow of his verse, its flawless composition, and its deceptive simplicity are held up as an exemplary standard in its genre.[27] With the exception of nine poems, and the short pieces (see Poems 42.1–46.2), his work is firmly devoted to the subject of love, or rather "the pursuit of amorous passion" (*ṭard al-hawā*).[28] In some poems he explicitly mentions Bedouin girls as the object of his desire. In other poems, the same meaning is conveyed through scenes of the departing tribe that carries away his beloved and the sight of the deserted camp at Nifī's wells; or it is implicit in the poet's description of the seasonal cycle of a year in Bedouin life (see Poem 32).

Ibn Sbayyil dwells on his position as a villager vis-à-vis the Bedouin to emphasize the impossibility of his love, and his consequent heartbreak. As he puts it antithetically: the drought that pushes the Bedouin to Nifī's wells heralds the springtime of his heart, and their departure at the first reports of rain ushers in the season of the poet's drought.[29] For the Bedouin and the village folks these months of residence at Nifī's wells were an occasion to catch up on friendships. In poetry, this is also the time for amorous glances and furtive contacts. Ibn Sbayyil describes how young Bedouin women, in their tight-fitting dresses and gaudy colors, could be counted on to create a sensation in Nifī's market street.

These ninety days of merriment and buzzing social life would come to an end in September when the star Canopus, Shēl (CA Suhayl), made its appearance on the horizon. For this reason the star has been cursed by all Nabaṭī poets,[30] the settled bards as well as those of Bedouin stock: clans would take off in different directions, each in search of its own pastures, interrupting—perhaps for good—budding acquaintances between lovers generally too shy to declare their love.

Ibn Sbayyil watches the camels and their precious cargo disappear over the crests of hills in the distance while he is plunged into the depths of despair at being cut off, possibly forever, from the object of his desire—identical to the abandoned-camp scene in the *nasīb*, the elegiac prelude of classical poetry. It is certain that such scenes were part of his real life. And this experience is mined for material to enliven his ghazals. The suffering of the poet's heart is compared to the strain on the rope of a heavy bucket that is hoisted from a well by a strong, untrained, vehement camel. This and other extended similes create similar impressions of vivid action.[31] The simile may become the real purpose of the poem, but more often it is part of a prelude to the poet's musings on his predicament.[32]

The beloved's beauty is mostly a summing up, a "descriptive catalogue,"[33] of her physical features, but with some original touches. She is painted as an exotic bird that lands on the outskirts of town on its yearly migration. She stirs things up, rendering the men speechless as she strides onto the village stage in her tight red dress. With a gentle sway, she walks by the men at a maddeningly slow pace, not because of high heels, but because of a heavy behind that slows her gait. Moreover, she has the built-in handicap that her firm, protruding breasts stretch her dress tight in front while her buttocks do the same from behind, in a tug-of-war, as she attempts to take a step (§34.10).[34] She throws the poet into confusion by lowering her veil slightly and shooting glances at him; or by unfastening one button of her dress so as to release the pressure, and thereby opening a view on the creamy white of a bosom the size of a she-camel's full udder. She strikes the poet as a mass of femininity that struggles mightily to maintain forward momentum lest she starts sliding backward. Or like the excruciatingly slow steps of the imam as he measures the length of the shade to determine the time of the afternoon prayer. And he can have had no other imam in mind than Ibn Sbayyil's neighbor, Sʿēdān al-Muṭawwaʿ, the poet known as Muṭawwaʿ Nifī.

In spite of some exchanges of vicious invective between the neighbors, they seem to have found common ground in the view that life would be immeasurably poorer without amorous activity outside of wedlock. They also seem to have agreed that putting some of this content in a religious context would add spice to their pursuit, but without undue emphasis and ingenuously, in the way that religion was part of the town's unchanging routines and seasonal cycles. S'ēdān, at least, did not shy away from extending his jocular ways to religious practice—for instance, when a shaykh from al-Qaṣīm passed through Nifī and performed Friday prayers in its mosque, and he admired the imam's chanting of a Qur'anic verse. Upon being informed that the imam's voice was even sweeter when he chanted frivolous poetry—such as the imam's assertion that the holy war waged by his heart and soul on account of a girl with luscious breasts was more savage than the onslaught of Shaddād ibn 'Ād—he was shocked, and declared prayer behind this imam null and void. S'ēdān replied in verse, saying that he had no intent to cause a scandal, but that a devotee of passion, even if he wished to repent, did not have the power to shed his habit. The only way to keep up appearances was to disguise it as jest.[35]

Ibn Sbayyil occasionally spices descriptions of lusty love with religious imagery (§§7.22–23):

At night, the vision of her makes me start.
  At prayer time, her specter floats before me—
It happened last in the evening,
  when the imam spoke the closing words. [36]

He subtly plays with the concepts of love and religion in a way that suggests a reversal of the usual hierarchy of values. Instead of seeking salvation and admittance to paradise through religion, the poet affirms his belief that there lies "heavenly fruit between her breasts" (§7.20). In a bid to move his beloved to tend to his wrecked body, he beseeches her (§§6.6–7):

A honeyed lick above the buttons on the breast,
  then the preacher's recitations.
If she fears God, if Islam is truly her faith,
  for her salvation on Judgment Day . . .[37]

The poet's intent becomes clearer when he suggests recourse to legal arbitration. While he asks to submit the dispute with his beloved to a Shariah court, she insists on applying tribal customary law; that is, he must prove his innocence by licking a red-hot iron without burning his tongue (§36.10).[38] His preference for Shariah law seems incongruous, but must be understood in the context of his advocacy of the lover's pursuit as his true "religion." That is, he is in the right, while his beloved follows cruel, heathen Bedouin rites. The relation between religion and the game of love, as the poet sees it, is (§§28.17–18):

> My refuge is with you; let bygones be bygones,
> if a shred of religion remains in your heart.
> You turned me from a student of the Qur'an into a silly poet!
> Before, I was known as sedate and solid.[39]

These last verses epitomize the fundamental ambiguity in Ibn Sbayyil's work. It is well-nigh impossible to tell where playful, teasing suggestion shades off into more deeply held views, if at all. Even the explanation given by Muṭawwaʿ Nifī—that he had to dress up his lover's passion as jesting to protect his honor—does not answer the question, because this statement itself is made in jest. In Ibn Sbayyil's poetry the role of love and religion does not stand alone, but is part and parcel of his creation of an alternative reality.[40] Usual values are reversed and replaced by binary oppositions: poetry versus the religion of the Qur'an; tribal mediation versus Shariah law; the world versus metaphysical truth; passion versus social convention; predilections of the heart versus risk-averse calculation; dream versus reality.

In his poetic oeuvre as a whole, the thrust of Ibn Sbayyil's message is in favor of the first and in opposition to the second of these mutually exclusive concepts. Yet there are also cases where the poet positions himself on the other side of the equation. Sometimes he does so only to revert to his default stance in favor of the contrary choice, with the excuse stated so clearly by Muṭawwaʿ Nifī—that his heart really leaves him no choice.

The Valley of Love's Temptation

Ibn Sbayyil's love lyrics can be understood as the creation of a dreamlike alternative world: the valley of love's temptation. As he put it (§18.10):

> She is a moon rising from the valley of seduction,
> resplendent, layers of light on radiant luminance . . .

The Arabic word for "temptation, seduction," *ghayy*, has the connotation of "sinful, frivolous." Yet in Nabaṭī poetry it has a long pedigree as a conventional theme.[41]

In the early ghazals of the seventh-century Umayyad poet ʻUmar ibn Abī Rabīʻah, the lover is a Don Juan for whom women are as prey to be seduced. However, Ibn Sbayyil's poet-lover is in thrall to a beauty who plays cat and mouse with him—a conventional motif centuries before Ibn Sbayyil, but one that is at odds with Najdī social reality, as reflected in the work of the seventeenth- and eighteenth-century poet Ḥmēdān al-Shwēʻir.[42]

At times, the beloved appears as a coquettish ingenue, or even clever and adept at conspiring with the poet to keep their affair secret in the face of hostile enviers and society's omnipresent moral police—Arabic poetry's stock characters of the censurer (*ʻādhil*) and informer or slanderer (*wāshī*). But her gaiety and stunning looks are not the only attributes keeping the poet-lover in thrall. These traits would mean little to him were it not for her intellectual charms and ravishingly delightful way of conversing—her *taʻājīb*, "the wonders" she works in her sweet speech, accompanied by seductively refined gestures, such as the expression of her black eyes, *lijlāj sūdih* (§13.32 and §28.2).[43]

The sweet-tempered seductress reappears in a different guise when the lover is frustrated in his desires. Then she metamorphoses into a beautiful lady without mercy, who takes pleasure in subjecting her admirer to refined torments. The poet protests his innocence and pure devotion, but to no avail. At each turn she leaves him defenseless and cravenly beholden to her every caprice. Even his ultimate plea to accept him as her most docile and well-bred slave falls on deaf ears (§6.14).

If the beloved often shows a sadistic edge, with even greater justification it can be said that her lover derives masochistic pleasures from her cruelty to him. The word "ordeal" (*imtiḥān*) occurs in eight poems.[44] The poet prays to God to lighten his "burden of passion" (§12.8) and to cure him from his addiction to it.[45] His suffering is not only his greatest pride, but also a source of sensual satisfaction, as when he describes in detail how his beloved puts her red-hot branding iron to his liver and other internal organs—and he even dreams of doing the same to her (§§6.11–12). Invariably, the riveting scenes of the extended similes are hitched to the pain inflicted on the poet. In this way cruelty, as a metaphor for frustrated desire, became a motif in which Najdī ghazal poets competed to outdo each other. But Ibn Sbayyil also shows that the poet-lover is not powerless, even if the odds are stacked against him.[46]

To mollify her and protect himself from the belle's depredations, he points to the stigmata inflicted by her whims, coquetry, and cold indifference. But his first priority is to restore some order to his conflicted inner life. At first glance, he seems to adopt the censurer's reproving stance toward his heart's inclinations.[47] But in the dispute between mind, soul, and heart, the latter is in the seat of power, with eyes and feet at his beck and call (§20.13):

> The heart is a sultan with despotic powers:
> it rules at the pleasure of its whims . . .

Faced with criticism, the poet must confess: "I do my heart's bidding, whether right or wrong" (§9.17). The heart is the beloved's natural ally, united against the poet's rational mind and society at large, and they are equally willful.[48] If the poet's mind tries to make it see reason, the heart only becomes more obstinate. But in fact, the heart's ungovernable, independent nature provides the poet-lover with a handy excuse to plead his helplessness when censurers rebuke him for his irresponsible behavior.[49]

The object of the heart's desire also does as she pleases (§18.12):

> She twists the rope, then unties the knot, at will:
> I can't make head or tail of it.

With her push and pull, she attracts the lover and ensnares him in her web. The poet tries to keep his composure, but is powerless against the heart's dictates. The heart itself is at the tender mercies of the beautiful lady—it is she who holds the heart's strings. When the heart's pleas become too impertinent, she reminds it: "You're no relative of mine nor one of my kin" (§28.12). And for good measure she adds (§28.14):

> "If you die," she said, "that's fine by me."
> Should love be coercion, or reason and gentleness?

Goaded on by the beloved, the heart is in constant rebellion and efforts of the poet's rational self to gain control come to naught. Under pressure, the heart absconds, leaving behind an emaciated body and a mind that has been driven insane. But the poet does not just pine away: memories of happier times revive his flagging spirits. Carried away by a surge of rekindled passion, he boasts of his prowess as a lover and intimate knowledge of passion's hidden tracks (§33.16). This experience convinces him that the valley of temptation is not a temporary abode for youthful dalliance: for true lovers it is permanent, regardless of age—even if it is essentially an addiction to a dream.

The poet's mental trajectory transitions from one motif to the next, until the poem reaches closure. In consequence, many of these ghazals follow an emotional arc. The arc's shape depends on the sequencing—and the arc may also come full circle. For instance, the poet is left only with his memories and spleen, as the Bedouin carry away his love. Then, in one poem, he accepts the inevitable and pulls himself together (§40.6):

> Now I've gone gray and foresworn my old ways,
> drawn up my frayed ropes from all watering holes . . .[50]

But not for long. In the next line, he adds: "Except when haunted by memories of a buxom beauty." Flush with earlier memories, he revels in his former affairs and boasts that his wounds are the proud mark of a life in the service of passion (*āyat hawā*)—and since *āyah* also has the meaning of "Qur'an verse," the double entendre is that he is as devoted to love's pursuit as society expects one to be to religion (§§40.10–11).[51] On a more subdued note, he then admits that had he not vented his grief, he would have gone raving mad like other legendary Arab lovers (§40.13).[52] The poem closes with proverbial sayings about such lovers' characteristics, and ends on a note of resignation: the popular saying that wishful thinking is of no more use than sowing on a clay roof and expecting a rich harvest (§40.19).

The opening of yet another poem compares the heart to a piece of wood that is smoothed with a hand plane by a muscular carpenter and twisted into a bow (§§29.1–4). It is followed by a description of his paramour and the affirmation that he cannot detach himself from her: a glimpse of her teeth when she lifts her veil slightly makes him sit up and clench his fists, as a trained falcon clasps the leather cushion on his pole when he sees a morsel of meat being prepared for him. The poet then effects a transition by pointing out that hunters in the valley of temptation never tire of their quest: "for them, the hunt is treading on soft Persian carpets" (§29.19). Verses of gnomic wisdom are followed by an unexpected outburst: if it were not for fear of gossips, he would swoop down on her camp and elope with her. Having abducted her, he would indulge his craving "until belly ropes burst," (§29.26) and he would expertly satisfy her desires as well. Then the happy pair would rest, their "thirsty camels" watered, serene and without bearing grudges (§29.28). As reality triumphs in the first example, so does fantasy in the second. Indeed, most of the ghazals oscillate between such resignation and lover's bravura, even if it comes in the sublimated shape of a dream.

The poem's emotional arc may also come full circle in a humorous, ironic fashion. In one poem's first line he asks his beloved to revive his sagging spirits before it is too late. But she blows to him the crust of foam on a pool of fouled water that even thirsty camels would find hard to drink. Cruel death is all he can expect from her, and in the closing line he envies those who are blithely ignorant of such entanglements (Poem 41).

Another circular poem explains why regrets are not final. It opens with the observation that ends the previous poem. Here the irony works in the opposite direction. The first line expresses congratulations to a heart that is blasé and carefree (§38.1), but continues to compare it to a mule on its shady patch (§38.3)—

His heart's immune to stirrings of merriment and fun,
  not up to the challenge of her flirtatious game.

This is a prelude to a proud account of the poet's career in the school of love. Through a string of popular wise sayings, it arrives at the conclusion that a love affair must be based on mutual feeling. If the beloved coldly turns her back on the poet, he will kick the dust up into her face and return her the compliment. It ends with an affirmation of the opening verse (§38.17):

Only dogs grovel before displays of contempt;
  only oxen graze on without a care.

In his dream of love the poet transcends these paradoxes. Though he may groan like a she-camel that has lost her young (§8.18), and no matter how old he is, he will not abandon his pursuit of passion. The poet wishes that his heart "were placid with quiet joy," and then compares it to a full bucket hoisted from the well by an impetuous camel, banging against the stone wall such that the rope and the wooden crosspieces are torn from the bucket (§§2.18–23). Love is his way of life, and without it he would be condemned to a torpid existence. More to be feared than passion's agony is the mule's fate: to be a *dalūh*, placid and mindless among the walking dead.

At some point a heart that is alive with feeling must give vent to it or the lover will start raving. "Were I the only one, my beliefs would be in doubt" (§26.15). Then the poet reminds himself that before him mighty shaykhs were known to utter their despair and would give their all to attain their desire (§26.16). Vindicated by this thought, the poet regains the good spirits and slightly melancholy humor that characterize his work.

Correspondences with Early Classical Poetry

Two of the collection's longest poems do not fall in the category of ghazal. One is a poem in praise of Muḥammad ibn Rashīd (r. 1869–97), whose rule over most of Najd in the northern capital of Ḥā'il was the apogee of his dynasty. In Ibn Sbayyil's eulogy he is portrayed as fear-inspiring and marauding, and a lavish despot who punishes and rewards as he pleases, unrestrained by any checks on his power (Poem 23).[53] The other poem deals with the theft of a herd of the town's smaller cattle by Bedouin of the ʿUtaybah tribe, including some owned by the poet, and appeals to Nifī's "brothers" (Bedouin chiefs who are paid protection money) among ʿUtaybah for their return (Poem 5).[54] Unlike the scrupulously serious first poem, it evinces Ibn Sbayyil's trademark amalgamation of heartfelt interest with a sense of gentle and playful humor. Apart from short exchanges of invective verse with other poets (see Poems 42.1–46.2), seven more poems are on different themes.[55] Two provide wisdom on the subject of the "world" (*al-dunyā*) and its inequities.[56] One celebrates the victory of ʿAbd al-ʿAzīz ibn Saʿūd over the Rashīd dynasty. One is about the pleasures of coffee and smoking, mixed with some gnomic wisdom. And one is a colorful description of the Bedouin's seasonal migration patterns—usually this theme is part of a prelude to the subject of love, but here it has been developed into an independent poem.

The great majority of Ibn Sbayyil's poems falls in the category of ghazals, love poetry. Their tone, style, imagery, vocabulary, and phrasing are akin to classical Arabic ghazals—in particular as developed prior to the rise of the consciously urban (that is, non-Bedouin) and courtly poetry of the Abbasid period.[57] The mostly oral tradition of poetry in Arabia was not part of the literary canon, which may have contributed to the misconception that the pre-Abbasid poetic idiom of the desert and the Bedouin ended then and there, at least in a literary sense. In fact, the tradition was still alive and well more than a thousand years later, and widely practiced by Najdī poets such as Ibn Sbayyil in the nineteenth century, in the centuries before, and even in the twentieth century. One reason for this perdurability is that for a millennium the essentials of life in the Arabian interior hardly changed, at least not in ways that made a profound difference.

While it might be justified to call this idiom "antiquated" in the context of ninth-century urban and urbane Baghdad, this plainly was not the case in the vast Arabian interior, where Bedouin and sedentary oasis dwellers continued to eke out a living using time-honored means and abiding by unchanging codes of virtue.[58] Some political developments, like the rise of the Wahhābī movement in the eighteenth century, had a deep impact. Yet, as the poetry of Ibn Sbayyil and many others shows, the substratum of nonreligious values kept its popular legitimacy, while the desert and oasis economy remained intact and provided an ever-present store of imagery akin to that used by early classical poets.

Whether Ibn Sbayyil and his fellow poets of High Najd were influenced by early Arabic examples from written sources, directly or through oral transmission, is difficult to ascertain. But the poetry of his contemporaries and predecessors shows many traces of literate culture. And these influences undoubtedly percolated into his work as well.[59] It must be assumed that the poetic idiom of early classical poetry continued to be passed down from one generation to the next, even during the centuries when it disappeared in a literary sense; and that during this long period the oral tradition continued to draw on the literary tradition.[60] In any case, classical Arabic poetry up to the Abbasid period offers an indispensable perspective for the later Arabian tradition; and the study of premodern Arabian poetry and its milieu may offer insights that are useful for the interpretation of classical poetry.[61]

Ibn Sbayyil's ghazals exhibit various possible influences from the classical era, much of it dating back to pre-Islamic poetry. More interesting from a literary perspective are parallels with the early Umayyad Hijazi poetry of ʿUmar ibn Abī Rabīʿah—the straightforwardness and relative simplicity of expression; the lively impression created by the use of direct address; the gentle playfulness and deliberate ambiguity of intent as the poet draws his audience into his game of hide-and-seek; and the fair amount of common vocabulary, images, and phrasing that became part of ghazal poets' stock-in-trade. But they are fundamentally different in their attitude toward the beloved. While it is the conceit of ʿUmar ibn Abī Rabīʿah's lover-poet to strut on the stage as a lady-killer who measures his success by the number of women of high social rank who are vying for his attentions, Ibn Sbayyil is on the opposite pole: he delights in graphic descriptions of his torments, and declares his eagerness to serve as his sweetheart's slave.[62]

In eight of his poems, love is pictured as a trial that purifies the heart.[63] In its predilection for heartburn, his poetry is closer in theme and tone to early

Abbasid courtly ghazals, where the beloved is forever beyond the lover's reach and her despotic and cruel disposition toward him is a given.[64] But for Ibn Sbayyil this is one element in a broader spectrum of possible give and take in a complex relationship. She quasi-innocently manipulates the lover's feelings, driving him beside himself with desire; and the imagery of his torments makes for gripping poetry. But the beloved is also praised for her sweet speech, social discernment, psychological acumen, and ingenuity in finding ways to communicate discreetly with the lover.

The poet-lover insists that he will not pursue an affair unless it is based on some mutuality of amorous interest—a stark contrast with the courtly school represented by al-ʿAbbās ibn al-Aḥnaf and its "ideological" devotion to an unattainable ideal of love and unconditional submission to the beloved's cold and whimsical dictates.[65] Ibn Sbayyil, on the other hand, champions the proverbial saying that warns against groveling if one is given the cold shoulder. There is mention of trysts, erotic detail, the poet's aspiration to satisfy his desires and those of the beloved, and the occasional culmination of his endeavors in a dreamlike lovers' union.[66]

Proverbs and Sayings in the Poetry of Ibn Sbayyil

Ibn Sbayyil's oeuvre is frequently quoted in the Najdī proverbs and sayings collected by al-Juhaymān,[67] who seems to have had a particular liking for his poetry.[68] In about sixty-five instances his verses are adduced to illustrate a proverb or saying, some of which are clearly coined from his verse.[69]

As one might expect, the great majority of quoted verse has some relation with the theme of love. Some of these are particular to his time, such as "(her beauty is) unlike those who use makeup from Java" (§39.12); others are timeless: "even lovers cannot suffer beyond endurance" (§13.5). Perhaps one-quarter carries a more general meaning—and these are frequently cited. Sometimes it is not immediately obvious that a proverb is an expression of the poet's all-consuming passion, as in: "I said, 'Shariah!' and she, 'Fire of Ibn ʿAmmār'" (§36.10). In the proverb the opposition of religious law, Shariah, with Bedouin customary law (*ʿurf*)—here the practice of firelicking as a test of the accused's veracity—is explained as: "Trying to convince someone to take the more acceptable course," as symbolized by Shariah law.[70] Ibn Sbayyil adds another layer of complexity with the conceit that the pursuit of passion is his true religion—hence "Shariah" in his discourse must be considered the lover's code.

In one sequence of verse, each of which comprises a proverb, the poet explains that a love affair must be two-sided: he will not keep pining for a belle who gives him the cold shoulder, but any kind of response will be reciprocated by "hoisting my ship's sail." Then he effects a subtle transition to imagery from Bedouin life: he is disdainful of drawing water from a crowded well, where visitors are indistinguishable from the encamped tribes, but looks for the exquisite and unique (§§33.12–16):

> My taste is a drink from a rock hole in the mountain,
> reserved for rugged hunters who know its hidden trail.

The greatest density of proverbs is found in three poems, 13, 14, and 29. Two of these are relatively long, both addressed to a shaykh of the tribe of Muṭayr, Fayḥān ibn Zirībān, with whom Ibn Sbayyil maintained a "poetic correspondence." In time-honored fashion, the friends commiserate about the trials of love and join efforts in tracing the whereabouts of a runaway young she-camel, i.e., the beauty who haunts their thoughts. Some of these sayings can be applied to multiple situations and are therefore often cited, such as: "My hand is fastidious: any old cane won't do" (§13.34); "he has a disease of his own making" (§9.14), that is, "his problems are of his own making"; and "my wounds demand retaliation" (§6.12). The other, longer, poem in this correspondence is quoted eleven times for its proverbial expressions. Remarkably, all are of a general nature and not specific affairs of the heart—perhaps because this poem is about a shaykh's pursuit, while the poet provides commonsensical advice, such as the admonishment not to mistake one's fancies or excuses as a substitute for reality.[71]

Proverbial phrases, quoted in the collections together with their context of verses, are concentrated in a poem that through deft transitions transports the lover-poet from a state in which his heart flies like a shaving from the carpenter's hand plane to a triumphal outcome of his dreams (Poem 29; see also p. xxiv above). Its twenty-eight verses are interlaced with twelve proverbial sayings of a mixed nature—some uniquely related to love and beauty, such as walking with a "pigeon-toed gait." Others appeal to common sense, such as "sticks that do not bend cannot be changed," which in this case is synonymous with the saying that "a torrent that races down does not change course": it is no use trying to divert a love-stricken poet's attention from his quest. And in any case, "the amorous do not flag in their pursuit of passion."

Style and Language

A distinguishing feature of the poetry of Ibn Sbayyil, and other members of the "romantic school" of High Najd, as noted earlier, is the extended simile. In this edition of his diwan about fifty verses would qualify as such, varying in length from two verses to eleven.[72] Without exception, the similes are linked to the suffering of the lover-poet's heart. The transition to the simile is marked by the preposition *ʿalā*, with the meaning of "because of, on account of," and followed by the suffix *-k*, "because of you (the beloved)," or similar prepositional markers.[73] In essence, these formulas correspond to the classical and modern formula *wajdī*, "(my ardent heart) is in agony because of (my unfulfilled love)."[74]

The simile extends this formula and extrapolates it into dramatic scenes derived from the poet's natural environment in desert and oasis.[75] Obviously, among the poets of this group the extended simile was seen as a suitable arena for artistic rivalry. To the more common devices of the art, they added a touch of hyperbole—though one that generally did not cross the boundaries of probability.[76] For instance, in one poem (22) a frequently used formula that opens such descriptions, *ya-tall galbī*, "the pull or strain on my hearts is like" (followed by the simile), is employed four times to build tension. To heighten the tension, a cumulative effect is also used within the simile. For instance, in a scene of the hardship to which robbed camels are subjected on a forced march, the poet makes them cross "waterless wastes, already thirsting," until "dawn broke miserably, a terrible fate awaiting them" (§§18.3–4).[77]

Najdī critics have found Ibn Sbayyil's language and style much to their taste.[78] His verse's lyrical tone and deceptive ease keep the audience spellbound as it is carried along from one transition to the other in a flawless, rolling movement of meter and rhyme.[79] Wording and phrasing are mostly part of the well-known inventory of the ghazal genre. The inventory is used for descriptions of the beloved's physique, bearing, subterfuges, and seemingly artless but beguiling speech; for the mental states of the poet-lover that range from tottering on the brink of insanity to reckless bravado, and often end in the tranquility of resignation or serene, dreamlike vision; the elaborate vocabulary of push and pull, hiding and revelation, secrecy and divulgence, self-restraint and involuntary release, ailing conditions and restored health; and the game of hide-and-seek with the obnoxious breed of spies, informers, censurers, and well-meaning advisers whose common sense makes no sense to a lover who adheres to the internal logic of passion's code.[80]

At the level of imagery, vocabulary, and phrasing, Ibn Sbayyil employs his art to great effect in a subtle, almost imperceptible manner. In one poem, which ends with the poet's acceptance of his doom, the final words are a prayer for closeness to his beloved, with a musical timbre of soothing self-suggestion: "let the smiling gazelle roam close to me" (§19.21). The confusion sown by the conquering woman's wiles and whims has its parallel at the level of language: rapid successions of paronomasia, repetition of consonants, and other parallelisms, such as *yiǵfī w-yiǵbil, harraj w-darraj, yāʿid w-yibʿid*, and *wilfin w-jaflī*; parallel repetition of words, *yʿassifni* and *inʿasaf lī, asmaʿih* and *lā samʿ, mā aʿrf* and *ʿirfuhum* (§§41.5, 41.7, 41.10, 41.16). This leads the poet to the conclusion that the beloved plays with his feelings as with pieces on a chessboard. It also brings the poem full circle, in a mere sixteen lines, from its hopeful beginning, "Hey, what's-your-name (*yā-hann*), give me the stuff that revives," (§41.1) to the realization that on the contrary she will seal his fate, with an ironic repetition of the poem's first word in the root of the last word, *wā-haniyyih*, "lucky the man who is spared the torment of such affairs" (§41.16).

Ibn Sbayyil makes frequent use of direct speech, like ʿUmar ibn Abī Rabīʿah, in combination with other stylistic devices, such as in one poem the singsong, quasi-plaintive effect achieved by parallel syntax (Poem 9). Ibn Sbayyil is also a master in his manipulation of tone to achieve his rhetorical objectives. For instance, a poem may open on the grave note of the ancient poly-thematic qasida (§§40.1):

As the camel train disappeared over the spur of Abānāt,
I recalled and pined for my days with the wasp-waisted.

But already in the next line he brings a smile to the audience's faces when he wishes that his love would ride behind him on a camel, holding on to him or, if that were too much, then behind a companion on the other camel—presumably that he might have a better view of her. Ibn Sbayyil marks these transitions with a variety of formulas, mostly to signal that what preceded or follows must be understood at a level different from ordinary reality, such as dreams and wishful thinking, and should not be taken literally—only to substitute the imaginary scene for reality as if it were reality.[81] In the same poem, he explains two proverbial sayings in one line in their respective order in the next line; he then delves into the mystery of his heart's hidden wounds in a line that opens with a word that repeats the last word of the preceding line, but with a different meaning. Unlike many of his predecessors, who reveled in rhetorical flourishes, Ibn Sbayyil's work never leaves an impression of artifice pursued for its own sake.

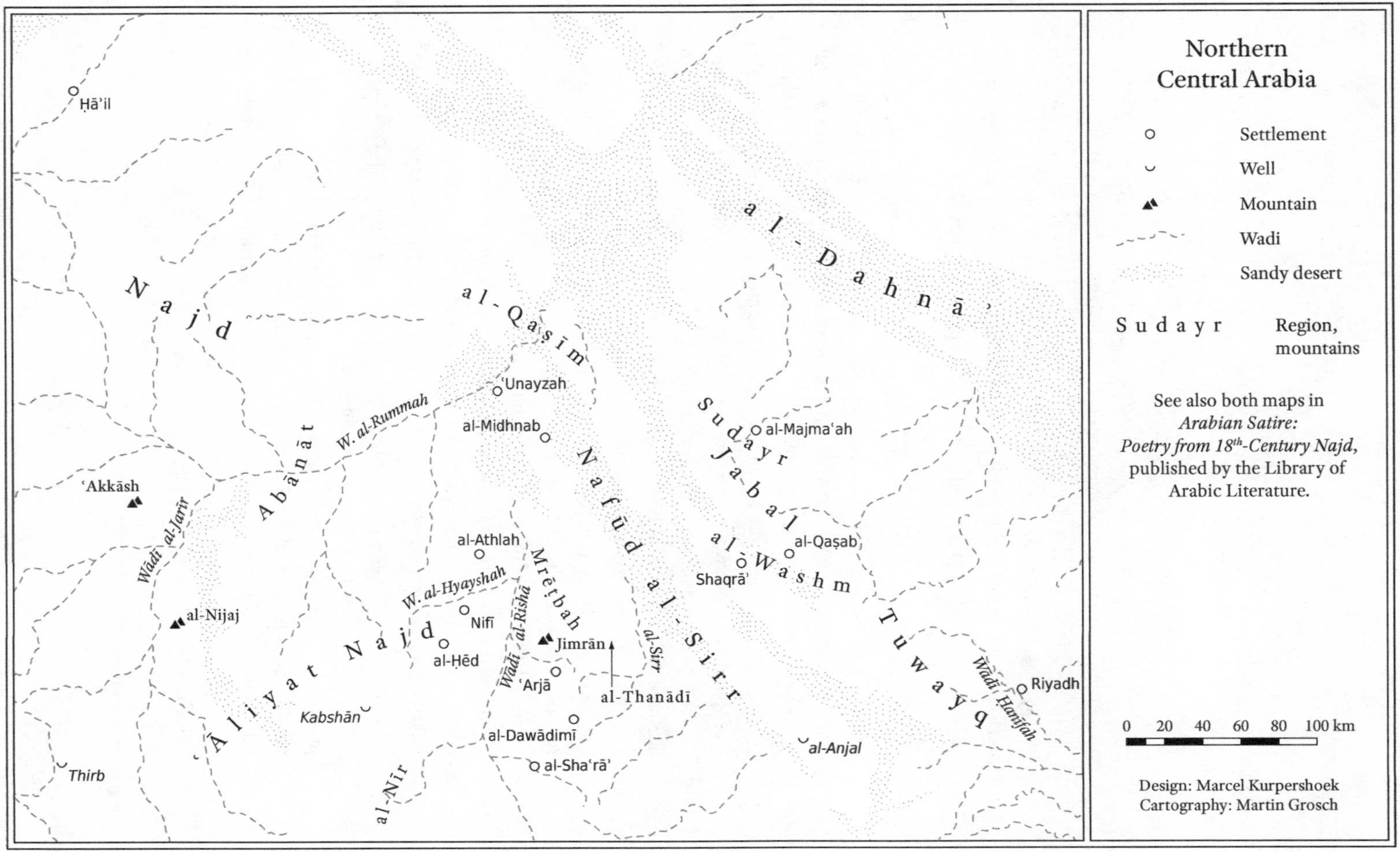
Northern Central Arabia
Settlement
Well
Mountain
Wadi
Sandy desert
Sudayr
Region, mountains
See also both maps in *Arabian Satire: Poetry from 18th-Century Najd*, published by the Library of Arabic Literature.
0 20 40 60 80 100 km
Design: Marcel Kurpershoek
Cartography: Martin Grosch
Ḥā’il
Najd
al-Qaṣīm
al-Dahnā’
ʿUnayzah
W. al-Rummah
Abānāt
al-Midhnab
al-Majmaʿah
Sudayr
Jabal
ʿAkkāsh
Wādī al-Jarīr
Nafūd al-Sirr
al-Athlah
al-Qaṣab
al-Washm
Shaqrā’
W. al-Hyayshah
Mrēṭbah
al-Nijaj
Nifī
Wādī al-Rishā
Jimrān
al-Sirr
Tuwayq
ʿĀliyat Najd
al-Ḥēd
ʿArjā
al-Thanādī
Wādī Ḥanīfah
Riyadh
Kabshān
al-Dawādimī
al-Anjal
al-Shaʿrā’
Thirb
al-Nīr

A Note on the Text

This edition's text of Ibn Sbayyil's poetry is mainly based on two manuscripts that comprise the works of many poets in the Nabaṭī tradition: one written by ʿAbd al-Raḥmān Ibrāhīm al-Rabīʿī from ʿUnayzah (d. 1981 at the age of ninety-three); the other by Muḥammad ibn ʿAbd al-Raḥmān ibn Yaḥyā from the Sudayr region (d. 1993 at the age of ninety). In addition, four other manuscripts were used.[82] Poems by Muṭawwaʿ Nifī are found in a manuscript by al-ʿUmarī, entitled *Dīwān Suʿaydān ibn Musāʿid, Muṭawwaʿ Nifī.*[83]

On a visit to Nifī and al-Athlah in June 1989, I recorded four of the longer poems by Ibn Sbayyil from ʿAbdallah ibn Nāfiʿ ibn Nmēsh al-Ghbēwī al-ʿTēbī, a Bedouin transmitter of the ʿUtaybah tribe in the small Bedouin settlement (*hijrah*) of Msāwī.[84] Remarkably, the recorded version hardly differed from the published poems.[85] At the time of my visit Ibn Sbayyil's daughter Sārah was still alive—she was the Sārah about whom the town's imam, nicknamed Muṭawwaʿ Nifī, composed some flirtatious verse to tease his neighbor.[86] I was told that as a little girl she used to listen from behind the door to Ibn Sbayyil's poems, because he did not want to let her attend his sessions with other men. However, when he noticed her talent and her capacity to commit poems to memory, he started teaching her his poems himself. Thus, she became an authority on his work and was a decisive voice in the edition of the collection published by his grandson Muḥammad.

In Riyadh, prior to my first visit to Nifī, several experts gave me their views and interpretations of words and passages in Ibn Sbayyil's verses that I had not fully understood, among them ʿAbdallah ibn Raddās, the editor of the excellent collection of verse by Bedouin women poets, *Shāʿirāt min al-bādiyah,* with many explanatory notes; Saʿd ibn Junaydil, the author of many works on poetry and Najdi traditional culture, including other poets in the general area of Nifī; the grandsons of Ibn Sbayyil, Muḥammad and Saʿd ibn ʿAbd al-ʿAzīz ibn ʿAbdallah al-Sbayyil (the latter is a Qur'an teacher); and Ḥamūd ibn ʿAbd al-ʿAzīz ibn Ḥamūd ibn Sbayyil, a cousin of the poet (and at that time a retired judge living in Riyadh). Muḥammad ibn Sbayyil was again generous with his time for explanatory comments during research visits to Saudi Arabia in 2015–17.

Translation

One long poem of Ibn Sbayyil (Poem 14) has appeared in English translation in Musil, *The Manners and Customs of the Rwala Bedouins*, 292–300, as described in Kurpershoek, "Praying Mantis in the Desert." Another poem (Poem 32) has been translated in Sowayan, *Nabaṭi Poetry*, 24–27. A limited number of translated verses have appeared scattered in other works. Apart from these few poems and verses, this is the first translation of Ibn Sbayyil's work.

In transliteration from classical Arabic, Ibn Sbayyil's name is written as ʿAbd Allāh ibn Subayyil. Because his work is in the idiom of Najdī vernacular poetry, called Nabaṭī poetry, his and other names are transliterated in a way that more closely reflects the pronunciation of this predominantly oral poetry (recited on social occasions), and that is accepted among specialists. In this introduction, names of towns and other geographical features mentioned in the poetry are transliterated according to their standard classical Arabic spelling to facilitate identification. Occasionally, as appropriate, names and words that occur in the vernacular text may be given in the introduction and the endnotes (e.g., if they occur in book titles or as official family names) according to the classical Arabic transliteration. For instance, the title and name of *muṭawwaʿ*, which is *mṭawwaʿ* according to the vernacular, is written throughout in accordance with the classical spelling—for the convenience of readers not familiar with the vernacular, and because the difference is minimal. Similarly, the classical spelling of a name is used where this is more convenient or recognizable for these readers. For instance, the tribal names ʿUtaybah and Muṭayr are ʿTēbah and Mṭēr in the vernacular, but will be written throughout according to the classical spelling, as chances are that in other English texts the spelling will resemble the first. The name of the poet Swēlim al-S'hali (CA Suwaylim al-Suhalī) will be written as Suhalī because otherwise readers might pronounce it as the initial consonant of the English "shall," while it should be pronounced as two separate consonants: *(i)s-ha-lī*. Similarly, the Arabic word for the star Canopus, Suhayl, is Shēl in the vernacular, pronounced as: *(i)s-hēl*. The transliteration in these parts of the volume will also hew closer to the classical Arabic practice in other respects and details: the name of Ibn Sbayyil's town will be written as Nifī, with macron on the final vowel, and not as Nifi, as is common in the transliteration of the vernacular where all final vowels are long by definition and there is therefore no need for a macron. In the notes, transliterated verses in the Najdī vernacular show affricated *g* (CA *qāf*) and *k* as, respectively, *ǵ* and *ć*. In the glossary both versions are given: first the vernacular, and then the classical in brackets. Poems and verses are referred to by the number given them in this edition. A full transliteration of the poems, according to the vernacular pronunciation and the system used for its rendering in transliteration, will appear as part of the web-based materials for this edition on the Library of Arabic Literature's website at www.libraryofarabicliterature.org. This will allow the reader to get a more precise idea of how this vernacular poetry is pronounced. For instance, it is not possible in a script developed to represent classical Arabic to render features such as changes in diphthongs or the merging of the phonemes *ẓ* and *ḍ*.

Notes to the Introduction

1 In Najdī perception, "Bedouin" and "sedentary" are generally presented as antithetical concepts. In fact, they are more often symbiotic: two aspects of one social and physical reality, with many intermediate shades. In the poetry of High Najd, the theme of romantic love in poetry was conventionally accepted as part of socializing between different groups. An example of such a setting is a description of a farewell meeting in the tent of a shaykh of al-Daʿājīn of ʿUtaybah, Mnāḥī al-Hēḍal, a daring raider and poet, when his Bedouin were about to leave the wells at al-Athlah, a village near Nifī, at the end of the hot season. They invited their sedentary hosts for the evening and everyone was asked to recite a poem or tell a story. Among the guests was the poet Fhēd al-Mijmāj (see also introduction, p. xv, n. 20 below, and glossary), whose father-in-law asked him to take his turn, as he claimed to be ignorant in this field. Fhēd then recited a poem in which he addresses his father-in-law with the words: "By God, when the Bedouin made up their mind to depart, and loaded the victuals on their white-shouldered camels! / Only yesterday they sojourned at our wells, their fires blazing like fiery flashes of lightning. / Now all we see are kites scavenging on the campsite, a deserted abode, as if no human ever set foot on it." The last verse is similar to this edition's §3.2. Al-Mijmāj ends with warm praise for al-Athlah's Bedouin guests. It was reported that all those present on that occasion were moved to tears. In a sequel to this poem al-Mijmāj sang the praises of his heartthrob among the Bedouin who carried her away. His opening line is: "By God, they have left their campground around the wells deserted, and now its emptiness stares me in the face." (Ibn Junaydil, *Min aʿlām al-adab al-shaʿbī, shuʿarāʾ al-ʿĀliyah*, 50–55). One of the last true Bedouin poets, Riḍā ibn Ṭārif al-Shammarī, who passed away in 2015, and who also might be considered one of the last representatives of this school, could still identify with such scenes based on the experiences of his own life. Instead of the kite, he has the classical raven croaking on the deserted site: "On the resting places of their herds, ravens hopped like little lambs" (*mirḥānihum gāmat ʿalēha tiḍūli, taḥājal al-ghirbān mithl al-garāfīsh*) (Sowayan, *al-Ṣaḥrāʾ*, 601). Thus, in High Najd, Bedouin and villagers shared the same lore and imagery, with a history of more than a thousand years, based on common experience.

2 Al-Masridī mentions that traces of the ʿUtaybah tribe's dialect are discernible in the poetry of Muṭawwaʿ Nifī. *Suʿaydān ibn Musāʿid (Sʿēdān ibn Msāʿid), Muṭawwaʿ Nifī, ḥayātuh wa-shiʿruh*, 83, n. 1.

3 See the article on Nifi in the geographical dictionary for the High Najd by Saʿd ibn ʿAbd Allāh ibn Junaydil, *Al-Muʿjam al-jughrāfī li-l-bilād al-ʿarabiyyah al-Saʿūdiyyah, ʿĀliyat Najd*. A popular saying is "for free-ranging camels the best pasture is Nifī's" (*mā l-al-hāmil ʿan Nifī*), used in reference to the tendency of people to be attracted to places where there is a relative abundance of what they need. Al-Juhaymān, *Al-Amthāl al-shaʿbiyyah fī qalb al-jazīrah al-ʿarabiyyah*, 7, 151.

4 See §27.2.40: "As for myself, I have no further knowledge about her: I am just a villager—they, redoubtable Bedouin." In fact, marriages between sedentary and nomadic lineages were quite common, at least among the more prestigious "pure" lineages. Al-Fahad, "The ʿImama vs. the ʿIqal," 39.

5 Khālid al-Faraj gives 1938 (1358) as the year of his death (*Dīwān al-Nabaṭ*, 165). The more likely 1933 date is the one given by Saʿd ibn Junaydil in his introduction to the edition of Ibn Sbayyil's poetry by his grandson, Muḥammad ibn ʿAbd al-ʿAzīz ibn Sbayyil (*Dīwān Ibn Sbayyil*, 14).

6 Al-Masridī, *Muṭawwaʿ Nifī*, 25.

7 The ode must have been composed toward the end of his rule. The battle of Thirb, mentioned in the poem, took place in 1894/5 when the poet was probably in his early forties. Ibn Sbayyil is said to have composed the ode in praise of Ibn Rashīd under duress, after having received a crippling beating from the ruler, see translation, n. 249.

8 Ibn Sbayyil's political views progress, and can be traced through his poems. Assuming that Poem 23 was composed around 1895, at the zenith of Muḥammad ibn Rashīd's power, the next poem is his exchange of invective verse with a poet of the ʿUtaybah tribe on the occasion of Ibn Rashīd's death in 1897 and the succession of ʿAbd-al-ʿAzīz ibn Mitʿib al-Rashīd (Poem 43.2). While in this exchange he speaks in flattering terms about the Rashīdī ascendancy in Najd, he does not respond to an insult in a poem by Minīʿ al-Giʿūd in celebration of the Rashīdī raiding expedition near Nifī in 1902 (Poem 44). Perhaps his reply was lost, but it is possible that he was dismayed at the Rashīdī behavior at the gates of Nifī. Also, it had become clear in the intervening years that ʿAbd al-ʿAzīz ibn Mitiʿib could not hold a candle to his uncle Muḥammad and that Rashīdī influence was on the wane, as explained in the manuscript of al-ʿUbayyid, *al-Najm al-lāmiʿ li-l-nawādir jāmiʿ* (see translation, n. 504). Moreover, ʿAbd al-ʿAzīz had reconquered Riyadh from Ibn Rashīd in January 1902. And toward the end of 1904, with the Rashīdī discomfiture to the south of al-Qaṣīm, he had switched his allegiance to Ibn Saʿūd's rule,

as expressed in his short poem on that occasion (Poem 25). As a literary achievement, this piece cannot bear comparison to his earlier great ode in praise of Muḥammad ibn Rashīd. It is likely, therefore, that the poetry on which Ibn Sbayyil's renown is built dates from an earlier period, roughly between 1880 and 1900. Most of his ghazals were probably composed before 1895, when he was in his forties—though his assertion in the first verse of his ode to Ibn Rashīd that "I am done with the subject and pursuit of love" is a standard trope. In any case, it is unlikely that he continued composing on his earlier "frivolous" note into his fifties, given the rise of the movement of the *ikhwān*, the settled Bedouin who were instrumental in most of the Saudi conquests, who imposed an implacably strict adherence to Wahhābi tenets, and who frowned on such poetry.

9 The theme of Poem 5.

10 See al-ʿUbayyid, *al-Najm al-lāmiʿ li-l-nawādir jāmiʿ*.

11 Ibn Junaydil, *Aʿlām*, 17–23, and *Khawāṭir wa-nawādir turāthiyyah*, 161–63, where the author avers that this poetry, with its mixture of lightheartedness and amorous sentiment, made the relentless toil and hardship more bearable.

12 Verses by members of this group, among them Ibn Sbayyil, are presented in Kurpershoek, "Heartbeat: Conventionality and Originality in Najdi Poetry."

13 Hereafter spelled al-Rūgah for al-Rūqah, Bargā for Barqā, and al-Bgūm for al-Buqūm.

14 He grew up in the village of al-Burūd in the al-Sirr region, where his father had married the sister of a poet of the al-Mrēkhāt branch of the Muṭayr tribe, ʿBēd ibn Dūghān al-Mrēkhī. After his father died, he moved in with the family of his uncle in al-Athlah. Ibn Junaydil, *Aʿlām*, 67–68.

15 Sowayan, *Fihrist al-shiʿr al-nabaṭī*, 234–35. His descendants have adopted the diminutive al-Sʿēdān as the family name (al-Masridī, *Muṭawwaʿ Nifī*, 20).

16 Among the books he read with his community in Nifī were Ibn al-Jawzī's *Dhamm al-hawā* (*Censure of Passion*)—a book he honored in the breach if one goes by his ghazal poetry—and *Laṭāʾif al-maʿārif* by Ibn Rajab. Al-Masridī, *Muṭawwaʿ Nifī*, 15.

17 Ibn Sbayyil had achieved some level of literacy, according to information provided by members of his family, and according to letters addressed to Ibn Sbayyil that are included in his grandson's diwan of his work.

18 This kind of friendly, and sometimes not so friendly, barb among poets is called *ʿayārah* (from the verb *ʿayyar*, "to insult, taunt, revile"), a word that denotes playful impudence, an unconventional demeanor, a trait that Ḥmēdān al-Shwēʿir mentions as his signature quality in the opening verse of one of his poems (Kurpershoek, *Arabian Satire*, 41, §14.1). Ibn Khamīs writes that Sʿēdān al-Muṭawwaʿ is a poet known for "his gaiety and delightful jesting" (*Taʾrīkh al-Yamāmah*, 5, 398).

19 Hence the popular saying "more expensive than the mortar of Muṭawwaʿ" (*aghlā min nijr al-Muṭawwaʿ*). Al-Masridī, *Muṭawwaʿ Nifī*, 16. See Poem 42.6.

20 In an anecdote that is adduced as evidence of the respect he enjoyed as a trustworthy person and skilled poet, Muṭawwaʿ Nifī is presented as the arbiter in a competition among four poets: Slēmān al-Ṭiwīl, Ibn Sbayyil, Slēmān ibn Shrēm, and Fhēd al-Mijmāj. Each was asked to compose two lines of ghazal (Ibn Sbayyil's two lines are §§22.19–20), and al-Mijmāj was declared the winner. This story was first published in an article,"Muṭawwaʿ Nifī Organizes a Competition among the Champions [*fuḥūl*, lit. 'studs'] of Poetry," *Al-Riyadh* newspaper, 2008, by Ṣalāḥ al-Zāmil, who recorded it from Rḍēmān ibn Ḥsēn al-Shammarī (al-Masridī, *Muṭawwaʿ Nifī*, 30–33). It is an example of how some poets, even relatively recent ones, are turned into protagonists of stories that cast them as a certain type of character—in this case the jocular type and the maverick who offers a delightful contrast with what one would expect from a religious functionary and turns him into the hero of curious anecdotes, *rāʿī ṭarāʾif*—as studied by Sowayan in his chapter "Tadākhul al-taʾrīkh wa-l-usṭūrah" ("Enmeshment of History and Legend") in *al-Ṣaḥrāʾ*, 320–73.

21 See n. 8 above.

22 On Swēlim, see n. 25 below. The first student to draw attention to these poets as a specific group is Saʿd ibn Junaydil (1925–2006), who in the 1980s kindly assisted me with additional glosses to his anthologies. He is considered the principal historian of High Najd, and authored one of the best Saudi geographical dictionaries, *ʿĀliyat Najd* (*High Najd*). His father, ʿAbd Allāh ibn Junaydil, was well acquainted with the poetry and person of Muṭawwaʿ Nifī, with whom the family was related through marriage (al-Masridī, *Muṭawwaʿ Nifī*, 45). He was a trader who moved from Shaqrāʾ to al-Shaʿrāʾ, at the heart of the Bedouin country sung about by the poets whose work he collected. He belonged to Najd's sedentary classes, but it is evident that he fully shared the romantic vision of Bedouin life that transpires from the work of Ibn Sbayyil and other poets of this group, whether sedentary or Bedouin, in his well-annotated anthology, *Min āʿlām al-adab al-shaʿbī* (*Highlights of Popular Literature*). Though the title suggests otherwise, it exclusively deals with five poets of the "romantic school": Fhēd ibn ʿAbdallah ibn Fhēd al-Mijmāj al-Tamīmī, Mashʿān al-Htēmī, ʿBēd ibn Hwēdī al-Dōsirī (whose work was continued by his son, Ibrāhīm ibn ʿBēd ibn Hwēdī), Ḥwēd ibn Ṭihmāj al-Wāziʿī, and ʿAbdallah ibn ʿWēwīd.

23 Kurpershoek, "Heartbeat," 36, where parallels between the lyrical style of Ibn Sbayyil and other members of the "romantic school" and the poetry of al-Dindān are pointed out.

24 For the term "Nabaṭī poetry," see n. 82 below. A prominent representative of literate Nabaṭī poets who strove to embellish their verse with rhetorical flourishes (*badīʿ*) was Mḥammad ibn Liʿbūn (1791–1831/2). Before him, the poet Miḥsin al-Hazzānī (1718–1795/6) contributed to this trend. Its influence is still conspicuous in the poetry of Muḥammad al-ʿAbd Allāh al-Qāḍī, who died in 1869. These literate poets were firmly embedded in a sedentary culture and exhibited far less Bedouin influence than Ibn Sbayyil and his fellowpoets of High Najd, see Sowayan, *Nabaṭi Poetry*, the chapter "Nabaṭi Poetry and the Classical Literary Tradition," 168–82. The poetry of Ibrāhīm ibn Jʿēthin (1844–1943) from al-Tuwaym in Sudayr uses some of the same stereotyped ghazal language as Ibn Sbayyil, though without the latter's skills as an artist. Significantly, the extended simile is entirely lacking in his work.

25 See Sowayan, *al-Ṣaḥrā'*, the chapter "The Historical Dimension," 94–96, on the stylistic use of the extended simile (*al-uslūb al-istiṭrādī*) in classical and Nabaṭī poetry. Sowayan points to an early and already developed example: the elegy in which Abū Dhu'ayb al-Hudhalī mourns the loss of his sons with three consecutive such similes. He considers Ibn Sbayyil and Swēlim al-ʿAlī al-Suhalī (on the spelling of his name, see introduction, p. xxxv) the masters of this device (ibid., 261). A late flourishing of the school is the oeuvre of Swēlim al-ʿAlī al-Nwēṣir al-Shalī (Suwaylim al-ʿAlī al-Nuwayṣir al-Suhalī, 1916–86), who outdid all the other poets with a double extended simile of great length—one with a description of a Bedouin who loses his possessions to a raiding party, and the other on a sudden hailstorm that wiped out many months of farmers' toil (for detail and a translation, see Sowayan, *Nabaṭi Poetry*, 113–17). Swēlim preferred to live in the desert and his poetry is hardly influenced by the changes that occurred since the time of Ibn Sbayyil. Other poets who lived in High Najd or its periphery, like ʿAbdallah ibn Dwērij and Slēmān ibn Shrēm, do not qualify as members of the group on stylistic grounds, such as the absence of the extended simile in their work.

26 Saad al-Bazei wrote that Ibn Sbayyil composed "some of the most lyrical poetry in the colloquial Arabic of the Najd region. He is still widely remembered as an exceptionally talented poet [. . .] with thousands of people memorizing his lines and reciting them either to substantiate a wisdom, or simply to express a sentiment" (*Riyadh Daily*, 24 September 1994). Khālid al-Faraj, the first editor of his poetry, praises Ibn Sbayyil as "the seal of the great poets who became famous during his life and whose words were carried far and wide by travelers on camelback." Another early editor, al-Ḥātam, concurs: "One of the great names in poetry, Ibn Sbayyil is among the foremost of the later Najdī poets" (*Min al-shiʿr al-Najdī*, 5). And Sowayan writes: "The settlers' romantic and nostalgic view of nomadic life is reflected in the compositions of settled Nabaṭi

poets, some of whom dedicated the major share of their poetry to describing the ways of nomads and their patterns of migration. The best representative of this school is ʿAbdallah al-Ḥamūd Ibn Subayyil" (*Nabaṭi Poetry*, 24–27). Sowayan notes that his grandfather knew five poems by Ibn Sbayyil by heart (ibid., 121), and avers that the genre of poetic correspondence reached its apogee in the exchange of poems between Ibn Sbayyil and Ibn Zirībān (ibid., 182).

27 Indeed, Ibn Sbayyil appears natural and easy at first, but this impression of polish results from a complex of artfully structured and integrated factors that becomes apparent only on closer engagement with it.

28 This is the central theme of Ibn Sbayyil's work. Therefore, this pursuit is by and large presented in a positive light, in spite of the agonies it entails. The poet's "heart," "soul" (*al-nafs*), and "eye"—with the double meaning of "inner self," or "eye/self-I" (Homerin, "Mystical Improvisations," 112)—are united in their pursuit of love, as expressed in §2.13. The attempts of the poet's "ratio" to temper their zeal remain futile. There is no hint of moral scruple as to what classical preachers condemned as "the passion of concupiscence" (*al-hawā li-nafs*), as detailed in Homerin, "Preaching Poetry."

29 Similarly, in early Arabic ghazals drought and springtime are metaphors for the absence or presence of the beloved, e.g., in verses by the Hudhalī poet Abū Dhu'ayb: "A land where you are not dwelling seems barren to me, even if it is moistened by dew and flourishing" (Jacobi, "Time and Reality in Nasīb and Ghazal," 3). The ʿAbbāsid poet al-Buḥturī metaphorically located the "deserted campsite" in his heart. Ibn Sbayyil adds another layer by connecting the motif antithetically to the Bedouin's seasonal migrations and their pedestrian concerns with pastures and wells.

30 For many examples, see Muḥammad ibn Nāṣir al-ʿUbūdī, *Muʿjam al-anwāʾ w-al-fuṣūl*, 123–30, and his *Muʿjam al-uṣūl al-faṣīḥah li-l-alfāẓ al-dārijah*, 462–68. There is also evidence that villagers would expect the Bedouin to depart, see n. 373 to §32.12.

31 The well, its equipment, and ways to draw water from it are an inexhaustible source of inspiration, images, and similes for the Najdī poet. These are generally used as metaphors for the poet's inner state of mind, and in particular the suffering of his soul. Sometimes the poet's inner world is directly linked to the well and its accoutrements, as in a verse where al-Mijmāj speaks about "the pulley wheel of my gushing feelings" (*maḥḥāl al-ḍimāyir*), following his love's departure. A famous early classical example is a section of seven verses on this motif by Zuhayr ibn Abī Sulmā, *Sharḥ dīwān*, 37–41, and verses by ʿAlqamah, Ahlwardt, *The Divans of the Six Ancient Arabic Poets*, 111 (see n. 61 below). The imagery of the well, the rope, and the bucket is also used as an appropriately ambiguous metaphor for sexual intercourse, see Kurpershoek, *Arabian Satire*,

index, 194, under "sex" and "well, sexual symbolism of." Thus ʿBēd ibn Hwēdī replies, when teased by girls on account of his stooped walk and cane, that he has not lost any of his interest in amorous escapades and keeps his "bucket, rope, and utensils for scooping up water from the well's bottom" ready at hand for "passionate romance" (*al-hawā*) (Ibn Junaydil, *Aʿlām*, 163).

32 It is typical of Muṭawwaʿ Nifī's buffoonery and jesting that his well features no less than four pulley wheels and four camels trained for the hard work of pulling up heavy buckets, driven by a wayward black slave, followed by advice to sell him off immediately (al-Masridī, *Muṭawwaʿ Nifī*, 80–82). See also n. 397 to §34.3. Scenes of mayhem at the well, generally introduced by a formula such as "How I cry for so-and-so," in his hands turn into hilarious parody: "The laments of three yearling camels, three shrieking pulley wheels, the howling of seven wolves, the groans of three she-camels bereft of their young, the lovesick cooing of two doves accompanied by the squeals of a one-stringed Bedouin violin: all this on account of a sweetheart who [. . .]," (*yā-wannitī wannat thalāthat mifārīd, w-thalāth maḥāḥīlin w-sabʿat dhyābih / w-thalāth khiljin kill ibūhin mawālīd, w-ḥamāmitēn w-thālithathin ribābih / ʿalā ʿashīrin* [. . .]) (al-Masridī, ibid, 88).

33 In the words of R. Jacobi, "Die Anfänge der arabischen Ghazalpoesie," 31. An early example involves the thirty-three verses devoted to a picture of the beloved in a poem by al-Marrār ibn Munqidh: its centerfold displays five verses that detail one element of this ideal of beauty, the beloved's voluminous behind, in almost phantasmagorical detail (*Dīwān al-Mufaḍḍaliyyāt*, 1, 155–59; 2, 53–54).

34 The motif is succinctly expressed by ʿAbdallah ibn ʿWēwīd: "Her firm breasts protrude as round as apples; if she wants to unbutton her front, she is obstructed by the pressure from her bulging behind" (*ibū nhūdin fī ṣadrih ṭalʿ tiffāḥ, yibī zarr thōbih w-ar-ridāyif yʿawwiginnih*) (Ibn Junaydil, *Aʿlām*, 81). And ʿBēd ibn Hwēdī al-Dōsirī: "Her movements make her tight dress wrinkle in layers over her buttocks, may God help her to carry the weight of that behind" (Ibn Junaydil, *Aʿlām*, 144). Nöldeke, in his comments on the name of Dhū l-Rummah's beloved, Kharqāʾ, explains that it was seen as desirable for a woman to be inactive "in order to allow her posterior to balloon so that she would walk with a wobbly gait and pant from exertion, and leave the domestic chores to slave girls" ("Dhurumma," 183).

35 Al-Masridī, *Muṭawwaʿ Nifī*, 68–69. The author muses that his fame can probably be partly ascribed to the seeming incongruity of an imam who composes poetry, and love poetry at that, "since it is well known that those trained in Islamic law stay away from composing this kind of poetry" (al-Masridī, *Muṭawwaʿ Nifī*, 29). This is not entirely true. Other men of religion who were known as *muṭawwaʿ* were also famed for their

love poetry: Khalīl ibn ʿĀyiḍ, dubbed "Muṭawwaʿ al-Maskūf" (i.e., of a mosque in the old alleyways of ʿUnayzah) (Sowayan, *al-Shiʿr al-nabaṭī*, 493–94), and "Muṭawwaʿ Ushayqir," who died while composing his last love poem when he was forced to divorce the wife he had married from love against the will of his family (Ibn ʿAqīl, *Kayfa yamūt al-ʿushshāq* (*How Lovers Die*), 394–457; see also n. 441 to §40.15)

36 Similarly, §§10.4–5. Ibrāhīm ibn Jʿēthin (see n. 24 above and Kurpershoek, *Arabian Satire*, 69, §19.34) adds the same touch, albeit in a more bashful way by making it conditional: "If not for my fear of God, I would say seeing her is as good as my Hajj and fasting during Ramadan"; and: "Have compassion with me, she was my partner in praying and fasting" (*Dīwān*, 136, 124). The motif was widespread, therefore.

37 Similarly, §12.13 ("Slayer who needs no weapon, give the Muslim fair warning before taking his life!") implies that the poet follows the right religion—his devotion to the codes of love—and wishes that his belle would convert to it. The concepts of justice and the law of retaliation are employed by Ibn Sbayyil for similar purpose in §§6.10–12.

38 The procedure is explained in detail in Burckhardt, *Notes on the Bedouins and Wahabys*, 121–22.

39 The same sentiment is expressed by Muṭawwaʿ Nifī: "I wanted to be pious, recite with diligence from the scriptures, and stay away from silly acts, / but things beyond my power intervened and blocked my intentions. / A lover who reads scripture is just pretending: he only pines for a love who left." (al-Masridī, *Muṭawwaʿ Nifī*, 105–6). In another line that follows the standard verse about his suffering heart, he unapologetically brackets religious duties and poetry together in a matter-of-fact way: "Like prayers and associated duties, I want to declaim my well-crafted, flawless verses" (Ibn ʿAqīl, *Ḥadīth al-shahr*, 140). These exchanges echo classical debates, such as the criticism by al-Ghazzālī and Ibn al-Jawzī, in his *Kitāb al-Quṣṣāṣ wa-l-Mudhakkirīn*, of "the frequent recitation of love poetry during sermons" from the pulpit in the mosque (Homerin, "Preaching Poetry"). In some verses Ibn Sbayyil's method closely parallels the dalliance of the seventh century poet ʿUmar ibn Abī Rabīʿah. Both use religion as a foil to reaffirm—partly tongue-in-cheek—the seriousness of their devotion, e.g., *al-Aghānī*, 1, 205; *Diwān ʿUmar ibn Abī Rabīʿah*, 389–90.

40 Thomas Bauer's remark that literary testimony, if taken seriously, demonstrates that it is possible to make a distinction between secular and religious spheres in "Islamic" societies, is seemingly applicable to nineteenth-century Najd too. Bauer, *Liebe und Liebesdichtung in der arabischen Welt des 9. und 10. Jahrhunderts*, 6.

41 See for instance n. 221 to §18.10 and Kurpershoek, *Arabian Satire*, 105, §26.6.

42 In Ḥmēdān's long poem on women and marriage, for instance, the wife is expected to be strict in her modesty, frugality, and exclusive devotion to her husband and family. To walk in the street, even wrapped in a black cloak and veiled, and chat at other people's doors would expose her and, much worse, her husband, to shame and loss of status, "for a woman about town is like a fat sheep, eyed lecherously by hungry dogs, even by the puppies" (Kurpershoek, *Arabian Satire*, 71, §19.54).

43 Similarly, the seventeenth-century Najdī poet Jabr ibn Sayyār (see Kurpershoek, *Arabian Satire*, xiv) praises his beloved's spiritual qualities: "She is vivacious, fun-loving, and playful" (*ʿajjābitin mazzāḥitin laʿʿābih*), Sowayan, *al-Shiʿr al-nabaṭī*, 462.

44 The poet's example is Job, whose faithfulness is sorely tried by God, see Poem 1.

45 The only cure is in the hands of the beloved, see translation, n. 123. In §13.3 it is compared to the habit of smoking, something one wishes to give up, but willy-nilly keeps returning to.

46 Sowayan quotes from poems §§33.14–18, and §29.19, to argue that the energy the poet displays, as he braces himself for the hardships he will encounter on his amorous adventures, should be understood as a metaphor for the arduous task of composing poetry (*al-Ṣaḥrāʾ*, 209–10). Certainly in these examples a reading on one level does not exclude the others.

47 As in Poem 31's opening verse: "Leave off, you players of love's game, leave off! Abandon that worn-out charade; just stop!"

48 Society's common sense is reflected in the popular saying "If you marry a woman from love, you will soon loathe her" (*min khadh ʿishg khallā ʿyāf*) (al-Juhaymān, *Amthāl*, 8, 157). The view of traditional society in the settled communities on this question is detailed in Ḥmēdān al-Shwēʿir's long poem with marriage advice (Kurpershoek, *Arabian Satire*, 64–73).

49 That is, the poet deflects society's criticism, similar to countries that justify their external behavior by pointing to the constraints imposed on them by situations of domestic strife.

50 Similarly, "I have packed up my equipment at the well: let someone else take my job, if he feels like it" (Kurpershoek, *Arabian Satire*, 15, §5.15).

51 In a further subtle twist, the word *āyah* is a repetition of the last word of the previous line, where *āyah*, for *ayyih*, means "which one?"

52 Here he argues that it is not a novelty, *bidʿah*, with the religious connotation of "heresy"; and in further explanation, §§26.15–18, that he would feel remorse at being remiss in his religion, were it not that many famous and mighty lovers preceded him on this path. The same point is made by ʿUmar ibn Abī Rabīʿah, see translation, n. 439.

53 According to transmitted lore, Ibn Sbayyil had good reason to be on his guard for Ibn Rashīd, see translation, n. 249 for more background on this poem.

54 The poem is in a different meter and rhyme than normally used by Ibn Sbayyil.

55 The poems on other themes than ghazal are 5, 11, 15, 17.2, 21, 23, 25, 30, and 32.

56 Curiously, these two poems are not much cited in the Najdī collections of proverbs. Many of these poems' maxims correspond to the wisdom proffered by Ḥmēdān al-Shwēʿir, see Kurpershoek, *Arabian Satire*, xxviii.

57 Often referred to as the "modern school" (*al-muḥdathūn*). Sowayan, in *al-Ṣaḥrā' al-ʿarabiyyah*, 93, 395–96, 414–15, 437–44, draws comparisons between Ibn Sbayyil's poems and those of Dhū l-Rummah, al-Farazdaq, al-Aʿshā, Ṭarafah, ʿAlqamah ibn ʿAbdah, and Qays ibn al-Ḥadādiyyah.

58 If at the time of Dhū l-Rummah there was "a nostalgia for a mode of life about to disappear," as R. Jacobi avers in her *EI* article on the subject of Nasīb, then this applied only to centers of literary taste in Iraq and elsewhere. In the Arabian interior, Bedouin life and poetry must have continued very much unchanged for more than a thousand years.

59 In his verses Muṭawwaʿ Nifī mentions some earlier Nabaṭī poets—Nimr ibn ʿAdwān, Miḥsin al-Hazzānī, and Ibn Liʿbūn—who were literate and influenced by classical Arabic poetry (al-Masridī, *Muṭawwaʿ Nifī*, 96). So does the school's late representative, Swēlim al-Suhalī: "Before me, Nimr [ibn ʿAdwān] was not blamed for recounting his exploits, and Ibn Ribīʿah when his feats were told; / and Mḥammad al-Gāḍī and Miḥsin [al-Hazzānī] and their ilk, or Majnūn Laylā when he turned insane." (*Majmūʿat ashʿār al-shaʿir al-shaʿbī Suwaylim al-ʿAlī al-Suhalī*, 212).

60 The most thorough discussion of the early roots of the Nabaṭī poetry that originated in the early classical Arabian poetry is found in Sowayan, *al-Shiʿr al-nabaṭī*, based on comprehensive readings of manuscripts. It also provides many edited examples, a careful periodization, and detailed prosodic analysis.

61 For instance, both these interconnected traditions employ imagery derived from the use of animal traction for hoisting water from wells in a way that hardly changed until the introduction of engines in modern times. In her discussion of a poem by the pre-Islamic poet ʿAlqamah, R. Jacobi comments that in the prelude "the contrast between the nostalgic mood of farewell and the banal description of a scruffy camel pulling at the well has a jarring effect," and that here the simile "has no longer any relation to the poem's theme" (*Studien zur Poetik der altarabischen Qaṣide*, 20–21). In fact, for those acquainted with the environment, the simile might well serve to underpin the poet's overall intent. When the camel used for irrigation (*sāniyah*) has reached the point of exhaustion and almost collapses, it is sent to recover in pastures. When the camel returns to the labor at

the well, it pulls the bucket with renewed strength, and sometimes vehemence when it is driven by a laborer without feeling for the animal (a trait condemned in this poetry). This may cause additional strain on the ropes and uneven motions of the bucket, with the result that it empties with a violent splash into the catchment basin, as in Ibn Sbayyil's verse §13.20, which features an untrained, vehement camel that wreaks havoc at the well. Therefore, it is likely that ʿAlqamah's verses on the camel at the well are meant to reinforce the image of the poet's shedding of tears "pouring forth in streams." ʿAlqamah's simile transits with a marker, *min dhikri* (Salmā), "as I think nostalgically of," and so does Ibn Sbayyil with *ʿalā llidhī*, "on account of (a beloved)."

62 Ibn Sbayyil is always deferential and often submissive to his beloved in the style of the courtly poets who came after ʿUmar. ʿUmar's favorite hunting ground was the precinct of the holy Kaaba in Mecca, where he would accost rich and beautiful women, who appeared to have had considerable freedoms. The women are pictured as eager to meet him, in spite of rebukes on all sides, and keen to be immortalized in his verse. He is reported as having said that women fell in love with him, and his poetry is said to have "bewitched" women (cf. §33.9). Ibn Sbayyil would never permit himself ʿUmar's delight in impudence, such as his call on judges, "in fear of God," to hand down favorable testimonies to women with bulging behinds and to send those with slender buttocks to a camp deep in the desert so that Muslim men would be spared their sight, *Dīwān*, 13. Nor would Ibn Sbayyil ever be greeted by ladies as "you fornicator" (*fāsiq*), as is a character in the anecdotes of al-Iṣfahānī's *Book of Songs* (*Kitāb al-Aghānī*); or be called the "most disobedient to God" (*al-Aghānī*, 1, 108); nor would people pay him large sums to abstain from composing sinful verse (*al-Aghānī*, 1, 110). Ibn Sbayyil's poet-lover does not engage in ʿUmar's lively dialogue with his paramours, as for instance on his tryst with Nuʿm (*Dīwān*, 120–27); and his tone with the beloved is less intimate, and in that sense less "modern," than when ʿUmar tells her (*Dīwān*, 94): "I said, 'Don't be angry, I'd give my poetry and tongue for you, and whatever besots my heart; / Don't be mad at me, I'd give my soul for you, even my folks, my eyes, my children.'" Even though ʿUmar plays the role of lady-killer, his conquests often give as good as they get and make clear that they see him as the prize to be won—not that they are the poet's prey. There is a fine human balance in their affairs of the heart, and it is quite unthinkable that Ibn Sbayyil's beloved would beg him for mercy instead of him doing so (as in §6.13), in the way of Hind to ʿUmar: "May God help you, don't you have mercy on me, or has your heart turned to stone?" (*ʿamraka llāha amā tarḥamunī, am la-nā qalbuka aqsā min ḥajar*), *Dīwān*, 172.

63 The noun and verb for "trial, putting to the test," (*imtiḥān, imtaḥan*) is used. Cf. "Do not put my patience to the test (*lā tamtaḥin*) by forsaking me, because I have reached the limit of my endurance." Bauer, *Liebe und Liebesdichtung*, 395.

64 "The power of the beloved is however only the one pole of this play, the other being the lover's willingness to submit to and accept every whim, every crudeness and cruelty from the beloved." Bürgel, "The Mighty Beloved."

65 Bürgel, "The Mighty Beloved," 56 ff.

66 Ibn Sbayyil's work lends itself to a comparative listing of ghazal elements. But even a cursory view shows that it falls within mainstream Arabic traditions of this genre. Virtually every theme and motif categorized by Bauer has its correlate in Ibn Sbayyil's ghazals, down to the level of vocabulary and phrasing specific to the genre. Bauer, *Liebe und Liebesdichtung*, 208–527.

67 Al-Juhaymān, *Amthāl*. Some sayings are also found in al-ʿUbūdī, *al-Amthāl al-ʿāmmiyyah fī Najd*, but to a much lesser extent. Al-Juhaymān's work cannot be used as a guide to Ibn Sbayyil's work as such. Verses are quoted at random, according to the taste of the author; the same verse is sometimes quoted with somewhat different wording; and where readings differ from the version in al-Faraj, *Dīwān al-Nabaṭ*, it is usually inferior.

68 However, the Najdī collections quote more than twice as many sayings from the seventeenth- and eighteenth-century satirist Ḥmēdān al-Shwēʿir, whose work deals with social and political issues in a pithy and apodictic manner that closely parallels the expression of gnomic wisdom. Ibn Sbayyil is probably the second-most quoted poet in al-Juhaymān's collection.

69 If one uses a general correlation of meaning in comparing the diwan and the two collections of Najdī proverbs, one may arrive at about 135 instances of more or less close correspondence. The total number of verses quoted by al-Juhaymān is about 320. There is considerable overlap, however, as many are quoted several times to illustrate different proverbs. In addition, many of the proverbs are similar in meaning and wording. Therefore, the real number of proverbs and sayings quoted from Ibn Sbayyil's work is considerably smaller than the one these figures would indicate.

70 Cf. al-Juhaymān, *Amthāl*, 5:314–15.

71 E.g., "excuses do not fill the guest's stomach"; "shaking the bucket by its rope does not quench the camels' thirst"; "do not let cooler weather stop you from carrying a waterskin."

72 Cf. Swēlim al-Suhalī, who extends two consecutive dramatic similes to no less than twenty-one verses. Sowayan, *Nabaṭi Poetry*, 114–16.

73 One finds *ʿalēk y-allī*, "because of you, who (followed by a description of the beloved, as in the formulas that follow)"; *ʿalēk yā-*, "because of you, O so-and-so"; *ʿalā allidhī*, "because of one who"; *ʿalā ʿashīrin*, "because of a lady friend who," in Poems 2, 7, 13, 18, 22, 29, 33, 34, and 38.

74 An example of the formula's early classical usage is the line in the *muʿallaqah* poem of ʿAmr ibn Kulthūm: "A moaning camel mother who lost her young does not feel as much grief as I do, / nor does a graying woman whose nine sons all lie buried in a grave" (*fa-mā wajadat ka-wajdī ummu saqbin, aḍallathu fa-rajjaʿati l-ḥanīnā / wa-lā shamṭāʾu lam yatruk shaqāhā, la-hā min tisʿatin illā janīnā*) (al-Zawzānī, *Sharḥ al-muʿallaqāt al-sabʿ*, 122); or the line of Abū Ṣakhr al-Hudhalī: "On account of Laylā, my agony was double as much as the pain felt by a gray woman who lost her children and grew frail" (*la-qad wajadtu bi-Laylā ḍiʿfa mā wajadat, shamṭāʾu tathkalu baʿda l-shaybi wa-l-haramī*) (Dmitriev, *Das poetische Werk des Abū Ṣakhr al-Hudhalī*, 259). The related formula in §37.12, *wajdī ʿalēhum wajd*, literally "on account of them I suffer the torments of someone who," is followed by a long simile that features the dramatic and unexpected end of an intrepid desert knight, similar to one of al-Suhalī's similes mentioned in n. 25 above.

75 Viewed in this context, three poems in which Bedouin life is ostensibly the main theme, or partly so, might be considered an amatory prologue, *nasīb*, that acquired independent status and where the poet's lovesickness is externalized—though there are clues that hint at the poet's stormy state of mind. In Poem 2, such clues are the exclamations, "Why rejoice at their summering near our wells?" and "Woe to a heart perplexed by the Bedouin's departure!" and, at the end of the scene, "My eyes!" In Poem 24, the first three lines speak about the "drought" and "springtime" of the poet's heart, tied to the movements of the Bedouin in a contrary sense. Poem 32 opens with the negative version of the classical prayer for rain, that is, not to let it rain on nights that passed too quickly—explained in the second line as the reason for the separation of amorous hearts. The remainder of the poem is a representation of the cycles of Bedouin life as dictated by the seasons, without further reference to the sentimental tone struck at the beginning.

76 One exception is a piece by Muṭawwaʿ Nifī, see n. 32 above.

77 Swēlim al-Suhalī, who might be considered a later acolyte of Ibn Sbayyil, employs the same image for a man traveling alone in the desert, who loses his way and dies of thirst, as a simile for his failing success in love (*Majmūʿat ashʿār*, 213). A similar simile on getting lost in the desert is given in Sowayan, *al-Ṣaḥrāʾ*, 261; and Ibn Junaydil, *Aʿlām*, 95, about a camel rider who is thrown off by his mount and left alone in the desert. In addition to the extended simile, short similes are scattered throughout Ibn Sbayyil's verse.

78 See n. 26 above.

79 In contrast with poets like Ḥmēdān al-Shwēʿir and al-Dindān, Ibn Sbayyil's work uses few meters. The great majority of his poetry is composed in a variant of the classical *ṭawīl*, "the long meter," one of the best attested in Arabic poetry. A notable exception is a long poem with a strophic rhyme, called *mrawbaʿ*, with a meter that consists of only long syllables (Poem 5).

80 As Kuntze notes in a comment on Abū Dhu'ayb al-Hudhalī and the issue of common sense: "It is not even clear whether whoever is judging the lover's actions is himself not in a state of folly (*jahl*)." Kuntze, "Love and God."

81 As in Poem 29. In this example from Poem 40 the formula is *lētih*, literally "I wish that she (were with me)." Other markers used in the same poem are: *lōlā . . . lā*, "if not for, were it not that [. . .] I would become, do"; *lō . . . mēr*, "if . . . but," to mark antithetical stages in the poem's emotional arc; *illa* and *mēr*, to signal a reality in opposition to what preceded. The use of the particles *lēt* and *yā-lēt* (CA *layta* and *yā-layta*), "if only, I'd wish that," as a rhetorical marker is made explicit in this line by ʿBēd ibn Hwēdī: "To sigh 'If only' is useless, even when I say 'I'd wish that it was'" (*w-al-lēt ma yanfaʿ w-law gilt lētih*) (Ibn Junaydil, *Aʿlām*, 134). An early classical example is: "You should know that 'if only,' or 'how I wish,' and 'I would like,' will not catch anything" (*wa-ʿlam bi-anna lawa nnanī aw laytanī, wa-wadidtu lā tughnī ḥibālata ḥābilī*) (Dmitriev, *Abū Ṣakhr*, 181).

82 For a short introduction to the subject of Nabaṭī poetry and further information on the manuscripts of al-Rabīʿī and Ibn Yaḥyā, see Kurpershoek, *Arabian Satire*, xxxviii. The best introduction to Nabaṭī poetry in English, and one that makes for delightful reading, is Sowayan, *Nabaṭi Poetry*. For further detail on prosody and language, see also Kurpershoek, *Oral Poetry and Narratives from Central Arabia*. For linguistic aspects, and also their relation to poetry and narrative, see Holes, "Language of Nabaṭi Poetry," and also the chapter "Style in Spoken Discourse" in Holes, *Dialect, Culture, and Society in Eastern Arabia*, 3: 434–66, which is particularly relevant for these aspects in the poetry of Ibn Sbayyil.

83 The MSS by al-ʿUmarī (vernacular spelling: al-ʿMirī) are more in the nature of notebooks. They are kept in the library of the King Saud University in Riyadh. A copy of the manuscript was given to me by Masʿūd al-Masridī, an employee of the Saudi Ministry of Culture and the author of a study on the poet, *Muṭawwaʿ Nifī*.

84 His opening remark was: *al-giṣīd bi-flūs*, poems are given in exchange for money. Then I was told that it was a joke and that, because I was a guest, everything was free.

85 At the time, it did not occur to me to ask the transmitter about his sources. Perhaps he continued earlier oral transmission flawlessly, or he may have memorized the poems from written versions.

86 Al-Muṭawwaʿ Sʿēdān taught children reading and writing, and the Qur'an, at the village school. At the time of the poem on her she was about six years old. It is said that he wrote the verses on her slate and told her to show them to her father, knowing that he would reply in verse. Sārah passed away a few years ago, about one hundred years old. Al-Masridī, *Muṭawwaʿ Nifī*, 50.

Arabian Romantic

~ ١ ~

يالله ياكاشف عن ايوّب ما بِه من الضِرّ يا قابل مِطاليب يَعْقوب
يا ربّ يوسِف يا مصَدِّق جُوابِه يا مِظْهِره مِن ماقِعٍ فيه مَصْلوب
يا داعِي بِنْداه موسى واجابه ياجاعله غالب وفِرْعون مَغلوب
يا مِخْرِجٍ ذا النون يوم اكْتِرابه من غِبّةٍ قَلْبِه من الحُوت مَرْهوب
ولَيّن لداود الحَديد اكْتِسَى به ومِصَخِّرٍ لابْنِه من الريح مَرْكوب
تِفْرِج لِمِمْتَحِنٍ يبي مِنْك ثابه ضاق الفواد ودَكّ بِه كِلّ دالوب
الى بَرَد حَرّه يِزيد الْتِهابه ما يِبْرِده نَقْعٍ من السِحْب مَشْروب
يومٍ انّ خَتّال الزمان الْتِوَى به ما نِحْر الشَكْوى محبٍ ومحبوب
وَحَدْك يوم انّك خَبيرٍ تَرَى به ما يِرْتِجي لِحْذاك يا خير مطلوب
هاب الرِفيق اللي عَرَض لي جَنابه بالطيب واظِنّه من الطيب مَنْتوب
يوم اتّضح والَى الزمان مِتْشابِه صارت مَواعيده مَواعيد عِرْقوب

~ 1 ~

God, You saved Job from his predicament[1]
  and his tribulations; You answered Jacob's prayers.[2]
Lord of Joseph, You made good on Your promise:
  You rescued him from being caught in dire straits;[3]
You called to Moses in a loud voice and answered him:[4]
  making him victorious, and handing Pharaoh defeat.
You delivered Jonah from the clutches of terror
  when the whale swallowed him amid raging waves.[5]
You taught David to forge iron and make a coat of mail;[6]
  You taught his son to use the winds as vessels.[7]
I beseech You! Bring relief to a distressed man:
  his heart is oppressed and by sorrow beset.
If it abates, it will only burst into fiercer flames—
  a rain-filled pool would not quench its fire.
When he is waylaid by Fate's wicked plots,
  a true lover does not recriminate and whine.
You are the One and only to know his plight;
  to no one but You does he plead for succor.
He fears a companion who showed me kindness,[8]
  flowing, I thought, from his natural disposition.
Truth is, Fate's treachery came to light—
  The pledges were as vain as the promises of 'Urqūb.[9]

~ ٢ ~

وِشّ خانة المِقْطان لو قيل ما احلاه   صَيّور ما جا بالليالي غَدَتْ بِه
يا مِن لقَلْبٍ من شِديد العَرَب باه   بَوهَة غَرِيرٍ بالمِظامي رِمَتْ بِه
لا والله الّا صار لِلبَدو نوناه   وثَوّر عَسام الجَوّ مما عَفِتْ بِه
والبيت هَدّنّ الخَدَم زَين مَبْناه   طَوّن ذَراه وقَينة الزَمل جَتْ بِه
وشالوا على اللي بالمِبارك مشَنّاه   ما حِطّ فوق ظُهورها زَوّعَت بِه
مَظْهورهم كِنّ الطِماميع تَشْعاه   يَتْلي سَلَف خيّال من قَرّبَتْ بِه
يا قِرْب مِسْراحه وما ابْعَد معَشّاه   له شَدّةٍ راعى الغَنم تِشْتِمِتْ بِه
لو صَوّت الرَجّال ما تَسْمَع نْداه   من لَجّة المَرحول ما يِلْتِفَتْ بِه
مِقْطانهم امْسَت خِليٍّ رِكاياه   تَقْنِب سباعه والذواري بَنَتْ بِه
وَرْدوا على عِدٍ خَلّلهم بمَنْداه   لين انّ كلٍ من مِديده لِفَتْ بِه
يوم استخالوا نَوض بَرْقٍ بمَنْشاه   يِذْكَر لهم مِدراج سَيلٍ بنَتْبِه
ياعيني اللي في نِظَرها مشَقّاه   تاصَل الى مِشرافهم واشْرِفَتْ بِه
والعَين سَبْر القَلْب والرِجْل مِغْزاه   والى وُمَر قَلْبي لرِجْلي مِشَتْ بِه
رِجْلي على كِثْر التَراديد مَشْهاه   مامورةٍ والّا انّها مِسْتَعَتْبه
قَلْبي رِبيعه جَيّة البَدو ومِنْاه   ولا حَسَّب البَيعات وِش صَرّفت بِه

~ 2 ~

Why rejoice at their summering near our wells[10]
if the nights only will snatch them away?
Woe to a heart perplexed by the Bedouin's departure,[11]
lost like a helpless child cast into waterless wastes.
By God, once the Bedouin have made up their mind,
they kneel their animals, stirring up clouds of dust,[12]
While servants fold down their well-built tents,[13]
slave girls roll up tent walls, fetch the pack camels,[14]
Lift the loads onto the kneeled and fettered beasts
that rush off with goods and chattel on their backs.
The camel train, led by an intrepid knight,[15]
hurries at breakneck speed, as if urged on by bandits;
It left in the morning, its evening halt worlds away,
Leaving sheepherders seething with rancor.[16]
Before, if a man called out loudly, no one heard—
the sound lost in the din of a mass on the move.[17]
Now the summer camp around the wells lies deserted,
but for the wolves' howls and the drifting sands.
Their tents are pitched far off, at a well in lush pasture,
awaiting the arrival of the stragglers and their heavy loads.
They were stirred from our wells by the flicker of lightning
and by reports of torrents and sprouting shoots—[18]
My eyes, transfixed, knew misery and frantic despair,
seeing them fade into the distance from the lookout.[19]
Eyes are the heart's scouts; feet entice it away:
but at the heart's bidding, they will walk;[20]
What my feet like best is to saunter,
when ordered to, or to give satisfaction.[21]
My heart bursts into blossom at the Bedouin's return,
regardless of what we sell or how much they spend.[22]

العَصِر يومِ ان القَصِر مالَت افياه   في سُوقنا الثَوب الحَمَر وَقِّفَتْ به
يجِرّ ثَوب البَزّ واعِظِم بَلْواه   لو انّ قَلْبي مِمْحِلٍ رَبَّعَتْ به
هَنِيّ من قَلْبه دِلوهٍ ومِدْلاه   ما صفِّقت به رابِعه ولْعَبَت به
يا تَلّ قَلْبي تلّة الغَرْب لِرْشاه   على زَعاعٍ حايلٍ صَدَّرَتْ به
سَوّاقها عَبْدٍ ضَرَبْها بِمحْداه   امّا امْرِسَتْ بِرْشاه والّا وِطَت به ٢٠،٢
كِنّك على سَوقَه تِهِمّه وتَنْخاه   لا عَوّد اللّٰه ساعةٍ عَرِّفَت به
لَى اقْفى بها كِنّ الطِماميع تَنْخاه   كِنّ الدَلُو طَيرٍ الى نَزَّعَتْ به
لَين امِّزَع غَرْبه على حَدّ عِرْقاه   وجيلان بيره بالِمسوح لْعَبَتْ به

~ 2 ~

In the afternoon, when the shadows lengthen,[23]
their damsels come and linger at the shops, robed in red,
Trailing the hem of silk dresses. Good heavens!
They revive the parched heart like springtime!
If only my heart were placid with quiet joy,[24]
not battered and buffeted by worry and anxiety!
Ah, my heart is a well bucket dangling on a rope,[25]
pulled up by an unruly she-camel at full tilt,[26]
Beaten by a slave's cudgel as it hurries on the walkway,[27] 2.20
till the rope slips off the roller, or the camel steps on it.[28]
He castigates her as if goaded by battle cries—[29]
may God not let the animal fall into his hands again!
The camel hurtles down the path as if assailed by rustlers,
yanking the well bucket like a fleeing bird.
The wooden crosspieces on the bucket smash
as it scrapes and bangs the well shaft's stones.[30]

~ ٣ ~

يا عَـين وَين احـبابك اللي تودّين   اللِي الى جَوا منـزلٍ رَبَّعوا به
اهْل البيوت اللي على الجوّ طوفَين   عِدٍ خَـلا مـا كنّـهم دوَّجَوا به
مِـنزالهم تـذْري عـليه المَعـاطين   تَـذْري عليه من الذُواري هَـبوبه
عَهْدي بهم باقي من السَبْع ثِنْتَين   قَبْل الشـتا والقَـيظ زَلّ محُسوبه
قلّت جَهـامتهم مِن الجوّ قِسْمَين   الزَمل حَودَر والظَعَن سَـنّدوا به
ما احْـدٍ درَى عن نوّهم وَين ناوين   لَين انهّـم بِظَـعونهـم نـزّلوا به
يبْـغون مِـصفارٍ من النير ويمين   الله لا يجْزي طروشٍ حَكَوا به
قالوا من الوَسْمي نِباته الى الحين   ومن تالي الكَنّه تمَلّت دعوبه
شَـيّالة الكايد على العِسْـر واللِين   والَى وِطـاهـم مُوجبٍ رَحّبوا به
زاد الصِيف معهم بليّا مُواعين   وان شافوا الضيف المطَرّق عَدوا به
والَى تِـرَيّـض يَـذْبحون الخَرافين   ومن زاد بيت الله تْفَرّش عصوبه
ولا عَـطوا يعْطون رُوس البَعـارين   وان فات مِنهم فايتٍ ما حْسِبوا به
ما هم بـربعٍ بالغَنايـم قِـصِيين   لو الحَصـيل حمـار تحَاشروا به
يَشْـعَون مـالٍ فـاختَـتَه الحَوارين   يَشْدي تَـراطين الدُوَل يوم جَوا به
وِلحْدودهم بمَطَرّق الحَدّ حامين   وِقَبّ تبـدّا في بَـرايرِ كسوبه

~ 3 ~

My eyes, where are the loved ones you hold so dear,[31] 3.1
who set up camp and tarried,[32]
And camped in tents in two rows?
Now the well lies deserted, as if never visited; [33]
The resting places' cattle droppings have crumbled
to fine dust blown about the abandoned site.[34]
When last we met, two stars in Ursa Major were in hiding—[35]
not winter yet, but the dog days of summer long gone.
The mass of camels left the flat in two groups: 3.5
pack animals eastward, to stock up; caravan westward, upcountry; [36]
No one knows where they set their sights,
till the camels are kneeled and the camp is made;
They headed for the early fall pastures by al-Nīr—
may God's reward elude the bearers of such tidings,[37]
Proclaiming, "Herbage sprouted by winter rains;
at the cusp of the hot season, the gullies ran full again!" [38]
Stalwarts who do not flinch, either in hardship or ease,
ever ready to prove their mettle in the hour of need.
In late spring there is milk aplenty, straight from the udder: 3.10
if a wayfarer passes by, they rush to him with a bowlful;
If he lingers, they slaughter a sheep and serve it roasted,
entrails coiled around meat, upon a mound of rice.[39]
If they bestow gifts, then nothing less than camels:
so they lose some property—no matter!
If they harvest booty, they do not grab at the windfall:
if all they get is a donkey, it is gladly shared.
They drive herds of camels unhindered by calves,
champion racers that grumble in meaningless prattle.[40]
They protect their borders with blades of steel, 3.15
ride horses fed on choice milk from plundered camels.[41]

صاروا على بَعْض القِبايل عقوبه   والَى تعَـلَّوا فَوق مِثل الشَياهـين
مـثل المـعَشَّر راسـها عـند ثَوبه   لا تَلّهـا الراكب غدا الحَبَل ثِنْوَين
ما قيل يَسْعَل قَـينها وانْظِروا به   عقب النكايف كنّهن السَراحين
فالمـرْمِس اللي من قِديم ادَّعوا به   وان قيل عند قْطِيّهم يا هْل الدين
في المـاقف اللي بايَعوا واشْتِروا به   وتَواقِـفوا مثل الطُوابير مِـرْزين
كِلٍ يبى النومـاس قِدْم مْحَبوبه   رَدّوا عليـهم رَدّةٍ تِعْجِب العَين
وهـذي مـريح عـنانها زل صَوبه   الى ذاك مطروحٍ وذا فيه رِمْحَين
واللي تعَدَّتْه السهوم رْجَلوا به   وهـذا طِريح وذا شِـنيع الاكاوين
وضَبْع الخَلا ياخِـذ سِنينٍ ينُوبه   كِثْر اللَحَم للطير والذيب وحْصَين
لى اومَى لهم سَـبّارهـم رِثْعوا به   كَم عَـزَّلوا ذِيـدان بَـدْوٍ عَـزيـزين
وقالوا لرِعْيان الاخيذ ابْشِروا به   ولْحَقوا بِعيدين المِسـاريح عَجْلين
وتبـاشروا بالمَقْنَوي والجـلوبه   يا زَين تَشْويش العَـرَب بالمـغَنِّين

~ 3 ~

When they vault onto their falcon steeds,[42]
    they fall upon some tribes like a punishing scourge.
A pull, the reins go slack, the animal rears its head,
    like a pregnant camel's tail, touching the rider's shirt.[43]
When the raiders return, the steeds trot like untiring wolves:
    no one says, "What a din from the loosened horseshoes!"
When the shout rings out, "Onto their haunches, avengers!"
    grudges that lie buried are with vigor renewed.[44]
They are unyielding, like heavily laden camels,[45]
    in battle when dear life itself is bought and sold.[46]
The cavalry charged at the enemy with swagger,
    each vying to be his sweetheart's hero.[47]
One is struck down, another pierced by two lances;
    Reinless horses of fallen men run amok;
Here, scattered bodies; there, the grievously wounded;
    the unscathed are unsaddled, robbed of their mounts:[48]
An abundant feast for vultures, jackals, and foxes;
    enough food to last the desert hyena a long time.
They have despoiled countless tribes of precious herds:
    with a sign from the scouts, they rush in and lay waste.[49]
They bring lightning succor to their distant camels;
    their herdsmen are told to expect new booty.[50]
Cheerful they ride out, taunting their enemy in song,[51]
    vaunting the plunder they keep, or peddle.

~ ٤ ~

يا زَيد اشوفك عِقْب الاقبال صَدَّيت　　بعينك وقلبك ما اذري وَيش غَيبه
في خاطري لك واردٍ مار عَدّيت　　لا من يوَدّ العلم ولا من يجيبه
وانا لمارودك وعِلمك تَحَرَّيت　　ومثلك يخَبِّر صاحبه وش مريبه
لا تَحْسِب انّي عنك يا زيد سَجَّيت　　مانيب مِن يَنْسَى جمايل صِحيبه
انا على هاك الحَكايا تَلَوَّيت　　لو غَتَّرتْ سود العَوارض مِشِيبه
افْرَح الى منّك مع السوق مَرَّيت　　كِما تِفَرَّح مِذْهِبٍ في ذِهيبه
واكْرَه الى صَدَّيت وافْرَح الى جِيت　　تَرْحيبةٍ من روح روحٍ لِبيبه
من يمّكم فكّروا بي الناس وشْنيت　　ابْعد بعيد الناس واقرب قِريبه
في حبّكم يا مِتْرَف الروح ضِرَّيت　　نِصيبْ يوم الكلّ يَبْلَغ نِصيبه
احِبّكم والله عليمٍ بما اخْفَيت　　احبّ من مِهراع عَودٍ لِصيبه
الَى مَرَضْت وشِفْت زَولك تَعافَيت　　مثل المَريض اللي تِشافى لِطبيبه
كَميت جَرْح الوِدّ لَين اني ازْرَيت　　ولولا امْتحان الذيب ما اوْحَوا قِنيبه
ما مرّةٍ في هَرْجَة الوِدّ زَلَّيت　　من عِرفْتي روحي الى قَولِتي به
قالوا جَهلْت وقِلْت بالجَهْل قَرَّيت　　الجاهل اللي قال لي وِش تبي به
كم ليلةٍ جاني على ما تمَنَّيت　　ولا يِنْجِزي بالخَير من لامني به
والى نِصَحْني ناصِحٍ عنك ما اوْحَيت　　يزيد حِبّ مولَّعٍ في حَبيبه

~ 4 ~

Zēd, first you smiled, now you turn away from me.[52] 4.1
Why avert your eyes: has your heart absconded?[53]
I wanted to give you my news, but you avoided me:
no way to let you know or get your news.
I was waiting to learn from you what it's all about:
shouldn't you tell a good friend what's troubling you?
You shouldn't think, Zēd, that I lost interest:
I am not one to forget my sweetheart's favors.
Deep inside, I treasure the story of our trysts, 4.5
and will forever, even when my hair is flecked with gray.
If I see you walking in the street, my heart jumps
like a man's who spots his missing camel.[54]
I wince when you ignore me; I perk up when you come,
and welcome you from my heart of hearts.
When people look askance at me, it is because of you:
on your account, I was reviled by all and sundry.
Tender love and devotion to you wasted me away:
my inescapable fate is to suffer like all men.
Only God knows how deeply I felt for you— 4.10
more than a graybeard does for his grandson.[55]
When I am sick at heart, seeing you braces me,
like a patient by a doctor cured.
I hid my love's open vein till it became unbearable:[56]
when else does a wolf howl but when wracked with pain?
No slip of the tongue betrayed my feelings,
no word revealed what was on my mind.
"You fool!" they said. "And fool I'll stay!" said I:
it takes a fool to wonder at my infatuation.[57]
More than one night we spent as in a dream: 4.15
if I am blamed for it, let my faultfinders be damned.
My ear is deaf to staid advice:
my passion's only stirred the more![58]

قِم يا نديبي قَرِّبها   حَمْرا بِيضٍ مَحاقِبها
ما فيها رُودٍ يَقْضِبها   ارْكَب ما بيك تْثَنِّيها
ارْكَب ما فيك مْراواه   بادٍ لك عِلْمٍ تنصاه
ارْبَع راسه واخِذ وْصاه   منّي للضِيط تودِّيها
واللي غيرك ما وَصّيته   دَرْهم نَوِّخ علي بيته
وازْهم بالصوت الى جِيته   قِدّام الهرجه تِبدِيْها
وازْهَم مارق وصْنَيتان   وازْهم جِميع العِضْيان
ومن الخَمْسه كل اسنان   رَبْعٍ تِعْجب عَزاويها
والغيبَوي لا تَنْساه   والدِماسين العصاه
ربعٍ ما فيهم تلْقاه   كم بنتٍ تَنْعَى غاليها
والمَراشده القروم   عَوق العايل بالزحوم
كم مالٍ خَلّوه قْسوم   ان ثار المِلْح بْتاليها
هقْوة انّي ما خَلّيت   من الحَشْمه راعي بيت
زَبْن المضيوم الَى اطْرَيت   الى وَصلَت قواصيها
قِل له غَنَمنا تْنَخاكم   ولا نَدْري وِش وَراكم

~ 5 ~

Come, messenger, fetch your mount: 5.1
a light-brown she-camel, flanks white.[59]
Not easy to rein in the spirited beast;
let her run as she wills.
Set off without second thought:
your road is clear.
But wait; carry this message— 5.5
words to convey to al-Ḍīṭ:[60]
To you alone I entrusted them!
ride out, kneel your mount at his tent;
Call out in a loud voice
Before revealing your mission.
Call for Mārig and Ṣnētān to join;
call all tribesmen of al-ʿIḍyān to attend;
Call young and old of the clan entire,
men known for fearsome battle cries.
Do not overlook al-Ghbēwī 5.10
and others from indomitable al-Dimāsīn:
A kin group renowned for warlike feats,
in whose wake grieving young widows wail.
Call also for al-Marāshidah, fighters fierce
who block and repel the enemy's advance:
Herd after herd have they divided as booty,
seized amid drifting smoke of guns and shots.
Methinks I have not overlooked
any of the tent-dwelling worthies,
Men with whom the oppressed seek refuge
when, at wits' end, they face imminent death.
Tell him, "Our sheep call to you for help; 5.15
we are at a loss how this came to pass.

نَشْرَب الما في حَراكم   وامِ الوِرْعان نرجْويها
اخَذها وِلْد الخَرّاص   واحْتِدانا بالرصاص
اخسوا ما فيكم مِفْراص   يِنْقاها ولّا يِدّيها
ثَلاث مْيه مَعْدوده   اصْغَرهِن كِبْر المَفْروده
ما فيهن عَنْز ولا عَوده   يَشْهَد عليها راعيها
وَقّف بالقاع يقَسّمها   واشْبَع قومه من لَحَمها
تَخاوَر يوم يوَسّمها   كلٍ يَسْمَع تِشاغيها
سُودٍ نِجّود الّا روسه   خَلْفاتٍ واِكْبَر ديوسَه
لا مِخْفات ولا مَدْسوسه   يسَرّحها ويضَوّيها
واطْيَبْها عند وَلَد طامي   ابو ثِنْتَين القَسّامي
يومِ حِضْرَت للوَسّامي   سَبْع وعِشْرينٍ ناقيها
شيٍ دَسّه شيٍ باعه   وشيٍ دونه ما قط باعه
يا شيٍ تقليط مْتاعه   يا وجه الله يا طاريها
وان كان رَبْعه ما نَقّوه   ومعازيبه سَرّقوه
اخذ مِقْراه وشَقّوه   والسودا للي راضيها
شالوا مِزْهَبهم عَلْقَتها   بِبطون الستّه مِلْحَتها
ويدامهم اتلا حَلْبَتْها   يا عتَيبه هذي وِش فيها
مثل ابو ثِنْتين وجِنْده   طَرّدهم حَوّال بِزَنْده

~ 5 ~

Our only drink is water, and you are our last hope!
What do we tell our desperate mothers?
Someone from al-Kharrāṣ has rustled the animals:
he snatched them from us at gunpoint—
A despicable act! Isn't there a hero among you
to track them down and return our property?
The flock is no less than three hundred;
none are young lambs, none yet unweaned,
None goats or rams grown old;
pilferers know this only too well:
On the dusty plain he stood in their midst
And shared them as meat with his gang.
They bleated as he wielded the branding iron,
their plaintive baas heard by all:
Najdī sheep, black but for the head;
in milk, their fat udders a marvel.
It is no secret, no mystery about it:
they are driven to pasture early; later they return.
The pick of the herd is held by Ṭāmī's son,
of Abū Thintēn al-Gassāmī.
When they were lined up for branding,
he picked the twenty-seven he liked best;
Some sheep he penned up, others he sold,
to some he holds on to as to dear life itself.
These are the ones served for dinner—
what behavior! May God serve him his desserts.
Perhaps his clansmen had no hand in it,
yet they relished their host's stolen food.
They sat at the tray and tore off the meat:
shame on whoever condones such a deed!
Swinging their food bags onto their mounts,
six visitors departed, our salt in their bellies:
Their butter was from our sheep's last milk.
Well, 'Utaybah, how can that be?
Abū Thintēn came with his mounted horde;
armed rustlers drove them off at gunpoint.

وِبْجاد عَيّا باللي عِنده   يقول لي ماكولٍ فيها
الواحد يدّي لزومه   بْقوّة ذْراعه وعزومه
يَضْوي الحايف على قومه   ويطَلّقها ويسَرّيها
اما فكّوها ذِرْعيه   فبيوت عْتَيبه مَبْنيه
فكّاكة راع الجَنْبيه   اللي بالدمّ مْخَنّيها
واللي مِزْري واللي بايق   مثل اللي مكسور وذارق
ولا تْثَوّره المطارق   يناظرها ويْخَلّيها
مِنْهن شاتي واسِفا به   مَلاّية كُوز الحَلاّبه
عليكم منها جَنابه   والما ما يْنَظّف راعيها
مِنهِن شاتي راحت طَلّه   خَلّوها لبجاد رْضًى له
يقول امّي فيها عِلّه   تَبْغي صِحْيِنه يِبْريها
وان ادّوها في هَواهم   عن هرج الناس بْقِفاهم
وان خَلّوها ما تَشْناهم   كِنّ الذيب مْتَعَشّيها
ما تِسْوَى فِعل ومِجْراد   يِدّيها منهم روّاد
وان خلّوها لامّ بْجاد   الله بالدرّ يْهَنّيها
ما جَتْها مِنّي وِهيبه   من ورا خَشْمي غَصيبه
عَزل بْجادٍ من كِسيبه   قِدّام القوم مهاويها
ان ساقوا لي خَمْسٍ عنها   ولّا عِشْرينٍ ثِمَنْها

~ 5 ~

Bjād refused to surrender his share of the spoil,
    saying, 'These are the sheep I will eat myself.'
Shouldn't the dictates of honor prevail, 5.35
    through resolute force if needed?
Or by stealth—slink up to the culprit,
    unfetter the animals, and send them out!
Why not openly twist his arms?
    The tents of 'Utaybah are standing tall!
If a poor kinsman armed with only a dagger
    bloodies it, they save him one way or another.
Waste of time to deal with gutless traitors,
    useless as broken handles, as blobs of bird shit.
You cannot goad them with a stick; 5.40
    they just watch, not lifting a finger.
One sheep is mine; how I pine for her!
    Pull her teats and milk fills the bowl.
A prize animal that stains your honor:
    no amount of water can wash that shame.
Yes, this lovely sheep was stolen from me,[61]
    and gifted to Bjād to please him.
'My mother is ill,' he pleaded.
    'Boiled milk will make her better.'
They'd be wise to return them; 5.45
    they'd forestall whispers of scandal.
If nothing comes of it—too bad;
    we'll say, 'A wolf took the sheep for supper.'
I admit, she's not worth an armed clash:
    strong, upright men should be enough.
And if she stays with Bjād's mother,
    may God let the milk go down well with her.
But remember, the ewe was no gift,
    but grabbed from me by force:
Bjād's share from their brigandage. 5.50
    He whined and they let him have her.
Neither five sheep in compensation,
    nor even twenty, could defray my loss.

ان ماكَرَّعت بْلبنها   ما يزِلّ يومٍ ما اطْريها
فان زَلّ العِشب المَمْدوح   خَيبه تجي هم وِتْروح
لولا الزِبْده والصَبّوح   وِش ادوِّر يوم اشْريها
وان كان عَجْز ابو ثِنْتَين   خلَّى لومه شَوف العَين
وِحضَر البايع والضِمين   وراع الدَينه يِسْتافيها
ركب فيها زَبْن الخايف   ما اسْتَكفى بِخنَيف ونايف
ما عقّب مارق حَسايف   يا وَيلك ياللي حاويها
مِن حين ينَوِّخ يِدّون   مثل التَمْره بالماعون
حتّى الهَرْجَه ما يِبدون   كلٍ بالدِين يزَكّيها
مَقْروره عند ابن صايل   تَنْخا وافين الخَصايل
والعاني يِدّ الاصايل   وانا مخْتارٍ عانيها
من على شالح جَدّيه   ما هي دَخلَة الحَوليه
كان العِضْيان حْمَوِيّه   جَتْ ورْخيلتها تْتليها

I miss the long drafts of sweet milk—
every day memory stings:
This is not herbage withering in the heat:
that misfortune is no one's fault.
If not for butter and a morning draft of milk,
why for heaven's sake would I buy the ewe?
If Abū Thintēn can't muster the resolve, 5.55
his baseness will stain his honor.
The seller and guarantor will come forward
and let the lender redeem his loan.
Out rode the protector of the weak:
his escort not just common men.[62]
Mārig has always lived up to expectation:[63]
he'll make you suffer the consequences, thief!
As soon his camel kneels, the ewe is brought,
dumbfounded, more tranquil than dates in a jar,
They obey, keeping quiet all the while: 5.60
meek and diligent, they pay their due.
Ibn Ṣāyil can be your witness if you wish:
he answered the sheep's appeal to his honor.[64]
A pillar of strength who gives only the best:
I turn to the benefactor who answers the call.
Their reputation has ancient roots in Shāliḥ,[65]
not some parvenu who showed up yesterday.
If you appeal to al-ʿIḍyān for justice,
they bring the ewe, the frisky lamb in tow."[66]

~ ٦ ~

لا تَمْحَـنون القَـلْب يا عـاذلينه   الامـر لله والحَـكي ما يِشيبِ
لا خبَرْ عن باسـه ولا عـالِمينه   يَعْـلَمَ به اللي للدعا يِسْتِجيبِ
عـامَـين اِكِنّـه يوم انا مِسْتِهيـنـه   ولا وِدّي ابْدي للعرَب وَيش غَيبي
واليومِ يومِ انّـه تِبَـيّحَّ كِـنينه   فانا عَـليل وعِـلّتي من حَـبيبي
قـالوا مَرَض هـاتوا طبيب المِدينه   قِلت الشفا بشفـا طِبيبٍ قريبِ
لَعْـقـة عسَـل بين الزرار وجبِينه   وحَـرْف القران الى تَلاه الخَطيبِ
كـانه يخـاف الله والاسـلام دِينه   وله في نَهار البَعْث حَظّ ونِصيبِ
يـرِشّ قَـلْبي قَـبْل ذَوبه بحِـينه   عن مَيتتي من سَبّته وِش يـبي بي
مـا هوب يَرْحـم لا رِحْـم والدَينه   كَيّـه صَـبر يا ربّي انك حَسيبي
مـا هو نِصَف كَيّ الظِنين لظِنينه   بالمـاقَـع اللي مـاكُواه الطِبيبِ
عَـرّقى على كَبْدي وِسيمة مـزَينه   وارْكى عـلى قـلبي ثَلاث المغَيبي
كان الجرِوح قصاص واشَيب عَينه   كَوّيت قـلبه كَيّـةٍ مـا تِطيبِ
لا عـاد عِـرْفٍ صار بيني وبينه   ابْغي المروفه منه واذْهَب ذِهيبي
وانا له الْجـا من حَـدا والدَينه   واطْوَع من العَبْد المِـليك الاديبِ

~ 6 ~

Moralizers! Do not put my heart to the test![67] 6.1
The matter rests with God; talk is no use.
I keep silent about its fortitude; others have no inkling.
Only the One who answers supplicants is aware.
Two years I had the strength to hide my feelings,
conceal my inner life from people's gaze.[68]
Now these secrets have spilled into view:[69]
I am ill and my illness is the sickness of love.[70]
"He is diseased," they said. "Get a doctor from town." 6.5
"My cure lies with a doctor nearby," I replied—[71]
A honeyed lick above the buttons on the breast,[72]
then the preacher's recitations.[73]
If she fears God, if Islam is truly her faith,
for her salvation on Judgment Day,
She'll sprinkle my heart before it wastes away.[74]
Or is it her plan to let me die because of her?
She is merciless—may His mercy elude her kin:[75]
Her red-hot iron, Lord, tortures me to death!
How unjust—branded by one's sweetheart[76] 6.10
on a secret spot no doctor can reach!
On my liver, she burns the Mzēni's cross-shaped brand,
on my heart, her iron presses the three rings of al-Mghēbah.[77]
She should beware, lest my wounds demand retaliation—[78]
her heart would never recover from my branding iron.
Is nothing left of the intimacy we once knew?[79]
I beg for tenderness, and she chooses to drive me mad,[80]
Though I am closer than her parents,[81]
more servile than a docile, well-bred slave.[82]

~ ٧ ~

البـارحـه وَنّيت ونّـة يتيـمِ   مـا له جِـدا كود البكا والتّنَهّات
ابوه وامّـه صـايـرينٍ هَشيـمِ   ماتوا ولا في باق الاقراب مـاوات
ياللّه يا مُحْيي العـظـام الرِميـمِ   تِلمّني واياه من عِقْب الاشتـات
تَبْكي وانا ابكي صاحبٍ لي قِديـمِ   عَساي ما اهوبِل وارمّي بالاصوات
وعـليك كنّي يا الحبَيّب فِـطيمِ   تَبْغيني اذلَه مار ما عنك دَلْهات
اعْوي كِمـا تعوي ذياب القِصيـمِ   ليـا اجْرَهَدّ الليل وامْسَن مجيعـات
على اللذي بيـني وبينه وهيـمِ   دَوٍّ بِعيـد البِيد ذِلٍّ ومَـظْمات
خَمْص القِدم ما شِفْت جِنْسه عَديمِ   اقـدام وِرَامٍ بليـا شِكـيّات
ومشْيه معَلّمْه الحَمام تَعْليـمِ   يِدْني خطاه ويدِّرج فيه خَـطْوات
وساقين عَصْبَات الشَحم للحَشيـمِ   وفَخْذَين من جا بينهن ذاق لَذّات
هايف ونايف شٍ تشيله هَضيـمِ   وش هو يصير ان كان عينك مشقّاة
كَتْـفٍ ورِدْفٍ بيـنهنّ البـريمي   يِشْـبه لحَـزْمٍ بالمِصاحِف مـطوّاة
والخَدّ بَدْرٍ لا انْجلى عنه غَيـمِ   مِثْله ولَونه مار بالبَدْر نَقْشـات
والخَشْـم منها مثل سَلّة قَـدَيمي   يِنُوج منه المِسْك والعَطَر نوجـات
ابو ثِمـانٍ كـاللوالو نِظيـمِ   كِنّه طَعَم سِكرٍ على دَرّ خلْفـات

~ 7 ~

Yesterday I was in throes of tears and sobs, 7.1
like an orphan child inconsolable,[83]
Whose father and mother were swept away.[84]
They are dead, and he is homeless and alone.
Lord, You who resurrect bones, dusty and decayed,
unite again those who were driven apart!
She weeps, as I do, for an old love lost:
let me not become deranged, go raving mad.[85]
It is as if I am a baby you weaned, my love;[86] 7.5
you want me to relax, but how can I be impassive?
My wails are like the howling wolves of al-Qaṣīm,
overtaken by darkness, with nothing to eat—
All that lies between her and me are fields of terror,
waterless wastes of dread and thirst.
I have never seen the like of her: feet finely chiseled,
legs plump and with flesh of immaculate white.
Like a pigeon she walks, with a bobbing gait,[87]
swaying as she struts with willing hips,
On calves like fatty meat served to worthy guests,[88] 7.10
and on thighs brimful of succulent delights.
Swelling curves roll from bulges to flat tummy:
what to do when eyes are dazzled by such views?
Shoulder and buttocks, a leather belt between,
protrude like hills encased in rock;[89]
Her cheek is a moon that bursts from the clouds,
but without blemish—no craters, no spots.
Her nose: implacable and straight as a dagger's blade,
but fragrant with musk and rose.
Her teeth are like a string of pearls, 7.15
and taste of sugar mixed with camel's milk.

~ ٧ ~

يا عـين الادميّه ويا عِـنْق ريـمِ　　لا اخْطاهنّ القنّاص واقْفن مِريبات
له قِـذْلِةٍ تِعْـمَل بـريحٍ لِغَيـمِ　　والَى عَمَلها فوق الامتان سافات
احبّ صـافي اللون حِبٍّ عَظيـمِ　　رِبيـع قَـلبي يا الملا فيـه شـارات
حِبّ الهَوى والسَلْهَمه وتْخَميـمِ　　مَـصٍّ ورَصٍّ والجِدايـل مثنّات
ولوانّ بالدنيـا يِـذكَّر نِعيـمِ　　لاقول بين نهودهـا طَـلع جَـنّات ٢٠،٧
وقَـلبي خَـذاريفٍ بها وتْحَليـمِ　　عَساي ماانْطِق باسْمِهاوَسْط مَقْهات
ورُوياه تِقْعِـدني ولو صِـرت نَيـمِ　　وقِدّام عيني في فروض الصلاوات
اتلى الخَـبَر بـه في صـلاة العَتَيم　　يوم المـطَوَّع جـالسٍ لِلتحيـات
يالايمي جـعلك بوسـط الجحيـمِ　　ولا ذِقْت مَـزّ معَسَّلات الثِنيـات

~ 7 ~

She has the eyes of a mountain gazelle, the neck of a sand gazelle
that darts in panic when the hunter shoots.
Her locks wave softly on the breeze of a cloudy day,
the loosened plaits streaming down her back.
My love for the fair beauty knows no bounds:
it made my heart burst into flowering spring.[90]
Driven insane by languid looks, I want to hold her tight,[91]
entangled by her tresses, to suck and press her flesh:
Earth offers no greater luxury and delight, I daresay, 7.20
than the heavenly fruit between her breasts.[92]
My heart whirls like a spinning top in my dreams:[93]
let me not reveal her name in the coffee rooms!
At night, the vision of her makes me start.
At prayer time, her specter floats before me—
It happened last in the evening,
when the imam spoke the closing words.
If you find fault, may God cast you into the pit of Hell,
and may you never savor the taste of honeyed lips!

~ ٨ ~

يا صاحبي دونِك عَدُوٍّ الى جِيت   يَلْبَس عَلَيّ الجِلْد لِبْسِه عَباتِه
اقْفي الَى شَكَّيت وابْعِد الى اقْفَيت   ابْغي لَعَلّ السُوّ تِمْرِح وشاتِه
ابْعاد حَوم عن الحِذَف والمِشاخيت   والّا فلا قلبٍ سلا عن شِفاتِه
لو دَلّهوني ساعَةٍ ما تَناسَيت   اذْكِر عَجاريف الهوى وسْفَهاته
الَى تَوَسّع خاطري واسْفَهَلَّيت   وتِبَعْت هوِيات القِدَم وِشْهَواته
امّا سِمِعْت او شِفت ولّا تحَرَّيت   فَتْقٍ بقلبي فَزِّتِه والْتِفاته
أخْفَيت ما يَطْري لبالي ولا ابْدَيت   جا هاجِسٍ ما بين وَدّه وهاته
بي وَلْعة الصقّار عَدْي وتِصاويت   والّا رِضيع الدَيد يَذْكِر لباته
وِرْعٍ صغيرٍ راحت امّه عن البيت   مصطوم ملطومٍ قليلٍ سكاته
ما غير هَرْجه من فواده تَناهِيت   تِنِهِّت المظيوم عند شْرهاته
قالوا جَهَلْت وقِلْت بالجَهل قَرَّيت   الجاهل اللي ما تِذكّر طَراته
كم ليلةٍ جا لي على ما تِمنّيت   الله يَجْهَر لايمي بِجْهَراته
يا لايمٍ راعى الهوى ما تَعافَيت   طاري هواه مخاشِره في حياته
عَساه ما يُوحي يِقَع يُوحي المَيت   وابْكَم صديقك ما يِسَوّي سواته
يلومني خِبْلٍ هروجه سِفاريت   ما ذاق طَرْبات الهوى وسْفَهاته

~ 8 ~

Darling, if I come, mind the enemy, 8.1
who hides rancor under his cloak.[94]
If I have doubts, I'll turn and go far
as I retreat, to throw ill-wishers off my scent;
Even if I soar beyond the reach of pelting stones,[95]
my heart will not stray an inch from its desires.
It returns without fail after every distraction,
driven by memories of the daring follies of love: [96]
When I am calm, at ease and in repose,[97] 8.5
and make the rounds, sampling pleasures,
And catch a glimpse . . . or hear a hint . . .
it tears my heart! I start, grow tense.
My thoughts are invisible, hidden deep,
while "Shall I?" and "Shan't I?" buzz in my head.[98]
I am like a falcon hunter who runs and shouts,[99]
or a newborn yearning for its first milk,
Or a toddler left alone at home by its mother—
slapped and spanked, the child cries endlessly.
Sobs and screams pour from my heart, 8.10
from a breast heaving with unfulfilled desire.
"You fool!" they chided. "May I stay a fool," said I.
The real fool has no memories of love.[100]
Night after night I spent with her like a dream:
may God humiliate my critics in public view.
Harassing love's devotee will do you no good:
thoughts of his love never leave his mind.
Let the caviler go deaf until the dead can hear; [101]
go deaf-mute! A friend does not behave like this.
He aims to blame, but blathers silly nonsense: 8.15
he is ignorant of love's raptures and follies.

~ ٨ ~

انا الذي لو قالوا الناس سَجَّيت   ما اِسِجّ لَين القَبْر تِركَز حَصاته
كل النهار مْعبِّرِه مَشْي خِرّيت   والليل كله نَسْهَره ما نِباته
كنّي خَلوجٍ تَنْهَض الصوت وِتْهيت   وِحْوارها الراعي تَعَشَّى شواته
لَى صَكّه المِلْحاق واسْتَلْحق بْخيت   تَنْكِس عليهم لين تاصَل مِماته
كنّه يْنقَزّها عن الرِعْي عِفْريت   والشِرْب كِنّه تَنْقِره من صَراته ٢٠،٨

If people say, "You've lost the plot!"
 "Not so," I'll say. "Not till my grave is dug."
All day I pace up and down like a desert guide;
 my nights spent in bleary-eyed insomnia;
I groan like a camel searching for her calf,
 while her owner grills its meat.[102]
If a herdsman's sent to fetch her back,
 she returns to where the calf was killed.[103]
It's as if a demon startles her from pasture 8.20
 and she recoils from drinking foul water.

~ ٩ ~

يا الله يا اللي تَسْجِد الخلق لرْضاه   يا وامِرٍ عَبده على حَجّ بيتِه
تِفرِج لمن سَدّه على الناس ما ابْداه   راضٍ على مقْسومك اللي عَطَيتِه
من شٍ يِسِلّ الحال والجِسْم يبْراه   والناس ما يِشْفونه ان ما شِفَيته
قلت آه واجَرحاه من خِلّتي آه   وان حَمَّلوني حِمْل غَيٍّ قَوَيته
قالوا سِفا بالحال ويش اللي اغْواه   قِلْت آه ويش المِنكَر اللي وِطيته
قالوا جَهَلْت وبان عِلْمك لمَنْهاه   قِلت آه عِلمي يا ملا ما كِميته
قالوا طَلَبنا لك من الله معافاه   قلت آه وَحَّدْتِه وعَفْوِه رِجيته
قالوا هَله واحباب عينه نِصَحناه   قلت آه هذا وارِدٍ ما بَغيته
قالوا ندوّر لك من البِيض حِلياه   قلت آه لو غيره بكَفّي رِميته
قالوا نشاش العُود ما لك بلاماه   قلت آه عود المَوز بِيدي لَويته
قالوا تِزَوّج كود تَدْلَه وتَنْساه   قلت آه لو خَذْت ارْبَعٍ ما نِسَيته
قالوا من اقْصَى الناس وَين انت واياه   قلت آه ما انْسَى يوم جاني وجِيته
قالوا نشوفه عند هذا وهذاه   قلت آه عِمْره ما عَقَب حِجِر بيته
قالوا عليلٍ ناقلٍ داه بِرْداه   قلت آه باقْرابي وروحي فِدَيته
قالوا نشير ولا نِفَع ما حَكَيناه   قلت آه هرّاج النِمايم عَصَيته

~ 9 ~

Lord, people bow in worship to win Your favor; 9.1
you told them to perform pilgrimage to Your House:
Bring relief to a man who keeps his soul under lock—
a man content with whatever fate You allot to him—
From a thing that cripples him and wears him out;
human remedy is of no avail, salvation lies with You.
"Ah, how my sweetheart's stabbing hurts, ah!" said I.
"Though I don't shrink from enticement's burdens."
They said, "You're a sorry sight, what made you go astray?" 9.5
"Ah, what's the heinous sin I've committed?" said I.[104]
They said, "Your foolish acts are the talk of town."
"Ah, I made no secret of what's ailing me," said I.
They said, "We asked God to restore your health."
"Ah, there is only one God—I ask His forgiveness," said I.
They said, "We've advised her near and dear."
"Ah, that's the last thing I wished to hear," said I.
They said, "We'll find you another beauty just as good."[105]
"Ah, if another was in my hand, I'd cast her away," said I.
They said, "Why get involved with that graceful limb?"[106] 9.10
"Ah, with my hand I bent the banana stalk," said I.[107]
They said, "You should marry, and forget her."
"Ah, if I took four wives I'd never forget her," said I.[108]
They said, "She is not your class, what pretention!"[109]
"Ah, I can't forget the delights of our trysts," said I.
They said, "We saw her in the company of so-and-so."
"Ah, no, she sticks close to her house," said I.
They said, "He has a disease of his own making."[110]
"Ah, for her I'd give my family and my life," said I.
They said, "We are talking sense to you, but to no avail." 9.15
"Ah, I don't deal with slanderers," said I.

~ ٩ ~

قالوا كِثِر شَيبك وقلبك بعَمْياه   قلت آه لو قلبي غَريرٍ نَهَيته
مطاوعٍ قلبي بجَحْفاه وِقْداه   والَى عَطى مِنهاج دربٍ عَطَيته
يا ناس خَلّوا كل وادي ومَجْراه   قِلْتوا كِثير وقَولكم ما لِقَيته

They said, "Flecked with gray, and a heart still blind."
    "Ah, if my heart were erring, I'd chide it," said I.
"I do my heart's bidding, whether right or wrong;
    If it is set on traveling a road, I give it free rein.
Listen everyone: let each riverbed follow its course—[111]
    You're all talk, but none of it has any point."

~ ١٠ ~

يالله يا اللي ما لغَيـرِك تَـرجَّـيت   يا واحـدٍ مـا غـيره احـَدٍ رِجَيـتِه
قِد لي لِيالٍ كل ما اصْبحت وامْسيت   حِلْو الكَرى لا جا مَحَلّه محَيـتِه
في ليـل سـابع بالكَرى ما تَهَـنَّيت   النوم عـاديني مثل مـا عَـدَيتِـه
يوم اذَّن التالي غَسَـلْت وتحَرَّيت   واخَـذْت جِزْوٍ في يِدَيّ وقَـريتـه
ظهرت يمّ السوق من يوم صَلَّيت   مِـتْذكّرٍ لي لازمٍ مـا قِـضَيتـه
يوم انْقِضَى اللازِم تَرَيَّضت وانْويت   واخَـذْت من حِلْو المِبيع وشَرَيتِـه
جاني فلان وقال وِش فيك ما جِيت   ابو عَـلي بالمِخْـتِصَر مـا نِصَيتـه
عَجَلت ثُمّ امْـرَسْت ثُمّ تَعَـدَّيت   واقْفى الّذي جا بالخَبَر واقْتِفَيته
حالٍ وصلت الباب للباب طَقَّيت   فِتَح بِخَيت البـاب واقْفَت بخَيـته
قال البَطيني دِشّ داخِـل ودَشَّيت   وانا احْـمِد الله كِلّ دَرْبٍ مِشَيتـه
سَـلَّمْت سَـبْعِينٍ وانا ما تَواسَيت   ولَو زِدْتها سَبْعَ مْيةٍ مـا جِـزَيتِـه
سـلّم عليّ بلِين مَنْطوق واصْغَيت   واللي عَـليّه من هـدومي رِمَيـته
صِـفا لي المِذْرَى على مـا تمَـنَّيت   واللي بِـذَرْتِه من قِـديـمٍ لِقَيـتِه
وَرَّدْت عَذْب مْبَيسِمـه وارْجَهنَّيت   وِرِجَع عَلَيّ قَلْبي عِقِب ما جِزَيتِـه
الخَـدّ قِـنْديـلٍ يِعَبّـا من الزَيت   مـا قِيل لوَلّاعه ورا مـا جَـلَيـتِه

~ 10 ~

I beseech You, God, and You alone, 10.1
the One and only, hear my entreaties.
On many nights, from darkness till the light of dawn,
sweet slumber eludes me, seemingly forever.
In this seventh night without the slightest rest,
again I could not find it: sleep passed me by.
At the call to prayer I washed and waited,
Qur'an in hand, reciting a whole part.
My prayers performed, I went into the street 10.5
for some forgotten business.
My errand done, I tarried, then had a thought:
my eyes fell on delicious wares, which I bought.
So-and-so accosted me: "Where have you been?
Why haven't you visited Abū ʿAlī's private room?"[112]
I quickened, then rushed, was running;
the messenger turned; I followed suit.
I went straight to the door, knocked;
Bkhīt opened and discreetly withdrew.[113]
A hidden voice said, "Enter!" I obeyed; 10.10
Thank God I honed my skills so long!
I paid my respects seventy times, no less;
seven hundred more wouldn't be enough.
Her gentle greetings were music to my ears;
I took off my clothes, threw them down.
Fortune smiled on me—the winnowing went fine:
I harvested the fruits of what I'd sown.[114]
I put my mouth to her sweet lips and took a draft,[115]
and felt my heart come home from long absence.
Cheeks as luminous as a burning oil lamp, 10.15
with a gleaming light behind shining glass.

~ ١٠ ~

والعَين عَين اللي يرَفْرِف على البَيت   ياتي لِمبْياته بحَزَّة مِبيتِه

ياخِذ على جَول الحَباري مِشاخيت   هذي معَفِّتْها وهذي مِميتِه

~ 10 ~

Eyes like a falcon's that flutters about a dwelling,
 and lands on its perch when dark sets in—
A bird that plays havoc with a flock of bustards:
 One is struck down, the other already done for.[116]

~ ١١ ~

اجَل عَنْك ما الدِنيا بتُوخَذ بحِيلاتِ وانا شاطِرٍ باحْوال نَفْسي وحالاتِ
مشيحٍ مدِيبٍ باطنيٍ وظاهر بَياض النَهار وِمِحْيي الليل ما اباتِ
بالاشْغال والافكار والكِدّ والكِدا هَميمٍ فِهيمٍ في جِميع الحساباتِ
واعْرِف حَراوى الرِزْق واجْهِد بدُورته ولا صار لي فيها بِعيرٍ ولا شاتِ
لى اجْهَدْت في طَلْب المِعيشه على القِدا الازِم على اللازم مِقيم صَلاواتي
ولا ساعَفَت ما الْحَقْت نَفْسي حَسايف صِبورٍ بحكْمِه يا علِيم بِخَصّاتي
انا اشوف سِكّانٍ بِلَيّا ذَهانه قليلٍ تِصِرِّفهم قِريبين نوَهاتِ
مريحات خِطَّرهم وساعٍ صدورهم ولا ابْعدوا غِرْبات وارزاقهم تاتي
مَهاريجهم في عَدّهم راس مالهم لِقَوا به على حاجات الاجواد صَرْفاتِ
وهم ما يعَرْفون المُواجيب والقِدا ولا ينْلِقي فيهم من الطِيب شاراتِ
وناسٍ مِقابيلٍ دوامٍ ومِقافي ورْكابهم من كِثْر الادْلاج وَنْياتِ
شِفوحٍ بدُورة رِزْقهم كل دِيره وما ذِكرٍ بالدِنيا لهم فيه حِرْفاتِ
صَعاليك ما يَلْقَون ما ينْفِقونه ودايم مَواقِفهم على العِسْر صَعْباتِ
وناسٍ الَى جالسْتهم واحْتِضَيتهم تَكْشِف على دِخْلِيِّهم بالاشاراتِ
يِعْطون نِصْح القَول والصِدْق والنِقا وهم خلاف النِصْح ما فيه شِكّاتِ

~ 11 ~

The things of this world can't be gotten by mere tricks, 11.1
so I'm smart at handling my affairs.[117]
I make ends meet by striving in body and spirit,
when the sun is up, with little sleep at night.
I work, think, labor, and sweat without respite;[118]
diligent and shrewd, I calculate every step.
I know what it takes to make a living, to toil,
without owning so much as a camel or sheep.
I do the right thing to bring home the bread, 11.5
stick to the rules when performing my prayers.
And if things don't work out, then no regrets:
I submit to His decree, for He knows me well.[119]
I see people without a notion of what to do,
Living a life of torpor, devoid of ambition.
Their minds are at peace, they have ample leisure,
they don't venture out for gain—it comes to them.
They have no interest beyond counting their wealth:
it leaves them no time for noble acts.
They don't give a damn about doing what's right;[120] 11.10
they don't care a whit to practice virtue.
Others are always busy, running here and there;
their mounts travel all night and sway with fatigue.
They eagerly search for a living in faraway places;
they try their hand at each and every trade,
Yet remain vagabonds, forever penniless,
hard-pressed to find a morsel for their guests.[121]
Others whose company you thought agreeable
show their true face only on deeper probing:
They proffer advice with candor, 11.15
but flagrantly disregard their own words.

~ ١١ ~

لا جِيتهم ظَمْيانٍ اشافيك يابسه　　ونشَدْتهم قالوا قْرَبْنا مطوّاتِ

يوِدّون مَوتِك والصِداقه يقال لها　　وذا فِعْل ضِدٍّ مِعْلِنٍ بالعَداواتِ

فلا ايّاك يا صافي السريره تِودّهم　　تراهم ربا زَوده يعَوِّد خَساراتي

~ 11 ~

If you stagger in, your lips cracked from thirst,
    they bluntly say, “We’ve stowed away the waterskins.”
They’d rather see you dead, and call it friendship—
    for enmity pure and simple, look no further.
Beware, gentle friend, of befriending such men:
    they’re usurers, charging exorbitant rates.

~ ١٢ ~

يا لله تَجْعَـل كِـل دَرْبي سِـماحِ   بِهْداك تامِرني على اللي به اصلاح
خَلّيت من شَـفّي بخَفْضَـة جَنـاحِ   من يوم شِفت الشَيب في عارضي لاح
ياليت يَمحا لابيـض الشيب مـاحي   ويْـرِدّ وَقْتٍ فـات بالغَيّ سَـبّاح
وليت الهَوى للي يِـريـده مـباحِ   والعَصـر الاوّل يِنْثِني عِقْب ما راح
وعن المَراجل ما تِقِلّ المِشـاحي   خَـصٍّ به اللي للمُواجـيب نَطّـاح
الى تَوَسّـع خـاطري واسـتِراحِ   اخَـذْت لي مع طَورِق الغَيّ مِسْراح
اسْرَح ولا اذْري وَين هو بِه مَراحي   واخِـذ بلَيلي قِـدْم فلّاج الاصباح
مَشْـعوف واذاري هَـبوب الرياحِ   وحِمْل الهَوى ما فِكّ عنّي ولا طـاح
لَى ما دَعا حـالي كِمـا العُود مـاحي   فَضْلة حَديد سـتاد مِبْرَد ومِصْفاح
الى ذِكَـرْت اللي حَـديثـه ذِباحِ   وغِـرٍّ يورّيني عَسَـلهن وهو شـاح
واللبّـه اللي مِثـل بيـض المِداحي   اسْهَـر وكِنّ بنـاظـر العَـين ذِرناح
انا عَليـل الجَوف لو قيـل صـاحِي   عَضيض غِلْث وشاف له بارقٍ لاح
يا ذابح المِسْـلم بليّـا سـلاحِ   مـا تِسْـتِبيحه قبل نَـزّاع الارواح
خَـلّه يِشوف بصَـدرك الانشـراحِ   وقَلْبه عليك من الاغـاليل يِنْسـاح
قَـبْل الفـراق اللي شَـرابه مَـلاحِ   ومِحِبّ مـا يَسْـمَع حَـبيبه ولو ناح

~ 12 ~

I supplicate You to smooth my path, God: 12.1
guide me to do what's right and in my interest.
I renounced love's play and lowered my wing[122]
when gray hair showed and flecked my temples.
If only this white abomination would wash off
and the halcyon days of carefree dalliance return!
If only the pursuit of love were licit,
allowing us to revive the good old times.
Exertion is no obstacle to manly deeds 12.5
if you're inclined to tackle noble challenges.
When my mind is at ease and finds repose,
I take a stroll down dalliance's path:
To sally forth in the morning into the unknown—
white nights that last till break of dawn—
To wander lovelorn, blown along by winds,[123]
no relief or escape from the burdens of passion;[124]
They whittle me down to a sliver of wood,
as with a carpenter's rasp or plane.[125]
It kills me to think of her sweet conversation, 12.10
the rare honey that shows on snow-white teeth.[126]
Her neck is as white as the eggs of an ostrich:
it keeps me awake like a sting in the eye.[127]
They say I'm fine, but inside I'm afflicted:
infected by rabies, I see lightning flicker.[128]
Slayer who needs no weapon,
give the Muslim fair warning before taking his life![129]
Why not show yourself in good cheer
and bring relief that dissolves a heart's rancor,
Before he is forced to drink separation's brine, 12.15
and a lover's sobs are lost in the empty distance?

~ ١٣ ~

مـا لَومِ يا نفسٍ عن الزاد مِـعْـطـاه   والمـاي مـا يِبْـرِد لَهَبـها بـروده
لَين انْحَلَتْ بالحال والجِسْم تَبْراه   والقـلب شَـبَّت به سَـعايرِ وقوده
بالصَّدْر اِكِنّه كَنَّة الضَرْم مِخْزاه   سـاعـه ويِشْـرِب له ولَزْمـا يِعوده
لوان جَرْحي يِنْكِـمي كان اباكْمـاه   لا شكّ بي شَيٍ على الله ركـوده
اصْبِر ما دام اقْدِرعلى الصبْر واقْواه   ولا يِنْقوي صَـبْرٍ تَعَدَّى حـدوده
صَبر الهَوان الى تِذَكَّرْت فَرْقاه   ولا خبِر للفَرقا حِتِن ومَعْدوده
وَين انت ياللي تُوصِـل العِلْمْ مَـلْفاه   فَيحـان شَوق اللي تنَقّـض جعوده
عَوق الخَصيم وسِتْرٍ من تِذْهِل غْطاه   لا هَجّ من عَجّ السِـبايا قـعوده
ولا يِسْـنِد الّا مِـرْوِيٍ حَـدّ شَـلْفاه   يِمْـنىً على نَشْـر الدِمِيّ مْحَـموده
زَبْن الحصان الى إرْتَخى سَير عِـلْباه   يَشْـني وَراه ويِحْتِـمي كِـل عَوده
من راعي السابق الى شاف مِذْلاه   اللي عَـدايلهـا مجامـيع ذَوده
كِنّ السِـبايا يومِ تُوحِي مـثاراه   صَـيدٍ عن الرامي تِقـافى جـهوده
قِل يا سِعْد من جاه ما به مـناجاه   ابْدَيت لك سَدّي كِمـا انك سنوده
راعيه ما يِبْدي على الناس عَجْفاه   يَكْماه لَين انه بَرى الهَمّ عُوده
الِحبّ يومِ انك مِـقَـرّه ومَـرْسـاه   وقَـلبك مِـداهـيله ومَـرْكَزْ بنوده

~ 13 ~

I can't blame a soul who abstains from food:[130] 13.1
no amount of water cools its flames.
His health is undermined: body emaciated,
heart consumed by raging fire within.
Hidden deep in my chest lies a smoker's secret:[131]
if he stops, the craving nudges him back to habit.
If I could, I'd hide my injuries from view,[132]
but only God has the key to calm my affliction.
I endure as long as I can muster strength: 13.5
even lovers cannot suffer beyond endurance;[133]
How to live with blighted hopes after separation
if one is haunted by doubts about reunion?
Where are you, courier, to take my message
to Fayḥān, the heartthrob of a beauty who loosens her hair?
He blocks the enemy when a lady's veil slips off,
and her mount panics in the turmoil and dust.[134]
If he thrusts his lance, the blade gulps down its drink:
his hand is legendary for the blood it scatters.
When the neck muscles of lesser horses sag, 13.10
he rushes to the rescue and fends off danger:
A knight upon a steed that swoops and pounces,
fed on the milk of its own camel herd.[135]
When his battle cry resounds, the enemy's cavalry
flees at breakneck speed, like hunted game.[136]
Tell him: "O joy of those who seek you out,
I bare my soul to you, my pillar of strength.
To others I will not reveal what ails me,
but waste away until my ribs stick out.
You are love's shelter and haven;[137] 13.15
your heart is its haunt and pole of attraction.

~ ١٣ ~

لا هِنْت رَدِّد لي الخَبَر عن سِجاياه   حَيث انك الباخص بهُونه وكُوده
عن حال مَشْعوفٍ نِقَل داه بِرْداه   يَبْـغي الدوا والدّا خَطيـرٍ بـزَوده
يا تـلّ قـلبي تَلّتَـينٍ من اقْصـاه   تـلّ الوراد اللي حِـيامٍ وروده
يَمّ الطّوال اللي عـدوده مـطَوّاه   يـرُوع جَـذّابه مجاذِب عـدوده
على زَعـاعٍ مـا يسـانع بمَمْشـاه   مِسـتَصـعِبٍ مـا يَتْبَـع اللي يقوده
شَخْـصٍ بركّابه طِفوقٍ بمَمْشـاه   مَـمْشاه نَكْـدٍ والمحارف تكوده
لا قـال يا راع الجِمَـل زاد بخْـطـاه   امّـا انِقْـطَـع ولّا تِصَـرَّم عَـموده
على الذي بيـني وبيـنه مسـاداه   لا هوب رايدني وانا ازْرَيت ارُوده
ما غير يَرْعـاني بعَـينه وانا ارعـاه   والكـل مـنّا مـا يبـيّن سـدوده
لَيته الى كَـزّيت له خَـطّ يَقْـراه   ايضـا ويِعْـطيني حَـرايـض ردوده
كِثر النمـايم سَبّبَتْ قَصْرة خَـطـاه   واللي صِـفـا لي في لِيـالي سـعوده
لا سـاعَفَت راع النمـايم بدِنْيـاه   لَعـلّ حـاله تِنْـقِـرِض مـا تعوده
يا اهْل النمـايم من عَمل عَمَل يِلْقـاه   في مـاقِـفٍ يوم الجَوارح شـهوده
لا شكّ عنـده نُواطيـر وِعْـداه   اللي من اقْصى الخَلق واللّي جنوده
لو حِيل دونِه مـا تِبَدّلت بحْذاه   القـلـب مـا له رَغْـبةٍ عن ودوده
يا عُود رَيحانٍ على جال مِسْقـاه   من اين مـا هَبّ الهوى لان عُوده
لوطال ياسِه ما هَـقيت اني انسـاه   اذْكِـر تَعاجيبه وِلجلاج سُوده
من ذاق حِبّ السَلْهَمه ما تَناسـاه   من الكِبر يِذْبح وهو له طِروده

~ 13 ~

Instruct me, please, in the mysteries of passion:
you are steeped in its pleasures and rigor;
Of the malady man keeps within him,[138]
he yearns to be treated, but it only consumes him more."
Ah, the pull on my heart comes from deep down,
like water drawn for camels frantic with thirst,
From al-Ṭwāl, deep wells with stone casings:
a daunting challenge for those heaving the ropes,
Tied to a strong and impetuous she-camel:
an intractable beast for the man directing her,
She shies with the rider, bolting right and left;
steering her is hell, turning her worse.
When they shout to stop, she picks up the pace,
breaks the rope; or else the well beam cracks.[139]
I feel such pain for her—we are in touch;
but she neither visits me, nor can I go to her.[140]
She just gives me the eye, and I look at her:
the two of us keep our secret locked away.
If only she'd read my scribble, if I sent one,
and promptly send me a note in response!
But whispers and aspersions made her wary,
my darling of many ecstatic nights.
Let the rumormongers come to grief,
or better yet, be rooted out for good.
The backbiters will get their just deserts:
on Judgment Day, wounds will bear witness.[141]
Though she is watched by enemy guards,
distant kinsmen and clan members,
Who keep her from me, I cannot change how I feel,
and I cannot force my heart not to love her.
Ah, my sweet stalk of basil by the stream,
swaying on breezes that gently bend its stem:
Even though my chances are bleak, I cannot forget
her joie de vivre and sparkling black eyes.]
A lover who's tasted the love of the dreamy-eyed[143]
remains obsessed even when bent by old age.

شَـرْهَه يِـدي ماكل عُودٍ تَعَصّـاه   ولا هي على عُوج العِـصِيّ مْحَدوده
المِـطْرَق اللي يِبْتِـغي وَين ابا اَلْقـاه   عَيـني لهـا طَفْحـه ونَفْسي شِـروده
الشـاهـد الله ما تَغـاليت مَشْـراه   لا شكّ واقِفٍ السِـببَ عن وجوده
ازْوال واجد مَير ما هيب مَشْهـاه   النفس ياقَـف لَه عـيافٍ يـذودَه
ما صـار من بيـني وبيـنه مـناباه   ما حَسَّـف الخـاطر تِوِقِّف وروده
الرابح اللي مـا دَرى وَيش بَلْواه   دِلوه مِـبْعَـد وَجْعتِـه من حَسوده
وانا ومِثْـلي بَيِّنـاتٍ كُـواياه   غـير الضِـمان اللي تِبَـعَّث لهوده
هذا مِـضى والخـاتمـه عنـد مَولاه   ولا شٍ يصـير الّا بحِكْمَـة وجُوده

~ 13 ~

My hand is fastidious: any old cane won't do;
the choices are many, not just crooked sticks—
But how to find one that is the perfect fit?[144]
My eyes dart about and I am hard to please.[145]
As God is my witness, I'd pay any price for her,
but penury keeps her beyond my reach.
Stunning looks abound, but they leave me cold:
my soul is repulsed, then turns away.
Not a word passes between her and me:
it breaks my heart not to have her news!
Good fortune is never to know such misery:
blissfully serene, unpestered by the envious.[146]
On me and those like me the brands are deep:
ghastly yellow pus gushes from our sores.[147]
This is my tale. Closure is in the hands of the Lord—
not a thing happens outside His will and benevolence.

يا راكبٍ من عـندنا تِسْـع مـايات   تِسْـعين مع تِسْعين والْفٍ تـزادِ
يـرْعَنّ من عَرْجـا الى ادْنا القـريّات   وان سَـنِّدَن للِشعْب وارضٍ حَمـادِ
فوق المَخـارِمِ قَيـظها مِسْـتِريحـات   عِرْوات لَين سُهَيـل شِفناه بادي
يِلْفِنّ من عنـدي زِبون المـعَـنّات   ابن سبيّـل ريفـــ هِجْنٍ ردادِ
جـَنّك رِكايبـنا عـَراوي معـرّات   وَلِّمْ لِهن من الاواني عَـدادِ
يَبن خَشيب وصوف وِجلود وآلات   وِحديد وعيالٍ خَفـاف التنـادي
عِدّ القوايـم عـدّة العِقـل وَلْمـات   عَقِّل عَـراقيب النـضا والعضـادِ
عَجِّل رواكيبٍ ولاشغـالهم هات   واِحـذَر عن الشـايب ووِلْد الردادِ
خَـذَنّ في دارك لِيـالٍ مقيمات   وارْكَـب على هِجْنٍ تفوت الريادي
وانْتَـه عَـقيد الرَبْع يا طَـيِّب الذات   دَوِّر عَشيري يا مـرُوِّي الهَـنادي
تَـراي من فَـرقاه دَرْكٍ بِمظْـلمات   ما اسْمَع ولا ابْصِر لو عيوني حـدادِ
دَوِّر ظِنين الروح عَذْب الشِفَـيّات   هـا في الحَشـا يِشْـبِه ظَبيّ الحَمـادِ
الَى ضَحَك لي بالثِمان الرِهيفـات   يِنْسِـين هَـمٍّ لاجيٍ في فوادي
روحوا لِمَكّـه والدِيار البِعيـدات   من ديرة الشِنْبِل لدار ابن هـادي

~ 14 ~

Poem by Fayḥān ibn Zirībān[148]

Rider who sets out with nine hundred mounts, 14.1.1
ninety, ninety more, and another thousand!
They pastured from ʿArjā to near al-Grayyāt,
in the uplands of al-Shiʿb and the gravel plains.[149]
They roamed on pristine grounds in the hot season,
grazing until Canopus winked low on the horizon.[150]
Take these camels to a host who cares for tired mounts,
Ibn Sbayyil, where exhausted camels will regain their strength.[151]
My riders came to you on animals bare of trappings:[152] 14.1.5
now it falls to you to outfit them:
Wooden saddle frames, wool, leather, gear,
metalware, and brisk lads eager to help.[153]
Make sure you have enough rope to tie them!
Hobble the hamstrings and limbs of the hardy ones;
Lose no time! Hurry the camel drivers on,
and beware of graybeards and good-for-nothings!
They took their time getting ready at your place:
ride the speedy racers into the endless wastes.
You, my fine fellow, are chief of a close-knit band: 14.1.10
drench your blade in blood, seek out my love![154]
I perish from thirst in waterless deserts since her loss:
hearing and vision are gone, yet my eyes stay sharp.[155]
Go, find my sweetheart, with her sweet lips
and wasp-like waist, graceful as a plains gazelle.
When she laughs and shows her finely chiseled teeth,
any sorrow lodged in my heart is swept away.
Have them run toward Mecca, to far-flung lands,
from al-Shunbul's home to where Ibn Hādī holds sway,[156]

ومن دِيرة حسَينٍ ودار الاغاوات   لاخوان ساره مِقحِّمين الطرادِ   ١٤،١،١٥
وقِّف على اللي يَشْغَل المارتيّات   وقّف على السِلْطان واهل الجهادِ
وجميع مِن في نَجْد يَبْنون الابيات   البَدْو واللي ساكنين البلادِ
ولى لِقَيت ضْخَيِّف الروح لي هات   من فَوق ما يَقْطَع بِعيد الريادي
لا جِيت مَظْنوني وهو ما بَعَد فات   ابيَض ولا يِقْدَر عليك السُوادِ
ان ما لِقَيته حَيّ تلْقاه قِد مات   خَفِّف عليه القَبر وارْم الهوادي   ١٤،١،٢٠
والا تراني مَيّتٍ كان هو مات   كِنّي طِريح مُخَضّبين الهَنادِ
تراي ما قِلْته مدَوّر حيالات   الا ولا طاري القِصا بك مرادي
مَير ابعِد الحِرْوه وارَمّي بالاصوات   اخاف من حَكْي الكِذوب الربادي

يا راكبٍ من عندنا صَيعريات   من ساس عَيراتٍ عرابٍ تلادِ   ١٤،٢،١
بَنات حرٍّ لَحَّلوه الشَرارات   بالجَيش تغني له جميع البُوادي
بِيض المَحاقِب والغَوارِب مْشيبات   للتِلُو ما سوّوا لهن التُوادي
لِجّ النحور وروكهن مِستِقلّات   خِضع الرقاب مْفتّلات العْضادِ
بالشَدّ وَنيّاتٍ وبالمَشي طَفْقات   غِزّ المسامِع والنواظر حْدادِ   ١٤،٢،٥
عامين يرْعن في حيا نَجْد مَشْهات   من حدّ الانْجل لِلنّجِ باستِنادِ
والى حَصل بين الحَفيفَين غَيظات   يَرْعَن زَهَر ما لاق في كِلّ وادي

~ 14 ~

From the quarters of Ḥusayn and Turkish lords, 14.1.15
to the brothers of Sārah, indomitable horsemen.[157]
Stop off at your friend's known for his rifles;
stay awhile with al-Sulṭān and his tireless warriors,[158]
And all those who have dwellings in Najd:
the Bedouin as well as the sedentary folk.[159]
If you find my heart's delight, bring her at once
on your camels across the vast expanses.
If you find my sweetheart alive and well,
I'll plant a white flag for your noble deeds.[160]
If you find that she is no more and has passed on, 14.1.20
lighten her grave, strew sand over the cooking stones.[161]
I declare, if she has died, count me dead as well,
like a warrior struck down by Indian swords.[162]
Mark my words, I am not playing games,
nor do I want to come down hard on you: [163]
I am blabbering on to keep them off scent,[164]
lest some rumormonger ferret out my secret.

Ibn Sbayyil's reply to Fayḥān ibn Zirībān

Rider setting out on a Ṣayʿar camel mount, 14.2.1
fast and hardy, offspring of the purest breed—[165]
Noble she-camels, sired by studs of al-Sharārāt,[166]
racers coveted by all Bedouin for desert treks.[167]
White below the belts, gray on their shoulder blades—[168]
never a calf suckling at their udders: [169]
With broad chests and freely moving haunches,
they run with necks low and muscles twisted.
Calm when being loaded, sprightly on the run, 14.2.5
alert, with ears pricked and eyes sharp.[170]
Two years they pastured in Najd to their heart's delight,
from al-Anjal's edge toward the highlands of al-Nijaj;
No matter if enemy tribes clash and fight with fury:
they graze undisturbed, bellies full.

مِـرباعهِن ما بين عـرْجـا وابانات   وان حـدَّرن لِمْـريَظبه والثـنادي
مِصْـيافهن كَبْشـان للبـدْو مَشْـهاة   لى كِنّ مِزْن الصيف بِقْران حـادي
مْعـفَّيـاتٍ قَـيظهِن مِسْـترِيحـات   ليا ما بِـدَا نَجْـم السويْبِع وِكـادِ
جا حَقّنا فيهِن وهِن حَقّهن فات   قَـطْع الفَيـافي والحزوم البعـادِ
والصِبحْ من بطْحا نفي مِسْـتِقِلاّت   يَشْـدِن نعامٍ جافـلٍ مع حَمـادِ
والعصْر في دار ابن عَسْكَر مْويقات   خفـافٍ يجَـفِّلهن سِمار البلادِ
حُطّوا على اللي للمـراكيب مَشْـهاة   ذولا مَـراويح وذولا غوادي
ابن حَسن راعي طروقٍ مْخـلاّت   عبـد الله اللي للمـعـاني نفـادِ
له دَكـّةٍ فـيها دلالٍ مْـراكات   ونارٍ سَناهـا طول ليـله ينـادي
ومِحْماسةٍ دايـم على النار مِحْماة   ونِجْـرٍ يقلْقِـل راسـيات العَقـادِ
ومْبَهّرٍ كِنّه خضـاب الخُونْدات   يَبـراه مِختاره لِيـال الجِـدادِ
ومَـناسفٍ فيـها صحونٍ مـمَلاّت   يـرْمَى بهِنّ اذناب حِـيلٍ وزادِ
والصِبحْ دَنوّهِنّ تقِل مِسْـتذيـرات   من حـايـط الديره لِهِنّ اجْـتلادِ
غِبّ المسير مْعَزّلاتٍ وضَمْرات   مِثْل الحَنايا لا حَـناهـا سـتادِ
سِيروا وخَلّوهِنّ مع الجامع افوات   مِسْراحكم طـاروق وارضٍ حَمْـادِ
قِدْم المعَشّى مِـقْبِلينٍ على ابيـات   مـالٍ كِمـا الحَـرّه وقِبٍ جيادِ
عِلوى مَعاويدٍ على الحَرْب وعْصات   وساع النَحايا سِقْم عَين المـعادِ
نَصُّوهِن الرِخْمـان والعلم ما فـات   جمال التَخوت ان شال حِمْـلٍ وِكادِ

Their spring pastures are between ʿArjā and Abānāt,
and downcountry toward Mrēṭbah and al-Thanādī;
In early summer they roam at Kabshān, a Bedouin's dream,[171]
as if fed by rains—not of summer, but of the winter star.[172]
Unburdened, they spent hot summer in relaxation 14.2.10
until Ursa Major's seventh little star twinkled bright.[173]
Their right to idle at an end; it was our turn—[174]
we drove them across wastes and desolate rocky hills.
In the morning they set forth from Nifī's sandy watercourse,
running like ostriches fleeing across an empty plain.
At afternoon they looked sideways at Ibn ʿAskar's place:
frisky and light, shying from the oasis's dark shapes.[175]
Head for the travelers' favorite entertainment spot!
Mounted parties arrive, pass others departing:
No wonder! It's ʿAbdallah ibn Ḥasan, unrivaled nobleman,[176] 14.2.15
who probed every virtue to its core.
In the open welcome area, decked out with coffeepots,
a fire burns all night, its flames a beacon for guests:
A roasting pan for coffee beans always on the fire,
The house's sturdy domes shaken by the mortar's pounding.[177]
Coffee mixed with spices, the color of henna-dyed beauties,
served with freshly harvested dates;
Then platters chock full, heaped with roasted meat,
topped off with sheep's fat tails high on the rice.
In the morning, mounts are brought, nervous and edgy,[178] 14.2.20
ready to run at pace through the town gate.
Skin and bones from the journey's rigors,
like litter poles bent by an artisan into a bow.
Go on! Steer them single file past the mosque,
on well-trodden tracks through the plain.
Before supper you reach an encampment,
herds numerous as lava stones, and noble steeds.
ʿIlwā! Battle-hardened and indomitable tribesmen,
they wander far and wide, ever their enemy's plague.
Turn to al-Rikhmān of high repute, 14.2.25
like stud camels that carry litters into battle.[179]

ثُم انْصوا اللي بالقِسا يذْبَح الشاة   فيحان ابن قاعد حَريب الرِقادِ
عَطُوه رَدّ العِلم قَبْل التّحيّات   مِثايلٍ ما هيب بَعْض الدُوادي
يا زَين بالرَدّه هل الدوبليات   الى رَهَبهم حِسّ راعي جُوادِ
كَزّيت لي جَيشٍ عَراوي معَرّات   عِندك خَبَر مَحْسوبهِن و العَدادِ
ما بين بَحر وصوف وِجلود وآلات   وحديد وعيالٍ خفاف التَنادِ
تَبي تَعْجِزْني على كلّ مَشْهات   تِحِطّني ما بين قافٍ وصادِ
ونَهار جَنّي صار بالصَدْر فَرْحات   ليلٍ علينا مِثْل ليل العَيادِ
من يوم جَنّي والنَجاير مسوّات   الخَرْز تَرْز وراعي الصوف سادي
شِغْل النِصارى والزَهَب مِسْتِعِدّات   هَلْهِن على رِجْلين ما من قَعادِ
وعَصِيّ اهلهن كِلّهن خَيزرانات   وقِلْصان اهَلْهن كل ابوهن جدادِ
يوم اسْتَعَدّينا وهِن مِسْتِعِدّات   غَرَضك كِنّي قاضبه بالايادِ
الله يوفّقنا السعد والسلامات   ويسَهّل المطلوب ربّ العبادِ
وَجّهت بالامصار وارضٍ بِعيدات   وارفاض وديارٍ وَراهم بعادِ
عَطيت راع التَيل عِدّة ريالات   وطَقّه شِمال وشَرق واجْنَب واعادِ
ونِشَد هل البحرين واهل البضاعات   وكلٍ حَلَف لي عنه دِينٍ وِكادِ
خَلّيت نِصْف الجَيش رَذْيا وحَفيات   والنِصْف الآخر جا لهِنّ ارْتعادِ
ثُم انقلبت لنجد شِيخان ورعاة   من شافني قال انت وَين انت غادي
خَلّيتني بين القبايل ميادات   عَذّبتني واذَيتني باجتهادِ

~ 14 ~

Head for the butcher of sheep in times of dearth:
  Fayḥān ibn Ǵāʿid, who fights off sleep like a fiend.[180]
Give him my response before greeting him,
  my instructive verse, untarnished by claptrap,
To the protector of horsemen, swept up like flotsam,
  who cower at the cries of the charging knight:[181]
You dispatched a troop of barebacked camels—
  their exact numbers and details you know best—
In need of wooden parts, wool, leather, gear,
  Metalware, and brisk lads eager to help.
No, fool, I know you are out to confound me,
  to show that I am not up to your challenge.[182]
At their approach, my heart leapt with joy;
  that night my mood was merry and festive.
As soon as they arrived wooden saddles were made;
  leather bags were stitched, sack wool was spun;[183]
Firearms crafted by Christians, ammunition readied[184]
  by men who rushed about without a moment's respite.
The riders' sticks are cut from thick reed,
  the bucket-shaped leather bags brand new.
Once we were all set and the camels fitted out,
  I felt the chase's purpose in our grasp.[185]
May God make our enterprise fortunate and safe:
  the Lord's might paves the road for His servants.
I turned my attention to distant towns and lands—
  to the followers of the Shiite rites and far beyond:[186]
I paid some riyals to the telegraph operator,
  and he tapped away, north and east and back again;[187]
He inquired of folk in Bahrain, of merchants—
  all swore ignorance by Almighty God.
I drove half the camels to shreds, soles bleeding;
  the other half trembled with exhaustion.
When I returned to Najd's commoners and chiefs,
  they stared and asked, "What's wrong with you?"
You made me a laughingstock among the tribes,
  haggard from exacting demands and incessant toil.

مَذموح كِذْبك يا معزّي سَلامات مَـذموح كِذْبك يا مِـظَنَّة فُوادي
راعى الهَوى كَذّاب وابْليس ما مات دَوّر عَشيرك من فِريقك وغـادي
الهَـقْوة انّك تَنْظِـره بالحَبيبات من المْـراح الى الذَرا والهَوادي
والّا مع اللي بالحِجَر مِسْتِكِنّات والهَـقْوة انّـه يَسْمَعِك لو تنـادي
بينك وبين صويحبك خمسة ابيات وَزن القِـليب ومَنْـزِله بالركـادِ
حَيّ ولا بي من حَـلالك مجـازاة الّا حَـياتك والسَـلامـه مـرادي
ان مـا عِـطِـيت اياه والمَنّ فَوّات خِذْها انت قَبْلٍ من سَنا الصِبْح بادي
فان كان ما عندك لَحايق وِحشْمات ازْبِن على اللي مـا مِشَوا بالقِصـادِ
دُوشان عِلْف سيوفهم كلّ جِمْهات على القِـدى ولّا على غَـير قـادي
ولّا على اللي هـم وعِلْوى حَرابات ما بينهم غير اصْطفاق العَوادي
والَى عَـزَمْت لِحَطّ للرِجـل مِرْقـاة من خَوف يَدْري بك خَطاة الرَبادي
ولا تاخِـذ الدِنْيـا خراصٍ وهَقْوات يَقْـطَعْك من نَقْل الصِميـل البَرادِ
لك شَوفةٍ وَحْده وللنـاس شَوفـات ولا واديٍ سَـيله يفَـيِّض بوادي
الِحبّ كـلّ ذايقٍ مِـنْه لَيعـات من عَصْر نُوح وجاي ما له حـدادِ
مَشْعوف قَلْبي قِدم قَلبك وهَيهات مـا نيب مِـثْلك يا رِدي الجَـلادِ
ولا يَنْفـع المَحْرور كِثْر التِنَهّات ولا يِسْقي الظامي خَضيض الورادِ

~ 14 ~

Your lies are forgiven, my dear, salutations to you;[188]
  your lies are forgiven. I treasure you in my heart:
A lover must dissemble, for the devil's still around:[189]
  look for your darling with your relatives and kin![190]
Likely you'll spot her among lovely friends,
  moving from resting herds to tent flap and cooking stones.[191]
If she stays hidden from view in the women's quarters,
  chances are she'll hear you if you call her name.[192]
Your love is but five tents away:
  hers stands firmly pitched by the wells.
She is alive! No need to reward the messenger:[193]
  Enough to wish you long life and good health.
If you're not given her hand—for a promise is a debt—
  then grab her and elope before the break of dawn!
If middlemen and worthies fail to plead your case,
  turn to those who can arrange things:
To Dūshān, whose swords are drenched in enemy blood,
  winners, peaceably or through force.[194]
If all else fails, seek out their implacable foes:
  between them nothing but clash of men and steel.[195]
Once resolved, ready yourself with care and stealth,[196]
  lest some waffling fool gets in your way.[197]
Do not act from surmises and guesswork:[198]
  a cool spell is no reason to travel without a waterskin.[199]
Don't forget: if you hold a view, others have theirs:[200]
  like floods racing down valleys, each follows its own course.
As for love, no one has been spared its pangs:
  since Noah's time, it has heeded no bounds;
My heart endured passion's torment long before you;
  in such trials as these, you're no match for my grit.
A man ill with fever will not be cured by his groans,[201]
  nor does dangling the rope in a well slake one's thirst.[202]

~ ١٥ ~

تَرى حَلات الكَيف يا مِشْرِبٍ لِه لا فارِقوك اهل الحَسَد والنِجاسِه
لا صار شَغّاله ظِريفٍ بِزَلّه وذَرْبٍ بتَقْليطه وقيمة قياسِه
والى قِضَى حَبّه على ما شَغَل لِه تلْقَى على الفِنْجال رِدْعة لَعاسِه
يِقْفاه ما يِبْري الضَرَم مَزّةٍ لِه يِبْرِد لِهيب القَلب حَرّة وَناسِه
والَى شِكا شَرّابة العَظم قِلّه تلْقاه مع من يَنْقله عِقْب ياسِه
خَطو الوَلَد تَوّه على شَبّةٍ له جميع هَومات المَراجل براسه
يقوم بالمعروف دِقّه وجِلّه والله مهَيّن له على قَوّ باسه
وخَطو الوَلد رِجْمٍ على غير حِلّه لو جاز لِك مَبْناه بَرّق بساسه
خِضَرة عَشَر ما هو على شَوفةٍ لِه يِزوم رُوحه واحَسايف لِباسه
سَنْحِه الى شِفْتِه يناظِر لظِلّه تقول ذا من طالبين الرياسه
يدخل مع الخَفْرات بالعِلْم كله ومْعَلِّمٍ نَفْسه دروب الهياسِه
مَير إنْصِحِه يا موصّل العِلْم قِل لِه عن كَثْرة الشَوفات راسِه حَساسِه

~ 15 ~

If you drink to lift your spirits, connoisseur,[203]
    do it after mean-spirited grousers have left.
Have it prepared and served by a skillful lad,
    deft at pouring and serving just right.[204]
The roasted beans, treated with care,
    leave their dark imprint on the porcelain cup.
Satisfy your craving by lighting up, and draw: [205]
    its intimate glow cools a burning heart.
If the pipe-puffing crowd complains they're out,
    despair turns to joy with the arrival of more.
One boy, just old enough to light a fire,
    Is already alive with manly ambitions:
He performs noble deeds, big and small;
    aided by God his strength keeps growing.
Another's a cairn that's not properly secured;
    before building him up, inspect his foundations:
Like giant milkweed, he is not as he seems—
    he towers in the air, but fails to deliver.[206]
He and his shadow stride with such pomp:
    you'd say he's running for president.
He and women are from the same mold;
    his ways are tortuous—none runs straight.
You must warn him, carrier of my words,
    that his ostentation brings its own risks.

يا راكب اللي مَشْيهنّ اجْتِواشِ   لابن سبيل عانياتٍ من الطاش ١،١،١٦
لا رَوّحَن مثل الطَخاخ النُواشِ   وِلْهن مع الوادى السَناوي تِجِهْواش
مَلْفاك من يِنْبي لهنّ بالغباشِ   يِفِزّ باللافي ليا جاه طَرّاش
ضَيّعت لي بين المِظاهير حاشي   ومن غَدْية الحاشي وانا ما اقْدَر اعتاش
وَصْفه ثلاث رقوم ما غيرها شي   غير الوسوم البيِّنه ما عليهاش ٥،١،١٦

تَرى المِطَر باوّل سَحابه رِشاشِ   وتاليه وِدْيانٍ يِشيلنّ الادباش ١،٢،١٦
ان جِيت انا باخْبِرْك عمّا بِجاشي   دَرْب السِعه ضَرَّبْتِني دَرْب الابلاش
تَراه ما يَنْفَعْك حُبّ النُواشِ   اقْعِد رِفاض وخَلّ عَنْك التِوحّاش
لِقَيت بَيّاع المَعَزّه بَلا شي   يَسْرح على ما لون ويَضْوي على ماش
يا وَنّتي وَنّة من الغَوش ماشي   ابوه مات ولا وِرِث عِقْبه ادباش ٥،٢،١٦
ابوه مات ولا وِرِث غير حاشي   وحَرْبَش على الحاشي ومن عِنْده انحاش
خَرْفَش على الحاشي وطَقّه خراشِ   واتْلى العَهَد بِه هَفّ مَعَ حَزْم عَكّاش

~ 16 ~

Poem by Fayḥān ibn Zirībān

Rider of camels at breakneck speed[207] 16.1.1
running to Ibn Sbayyil from the world's far end,
Like small clouds scudding over the plain
and desiccated wadis, hell-bent to arrive
At your coffee mortar, which sings all night—
for travelers, you jump up with open arms.
I lost a young she-camel among the caravans:
after she went missing, life lost its meaning.
She is branded with three little rings, that's all: 16.1.5
other than these, there's not a mark on her.

Ibn Sbayyil's reply

When clouds roll in, the rain starts with a drizzle; 16.2.1
but it ends up sweeping herds of cattle away.[208]
Come, I'll tell you why I am seething:
I long for calm but you plunged me in troubles.
You don't want to make do with bits and pieces:
steel yourself for the long haul, don't panic!
A man who'll sell his honor cheap
starts out with nothing and ends up with less.
My sobs and tears are those of a forlorn little boy 16.2.5
whose father died and left him without a herd;
His father died and bequeathed just one camel;
young and maltreated, the animal ran away—
After a smacking, the poor thing went berserk:
it was last seen hurtling down ʿAkkāsh's slopes.

عَيني وقَلبي بينهِنّ اهْتِواشِ   وازْرَيت انا افْرِق بينهن ظَبْيَ الاوحاش
قَلبي يقول اشْقَحَ وفيه النِشاشِ   وعَيني تقول ابيْض ِكما قِطْعة الشاش
ان كان هو جاني فيا بِرْد جاشي   وان كان ما جاني فلا باردٍ جاش ١٠،٢،١٦
يا زَين عَطْني حِبّةٍ لو نُواشِ   احْيي بَها قَلبٍ مِحيمٍ ومِعْطاش

~ 16 ~

The warfare between eye and heart wears me down—
in the dust of battle, I lost sight of the shy gazelle.
My heart says, "She is a shade of white, with a touch of rose";
my eye says, "She is pure white as a cotton sheet."
Her arrival cools the smoldering inside me: 16.2.10
without her I can never have sangfroid.
My beauty, let me steal a kiss, just a little one,[209]
to revive a delirious heart overcome by thirst.

~ ١٧ ~

اللهْ يبيِّض وَجْه طامي بن قِدْران   عَشّى ذِلولي مع مِـطِية قَـراريش ١،١،١٧
وابن سبيِّل شَوق مَدْعوج الاعيان   اللي حجاجِه ضاحكٍ للطَّراريش
ياليت لي معهم بِني عَمّ واخوان   نِعْمٍ بِخطلان اليَدين الهَشاهيش
سَلامْ واحدهم لِباقه وصِفْطان   ما هوب مِثْل اللي سَلامه تَناويش

يا راكبٍ من فوق سَلْسات الاقْران   ما قَرَّبوهِن للسرا والمَغابيش ١،٢،١٧
نَقْوَة حَرارٍ من ضَرايب سِحَيمان   راعيه يِعْطا غير ما قال بَخْشيش
ما دَرَّجَن مع تالي الطَّرْش حِيران   رِمْلٍ الى هاج الجْمَل دونهن هِيش
مِرْباعهن ما بين عَرْجا وجِمْران   وما يَرْفع السَّرْحى وما طَمَّن الهِيش
ومَقْياظهِن وان قَصَّب العُود فِيحان   وادي نِفي عَلّه صِدوق المَراهيش ٥،٢،١٧
ومَيارِكٍ تِنْهِض عن الرِجْل وِلْيان   وِخْروج نَصْباتٍ هَدَبْهِن مِشاويش
رَكّابهِنّ فلان وِفْلان وفلان   ما هُمْب اهل هَمْزٍ ولَمْزٍ وتَوريش
ما يِمْلكون ظهورهِنّ لولا الارسان   لِكِنّه يوَحِّشْهِن من القَشْع تَوحيش

~ 17 ~

Poem by Mas'ūd Āl Mas'ūd from al-Sha'rā'

May God whiten the face of Ṭāmi ibn Gidrān, 17.1.1
who fed my mount and those of the grass cutters,[210]
And Ibn Sbayyil, admired by black-eyed beauties:
his eyebrows jump with joy when travelers arrive.[211]
I wish they were my relatives and brothers:
accolades to those big-spending and warm hosts.
My greetings to each of them, spoken with sincerity;
not one of those tepid handshakes and a murmur.

Ibn Sbayyil's reply to Mas'ūd Āl Mas'ūd from al-Sha'rā'

Riders of smooth, fast camels, 17.2.1
not the kind that toil all night at the well,[212]
The pick of pedigrees sired by Sḥēmān: [213]
the stud's owner was paid more than just a tip.
They weren't trailed by calves at the herd's tail;
rutting bulls never came close.[214]
Their spring pastures are from 'Arjā to Jimrān,
up from al-Sarḥā and down from al-Hīsh; [215]
When heat snaps the stalks, they seek the oasis, 17.2.5
the wadi of Nifī, may it be drenched by rains.
Cushions protect their fur from the riders' feet; [216]
the balanced saddlebags have fluttering fringes.
The riders aren't just anyone, but men of high repute
and upright character, leery of winks and whispers.
Their mounts are unladen except for the reins,
as if they are in mortal fear of baggage and clutter.

~ ١٧ ~

لا رَوَّحَن مع عِبْلِةٍ شَوفها بان　　يَشْدِن نَعامٍ جافلٍ مع نِشانيش

تِلْفي لنا رَبْعٍ بِفَيّه مسَيّان　　اهَل قصورٍ رَفَعوها بتَنْعيش ١٠،٢،١٧

ما يَذْبِحون الّا طِويلات الاثْمان　　ما دَوَّروا عنْهِن رِدِي القَرافيش

ما قِلْت غير اللي نِظَرْته بالاعيان　　ما نيب وَفَّادٍ بقَولي ولا ابيش

هذا جِزا مَسْعود في رَدّ الافنان　　شَوق الطِموح اللي تِقضّ العَكاريش

When they cross featureless plains at full stride,
    they are like ostriches fleeing over flat wastes.
You'll reach friends of ours as evening shadows fall,[217] 17.2.10
    in lofty mansions built by expert hands.
For guests, they slaughter the pick of the herd;
    it is beneath them to fob off little lambs.
I wished to say what I have seen with my own eyes—
    no other motive have I, nor reward do I solicit.
This is a grateful reply to artful verses by Masʿūd,
    the dream of sulking wives with loosened tresses.

~ ١٨ ~

الله لَحَـد يا تَـلّ قَـلْبي من اقْصـاه   تَـلّ القِطيع اللي شَعَوه الطِـماميع
زاعَوه من مَـفْـلاه حَـزّة معَشّـاه   وتالي نهـاره ضَـرّبوه المَـهاييع
وَطّوا به المِتْياه من عِقْب مَظْماه   واقْـفَوا يِلوعونـه مع الدَرْب تَلْويع
غِبّ المَراح وراحَتِه طال مَسْراه   واصْـبَح على فـاله بخُبْث التُواقيع
او تَـلّ زِمْـلوق الشِـفـا يوم لَوّاه   لاهوب صَيفٍ وحاميات الذَعـاذيع
على عَشيـرٍ عَـوّقَـتني هَوايـاه   بسهوم نِجْلِه مَـزَّع القَـلْب تَمْزيع
في مِـعْتَرَض سُوقٍ لِجاني مفاجـاه   والْحَق عَـليّ باعْـتِراضٍ وتَـرْبيع
واقْفي يَحَسْب خطاه طَرْبٍ لِمَمْشاه   وانا مْخَلّيني جِـضيع التُواجيع
يِدير عينه بي وهو يِدْرِج خطـاه   واشـار لي بِمْخَضّبات الاصـابيع
بَدْرٍ بـدا من وادي الغَيّ مَـنْشـاه   جَهْـرٍ غَشـا ضَوحه لنوره شَعاشيع
الخَـدّ بَـرْقٍ ناض نَوّه بِمَـثْناه   ينْشـاف في عِمْق الطَـها لِه تلاميع
المِـتْرَف اللي مِخْـلِفَـتْني سِجـاياه   يَفْتِل وينْقِض ما لِهَرْجه تِسانيع
ابو ثِليـلٍ فوق الامـتان يَغْـذاه   بالمِسْك وينَـقّـع له الوَرد تَنْـقيع
يَشْدي سِبيب كروش وَصْفه وحِلْياه   لا سـمْعت الصَيّاح وَقْت المِفازيع
سَـمعَت نِجايِج العَـرَب والمـناداه   مع قَول دَنّ المِـعْـرِقه والمِصـاريع

~ 18 ~

Almighty God! My heart is pulled from its roots, 18.1
like a herd of camels driven off by rustlers.[218]
They snatched them from evening pasture;
next day they filed through mountain spurs
Toward waterless wastes, already thirsting;
after a restful life, they were beaten furiously,[219]
Galloped down the track and ran all night long;
dawn broke miserably, a terrible fate awaiting them.[220]
Or is it distress felt by a desert stalk that withers, 18.5
lashed by gusts of fiendishly hot summer winds?
These are my feelings for a love that crippled me:
the arrows from her large eyes ripped my heart.
In the middle of the market, she took me by surprise;
catching up to intercept, hesitating a moment.
Then she walked on merrily, counting her steps;
leaving me poleaxed, as if smitten in battle.
She dawdles, then turns her eyes on me,
subtly gesturing with hennaed hands.
She is a moon rising from the valley of seduction,[221] 18.10
resplendent, layers of light on radiant luminance;
Cheeks like gleams from the depths of a cloud,
lightning that flashes in the misty fringe.
She twists the rope, then unties the knot, at will:[222]
I can't make head or tail of it.
Her plaited tresses tumble down her back,
musk-scented and sprinkled with a whiff of rose,
A cascade of hair like the tail of an Arabian horse
when cries of alarm resound and chase is given—
Shouting, din of arms, and loud voices of men 18.15
giving orders: "Hurry, bring saddle and reins!"

~ ١٨ ~

مِـتْبَصّـرٍ ربّي بخَـلْقـه وسَوّاه   لاهـل الهَوى زَود امْتِحانٍ وتَوليع

اللهٰ عـلى مَـزّة شِـفاياه بِـرْضـاه   حَيثي شِفوق وفيه ما اسْمَع ولا اطيع

وعِـرِفْت انا مَضْمون قَلْبه وقَصْياه   وانا لمـا يَهْواه سَـمّاع ومْـطيـع

وانا زِبون التَـرْف لو غِلي مَشْـراه   اسوق به من باب مَصْـرٍ الى الريع

وصـلاة ربّي عِـدّ خَـلْقه وطَـرْياه   عـلى النِبي الهاشـمي خَيـر مِن طيع ٢٠،١٨

My Lord keeps a close eye on His creation,
with special trials and heartache allotted to lovers.
By God, if I could only taste her lips, freely offered,
besotted and defiant, I'd refuse to obey reason.
I know what she harbors in her heart of hearts:
for her every desire, I am at her beck and call.[223]
I make my bids for the maiden: no price too high:
for her I scour markets from Cairo's gates to Mecca.[224]
I close with prayers—as many as there are people saying His name— 18.20
for the Hāshimī Prophet, who is man's best example.

~ ١٩ ~

حَلّ الفراق وحَنّ رايم لمَزْيوم وقَوَى الفراق اللي كبارٍ دفوفِه
امْسَيت انا عيني حَريبٍ لها النوم كِنّ الاداوي بالنِظير مُحَذوفِه
ابْكي بكا وِرْعٍ عن الدَيد مفطوم عاجاه غَير امّه وكَثْرَت صدوفِه
غَدَيت مثل اللي بمَسْراه مَنْجوم مِنّي مَعاليق الضِمير مُخَطوفِه
ونَفْسي غَدَت لا هِيب مَنٍّ ولا سَوم وجِسْمي نَحَل كِنّ السَعاير بجَوفِه
والقلب جارٍ له سُواميح وِهْموم ومن القَراده كِلّ طارٍ يلوفه
على الذي جاني منِه ردّ وِعْلوم شَرْهٍ عَلَيّ اللي جِميلٍ وصوفه
ولِه الشَرَه لوكان ما جيت مَثْلوم اصبِر على عَجْفاه لاجْل مْعَروفه
لو بيّن الجَفْوا فانا عنِه ما اشُوم لَين اتعَذّر منه واجْلِي الحسوفه
حَقٍّ عليّ رادع شِفاياه بِرْقوم يِروف بي وانا بحال المِروفه
وحَقّه عَلَيّ الى هَرَجْت ابْعِد الحَوم اغْضِي ولا كِنّي مع الناس اشوفه
انا الذي يا ما اتمَنّاه من يوَم وهو الِذي نَفْسِه لغَيري عَيوفه
ان مِتّ قَبْله قال لي زيد مرحوم وان مات قَبْلي ما الحياة مْخَلوفه
كِنّ اللوالو بين اشافيه مَنْظوم اوضِيق وَبْلٍ مُحلّتِمٍ في قنوفه
والخَدّ قِرطاسٍ عن اللِمس مَكْموم والعِنق عِنْق اللي تلَنّه خشوفه

~ 19 ~

Separation tore us apart and left me wistful with desire,[225] 19.1
but strong enough to endure, though advanced in years.[226]
When I lie down for the night, my eyes fight sleep,
as if the pupils are peppered with hot medicine.[227]
I cry like an infant just weaned from the breast—[228]
a foster mother's, not his own—leaving him in agony.
Like a traveler at night, lost among stars, I straggle,[229]
deranged as if my heart's arteries were plucked out.
My soul went missing—not as a present or bargain— 19.5
and my body is emaciated, as if flames lick its insides.
The heart is buffeted by misfortunes and anxiety,
beset on all sides by premonitions of disaster,
Because of her reply and bits and pieces of news
that leave no doubt about the damsel's displeasure.
She may feel vexed, but I did her no wrong:
for the sake of her kindnesses, I bear with her faults.
When given the cold shoulder, I do not forsake
but offer apologies to clear misunderstanding.
The damsel with blue tattooed lips owes it to me 19.10
to treat me gently since I need her tender care;
I owe it to her not to raise the slightest suspicion:
I speak and look as if she is unknown to me,
When in truth she's never out of my thoughts,
and she feels distaste for all but me.
If I die first, she says, "So-and-so passed away";[230]
If she dies first, my life loses meaning.
Her lips hide teeth strung like pearls,
or like hail from clouds in a pitch-black sky.
Her cheeks are as translucent as untouched paper; 19.15
her neck that of a gazelle trailed by fawns;

~ ١٩ ~

وَالعَين عين اللي على راس مَلْموم   ما جِيب لِه من كِلّ نَسْرٍ عَلوفه
حِرْش المَناكب لابْرَق الريش صَيروم   حِرٍّ مَلَك موت الحَباري كفوفه
ابو نهَيد بِلَبّة الصَدْر مَزْموم   بَيض الحَمام اللي رفاعٍ قيوفه
هافي حَشَى كِنّه عن الزاد مَحْروم   والثَوب يَشْكي ما نِبا من ردوفه
والزَين في مَقْرَن حجاجيه مَرْشوم   رَشْمة مَهَر شَيْخٍ شِبِع في مِضوفه ٢٠،١٩
يا جاعلٍ موت المَخاليق مَحْتوم   قَرِّب مِداهيل العَنود الهَنوفه

~ 19 ~

Her eyes those of a falcon high on its rocky perch,
    not a captive bird fed pieces of meat,
Shoulders rough, and claws fatal to bustards:
    angel of death for its brown- and white-spotted prey.
Firm breasts protrude below a gracious line of neck,
    like pigeon eggs in nests high on sheer cliffs;
Her waist is slim as if she is deprived of food,
    while her behind stretches her gown to bursting; [231]
Between her eyebrows, beauty has left its mark, 19.20
    like the stamp of a sated shaykh among his guests.
You made death a certainty for Your creatures;
    I pray, let the smiling gazelle roam close to me.

~ ٢٠ ~

اللّٰه من عينٍ تهِلّه عَبارِ　　يِشْبِه هَماليل السَحاب اندِفاقِه
على الذي بَيني وبينه مِداري　　شَوفِه الَى مِنّي بَغَيتِه شفاقِه
رِدْفه كِما طِعْسٍ على جال ذاري　　لى لافه الغَرْبي تِكَوَّم دقاقِه
يا شَيب عَيني يوم شِفْتِه يداري　　من ثِقْل رِدْفٍ لا بَغى المَشْي عاقِه
والهَرْج ما يَنْفَع ولا هوب قاري　　ولا يِسْتِوي حِبٍ بليّا لباقِه
لِلحب في وَجْه المقابِل مُواري　　ضِحْك الجحاج ورَفْعَته وانطلاقه
خَصٍّ الَى لَقّاك وَجْهِه نَحارِ　　واشْرَف على غاية غَلاه ونِفاقه
والّا من المِبْغِض تشوف النِكارِ　　ياله فِراقِك وانت تالَه فِراقِه
والهَرْج ياتي له دروب ومِجاري　　لا كان ما يَفْقَه خطاة الهَقاقه
خَطْو السِدوح اللي بِغَيِّه يماري　　يقول لي مع كِلّ زَولٍ عَشاقه
والّا ترا العِيدي يغَبّي الاثارِ　　الَى بَغى له رَمْسِةٍ بانسِراقه
ولا هوب زَهّافٍ الَى حَلّ طاري　　يَفْرِق على غَيره بعَقْل ووِثاقه
القَلْب سِلطانٍ وحِكْمِه جِبارِ　　الَى اشْتَهى للدَرْب يِنساق ساقه
والعَين سَبْر القلب مع كِلّ طاري　　تارَد وتَصْدِر بين قوم ورِفاقه
والحِبّ بَلْوى والقِضايا جُواري　　ولا يَنْفَع المَصْيود كِثْر الحَذاقه

~ 20 ~

God help me with this flood of tears, 20.1
like sheets of rain pouring from the clouds,
Because of a love so shy it makes us hide;
When I try to speak she scares and freezes.
Her behind is like a knoll rising on a windy slope:
gales from the west collect its fine sand in heaps;
My hair stood on end as I saw her studied steps:
the weight of her rump made walking hard.[232]
Words are just words, what's the use of it all: 20.5
I don't crave a love without gentle touch.[233]
Love speaks the face's expressions: [234]
a laugh makes eyebrows jump with merriment;
It happens when you meet her face to face
and behold your very dearest treasure.
Faultfinders who begrudge you are bad news:
they like to see your back–you wish them away.[235]
Words choose a path, flow through channels,
even though an obtuse fellow doesn't understand:
An idler in the shade who brags and blusters, 20.10
saying, "I have an affair with all lovely girls."
A true aficionado would cover up his traces [236]
if he is on the prowl to catch a rendezvous.
He is no hothead, rushing at a rumor,
but stands out for his savoir faire and prudence.
The heart is a sultan with despotic powers:
it rules at the pleasure of its whims;
The eye is the heart's scout sent to check,
to-ing and fro-ing at the well from enemy to friend.
Love is an affliction in perpetual motion 20.15
that offers no escape to the smartest game.

~ ٢١ ~

يا العَبْد قَيِّس ما طَرا لِك على البال   دِنْيـاك لا تِلهيك عن تبَع دِينِك
واعْرِف ترَى ما قِسم لك ما بِه اشكال   يِجيك لو كِلّ العَرَب حاسِدينك
والمـال مِـثْل الفَيّ لا بِـدّ ينْـزال   مَـرٍّ عـليك ومـرّةٍ في يِمـينِك
والفَـرْق في تبْـريق ربّك بالاعـمال   في سـاعَـةٍ تَـذْهَل بها والدّينِك
واعْـرِف تـرا الدِنْيـا لها كَم خَـتّال   ولَقّـافـةٍ لا بَدّهـم صايـدينِك
تَعْـمَل بها اشغالٍ وهي لِك بالاشغال   وعِـقْب المَعَزه قَلّ فـيها عَوينِك
فـان سـاعفَتْ دِنْياك بالحال والمال   تَحَمّد الوالي وعِـذْ من قِـرينِك
وان كـان بك عَدلات الايام مِيّال   تمْسّي مْقِـلّ وغِـلْمةٍ ضـاهدينِك
لا تَشْكي احوالك ولو طَـقّك الحـال   الّا على الكاتب بعـالي جِبينِك
اللي الى مِنّـه حَشَـم عَـزّ وِجْـلال   تَنْفَعك حَشْماته ولا احْدٍ يِهينِك
والّا رِفـيقٍ صـاحيٍ مـا له امـثال   ما اضْمَـرْت به لازِمٍ تِشوفه بعَينِك
في حـزّة اللزْبات ما شِـلْت له شـال   والى اخْلفَتْ يصْبر بزَينك وشَينِك
وباق العـرب مِظْهار بابٍ ومِدْخـال   لا ناشـدٍ عَنْهم ولا ناشِـدينِك
واقـرابك اللي تمِـتِنيهم بالافـعال   وهـم بحَزّات الكَرْب مْمتِنينِك
معـهم جمـال ومـال والعَبْد عـمّال   ابنك حَتين فلان وابنه حَتينِك

~ 21 ~

Servant of God, weigh your thoughts with care: 21.1
beware a world that distracts you from religion.
Have no illusion: your allotted fate, that's it—
it will be yours, even if envied by all.
Wealth is ephemeral and passes like a shade: [237]
one day you're down and out, the next fortune smiles.
What counts is how the Lord views your work,
on Judgment Day when people forsake their own parents.
The world is a pit full of snares; 21.5
it is trappers on a relentless hunt.
While you're at work, the world is busy with you;
in vain the despondent seek help.[238]
If the world smiles on you with health and goods,
praise the Lord and take refuge from the devil.
If you're breezing along and things go awry,
if you're down and out, treated with contempt,
Though you're hard hit—do not complain,
except to Him who writes fate on your brow;
The Almighty kindness, if He esteems you, 21.10
brings benefits and will endear you to others.
You may trust a smart friend, the most faithful,
whose fine deeds live up to your expectations:
When push comes to shove, you and he share the load;
a partner in adversity, not a fair-weather friend.
Others come and go as they please:
you don't care and they don't give a damn.
You expect a helping hand from relatives,
and in dire straits they would look to you:
They own camels, property, and strong slaves; 21.15
your sons hold their own against their fellows;

او كنت دَبوّسٍ لهـم عَوق من عـال   تِفِكّ مِشْكلهـم وهم خـابرينك

تَفْـتِل لِك الدِنيـا كافـين وِعْقـال   ويِغْضون عَنك وِكَنّهم جاهِلينك

فاشْنَخ لِمِن مَـدّاتـه جْـزال وِعْجـال   يِمِـدّ لك يوم انّهم حاقِرينك

بَلْكي تِـذَغْذِع لِك على روس الاقْذال   وِتكيل وافي صـاعهـم في ثِمينِك

وايّاك والمِـرْسـال ومْقَـرَّبٍ سـال   من الراس حَيث الراس تِبْرِح قِرينك

ولا تِسْتِمِع في هَـرْج نَقّـال من قـال   خَـلّه يقِـلّ الحكي بَيـنه وبـينك

وسَـدّك فلا تِعْطيـه عَـمٍّ ولا خـال   كِم واحـدٍ بالهَـرْج يِبْحَث كِنينك

ومَقْعدك مع ناسٍ لهم عَنك مِنْزال   لا هُـمّب راجينك ولا خايفينِك

معهـم خَبَـرْك وكايليـنك بِمكْيـال   على العِسِـر والمَـيسره عـارفينك

هـذاك مـالِك به مِقـام وتِفِصّـال   اخَير ما تَفْعَل مِقـامك بِحينِك

~ 21 ~

You're a stalwart who keeps the enemy at bay;
you solve problems and enjoy great renown—
If the world is plotting to chain and hobble you,
people look the other way, as if you're a stranger.
Turn to One whose aid is ample and prompt,
who provides for you when you're scorned:
Perchance winds of fortune will stir about the hills
to reward you with a pound for your every ounce.[239]
Avoid messengers; do not seek go-betweens:
meeting face to face rids you of the devil.[240]
Never listen to rumormongers and backbiters:
be sparing with words when you deal with them.
Don't share inner thoughts even with an uncle:
many scheme to ferret out your secrets.
If you're among people who are not your sort,
who have no need of you, nor any fear,
Though they know you and your worth full well,
your generosity, in dearth or plenitude—
If they do not treat you with regard and distinction,
get up at once, leave without another word![241]

~ ٢٢ ~

يا تَلّ قَلْبي تَلّ رَكْبٍ لشِمْشول   رَبْعٍ مِشاكيلٍ على كِنَّسٍ حِيل
شافوا وَراهم مِشْعَل الشَيخ مَشْعول   وغابَتْ نجوم اللَيل واوْحوا رِجاجيل
قالوا وَراكم زَول واقفَن كِما الجَول   جَول النَعام اللي تِقافَن مِظاليل
يوم خَطِفوهِن رَوَّحَن طِفَّح جِفول   كنّه يِرَمَّى من تحتهن هَداميل
يا تَلّ قَلْبٍ من عَلاويه مَتْلول   تَلّ الرشا مِن فَوق عُوج المَحاحيل
ويا تَلّ قَلْبي تَلَّتَينٍ عَلى نُول   وثلاث نَتْلاتٍ بِتَلٍّ بتَنْتيل
او تَلّ حِصن مسَرِّب القَيظ بِحلول   كَنَّ النجوم وفاختوه الزِماميل
في مِطَّرَق مِسْهاج قاتل ومقتول   طاحَتْ حذاهن والمَوارد مِداهيل
خَمْسٍ مِسيرَتْهُم ولا طالَعَن زَول   وهادَنّ عِقْب ملافَخ العِرف والذَيل
تِشاوروا ما بين عاذل ومَعْذول   والعِدّ الادْنى حال دونه مَحاويل
تخَيَّروا مِن طيِّب الفود زِعْجول   والمِنْقِطِع خَلّوه مِثْل المَخاييل
الّا وكِنّ بحاجر العَين سِمْلول   كِنّه يرَكَّز في نِظَرها سِماليل
من شاف حالي قال يحَوِّل يحَوِّل   كِنّي ضِريرٍ طايحٍ عَنه ما سيل
عليك ياللي في تِمَذْريه مَجْمول   بِصْباه عن بيض العَواتِق تنافيل
غِرْوٍ عليه تلول والوَجْه مَقْبول   لو يِعْتِرِض لِصْحاح راحوا مَهابيل

~ 22 ~

My heart strains like a small herd of camels
flogged on by brawny men on hardy mounts,
Behind them the torch of a shaykh in hot pursuit,[242]
on a starless night, abuzz with men's voices.
Alarmed—"Shapes, behind!"—they rushed like a flock
of ostriches running in each other's shadows.[243]
The panicked animals skimmed across the plain,
as if scraps of cloth were thrown at their feet.[244]
Or is it the strain of a heart pulled out,
like a well rope running over pulley wheels?[245]
Woe to a heart wound tightly as threads on a spindle:
twisted thrice, another pull, and twice again.
Or strain on horses that missed the baggage train:
in the quivering heat of midsummer's sparking stars,
Where any encounter is a matter of life or death;
their horseshoes lost, the wells in enemy hands,
They walked five days without seeing a soul;
eerily quiet, mane and tail no longer shook.
The men stopped for counsel, recriminations flew:
waterless desert lay between them and the nearest well.
From the stolen herd, they picked the strongest camels
and left the rest, like scarecrows, in the emptiness.[246]
I feel as if a long thorn was stuck in my eye—
No, as if pierced by sharp wooden spines.
Whoever sees my condition says, "Woe, woe!"
as for a wounded warrior lying unattended.
Such ravages are wrought by a hip-swaying beauty—
in her prime, she outshines all white-shouldered damsels.
She's a curvy young thing with a lovely face:
even decent men who glimpse her go berserk.

احْسَن شَخِص لا قَصر لا عَرْض لا طول　　عُودٍ زها لينه بـزَين التَعازيل
تَوَّه بِغَض صَباه بِخَباه مَجْهول　　ما دِقّ في مَصْيون عِرْضه ولا قيل
الَى مِشَى بِـذْلول ياحيّ من زَول　　كِنّه من احْلَى النَبْت في مَنْقَع السَيل
الى مِشَى بِجْول والراس مَجْدول　　فَوق الردوف ارْداف شِقْرٍ عَثاكيل
والى ضَحَك باللي كِما ضِيق هِمْلول　　او قِحْوِيانٍ في مِـدامِث غَراميل
يِنْفاج لِه بابٍ من الصَدْر مَقْفول　　واشْتَلْت حِمْلٍ بالهَوى مِنْه ما شيل
لا صار قِدْمي صار في مَشْيِتي هَول　　وان جا خلافي رِحْت ما بي تَعاجيل
عَذَلْت قَلبي مَير ما يَسْمَع القول　　عن نِيِّتِه عَدْيٍ وهو ما بَعَد نيل
او هو بِعيد الدار حَولٍ ورا حول　　ارْجيه تاتِيني ظعونِه مِقابيل
لا شَكّ دونِه مِدْفَع الحَرْب مَكْيول　　لا تاصِله رِجْلي ولا مِن مَراسيل
بين النزول وخاطري عَنْه مَذْلول　　لا في يِدي قُوّه ولا لي مِداخيل
عليه حالي كِنّها حال مَسْلول　　نِضْوٍ بَرَك ما يِلْتِفِت للمَراحيل
مِن شافني مْسومِلٍ قال يَحَّول　　كِنّي عَليلٍ راخِصٍ عَنْه ما سِيل
يا لله ياكاتب على العَبْد مَرْسول　　يا مِفْنِيٍ جيلٍ ويا باعِثٍ جيل
اجْبِر صُوابي مِنْه يا مِبْهِل الشَول　　يا حارس اركان الحَرَم عَن هَل الفِيل

~ 22 ~

Her shape is perfect: not short, not broad, not tall;
a supple, juicy shoot of gorgeous chiseled outline.
She bursts into flower in her secret hiding place
That kept her immaculate and beyond reproach.
God Almighty, the coy coquetry of her gait!
No flower in the green torrent bed is so fragrant.
She strides with thick anklets, her hair in plaits:
the curly tresses tumble to her buttocks.[247]
Her laugh bares teeth white as hailstones
or chamomile blossoms in dips of soft sand.
In my breast's vault, a locked door swung open
and out I carried the heaviest load of passion.
If I see her walking ahead, I am terrified;
if she comes from behind, my step slows.
I berated my heart, but it paid no heed:
it made a run for it and could not be caught.
When they trek to distant places, year after year,
I am left to pray for the camel train's return.[248]
Loaded guns, ready to fire, block my way:
she's beyond my reach, even through a messenger.
She's among those tents, but I must concede:
I am barred access, without means and powerless.
She has struck me with paralysis:
a couched camel that can't be made to rise.
"O dear!" stammered those who saw me thus beguiled,
like a sick man who is left to his own devices.
You sent a messenger to Your servants, God;
You root out a generation and bring forth the next:
Heal my wounds! You make camels flow with milk;
You protected Mecca's sanctuary from the war elephant.

~ ٢٣ ~

بِدَيت بذِكرُ الله على كِلّ ما طَرا　　مجيب الدّعا مِعطى العَطايا الجِزايل
تَركت الهَوى ما عادابي طاري الهوى　　ولا قـايـلٍ بخيـار قومٍ مِـثايل
ولا عـاد لي في باقي الاشيا حَسايف　　الّا مشـاهَـد راس شيخٍ بْحـايل
محمّـد سلطان العَرَب مُوهِب الذَهَب　　هو خَـير من تافَـد اليـه القِـبايل
تْشَـدّ النضـا من كِـل فجٍّ تِجي له　　كِمـا تاتي البَيت الشريف الرَحـايل
من جـاه يَلْقى رَغْـبةٍ في جَنـابه　　ومن راح مَـغْلول يِـزيده غَـلايل
سَهْـلٍ على الدانين صَـعْبٍ على العْدا　　لَكِن عـيونـه صَـلو جَمْـر الشَعـايل
فِهيمٍ عَديمٍ يِـرْهِب القلب عـارِفه　　لكِنْ يَقـرا الغَـيب وافي الخَصـايل
ولا شَيّ غَير الخَمْس ما هوب عالمِه　　مِضَى من سِياساته وبِخْصه دَلايل
يِشُوف عَـيازٍ ما بِدا الّا صـدورَها　　ويِشُوف من المِـقْـفي نْحور الاوايل
كِنّ الامـاكِن كِلهـا وَسْـط كَفّـه　　وكِنّـه على مَـضـمون تَيـلٍ يسايل
الَى فِتَـل فـتلٍ بالاسـباب ناقـضه　　على كِلّ حـال ولا لِفَـتله محـايل
ولا كِيـل له كَيـلٍ قِصَـر دون قِيـمته　　وتِـزيـد مِكـايِيله على كِلّ كايل
غَـيورٍ على العِـلْيا جِـضورٍ من الخَنـا　　جِـزوعٍ رِثوعٍ لى اوْجَس الشدّ مايل
من رَثْعَتِـه يوم السـعود تمـايلوا　　واهْل القِصـيم وبان هَرْج الصِمـايل

~ 23 ~

First, the name of God in all of the world's affairs: 23.1
He answers our prayers and bestows gifts liberally.[249]
I am done with the subject and pursuit of love,[250]
nor do I sing verses in praise of the chosen few.
For other matters in life I have not the slightest care,
except standing in awe before a shaykh in Ḥā'il:
Muḥammad, sultan of the Arabs who pours out gold;
he is bounty hunters' most rewarding destination.
From wide desert tracks lean camels come racing to him 23.5
as do caravans to Mecca's holy shrine.
On arrival at his lordship's their desires are fulfilled,
but he leaves the spiteful stewing in their juices.
Amiable with subjects, indomitable toward foes,
his eyes are ablaze like red-hot embers.
Shrewd and intrepid, he strikes fear into hearts,
as if knowing the unknown is one of his skills.
Nothing but God's select five are beyond his reach;[251]
witness his masterly policies and penetrating wisdom.
From afar, he sees the haunches of those approaching, 23.10
and he sees the front of groups retreating,
As if he holds all things in the palm of his hand,
or all news is read to him from a telegram.[252]
If the enemy lays a plan, he wrecks it at the root;
when he plots, there is no way around his scheming.[253]
Never is he given less than his proper due,
though his measure dwarfs others'.
Zealous in noble pursuit, impatient with the contemptible,
anxious and intractable when loads slide.[254]
The Sa'ūds wavered, like the men of al-Qaṣīm, 23.15
when his onslaught heralded the moment of truth.[255]

ذِبَح روسهم والحيّ مِنهم بحَبْسِه   خَذيلٍ ذِليلٍ بالرِدَى والفِشايل
مَلَك دارهم ومدارهم يوم دارهم   واللي شَرَد منهم رِمَى لِه حَبايل
يِصيدنّ حَذْرات الوحوش حَبايله   وصوايده ما تِذرِك الّا الجَلايل
مِثِل رَثْعَته بِمْطَير ما هي خَفِيه   نَهارٍ يشيب اطفال سِمْر الجِدايل
على ثِرْب يوم الله نَوَى بيذهابهم   تِمارَح العَزْبات بين النَزايل
عَقَّب مِبانيهم وضاوي حلالهم   وباقي الشَرايد يِطْلِبونه زِمايل
هذا جِزاهم يوم يَدْخِل عقولهم   على مِثْل عَمْل ابليس ما هوب طايل
اطاعوا لِمِن لا سَرّهم يوم ضَرّهم   غَشومٍ يشوم عن القريب المُوايل
كِثيرات رَثْعاته قِليلٍ سِليمها   الى طَنى ما يِسْتِمع للعَذايل
والَى بَغى امرٍ ما يِداري عَواقِبه   يِجي له دَجْرانٍ من الغَيظ شايل
الى شال غَيظه يِرْذي الخَيل والنِضا   تِطُول بُواريده بِعيد المَخايل
فيما يِغيظ الغَيظ الّا على العدا   بيومٍ يغطّ الشَمْس قَبو الدِبايل
تِضَعْ مِنه ذات الحَمِل والمِرْضِع اذْهَلَتْ   لَكِنّ فوق كبودهِنّ المَلايل
على شِفايا فَرّق البَين شَمْلهم   على راي من لا هوب عنهم بسايل
الى خَرّب الله كَيفهم ثمّ خَرّبِه   يِصبِح وِسيع البال والغَيظ زايل
اخذ مال ما حَسّاب يَضْبِط حسابه   وجَوّز عِزْبانٍ وطَلّق حَلايل
مِثِل ما مِضى ما هيب غِرٍّ فَعايله   ولا خير باللي ما مِضى له فَعايل
يهاوي ليال شْباط مع كَنْحَة الشْتا   ومن كَنْحَة الجوزا يهاوى القَوايل

~ 23 ~

He cut their throats and jailed the survivors:
humiliated by failure, they cowered miserably.
He conquered homesteads, ravaged the refuges,[256]
entrapped the scattered survivors.
Even cautious game is ensnared in his traps;
he hunts for mighty trophies.
The gruesome havoc he wrought on Muṭayr[257]
turned the hair of their fair ladies gray;
At Thirb, when God ordained their rout,[258]
though the flocks were safely couched at the tents,
He overran the encampments, looted their cattle,
and the survivors begged for pack animals.[259]
This is retribution for their cunning intent:
the mischief of devils will not stand.
They became meek when he meted out punishment;[260]
none but loyal followers are spared his violence.
His bursts of truculence leave few unscathed:
swollen with fury, he is deaf to council.[261]
Once decided, he is heedless of consequence
and lets himself be carried by fits of rage.
His wrath wears out cavalry and cameleers;
no target is too distant for his rifles.
His savagery targets none but the enemy;
it shrouds the sun in battle's swirling dust,
Pregnant women miscarry, breastfeeding mothers are dazed,
their guts grilled as if by glowing embers,[262]
From sorrow of separation from loved ones–
but he doesn't care about their fate.
Their snug life is ruined by God, then by him,
before his anger tapers and his mood brightens.
He drives off spoils too rich to be counted;
singles are married, couples divorced.[263]
No surprise—his deeds match earlier exploits:
Without armed feats there can be no claim to fame.
In midwinter nights he goes raiding in icy winds;
in summer he prowls, heedless of blistering heat.

الى عَنّى بالشَرْق والغَرْب واليِمَن   وطاعوا وراعوا عِقب ذَبْح وسَحايل
تِجاحرت حَضْرَه وبَدْوَه تَخامروا   كُلٍّ يحَسّب وَيش لِه من جِمايل
وِمَرْهُم وحَذّرهم وهادوا وهيّدوا   وصِفوا له وزَكّوا له بِليّا فِضايل
تَعدّى هقاويهم وضَيّع هُجوسهم   يَبي عادتِه على خباث الدَغايل
لَكِنّه يُوحَى لِه مِن الله الى عَدا   يَعْرِف مِصارِعهم وما هوب نايل
ناسٍ ينَفِّعهم وناسٍ يضِرّهم   حَليمٍ بحال وحال عَبْثٍ وعايل
الى عال مِثْل الموت ما عنه فَرّه   والى عَطى يِعْطى المهار الاِصايل
صِخيٍّ مَناله كِلْمتِه من لْسانه   مَردّه على الكِتّاب يِغْني قِبايل
حَضَرٍ لِهُم تَجْره وبَدْوٍ تِدَبّشوا   سِبَبْه المِهر ولّا مَردٍّ لِقايل
عساي من اللي ما يقصّر بحَقّهم   عَنَيت لفَضْله والمِشاحي قَلايل
شِفاتي الى جيت اتَحَدّث بمَدّتِه   قِدّام اجاويد العَرب والرِذايل
ولا رايحٍ من عنده الّا بواجبه   وعاني لفَضْله مِثل راعي عَدايل
نِفادٍ لماله مِثْل ما قال والده   عسانا ما نِعْتاض غَيره بِدايل
وزاد المِضايف ما عِرِف لِه وِصايف   اقْعَ يوم نَفْخ الصُور ذِكْره هَوايل
واسلاف بَدْوٍ من مَحالٍ تَوَجّهوا   الى وادي نَبْتِه من الوَسْم طايل
ولا فَرْد يومٍ قَلّط الزاد قافر   عليها ظهور الخُور والسَمن سايل
وضُوانٍ فوق المتوع مْتقاضبه   كِنّه مع الشاوي عَطين الشِمايل
لَكِن طِبايخٍ تحاضي مِطابخه   وورودٍ ظُواميها صِحاف الشُوايل

His trail of destruction runs east, west, south,
Awing his enemies through slaughter and massacres,
Until villagers hole up and Bedouin cringe 23.35
as they grasp for what will work in their favor.[264]
At his commands and warnings they turned quiet,
paid their taxes in obedience without demur.
Thus he confounded them and upset their calculations,
to inflict his customary punishment for ugly treachery.
On the attack he seems guided by revelations from God,
hitting vulnerable spots, tracking down booty.
Some benefit at his hands, others get hurt;
at times he is indulgent, then wanton and violent.[265]
His charges, like death itself, offer no escape; 23.40
he bestows pedigree fillies as gifts.
A word from his mouth unlocks the gates of largesse:
an instruction to a clerk enriches entire tribes:
Trade for townsmen and cattle for the Bedouin—
his call, not at a hint from his advisers.[266]
May I be among those not disappointed by him;
a man of little means, I traveled to his kindness.[267]
My wish is to tell people wherever I go,
noblemen and the lower ranks, of his liberality.
From his court no one departs empty-handed; 23.45
his bounty flows like the milk of large-uddered camels.
Like his father, he burns through his wealth:
we pray that his rule last forever.
No sight more wondrous than his lavish kitchen
till the horn blows at Resurrection;
And so the Bedouin throngs flee the desert,
toward the lush green of his rain-drenched valley.[268]
No one leaves his tray without tasting meat:
roasted camel backs washed by molten fat,
Heaped with full-grown sheep, legs interlocked, 23.50
like a shepherd's flock couched around the well;
In the kitchen, cooks jostle about
like thirsty camels pressed around a waterhole

على ابيار عَوهاتٍ عسارٍ مجاذبه   ولا يَشْرِبون الّا بشِطْن ومَحايل

اعَدِّد خصال الجُود وازْرَيت اعِدّها   اثِرْ ما يحَسِّب جُوده الّا الهَبايل

شِجاعٍ تورَّخ بالاماكِن فعايله   كِما ورِّخوا للسَلْف الاوّل فَعايل

وهو خاتَم الشِيخان لا شَيخ بَعْدِه   اشارة سِمِيّه نِزِّلَت بالرِسايل ٥٥،٢٣

وخَتْمة جُوابي بالصلاة على النبي   عِدّ النبات وعِدّ وَبْل المَخايل

~ 23 ~

With deep shafts and a bottom hard to reach
    by strong-roped buckets drawn over pulley wheels.
I fail to do justice to his generous traits,
    but I'd be foolish to think I could succeed.
The exploits of this hero are chronicled far and wide,
    like the chivalrous acts of the ancients.
He is the seal of the great leaders, no shaykh after him, 23.55
    like his namesake who brought the heavenly message.
In conclusion, prayers for the Prophet,
    as many as there are leaves of grass and rain-carrying clouds.

~ ٢٤ ~

يا ذعـار انا قَـلْبي من العـام حَوِلِه　　لليوم يَنْقِـص مـا بِقى الّا قِـليـلِه
مِثْل الشِعـيب اللي تِقـافَت محُولِه　　مِسْنٍ جَـنابه يابسٍ حَـنْـظِـليـلِه
رِبيـع قَـلْبي جَـيّة البَـدْو حَولِه　　وتِقيـرِب المِـقْطـان واحُبّـني لِه
السُوق يِعْجِـبْني ليـا شِـفْت ظَوله　　مِثْل النِظيـم المِخْتِـلِف عَن مِـثيله
ذولا لهم حـاجه وذولا بِـدوا لِه　　يِلْهَون راعى الوارده عن قِـبـيله
وش خـانة المِقْـطـان في كِلّ جَوله　　حَـزّ الرِبيـع الَى تِـزايـد نِـزيله
رِبيعـهـم قَول العِسوس ارْحَـلو له　　عِشْبٍ جِديد ولا بَعَد جَفّ سَيِله
والصِبْح سَحّين الوجيه حْقَـلوا له　　عَطّ السَلَف واسْتَجْنِبوا كِلّ اصيلِه
وكلٍّ لاهـل بيتـه يِنوّخ ذِلوله　　ونَوّخ خَـفيف الزِمْـل واقبَل ثِقيلِه
والبـيت يِبْنَى فـارْقِه كِبـر زَوله　　لا بَـدّ شَرّاب الحَشايش يِجي لِه
والمـال مـا يَضْوي له الّا زموله　　قَـفْـرٍ تسَـنّد بـه وقـفـرٍ تميـلِه
في رَوضـةٍ صَكّت عليـها نـزوله　　والنَـقْع قِدْم البـيت ما يِنْعَني له
تَلْوَة نَهـار وكِلّهـم سَـيَّروا له　　والخَيـل من تاعَى لَهـا تِـرْعَوِي له
ما قيل يا راعى الحصـان اقْهَروا لِه　　باطِـرْتـه النِعْمِه مـديمٍ صِـهيلِه
باغٍ ليـا مـا وَقّـف العِـلْم طوله　　وتَنـافِـضت بين العَـميل وعَميـلِه

~ 24 ~

Dhʿār, in the full year that has passed today 24.1
my heart pined away and shriveled miserably,[269]
Like a watercourse after a long period of drought:
bone dry—even the bitter apples are desiccated.[270]
My heart's springtime is when the Bedouin arrive:[271]
how I love the approach of their summer camp!
I delight in watching crowds in the market,
colorful, like myriad threads woven into woolen cloth.[272]
Some are on errands, others draw close to me:[273] 24.5
how to restrain a roving eye when in conversation?
Alas, my joy from their time at the wells is short-lived:[274]
at spring's arrival, their camps break up and disperse.[275]
Their spring starts with a scout's cry: "Pack up and leave:
there is grass aplenty and pools haven't yet dried up!"[276]
At first light, the noble visitors have left;
armed men on camels first, leading mares by the rope.[277]
Once there, riding camels kneel at the camp;
light pack camels are unloaded first, heavy ones last.
They put up a large, conspicuous black tent, 24.10
which attracts flocks of addicts craving a smoke.[278]
Only pack animals spend the night in camp:
The other camels roam on pastures low and high.[279]
They alighted at a meadow crammed with camps;
water nearby—the pool in front of the tent.
At the end of day, visitors arrive in droves;
if a man calls the horses, they come at a trot.
No one is told to rein in his stud:[280]
it bristles with energy and neighs with delight.
The steed is ready if things come to a head—[281] 24.15
when friends loosen ties and turn into foes.[282]

نَبَّب على اطْراف العَرَب وِجْمَعوا له　　نَمْرا تِصَهْرَج مِثْل نوّ الرِفيله
والسَبِرِ راح ورَدّها في حلوله　　ودَرْهَم عليه الشَيخ واشْتال شَيله
وشافوا عياله يوم قَرِّبوا له　　صَفْرا تِكِفّ الخَيل عن كِلّ عَيله
قالوا مطالِع قال الآخَر يِقوله　　تَعايَلت قِدّام يُومي شِليله
وفاضوا على طَرْشٍ وساعٍ خلوله　　من دَنّة الغاره تِزايد جِفيله
حَوّوا ورَدّوا باوّله وِقْهَروا له　　ما عنده الّا من يَحَلْب بصِميله
يوم اوسَعَوا لِحَقّ الطَلَب وارْجَحوا له　　كِلّ ابْلَج ياخِذ عليهم دِبيله
كِم مايقٍ بِرْماحهم سَبِّقوا له　　مِطْغِيته الدِنيا يَحْسَبه طِويله
هَوَّد وعَوَّد كاثراتٍ عذوله　　كلٍّ بِقَلْبه واهِجٍ من غَليله
الشَيخ مُوقِفهم يقول اعْزِلوا له　　يِزِّيه من سَرْب المِكاسب حَصيله
يَمْشون مَشْي اللي ثقالٍ حموله　　زَمْلٍ من الوَزْمه رِخِيٍّ مِكيله
يَتْلون شَيخٍ ماضياتٍ فعوله　　يَسْري وِغبّ سَراه ما يِنْدري له

~ 24 ~

At the call to arms, kinsmen near and far amass,
troops thick and dark like thunderous clouds.
A scout reconnoitered and reported promptly:
the chief hurried to meet him and hear the gist.
His men watched as they brought the shaykh's horse,
a white mare that brings enemy cavalry to heel;
"I see it!" they cried. "Right you are!" said another,
and sped off before the chief had waved his shirt,[283]
Storming to herds spread out on their pasture: 24.20
the camels ran, panicked and startled by the din,
Were encircled, rounded up, and halted;[284]
their shepherds carried only milk skins.[285]
The owners rushed in; the raiders faced them down:
they rubbed the noses of so many braves in the dirt,
Cut legions of swaggering braggarts down to size—
deluded praters who live in a fool's paradise.
Crestfallen and angry, the pursuers scuttled away,
nursing a smoldering fire of resentment.
The shaykh told his men to divide the booty, 24.25
taking a fair share of the haul for himself.[286]
They march at leisure, like heavily laden camels
with plentiful loads on the way back from markets.[287]
They pay fealty to a shaykh renowned for warlike feats;
After trekking all night, at dawn no one asks "Where to?"[288]

قال مِن غَنّى وغَرْهَد على رُوس العدام   واوْنَس البارد بكَبْده عِقِب لَفْح السموم
يا وجودي وَجْد مِن صام بايامِ التِمام   مِشْفِيٍ بالشِرْب والشِرْب من قبْل مَعْدوم
يا لِطيف الحال عِقْب السَهَر عيني تَنام   بارَحَت ما عاد فيها بثار ولا هَزوم
حَرْب بِن بَسّامِ سَبَّب على الرَبْع الحشام   جا لهُمِ مثل الصَنَمِ وِعْبِدوه وزاد زَوم
وشاله المِبْعِد الَين اوْصَلْه عِرْق الحَمام   وكافَخ ايامٍ قَلايل وباع بْغَير سَوم
يومِ ابن مِتْعِب نوى نَجْد بالرُومِ الطَغام   وساقت المَظْهور شَمَّر معَلّقة السهوم
يومِ جاب حْسَين صِبْيان اهَل حايل نِظام   مِثْل تِجّارٍ تَغانَمِ تبي بَيع القِدوم
جاك طايش شاربٍ لِه قِدَح خَمرٍ حَرام   ثُمّ نَبَّب قال يا قَومِ لا تاطون قوم
يومِ كلٍّ نَزَّله مَنْزِله والطَير حام   جاهمِ اللي حَطّهم بايْسرِ الفَيضه رجوم

~ 25 ~

I sing these verses, warbling on a high dune,[289] 25.1
refreshed after a hot wind's poisonous blasts.
I suffered, as one who fasts in the hot season
yearns for a drink when there isn't a drop.
What relief! My insomnia has been cured
by healthy sleep—boils and inflammation gone.
Ibn Bassām imposed his war on venerable men: [290]
idol-like, he basked in adulation and grew arrogant;
Carried by the devil, he landed on top of a mud house,[291] 25.5
sat flapping his wings, then beat a hasty retreat.
Ibn Mitʿib and his Turkish filth assaulted Najd,
while sharpshooting Shammar brought up the rear.
And Ḥsēn marauded with a troop of Ḥā'il youngsters,[292]
greedy like traders who want the first shot at bidding:
The madcap rushed in, drunk on sinful wine,
advising his men: "Don't trample each other in the charge!"
When the armies clashed and the vultures circled,
their nemesis slaughtered them to al-Fēḍah's right.

~ ٢٦ ~

يا مِن لقَلْبٍ طارعنه اليِقين   من يوم قَفَّنّ الظَعاين زَهازيم
هَفَّنّ أوايلِهن مع القِنّتَينِ   واتلاهِن اللي بالشِفا كِنّه الغَيم
وذكَرْت مَنْزِلهم علينا قِطينِ   ايام عندي بين شَدّاد ومُقيم
وجَيَّة بَنات البَدو تِسْيارتِينِ   وتَواجِبَن ما بين رَدّه وتَسْليم
الى مِشَن كِنّه تِخطِّي الجِنينِ   والا المطَوَّع يَقدِم العَصْر تَقْديم
عَشْر الخطا يمْشِن بَها ساعَتَينِ   كِنّ المِسير خلاف لولا التَعازيم
وبهِنّ لطلاّب الهَوى شارِتَينِ   السَلْهَمه واظْهارهِنّ المِقاديم
والبخنَق اللي تَفْصِله طَرْقَتَينِ   دون الشِفايا والثِمان المَناظيم
والى تِفاهَن به لعانِيّتَينِ   والا انْطَلَق مَقْرَن شباق التَلازيم
تَشْعَف قلوب اهْل الهَوى الحاضرينِ   ومَعْهن سهومٍ تَصرِم القَلْب تَصْريم
وآخِر مِزَرّ جيوبهِن فِرْقَتَينِ   عن مِثل دَرّ مُعَطّفات المَرازيم
ومعْهن لِمثْلي حَيرةٍ ما تِبينِ   ولا مِن مِفَرّ عَن القَدَر والمِقاسيم
ما اقول شَيٍّ ما نِظَرْته بِعَيني   والى اقْبلَن ما عن لقاهِن مَهازيم
الحِبّ بِيّح كِلّ قَلْبٍ فِطينِ   كم واحدٍ قَبْلي تِبَيّح ولا ليم
لو ني لحالي قِلْت اشَكّك بديني   مير اخْلفَت قَبْلي رجالٍ مَلازيم

~ 26 ~

Poor heart abandoned by its wits, 26.1
as camel trains moved away at a brisk pace:
The camels in front swooped down the crest,[293]
the caravan's tail like a cloud on the hill.[294]
I remained, lost in memories of their summer camp,
and how they used to come and go at our wells;
How their young Bedouin women would visit,
walking over to greet and chat, each in turn,
Gently and slowly, step by step, like a toddler, 26.5
or an imam who measures shade to set the prayer time,
As if taking ten steps would take hours,[295]
and they'd slide back but for their mighty struggle.
In love's game one should watch out for two signs:
sideway glances and a show of dangling forelocks.
Their veil has two layers,
shielding lips and rows of teeth from view.
Moments of inattention are for double purpose:
either the hook of the veil slips from its knot,
Playing havoc with amorous admirers, 26.10
whose hearts are pierced by glances' arrows;
Or loosened buttons on the sides of both breasts,
showing flesh white as the milk of groaning camels.[296]
Lovers like me might conceal their confusion,
but one does not outrun his allotted fate.
I tell nothing I did not see with my own eyes:
at their approach, you're trapped with no escape.
Love lays bare the secrets of prescient hearts:
disclosure was never a reason to blame its victims;
Were I the only one, my beliefs would be in doubt, 26.15
but it afflicted men beyond reproach well before me.[297]

~ ٢٦ ~

عـيال الشِـيوخ مْبَيّحين الكِنـينِ   وتِبـايَعوا لِشْراه شِـقْح ومِجاهيـم
اللي لُهُـم رَسْـمٍ عـلى الأوَّلينِ   وِلْهم على حَضْر القَـرايا مَعـاليـم
مِـرْوين حـَدّ مْـذَلّقـات العـرَيني   وِالعُمِـر يَرْخَص بالمَواقف الَى سـيم

Great chiefs betrayed their spleen,[298]
    sold white and black camels to pursue their fancy;
Scions of a noble race from ancient tribal stock,
    They levy tribute from settled village folk; [299]
Their sharp-pointed spears are dipped in blood; [300]
    they make light of their lives when they join battle.

~ ٢٧ ~

يا من لجَفْنٍ ساهرٍ ما يِباتِ ‏ ‏ ‏ سَهَرْت لَين انّي تِضاحَيت فَجْران
يا وَنّةٍ منها ظنونٍ حياتي ‏ ‏ ‏ من واهِجٍ بين المَعاليق يَصْلان
واوجَس جروحٍ بالحَشا خافياتِ ‏ ‏ ‏ ولا فاد بجُروح الهَوى طِبّ وقْران
طبِّي ومَوتي عند دَمْث الشِفاتِ ‏ ‏ ‏ عَبْثٍ الى مِنّه مِشَى تَقل سَكران
لاحَق بها مِروين حَدّ الشِباتِ ‏ ‏ ‏ اهْل المُواقِف يوم زَوغات الاذهان
اقْفوا مع الرَيدا والاقْدار تاتي ‏ ‏ ‏ ولا عاد لي حِيله وانا صِرت حَيران
نهار قَفّوا والظَعَن مِقْفِياتِ ‏ ‏ ‏ لَكِنّ يَضْرِب ضامري مِطْرَق الزان
يا راكبٍ من فوق عَشْر نَظْواتِ ‏ ‏ ‏ حَرايرٍ تِنْتَب على ساس ظَبْيان
مِثْل المَها وان دَبّرَن ذايراتِ ‏ ‏ ‏ لا اقْفَن مَع الخَبّه كما وَصْف غِزلان
والّا فَرِبْدٍ رَوّحن جافلاتِ ‏ ‏ ‏ شافَنّ قَنّاصٍ لِقفهن مسيّان
ومْدَوّرات خفوف ومْقَولَماتِ ‏ ‏ ‏ ما يَبْرِكِنّ الا على كُوع واثْفان
حداد الاذان ان شَبْهَرَن شايفاتِ ‏ ‏ ‏ وعيونهن فيهن كما قَدْح ضِيّان
وفَجّ الزغون ورُوكهن نابياتِ ‏ ‏ ‏ وفُخوذهنّ ليا ادْبَحَن تِقل بيبان
ووَسوطِهِنّ من الوَنا ضامراتِ ‏ ‏ ‏ لا طالت الفِرْجه يجيهن ديدان

~ 27 ~

Poem by Ibn Zirībān[301]

Pity eyelids that do not close at night 27.1.1
and remain sleepless well into morning.
I groan as if my life hangs by a thread,
seared by flames that consume my insides.
I suffer the pains of wounds deep within—
from love, incurable by medicine or Qur'an recitation.[302]
My cure, or my death, lies with a soft-lipped belle,
a whimsical creature with a drunk-like gait,[303]
Held by men who dip their spears in blood 27.1.5
when horrors of battle drive warriors insane.
Her caravan vanished into the desert, as fate decreed,
leaving me powerless and prey to confusion;
As the camel train shrank into the distance,
I felt as if a lance had pierced my soul.
Rider of ten purebred and hardy camels,
of noble race, sired by Ḍabyān pedigree,[304]
That hurtle along like wild cows when startled,
as gazelles that bound down a tract of soft sand,
Or ostriches streaking away at a panicked pace 27.1.10
on seeing a hunter close in at the onset of dusk.[305]
Their hooves perfectly round and well-clipped,
they kneel on their bodies' well-made calluses,[306]
Ears sharp and their gaze intense—
you'd say a fire sparkles in their eyes;[307]
Armpits widely spaced and haunches bulging;
on the move, the thighs are like massive doors;
The middle is gaunt from grueling desert treks:
the longer the crossing, the more spirited the pace.[308]

~ ٢٧ ~

الصِبح من طاش البَحَر سارحاتِ   والظُهر عَدّى سَيرهن رِجْم طيسان
والعَصْر يَمّ المَجْمَعَه خاطراتِ   ومن حين دَنّوهن يجيهنّ عِثْمان
يَفْرَح الى شاف النِظا مِقْبِلاتِ   فَرْحة كِريمٍ للخطاطير شَفْقان
ويروّحن من عندهم مِقْفياتِ   ويلفنّ رِيف الهِجْن مِرْوي شِبا الزان
عبد الله اللي يَنْطَح المُوجِباتِ   عَشير من قَرْنه على المَتْن سِيفان
عَطوه خَطّي واخْبِروه بْحَياتي   قلْبي غَدا باسناع مدعوج الاعيان
جَنّك ركابي ضمّرٍ عانياتِ   وِيْنَشّدِنّك عن ظَعَن مِطْرَق البان
حَيث انّ لاهل الودّ عندك دَعاتِ   وللصيد في قَصْرِك مِقَرٍّ ومِسْكان
دوّر لي المَجْمول قَبْل الوفاتِ   عَجِّل تَراني من هوى الترف عَيّان
وفَرّق ركابي يا عَطيب الهواةِ   مَع كِلّ فَجٍّ دَوّروا عَذْب الاسنان
مِنهنّ خَمْسٍ روّحن مِشْمِلاتِ   يَبْرَنّ مِن مَكّه ليا قَصْر بَرْزان
والخَمْس الآخْرى روّحن مِجْنِباتِ   يَبْرَن من الشِنْبِل ليا سوق نَجْران
وان كان جَنّ رْكابنا مِفْلِساتِ   حُطّوا على قبري صِفايح وعِيدان
وتَرحّموا لي يا عَشير البَناتِ   ولا باقيٍ غير الوِلي عالي الشان
وختامها منّي سلام وصلاتي   على النِبي ما هَلّ بالخَدّ وَدّان

~ 27 ~

In the morning, they set out from the rim of the sea; 27.1.15
by noon their speed had carried them beyond Ṭēsān.[309]
Late afternoon, they called on al-Majmaʿah's folks:
at their approach, ʿUthmān rushed to welcome them:
He rejoices at the sight of emaciated desert cruisers,
as a generous host thirsting for guests to entertain.
They depart, well-prepared to reach their destination:
the lance-thrusting knight, haven of worn-out camels,[310]
ʿAbdallah, without flinching, tackles his noble duty;
friend of a beauty whose tresses cascade down her back.
Give him my letter and tell him the news, by my life! 27.1.20
My heart has forsaken me for the black-eyed damsel.[311]
I sent you my lean-bellied camel mounts for help,
to ask about the caravan of the slender ben tree twig,[312]
Since lovers are in league to seek your guidance
at your home, the haunt of passion's devotees.
Go in search of the fabled belle before I die.
Make haste: I am sick with love for the tender lass!
You, my marksman of love, let groups of riders
scour every nook and cranny for those luscious lips.
Let five of the mounts hurry toward the north, 27.1.25
vying for speed from Mecca to Ḥāʾil's palace of Barzān;[313]
And set the other five on a southward course:
from al-Shunbul to the market of Najrān.[314]
If our camel riders return empty-handed,
raise slabs of stone and sticks on my grave.
Have mercy on me, confidant of lovelies,
for besides you, I only have the Magnificent Lord.
I conclude with greetings and prayers
for the Prophet, as many as rains on the plains.

يا راكبٍ عَشْرٍ من الهارباتِ   ما وَقّفوهن بالمِبايع للاثمان
اسنان من خامِس زِمان لقُواتِ   اسداس ما شافوا لهِن طَلْع نيبان
عن الجمال شمال ومْعفّياتِ   رُمْل التُوابع ما تلاهِنّ حِيران
عامَين يَرْعَن بالحمى مِهْمَلاتِ   لين ارْتكب نَيّ الشَحَم فوق الامتان
حراير اصْل جْدودهن كاملاتِ   لهِنّ في غربي شِفا نجد مِسْكان
هَلْهِن شَراراتٍ عليهن جَناةِ   طَلْبهِن الحاكم وجَنّه بكرْهان
ها يوم رَبّي جابهِن يا عَزاتي   شِيلوا عليهِن ضارب الدَرْب مِشْتان
الصِبحْ من بَطْحا نفي سارحاتِ   زَهاب اهلهِن فوقهن تمْر ودهان
لا عندكم خيفه ولا وانياتِ   حطّوا سدَير يمين من غَير حِقْران
والعصْر بالصُمّان عَدْل المشاةِ   تلْقَى لعِلْوَى به طُوارِف وعِربان
والى نِطحْكم واحدٍ للمِباتِ   قولوا نخطّرِهن على ابن زريبان
رِدّوا سلام بكاغدٍ من دواةِ   على ذُوي ناصر وخُصّوه فيحان
اهَل بيوتٍ بالقِسا بيّناتِ   يَفْرَح بهِن اللي من البعْد صَلْفان
رْباعهم مَذْهل هَل المُوجفاتِ   ولا شَدّن الّا مِستِردّات وبِدان
اهَل صحونٍ للفضايل مُواتي   يِرْمَى بهِنّ اذْناب حِيلٍ من الضان
نَدْوَه باثر نَدْوه يجُون سَبحاتِ   ولا يِفْهَق الّا محِتري السُور شَبْعان
الراويه تِدْهن من الفارغاتِ   والبَيت ياكِف مِقْدمه دَثْر الايمان

~ 27 ~

Ibn Sbayyil's reply to Ibn Zirībān

Camel rider with ten mounts chosen for speed, 27.2.1
priceless racers, not the sort that are bought and sold;[315]
Some of them in their sixth year, fertile animals;
others in their seventh, before eyeteeth break through;[316]
Nets on the behinds keep studs away: desert racers
are spared the chores of pregnancy and suckling.
Two years they roamed at will on protected pastures
till the humps towered high above their shoulders,
Purebreds, blessed with flawless pedigrees, 27.2.5
from deserts high on Najd's western edge,
Bred and raised by Sharārāt who fell afoul of the ruler,
parted with the animals at his command.[317]
They became ours by the grace of the Lord, what joy!
Ride out on them; take firmly to the road![318]
At dawn, they set out from Nifī's dry watercourse,
loaded with provisions of dates and fat;
Have no fear and don't let your spirits flag!
pass by Sudayr on your right, no harm no foul,[319]
Traveling straight ahead, by noon, at al-Ṣummān, 27.2.10
you will arrive at the first tents of the 'Ilwā tribe.
Expect to be assailed with offers of hospitality;
tell them, "We are entertained at Ibn Zirībān's."
Give them my greetings, read from ink on paper,
To the clan of Dhuwī Nāṣir and especially Fayḥān!
Their tents beckon to worn-out travelers in times of want:[320]
visible from afar—a signal that bolsters flagging spirits.
Riders of swift mounts flock to their coffee rooms,
rest and depart, well-fed, with renewed vigor.
The hosts carry in heavy platters, piled high with food: 27.2.15
tails of fattened sheep thrown on top.[321]
Group upon group squats to be served in turn;
the leftovers easily sate the lesser guests.
Enough fat remains to coat large waterskins
and drips from the tent flaps where hands wiped;[322]

ومَـنارةٍ كِنَّـه نِشيلة هَـباةِ   ونارٍ سَـناهـا مِـثْل صِـبْحٍ الَى بان
مَـرْكَى دلالٍ بْجَرهِن مـا يبـاتِ   مْحَمـاسهِن دايـم على النارحَمْيان
من البِنّ يِصـفَق به ثَلاث غَـرزاتِ   تِنْسَـف على المِبْراد والكِيس مَلْيـان
وان فَـرَّغ الطَّبخـه والا ذيك تاتي   ولا نازِح المَجْلِس عليهـا بشَفْـقـان
ثُـم انْشـدوا فَيحان سِتْر البَـناتِ   لا فَـرَّعنّ وطـار عـنهِن الايقـان
شَوق الطِـموح اللي عليـها شِفـاةِ   عـافت بَعَلها ما تبي منه وِرْعـان
جـاني خَـبَرَ يا حـامي الجَـاذياتِ   عمّا جَـرى لك بالمِوَدّه ومِن شـان
البَـكْرة العَـفرا الشَـناح الفِـتاةِ   اللي غَـدت لك بين راحـل وقَطّـان
دَوّرت لك بِمْـقَوّمـين الصَـلاةِ   اتْعَـبْتِني مِن بَين حَضَـرٍ وبِـدْوان
وقـالوا تَـراها مع فِـريق عَـطواتِ   ولّا يِقَـع شَـيفت مَـعَ وِرْد كِرْزان
هـا ثُـمّ جـاني من رِفيقٍ وصـاةِ   قـالوا لها مع نَـزْلة الهَـيضل الوان
طَـرّشْت ابا العِقـلان قَبْل الفَواتِ   والّا فـانا ما لي مع البَدْو غِـرْضـان
اثْـر الطـروش عـلومهم بايهـاتِ   الله لا يَجْـزي بَعَضهـم بالاحسـان
هـا ثُـمّ جـاني رَدّ عِـلْمٍ ثِبـاتِ   ورَدّيت عِـلْمٍ وجـاني العِلْم وِكْدان
قـال البِشـايـر قِلْت له حـاصلاتِ   لا شَـكّ مـا شَيّ على غَير بِـرْهان
وَصّـف لي البَكْره عن الواهـياتِ   قال احْتِرف ما جِيت بِعْلوم سِفْهان
قِلت ايّ من تَـرْعى مَعَه يا شِفـاتي   قال اسْـتِقَرّ العِلْم ما فيه جِحْـدان
يـرْعَونهـا عِلْوَى هَـل الطـايلاتِ   رَبْعٍ ليـا رْكَبوا عـلى الخَيل فِرْسـان

~ 27 ~

The heap of ashes is like a mound of dug-up earth,
because his fire's flames turn night into break of day.
The roasting pan is always held over the fire's embers;
At the coffeepots' side, the mortar never sleeps;[323]
Three handfuls of coffee beans are scattered in the pan;
freshly ground coffee bubbles in the pot, and still the sack is full.
As soon as one brew is finished, the next is made:
men at the circle's far end don't hanker in vain.[324]
Now, address Fayḥān, the protector of his womenfolk
when they loosen their hair, distraught and terrified;[325]
He's the dream of attractive married women
who loathe their husbands, refuse to bear them children:[326]
"News reached me, O defender of crippled warhorses,[327]
about the adversity you suffered on love's account:
That creamy, shapely young she-camel of yours[328]
went astray among the Bedouin's comings and goings.
I sought among upright Muslims everywhere;[329]
for your sake, I tired myself among villagers and Bedouin.[330]
I was told, 'She is encamped with Dhuwī 'Aṭiyyah,
or perhaps with the camels of Kirzān at the well.'[331]
Then I was given a tip on good authority from a friend:
they said, 'Her likeness was seen at al-Hēḍal's camp.'[332]
I sent for her, hoping to hobble her before escape,
though I have no business mingling with the Bedouin.
Alas! These wayfarers' tales were untrue:
may God withhold His rewards from those miscreants!
Finally, a piece of irrefutable news came;
I returned a query, and lo and behold, it was confirmed.
'The messenger's reward!' he insisted. 'It's a deal,' I said.
'But something for something, nothing without proof:[333]
Describe the svelte she-camel beyond any doubt!'
'Pay close attention,' he replied. 'This is no empty talk.'
I said: 'In what Bedouin company is she?'
'The reports are firm, and admit no doubt,' he said.
'She's been put to pasture by 'Ilwā, men of great feats,
who mount steeds to perform chivalrous deeds.

~ ٢٧ ~

مِرْكاضهم تَشْبَع به الحايماتِ　　الشاهد الله يومْ زَوغات الاذهان
بانت وراعيها بْن قاعد زناتي　　وعندك خَبَر عِلوى بِدايد وسِلْفان
امّا عَطوك اياّه بمْشايماتِ　　فالخَيل قِرَّح واجْرَد الخَدّ مَيدان
ياخِذ ورا حَقّه على كِلّ عاتي　　ما هو بِمحْتاجٍ مِثاوير واخْوان
ولا عاد لي فيها من الوارِداتِ　　حَضَيري وُهُم بَدْوٍ على الحَقّ عِيّان ٤٠،٢،٢٧

In the wake of their charge, vultures eat their fill,
may God be my witness, when minds go berserk.[334]
She is clearly with Ibn Ǵāʿid of legendary fame; [335]
you know ʿIlwā well, their lineages and ancestors:
They might offer her to you in an agreeable manner,
or else warhorses will thunder on flat, hard terrain.[336]
They claim rights by force, crushing lions in their path,
without appeals for help from friends and kinsmen.'
As for myself, I have no further knowledge about her: 27.2.40
I am just a villager—they, redoubtable Bedouin." [337]

~ ٢٨ ~

اسباب ما فاجى الحَشا وابتِلاني   غِـرْوٍ طَـغَى بالغَيّ طَـلْقٍ لسـانِـه
طَـلْقٍ لسـانـه لَيّنٍ مِـهْـرِجـانِ   مِتْداخِلٍ مع زَيْن هَـرْجِه ذَهـانِـه
عَـبْثٍ وعَجّـابٍ من اهْـل الجِنانِ   من حسْن خِلْقه ما يعْرَف الجِبانِه
يِـديـر عَـينه بي وهو قِـد رِمـاني   اعْـلَق صُوابه قَـبْـل تِـرْمِش عَـيانِـه
غِـرْوٍ يهـايف للْهوى واغْـتِـزاني   كم طـارِدٍ للغيّ داسِـه حصـانِـه
الى ضحَك ثـمّ ابْـرِقَنّ الثِـمانِ   كِنّ الجِواهِـر تِنْـتِـثِر مِن وجـانِـه
الوَسْـط هـافي والمِـبادي مـتانِ   مـا فيه لولا كـاملٍ في زِمـانِـه
عَـرّض ولاقَـيته وهو مـا يِـداني   مثل الوَحْش يجْفِل ليا انكَر مِكانه
قِلْت السـلام ورَدّ لي مـا نِسـاني   لا شكّ من يَمّي وِسـيع بطـانـه
هو رَيّـضٍ عَـنّي وانا الموت جـاني   مِسْـتَـصْـعَبٍ تَوّه يلاوي عـنـانـه
وان جِيت ازورِه قال يوم انت عاني   من كـان له حَقٍّ فياخذ بَيـانـه
لا انت بْقـريبٍ لي ولا من خواني   ولا طـالبٍ دَينٍ ولا لك ضِـمانـه
قِلْت البَـلاوي لا بَلاك الزِمـانِ   ما ذِقْت لَيعـات الهَوى وامْتِحـانـه
قـالت تموت ومَوتك اللي هجـاني   هو غَـضَـب والّا بالهـدا والليـانـه
كان انْتَشَـر دَمّي يِجي له عِيـاني   طَـلّابـةٍ لازِم يجون بحـيانـه

~ 28 ~

A sudden shock upset me, slashed my insides: 28.1
the seductive tyranny of a honey-lipped girl,[338]
A well-spoken, supple, and soft tattletale:
with her looks come intelligence and eloquence;[339]
Capricious, amazing, a companion from Paradise,
She is well bred and stands her ground.
Her eye has taken aim at me and shot its arrow,
wounding me grievously even before she blinked.
Given to dalliance, she forayed into my heart: 28.5
many philanderers end up trampled by her assaults.
When she laughs, and lets her white teeth flash,
scintillating jewelry scatters from her cheeks.
Her svelte waist is set between firm curves;
she is simply this age's paragon of beauty.
I faced her when she paraded, but she shied
as an antelope startles at the sight of danger.
"Greetings!" I said; she knew me and replied:
a sure sign that she harbored some affection.
She lingered along the path; I was ready to die: 28.10
she's an untamed filly that bolts from the rein.
On my visit, she said, "You came for a reason:
if you have a rightful claim, it will be honored.
You're no relative of mine nor one of my kin;
nor are we bound by any loan or obligation."[340]
"Bad news," I said. "May misfortune pass you by;
may you not suffer the lashes and trials of love."
"If you die," she said, "that's fine by me."
Should love be coercion, or reason and gentleness?
If my blood is shed, my supporters will come: 28.15
avengers who rush in to pay you back.[341]

يا زَين لا تَقْطَع سِبيـل الحَسـاني   خِف بي من الله يا ظَبيّ العَدانـه
دِخيلك اللي كِد مِضى لي كِفـاني   ان كان قَلْبك مـا خَـلا من دِيانـه
سَفَّهتِني بالشِعْر عِقْب القرانِ   والّا فـانا قَبْـلِك وِثيقٍ تِكـانـه
تَـراي مِـعْطِيك الرِسَن والعـنانِ   يا حَيث قَلْبك راكدٍ للخَزانـه
طـالِبْك تَقْبَلني عَسى اللي هَـداني   يِهْديك لي عِقْب القِسا بالِليانـه
مـا شِفْت من اللي لا بَغَيته بَغـاني   والّا فغَيره مـا حَـصَل لي مِيـانـه
يا الله يا اللي وان طَلَبْتِه عَـطاني   يا خَير مِن نَرْجي العَفو من حَسانـه
تَبْـلا بحِبيّ مِن بحِبه بَلاني   والّا تِكِفّ الحِب عَنّي وشـانـه
لا عـاد حَـظّي ما تلايم وشـاني   باجُوز من طَـرْد الهَوى وامْتَحـانـه
تَمَّت وصَـلّوا عِـدّ حَيٍّ وفـاني   على نِبيٍ قِـد سِـمِعتوا قـرانـه

~ 28 ~

Please, my love, don't close the open door;
  fear God for my sake, my antelope of heaven!
My refuge is with you; let bygones be bygones,
  if a shred of religion remains in your heart.
You turned me from a student of the Qur'an into a silly poet!
  Before, I was known as sedate and solid.
I give you free rein and all my trust,
  since your heart is a strongbox for secrets.
I beg you, accept me! I beg the Lord who guided me
  to turn your severity into silkiness.
The one I love doesn't requite my feelings;[342]
  still, I do not care a whit about any other.
O God, when I plead with You, You give;
  beneficent Lord, be kind and forgive us:
Afflict her with the feelings I have for her,
  or lift love's sorrow from my shoulders.
This life, beset with ill fortune, has lost its savor:
  I should abandon love's pursuit and its trials.
Lastly, prayers—as many as there are living and dead—
  for the Prophet whose Qur'an is recited.

~ ٢٩ ~

يا جرّ قَلْبِي جَرّة القَوس حانِيـه   ظَـرْفٍ مِطـاوِعْـتِه يِدِه بِلْعَـبانِـه
مَـرٍ يبـاعِـد بـه ومَـرٍّ يدانِيـه   آخِـذْه بالحِيلات لَين اسْـتِهانِـه
ويا بَرْي حـالي بَـرْيَة العُود باريه   حَـدٍّ حَداه سـتاد بِـزْعَيـمانِـه
لا وَرَّد القَدّوم يـكْـرِب عَـلابيـه   ويِـرْخي ذراعِـه يَصْفِحِه لَين مـانِـه
ما هو وِجَع واخْبِر هَلي عَن مِشاكِيه   اسباب مِن صَوَّب ضِميري وكانِـه
عَـليك يا اللي تايـهٍ في تِمـدْريـه   دَغْـدَغ هَواه وضـاحِكٍ لِه زِمـانِـه
لوكل مِن صَوَّب صِوِيبٍ يـداوِيـه   ويجارِحِه قِلْت اوْصِلوني مِكانِـه
كلٍ يعْـرْفـه مَير ما وِدّي اطْـريـه   والّا بهـا سـيد العَـذارى بَيـانـه
الى مِشَى كِنّه غَـريـرٍ تِخَطّيـه   والّا مـعَلّمْـه الحَمام دْرِجـانـه
حِبّه بقَـلْبِي مِـرْسِيٍ مَيـر كانِيـه   ما نيب مِن يِظْهِـرعَويله لسـانـه
يا عـاذل المِشْتاق من دون غاليـه   لا تِكْثِر الوارد يـزيـد امْتِحـانـه
واللي يعْرِف العِلْم ما هوب خافيـه   ما يِنْـعَـدِل عُودٍ بلَيّـا لِيـانـه
نفسي مـهاوِيتِـه وعَيـني تراعيـه   وعـليـه قَـلْبِي ذاهبٍ ذَيـهبانـه
لو دَلَّهوني عَنْـه مـا نيب ناسـيـه   ما نيب وِرْعٍ دَلّهِـه قَـرْقَـعـانـه
ولا بَغَـيت اتْرِك مجاله وطاريـه   عَـيّا قـراني يِنْطِـلِق مِن قـرانـه

~ 29 ~

My heart is being bent like a bow by a craftsman;
adroit, he shapes it with his deft, playful hand;
He holds it up, then hunches over it,
using all his skill to shape it to his taste.
My frame's been pared down like wood that's planed
by a carpenter who cuts and shaves with all his might: [343]
When he pushes the blade, neck muscles swell; [344]
his arm slackens as he gives it a smooth finish.
This is not a pain I'd want to tell my family about,
one that struck and wounded me deep inside—
It is you, bobbing along with your swaying gait:
caressed by lucky breezes, smiled upon by fortune.[345]
If she could treat grievous injuries and wounds,
and nurse the sufferer, I'd say, "Bring me to her!"
She is known to all, but I won't drop her name:
she is simply the princess of all pristine beauty.
She walks like a child when it takes its first steps,
or as if a pigeon had taught her to point her toes in.
Her love is lodged in my heart's secret moorings,[346]
and I'm not inclined to blurt it out in an anguished wail.
Why chide a lover in thrall to his treasure?
Faultfinder, your harping adds to his ordeal.
It's a fact well-known, no mystery about it:
a stick that's not supple cannot be straightened.[347]
Head over heels in love, I keep watching her,
while my heart absconds like a runaway camel.[348]
If I was distracted, still I would not forget:
I'm not a boy kept happy with a clattering rattle.[349]
Even if I wished to drop the subject, stop talking about her,
my cord cannot be detached from hers.[350]

فـلا وِمَـرْه الله يـِرِدّه وِيْشْنيه   ارْخَى لثـامـه لَين تَبْـدي ثِمـانِه
وَرَيَّعْت لِه تَـرْيِيع طَيـرٍ لِداعـيه   لا شـاف نَسْره واجْهَـره بِنْدِبانه
ومن الحَرَص جَوَّد سبوقِه بِرِجْلَيـه   وِمْبَرْقِعِـه عَن نورَتِـه وِكْفَخانِـه
المِـهْتِوي طَـرْد الهَوى مـا يعَـنِّيه   كِنّـه علـى زَلّ العَجَـم بِعْـدِيانِه
سَيل النَحـا ما يِنْعَدِل عن مِجاريـه   ليـا عـارَض السَـنْدا يِكود عْلِوانه
تِمَـنّي المَخْـلوق مـا هوب يِغْـنِيه   ان كـان ما شَيٍّ تِحُوشِه بَنـانـه
والرِمْح لوهو يَطْعَن الخَيل راعـيه   ما صاب قِنْطارِه الى اخْطا سنـانـه
والضَيف عِـذْر معَزِّبِه ما يعَشِّـيه   بالحَقّ يَنْطِف شارِبِه من دَهـانـه
والله لو لا الهَـرْج واذْرَى قُوافيـه   من مِـبْغِضٍ يَـرْكَب عَلينا حصـانـه
لا خـايفٍ رَبّه ولا هوب راجـيه   رِبيـع قَـلْبِه غَـيبِتِـه وهْـذَيانِـه
لا ادوس غِـرّاتِه علـى كِرْه واليـه   واشْفي فوادي لَين يَقْـطَع بطانـه
كان الرضا هو سِيد الاحكام راضيه   فانا عَـرَفت رْضـاه سِرّ وَعْلانِـه
الكـل مِـنّا واردات ظُوامـيه   مـا بِـه من الغَـيظـه وَزِن ذَرّتانـه

~ 29 ~

If, God forbid, it comes untied and swings back,
she allows the veil to slip and reveals her teeth:
I look up, like a falcon that turns to its master
and screeches loudly on seeing its piece of meat;
Clasps the leather loops on its feet from desire,
jumps, and flaps its wings, until it is hooded.
The amorous do not flag in their pursuit of passion: [351]
for them, the hunt is treading on soft Persian carpets.[352]
A torrent that races, that does not change course: [353]
it cannot climb elevations that block its path.
Wishful thinking does not bring you riches,
unless it's something you can grab with your hands.
A lance thrust with the butt first, not the tip,
scores no hit against charging horsemen.[354]
A host's excuses do not serve a guest as supper: [355]
he has a right to a mustache dripping with fat.
By God, but for my fear of rumormongers,
and ill-wishers lying in wait, ready to pounce—
Men who do not fear or beseech the Lord,
gleeful at her absence and his delirious sobbing—
I'd surprise her warden and snatch her up,
sate my heart with her until belly ropes burst.
Amicable arrangements are best, I agree: [356]
I know her stated wishes and secret desires.[357]
If the two of us water our thirsty camels,
Neither of us harbors the tiniest speck of anger.[358]

~ ٣٠ ~

سِنْعوس وِش عِلمِك بِمَشْيِك تَرَدَّيت　　ما ذا بعِنْدِك يومِ انا اقول بالهُون
الفاطر اللي باوّل الوقت سَبَّيت　　اليومِ عِندك جِلدها تِقِل مدهون
اِصْلِف عليها كِلّما اقْبَلت واقْفيت　　الزَرْع يبغي الما وراعيه مديون
والَى لِحِقْت الما بمَشْيِك تدَرَّيت　　وِيْدَيك كالحايك ومَشْيك على الهُون
لا بِدّ ما تَرْقِد صطاحي الَى اصْحَيت　　وهُم بِمَمْشاك القِديمي يهَرْجون
امّا الى جَت حِرْفَة الزَرْع خِلِّيت　　وِلّا خَذَوك وفي مِقامك يِزيدون

~ 30 ~

Hey Sinʿūs, what is this leisurely pace! 30.1
I didn't mean it when I said, "Go easy!"[359]
The old camel that you cursed at first
is now sturdy, as if greased with fat.
Set a strong pace, up and down.
The crop needs water; I must pay my debt!
Watch your step on your way to the well:
handle the ropes deftly, and slow down![360]
Work done, sleep like a log, wake rested, 30.5
and people will mention you with respect.
Next season, either you won't be hired,
or, if you do well, you might get a raise.

~ ٣١ ~

يا طالبين الغَيّ خَلّوه خَلّوه   خَلّوه يومِ انّه سِجَ لا تِبُونِه
خَلّوا حَشاويله لِربْعٍ تِبَلُّوه   هو نايرٍ عَنْهُم وهُم يَطْرِدونِه
تَوَلَّجوه بْنَصبِهم لَين جَلَّوه   عَنْهم جَهَم قَبْل امْس ما يَلْحَقونِه
شَبَّوا وشابوا ما لِك الله تَحَلَّوه   ولا حَصَّلوا كود العَنا والِمهونِه
عِشْب الرياض القَفرما قطّ فلّوه   يومِ الحَيا مَنْجوع ما يَنْجِعونه
يَقْصِر عن الما حَبْلهم يومِ دَلَّوه   لو وَصَّلوا المِرْقاب ما يِشْرِفونه

~ 31 ~

Leave off, you players of love's game, leave off![361] 31.1
Abandon that worn-out charade; just stop![362]
Leave its dregs to sully other boneheads:
love is on the run; they are giving chase.
They plunged in with their wiles but, the night before last,
love left them behind and they can't catch up.
Youngsters turn gray, God help you, without seeing it:[363]
all they are left with is sorrow and shame.
For them flowering desert meadows are just hearsay: 31.5
when others trek to the spring pasture, they stay put.
Their rope's too short when they lower it into the well;
at the base of a lookout, they're too sluggish to climb.

~ ٣٢ ~

الله لا يسقي ليالٍ شفا شيف   ايام راعى السمن يخلص ديونه
فرّاق شمل اهل القلوب المواليف   وكلٍّ على راسه يباري ظعونه
والى نشد عن واحدٍ قيل ما شيف   ازروا هل القعدان لا يذكرونه
الشيخ كنّه صايلٍ يتبع الريف   ياخذ سبوع البيت ما يبتنونه
يتلون مشهاة البكار المشاعيف   وكلٍّ يبي قفره قدم يسهجونه
سقوى الى جت نقضة الجزو بالصيف   وابعد ثرى تقعه وكنّه مزونه
والعشب تلوي به شعوفٍ من الهيف   والشاوي اخلف شربته من سعونه
وجتنا جرايرهم تدقّ المشاريف   البيت يبنى والظعن يقهرونه
وتقاطروا مثل الحرار المقاييف   وراعى الغنم عن مرحهم يفهقونه
وتواردوا عدٍّ شرابه قراقيف   العدّ لو هو بالفضا يشحنونه
وكلٍّ نصا القريه يدور التصاريف   واللي له احبابٍ لبابٍ يجونه
تسعين ليله جانب العدّ ما عيف   ولا للشديد مطرّي يذكرونه
وهبّت ذعاذيع الوسوم المهاريف   وسهيل يبدي ما بدا الصبح دونه
وجاهم من القبله ركيبٍ مواجيف   وحضور يوم انّ النخل يصرمونه
والعصر بالمجلس مضال وتواقيف   وامسوا وتالي رايهم يقطعونه

~ 32 ~

May it not rain on late-summer nights—the mad rush[364] 32.1
when Bedouin demand payment for their butter; [365]
When hearts, bound by affection, are torn apart,
all hasten to join their group's camel train.
If you search for someone, they say, "I have no idea!"
Too busy, even mounted herdsmen cannot tell.[366]
Like a rutting stud, the shaykh speeds to desert green,
not troubling to pitch his tent all week long,
While chasing his young she-camels' pastoral dream: 32.5
virgin track of desert herbs, as yet untrodden.[367]
Blessings when summer's scorch dries up the sap,[368]
the ground's moisture dissipates and clouds evaporate,
Grasses wither in the gusts of hot southerly winds,
milk skins no longer slake the shepherds' thirst.[369]
And nomads' caravans dot the crests and slopes: [370]
pack camels are brought to a halt, tents rise on their poles.
They come in droves, a black mass like hills of lava rock,
shoving aside the pens set up for small cattle: [371]
They make the well and its cool water their own, 32.10
filling the surrounding terrain.[372]
Next, all head to the village to trade and shop;
if they have friends, they call on them first.
Ninety nights the wells' sides are bustling; [373]
there is no mention of breaking camp and moving,
Until the first breezes redolent of autumn rains,
and Canopus twinkles before the light of dawn.[374]
From the southwest come mounted men, riding hard,[375]
while people gather for the date harvest.[376]
Afternoon, they throng the village square; 32.15
at night, after long discussion, the die is cast.[377]

الصِبحْ طَوَّنْ البيوت الغَطاريف   والمال قِدْم طْلاقِته يَصْبِحونه
راحوا مع الرَيدا وساع الاطاريف   يِذْكَرْ لهم مَنْدىً شِبيعٍ يبونه
مِقْياظهم خِلّي بليّا تُواصيف   قَفْرٍ عليه الذيب يَرْفَعْ لحونه
اوَيّ جيرانٍ عَليهم تَحاسيف   لولا انّهم قَلْب الخَطا يَشْعَفونه
وِلْهم على حِلّ المواسِم مَحاريف   والَى جِذَبْهم قايدٍ يَتْبَعونه ٢٠،٣٢
والى تَعَلّوا فوق مِثْل الخُواطيف   كم مايقٍ بارماحهم يَزْعَجونه
هذي مَغاويرٍ وهذي مَناكيف   وهذا يِبيعونه وذا ياسمونه
والى تِقَضّوا ما عليهم تَحاسيف   ومن اَين ما طاح الحَيا يَنْجِعونه

Morning, the imposing tents are folded up,
the animals watered and untethered;
Then off they go, into far-flung desert plains,
driven by glowing reports of wholesome pastures.
Their summer camp lies empty, featureless:
a wasteland silent but for the wolf's howls.
One is sad at seeing such neighbors leave,[378]
no matter how they pained the amorous heart.
They have a habit of turning with the seasons: 32.20
a leader with resolve makes them come along.[379]
When they jump on their raptor-like steeds,
many haughty fellows are felled by their blades.
If one party sets out on a raid, the other returns,
with booty to sell or animals to brand as their own.
Once they are done, they pack up, light of heart,
and wander in the tracks of life-bringing rains.[380]

~ ٣٣ ~

يا تَلّ قَـلْبي تَـلّ رَكْبٍ لِشِـرْشوح　　ذَودٍ عَلى تالى الدِبَش خـاطـفـينه
عِقْب العَتِيم مشَعْشَع البَدْر لِه ضَوح　　وشـافوا وَراهم مِشْعَلٍ ِ شاعِلينِه
شافوا وَراهم مِشْعَل الشَيخ لِه ضَوح　　وتَنَحَّـروا ضِـلْعٍ زِمَى زابِـنـينِه
شَلّوا خَـفـافه واِدِّرِج كِنّـه الدَوح　　ايضـا ومـاش مُبَـنْدَقٍ مِرْدِفـينِه
وقالوا تَرى مِن فاخَتْ الجَيش مَذْبوح　　رَبْع قـطوع ووَسْمِهـم عـارِفـينه
على الذي من دونها حـال ساموح　　وعَيـني بِكَتْ والقَـلْب بَجَّ كِنـينِه
وِدِّه يواجِهْني بِهَرْجِه ومَنْضوح　　لولا مِـقـاريـد العَـرَب مِخْلفـينه
له مِغْلَقٍ في داخـل الروح مَفْتوح　　وعن حِبّ غَيره مِغْلَقٍ صـارِفـينِه
سِيد العَـذارَى كامل الزَين مَمْلوح　　والِسحْـر في مَقْـرَن حِجاجه وعَـينه
والجِيد جيد غـزَيِّلٍ طـالَع شْبوح　　شـاف القنوص وجـاه مَجْرود بيَـنه
مـاني عَليها مِبْديٍ كِثْرَة النَوح　　لوكـان قَـلْبي بالوَلَع مِـرْهِـفينه
ولا نيب من يَتْبَع على غَير مَصْلوح　　يَـرْفـا لخِـلاّنٍ وهُـم نـاذفـينه
المِقْفي اقْفِي عنه لوكـان مَمْلوح　　والمِقْبِل انْهَض لِه شـراع السِفينه
مـا لي بعِـدٍّ طول الايام مَـمْيوح　　مـا يِنْعَـرف صَـدّارتِه من عَطِينه
عدٍ قِطينه ماليٍ كِل جـابوح　　صِبحٍ مِصـاديره وتَجْذِب دِفـينه

~ 33 ~

My heart is wracked like the hearts of rustlers 33.1
who snatched camels from the herd's fringe,[381]
Early in the night, in the moon's eerie shine,
they saw that a torch had been lit.[382]
Seeing the shaykh's torch burn so bright,
they made for a line of hills, seeking safety.
Riding the sprightliest camels, they tore off,
without cover from their comrades' guns.[383]
They said, "If you stray from the pack, you're dead: 33.5
They're ruthless; their camel brands tell it all."[384]
It's like the twist of fate that blocked my path to her:
I cry hot tears; my heart has spilled its secrets.
She yearns for a tryst—banter and serious talk—
but odious meddlers thwart our scheme.
Her secrets are under lock and key, except for me:
she keeps other pretenders at bay or fobs them off:
She is the queen of young ladies, she has no peer:
enchantment is enthroned in her brows and eyes.[385]
She has the neck of a gazelle spying shapes:[386] 33.10
hunters who wield the spear of her death.
I moan and wail, but not in her view,
though flames of passion lick at my frame.
To persevere in a lost cause is the height of folly:[387]
being nice to one's paramours, only to be rebuffed.
I don't want a face that's pretty yet cold;[388]
for a pleasant manner I will hoist my sails.[389]
What use have I for wells crowded with Bedouin and herds,
where you can't tell visitors from regulars?[390]
A well encircled with rows of tents;[391] 33.15
after the herds have been watered, all you draw is sand.[392]

شَفّي بشَرْبِة قَلْتِةٍ دونَها صَوِح   عَمْيا الصنوع ودَرْبَها خابِرينِه
گَمِ ليلةٍ غَدْرا خَطَرها عَلى الروح   نَرْعى حماه ومَرْقَبِه مِشْرِفينِه
واثْمارِه اللي ناعِماتٍ بلا فَوِح   حَدِر خَرامیس الدِجَى خارفينِه
نِمْسي ولا حِمْلٍ مِن الهَمّ مَطْروح   وِنصْبِح سلوم وِحمْلِهم جادعينِه
والله يا خِلٍّ عَطاني من الروح   لاعْطيه من روح روحي رِهينِه ٢٠،٣٣

My taste is a drink from a rock hole in the mountain,[393]
    reserved for rugged hunters who know its hidden trail.
Many moonless nights we braved the danger;
    as we looked over the beloved's tribal pastures,[394]
I enjoyed her fruits, silky soft and uncooked,
    picking them under cover of pitch darkness.
We spent the whole night weighed down with our woes,
    but awoke in the morning, our cares cast aside.[395]
If my sweet love gives me straight from her soul, 33.20
    then by God I vow to requite her from my soul of souls.

~ ٣٤ ~

يا تَلّ قَلْبي تَلّ رَكْبٍ لسَرّاق   مع دَعاجينٍ سَروا حايفينِه
او تَلّ حَبل السانيه عِقْب الاعلاق   سَوّاقها عَبْدٍ عضوده مِتينِه
حَدّاه بالمَسْنَى ولا هيب تِنْساق   لا شَكّ يبْغي يِهينَه الله يهينِه
عَليك يا سابي عَزا كِلّ عَشّاق   يا نافل الخَفْرات مِن كِلّ زَينِه
يا بو نهودٍ مِن على الصَدْر لَبّاق   يَشْدِن فَناجيلٍ تكَفّا بصينِه
وبَين الاجِحّا ناض يا تِقْل بَرّاق   يُوضي سَناه وماه هَمْلٍ غَشينه
ولا تِبَسّم ثُمّ تجْلِجَ بالارماق   ما اوْدَع بتالي قَلْبي الّا ثِمينِه
والخَشْم سَلّة هندي يَشْعَق شْعاق   والموت يِعْبا في مَحاجير عَينه
مَوّاق لا اقْبَل مَشْيِتِه لِه تِدِرْياق   يِشْبِه غصَين المَوز لِطْفه ولِينه
ولا مِشَى ثَوبِه على رِدْفِه اطْراق   الله على ذيك الرِدايف يِعينه
ويا هَنّ ما تَطْفي دَرَك قلب مشتاق   انْعش لِظا ولْفٍ يجَرِّع حَنينه

~ 34 ~

My heart strains like camels driven hard by rustlers 34.1
from the al-Daʿājīn tribe, who rode by night to steal them.[396]
It's pulled like a rope tied to a camel drawing water,
flogged on by a black slave with bulging muscles,
Who cruelly chases her along the sloping path:
he beats her to spite her, may God lay him low.[397]
Your fault: captivator of hearts, the bane of lovers;
in beauty's pageant, you outclass all contenders.
Pert breasts protrude from the neckline, 34.5
like earless porcelain cups upside down on a tray.
Between the eyebrows, her eyes flash like lightning
that sets the world ablaze and releases torrential rain.
If she smiles and winks by batting her eyelashes,
she ravages my heart, sparing only a whit.[398]
Her nose is straight like a sparkling Indian sword;
her eye sockets harbor Death itself.
She advances with a proud elegant gait,
gracious and supple, like a smooth banana stalk.
When she ambles, her rotund butt stretches the robe, 34.10
pushing up the cloth: God help her with that behind!
Hey, don't cut the lifespan of a lovesick heart;[399]
rather, rekindle an intimacy that groans and yearns.[400]

~ ٣٥ ~

يا عيـني اللي بالهوى عـذّبتني   تبكي واشوف الدمع حرّق وجنها
عذلت عيني بالهوى وعسرتني   مفتونةٍ في حبّ حيٍّ محنها
نفسي لها هويات ما طاوعتني   لين انحلت بالحال واكدت بدنها
عندل بطاروق الهوى ساعفتني   تنقاد لي قود العسيف برسنها
اهرع من المرضع الى هرّجتني   امّ الغرير اللى رضع من لبنها
تطرق برمش العين وان واجهتني   تعطيني الهرجه وتاخذ ثمنها
تخفي لي الهرجه الى كلّمتني   خوفٍ من اللي كلمته ما وزنها
بالصدق ما يسعى وكذبه فتنّي   ولا خبر له هرجةٍ ما دفنها
شاورتها على الجواز وهدّتني   تبغي لعلّه يبعد الحوم عنها
عطيتها علمٍ وهي خابرتني   لو اربع بالبيت ما جزت منها
خمسة عشر عامٍ وهي مالكتني   والخادم المملوك يومر ونها
هذا جزاها يوم ما ناكرتني   والّا فلا منها ولا من عدنها
الموجب انه بالهوى ولّعتني   لو لا غلاها ما سكنت بوطنها

~ 35 ~

Why, my eye, have you tortured me with love? 35.1
Now you weep hot tears that burn your cheeks.
I upbraided my eye for its rapture, but it mutinied:
it's in thrall to a person's seductions and torments.[401]
My soul follows its fancies, scorns obedience,
leaving me gaunt, my frame emaciated.
Gentle, she paved for me the road of passion:
she runs in lockstep, a tamed filly at the rein.
She speaks to me, as eager as a suckling mother 35.5
who picks up the baby to nurse it.
Seeing me, she flutters her eyelashes,
then chatters away, and peppers me with questions.
She's careful not to divulge what she's been told,
lest it be misunderstood.
Truth isn't her concern—I'm dazzled by her deceit—
but when told a story, she doesn't conceal it from me.
I asked her about marriage; she played it cool,
thinking that perhaps I'd change the subject.
She spoke with candor when I confessed to her; 35.10
even if I were married to four wives, I couldn't do without her.[402]
For fifteen years I have been beholden to her:
a servant slave who's told what to do, what not.[403]
This is how I requited her for ill-treating me,
though, truth is, I am not of her kin or league.
She inflamed my passion, that's the reason:
if not, my darling, I wouldn't live in your land.[404]

~ ٣٦ ~

يا اللّٰه يا عالِمِ خَفيات الاسرار   يا عالِمٍ ما يَطْرِق المُودمانِ
تِفِكّ حَبْل اللي مِن العام بِوْسار   وتِمْحَى مَوَدّة صاحِبٍ كِد بَراني
غِزْوٍ تِسَبَّب لي بِحَبْسٍ وِتحْيار   عَليّ صاغٍ ما اتَعَدَّى مِكاني
ما اعَرْفِه الّا يوم يِطْرَى بالأذْكار   لا عَوَّد اللّٰه جَيّتِه يوم جاني
ما شِفْت مِنه الّا العَزاير والامرار   وعيًّا قرانه يِنْطِلِق من قراني
للعَقْل سَحّارٍ وللشوف قَمّار   ولا يِنْعِرف رَطْنه من المِعْربانِ
والّا مع ذَلِك مجيحٍ ومَكّار   وازْريت اسَنِّع سِيرته قِلّباني
خِلّي وِسَرني وَسَرَة القِدّ للطار   ما فيه عَقْلٍ يَقْرَعِه مِطْرِبانِ
خَلّى فوادي مارِدٍ له وِمصدار   واضْرَيت حالي واللّٰه المِسْتِعانِ
قِلْت الشِرِيعه قال نار ابن عَمّار   يِبيني الحَسَها تحَرِّق لساني
ما اللي على المَتْن الشِمالي بعَذّار   وَيش انت شايف يا رِقيب الحَسانِ
ان كان ما انْتِب عاذرٍ عِقْب ما صار   باللّٰه وَيش اللي عليه تْهَداني
ابا اتَصَبَّر مَير ماني بِصَبّار   نَهَيت قَلْبي عَن هَواه وعَصاني
يِقول هَذي شَمْعَة البِيض والجار   يوم نْطَحَتْني تِعْتِرِض بِدْرِجاني
كِنّ القِدَم بالساق عِصْبٍ لْخِطّار   عِقْب النِجاح وقَبْل فَرْس اليِمانِ

~ 36 ~

You are privy, God, to the deepest secrets: 36.1
  You are no stranger to people's predicament.[405]
Loosen the rope that has fettered me for a year;
  efface my affection for a love that's worn me out!
A pretty little thing threw me into perplexity:
  her shackles forced me into confinement.
I didn't know her before, had only heard her name.
  I wish to God we had not met face to face:
All I got from her was chastisement and bitter woe, 36.5
  and yet her hook refused to leave my ring.
She bewitches the mind, gambles with one's eyes;
  her gabble means nothing to any Arab.[406]
Yet she's cunning and adept at winning an argument:
  I can't make head or tail of her baffling caprice.
This girl pinned me down like a skin on a drum,
  and in mindless rapture drummed away.
Her comings and goings to my heart's well
  made me ill: to God I turn for help.
I said, "Shariah!" and she, "Fire of Ibn ʿAmmār!"[407] 36.10
  She wants me to lick red-hot iron, sear my tongue.[408]
If the angel on my left shoulder does not forgive,
  what is your counsel, angel on my right?
If you cannot excuse me after all that passed,
  then, good heaven, what would you advise?[409]
I chose to suffer in silence but had no patience:
  telling the heart to calm down, I made it rebel.[410]
It said, "Among the fair she's the tribe's candle:
  she loomed before me with a swaying gait."
Her calves are plump like roulade served to guests, 36.15
  as yet untouched by hands, cooked to perfection

صَفّه ستادٍ صَفّةٍ له بها كار   قَصْبه قِليل وما فِهق منه ثاني
عَدْلٍ يِشيل الثَوب رِدْفِه الى ثار   ما هي مِن اللي كِبْرَها بالمثاني
هافي حَشاكِنّه عن الزاد مِخْتار   وِنْهود مِثل مْكَفّيات الصِيانِ
والعِنق عِنْق ادْمِيّةٍ تَرْعَى الاقْفار   اوْحَتْ حَساس ورَزّته بِجْفلانِ
والخَدّ قِرْطاس العَجَم ما به اسْطار   في يَد خَطيب وناشعِه زَعْفرانِ
راعي ثِمانٍ كِنّهن ضِيق الامْطار   والى عَطاني رِبع عِلِم قَراني
خَمْرٍ حَديثه لِلجسَد نافعٍ ضارّ   بَغَيت نَفْعه لين ضَرّه سِداني
والخَشْم سَلّة هِنْديٍ صَنْع بَيطار   يِحْفِيه لَبْسة بِخْنَقه ما يداني
وِزْمَيّمٍ فَوق المبَيسم بِشِنْكار   هَنيّ مِن وَرْد الثِمان بْثِمانِ
والعَين عَين اللي تَنَهّض ولا طار   في ماكرٍ عَسْرٍ عَلى كِلّ جاني
والراس ذَيل اللي يشَعْشِع الى غار   اشْقَر عليه قْروح ما هوب واني
حصان الشيوخ اللي مِن البرّ مِشْكار   ما يِنْقِهر لولا الرِسَن والعنانِ
جِمْلَة وصوفه نِظْف جَيبه من العار   ولا يِشْتِفي بِهْروجه المِسْنِحانِ
هَذي وصوفِه واعْذروني يا الاخيار   ومِن لا عَذر لا ذاق بِرْد الجنانِ

By a chef deploying his mastery,
  with almost no bones, unmarred by any blemish.
When she gets up, ballooning buttocks stretch the skirt;
  her mass is not packed around a flabby middle:
Her waist is slim as if she eats but little;
  her bust porcelain cups upside down on a tray;
The neck of a gazelle that forages on a desert plain,
  she hears the faintest sound and starts in alarm;
Her cheeks are made of unlined Persian paper, 36.20
  saffron-sprinkled, in the hands of a preacher;
Her teeth are white, like freshly fallen hail:
  I would exult at just a quarter of a word from her.
Her chatter is wine for the body, healthily noxious:
  looking for its benefit, I was drowned by its harm.
Her nose is like an Indian sword, well-crafted:
  its delicate skin chafes at the touch of a veil;
Her nose ring is fastened to a golden chain:
  heavenly bliss to suck her spittle mouth on mouth![411]
Her eyes are those of a falcon raising itself with a start, 36.25
  in a high nest, inaccessible to any thief.
Her mane waves like a charging steed's tail,
  a fiery, gold-colored, five-year-old bay:
A shaykh's warhorse, a hand-fed ball of fire,
  bristling with energy and straining at bridle and rein.
The quintessence of her nature is stainless honor;
  she wouldn't deign to speak to a devious idler.[412]
Such are her traits, so you must pardon me, my good people:
  whoever does not, may he not taste the coolness of Paradise.

~ ٣٧ ~

عَـدَّيت مِـرْقـابٍ بـراسـه رجومِ | مِـرْقاب طَلّاب الهَوى يومِ عَـدّاه
مِـرْقـاب من مِـثْلي بِقَـلْبه هشومِ | وعَـينه على بَعْض الازاويـل مِـغْراه
لولا الحَيـا لارْقَى طِويـل الرجومِ | واصِبّ صَوتٍ كلّ من حَولي اوْحـاه
لَى جَتْني الفَـزْعَـه تـريد العلومِ | قِلْت آه ذا حِبّ الحَبيّب وفَرقـاه
عليه قَـلْبي بَين الاضـلاع يُومي | اومـاي صَقّـارٍ لطَيـره ولا جـاه
الطَيـرعـانَق له طـيورٍ تحومِ | ثـمّ ارتِقَـع يَـمّ الخضَيرا وخَـلّاه
واصـاحبي عَنْـه ارْمِسَنّ العـلومِ | ولا اذْري وِش الله قال به عِقب فرْقاه
دارٍ سِكَنْها لا سِقَتها الغـيومِ | يِقْحِـط محَلّه بالمحَل لَين تجْفـاه
عِلْمي بهم بالقَيظ حامى السِمومِ | واليَوم عِشْب الوَسِم تَشْبَع رَعاياه
سَـقْوى الى جَو يَتْبِعون الرسومِ | وتطـاوِلوا وادى الهِيَيشه ومَجْراه
من يَمّهـم دَبّتْ عَـلينا السـلومِ | ومن له عَميلٍ جايبي منه مَقْضاه
وَجْدي عليهم وَجْد راعي بِحَومِ | تَلْحَق ولا تِلْحَق نَهـار المـثاراه
قَـزّاه صـيّاح السَرَق عِـقب نومِ | قالوا عَـطونا مِشْعَل الشَيخ نَقْفـاه
وِلحَق الطـلَب نَقْوة عيـالٍ قـرومِ | وشافوا سَرْقهم واذْهم الجَيش يَشْعاه
وتِقايِسوا بالكِثْر والكلّ دومي | وكلٍّ تحَـزّم واحْـتَزَب للمـلاقـاه

~ 37 ~

I climbed to the lookout, a peak marked by cairns— 37.1
a refuge for love's devotee who mounts its slopes;[413]
A lonely height for one whose heart was shattered,
his gaze fixed on silhouettes fading in the distance.
But for the shame, I would scale a precipitous high crag,
to scream so loud it would raise alarm far and wide.
If rescuers rushed up and asked me what was wrong,
I'd say, "I am pining for a sweetheart who decamped."
On her account, my heart flutters in its cage, 37.5
like a falconer waving to his bird to return, in vain:
It saw other falcons circling and flew to join them,
then all soared up to the blue zenith, leaving him forlorn.
Soulmate, signs of life from you were effaced.
I am ignorant of the fate that God bestowed on her.
May the clouds not release any rains on their camp—
punish it with severe drought and force her out!
The last time we met, scalding midsummer winds blew;
now herds feed on pastures of early winter rains.
What bliss when they return by roundabout tracks, 37.10
until they rejoin al-Hyiyshah's dry watercourse![414]
Once encamped, the Bedouin hasten to the settlement,
renew friendships with villagers, and go shopping.
Ah, I suffer the woes of the owner of a fiery steed—
a racer that can't be outstripped in bitter fight.[415]
Woken up by shouts raising a robbery's alarm,
they asked for the chief's torch and rushed off in chase.
The pursuing party, the finest pick of valiant youths,
caught sight of their animals driven by a strong force.
They took the others' measure, looking to settle scores in blood,[416] 37.15
each girded with arms and munition, ready for battle.

~ ٣٧ ~

طِريحهـم من بَينـهـم ما يِقومِ   خَـلّوه لِسحـم الضُواري تَعَشّـاه
وبانتْ فَعـايـل كلّ بَتْعٍ جِزومي   وتنَسّـلوا دِهْـم الفـرَنْج المخَبّاه
وحَوّل عـليـه مُـبَخّتٍ بالسـهومِ   وطـابَق مبَطّنْها على سـاق يِمْـناه
وِتكَرْسَعَت لغـيون زاهى الرقومِ   من كَفّ قَرْمٍ راعي الكُور يَنْخاه
وضـالوا عليه وعَـضّ روس البهومِ   وِتشـايَنوا صَـبْره ولَجّة يِتامـاه ٢٠،٣٧

A fighter falls to the ground; he does not rise again:
he is evening supper for sinister beasts of prey.
Resolute and intrepid, they launched their attack,
unsheathed dark barrels of rifles kept hidden.
Fortune smiled on a marksman who took aim and shot,
piercing the breast girth and into the right foreleg.
The horse was sent crashing, for tattooed ladies' sake,
by a warrior cheered on by camel-mounted friends.[417]
They surrounded the fallen rider who bit his thumbs in surrender,[418] 37.20
then, for the orphans' sake, thought better of killing him.

~ ٣٨ ~

هـنيّ من قَـلْبِـه دِلوهٍ ومَـمْنوح   حـاله كِما حـال البَغَل من غْذاهـا
بين الاظِـلّه كِنّه السَـدُو مَـطْروح   هَـمّه رقـاده والرُوابع نِسـاهـا
ولا شَعَب قَـلْبه تَعـاجيب ومْزوح   مِن طـالَبَة غيٍّ على مِسْـتِواهـا
والّا فـانا قَــلْبي من الوِدّ مَجْروح   وعَيـني تِـزايد دَمْعها مِن عَنـاهـا
قَـلْبي كِما وادٍ من الجِنْد مَـمْروح   لِيـال ما بِه قَشْـعَـةٍ ما رَعـاهـا
كِنّي بغِـبّات البَحَـر راكبٍ لَوح   تُومي بـه ارياحٍ زِعوجٍ هَواهـا
بتيـفـاق زِيـرانٍ من المَوج بِنْـطوح   وتاه الدِليـله والاناجِـر رِمـاهـا
على الذي بِعْيونِه النـاس ذِرْنوح   ما يِبْـدي الغـايه على مِن بَغـاهـا
وانا الَى جِيته غَـدا الصَدْر مَشْروح   يِبْـدي لي اسرارٍ على امِّـه كِمـاهـا
ولو ما هَرَج لي عارِفٍ كِلّ مَـنْضوح   عـندي طُواريق الهوى ومِعْـناهـا
واللّٰه يا خِلٍ صِـفَـط لي مِن الروح   لا اصْفِط لها من روح روحي جِزاهـا
مـا انا الذي يِـرْكِي رِفيقه على صَوح   مِـعْطي كِراب ايدَيه يبْغي مَـلاهـا
ولا ياصَل الحِرْوه اقَع كِلّ مَـمْدوح   وانا بِـراي اللّٰه لَاعَـدِّي وَراهـا
مِن خـاطرٍ ما عـارَضِه كِل سـاموح   الَى بَغَى لِه نِيِّـةٍ وانْتَواهـا
يِفْـتي بِـرايٍ يَجْمَع العِـزْب وِسْروح   وِتمْسي جِمـيع وِتحْـتِذِر من عَـداهـا

~ 38 ~

Blessed is the blasé heart—one that lacks for nothing,
like the mule when his nose bag's on.[419]
He lazes in the shade, like wool laid out for spinning,
with no ambition but to sleep. His mind's a blank, no worries;
His heart's immune to stirrings of merriment and fun,
not up to the challenge of her flirtatious game.
My gashed heart shows love's stigmata–
sorrow's tears stream from my eyes.
My heart is a valley that's crawling with locusts; [420]
at night, they strip every shrub bare of its leaves.
It's as if I'm in a wooden ship tossed by a raging sea,[421]
swollen by the storm winds that drive the surging waves:
When the gale-driven rollers launched their attack,
the pilot got lost and dropped the anchor.
All this for a girl who avoids people like a sting in the eye[422]
and who leaves admirers in the throes of despair.
On my visits, she disclosed her feelings,
telling me secrets she kept hidden from her mother.
Without words, intuitively, I know what she means:
I boast a long history of treading passion's roads!
By God, she's my soulmate! She's opened her heart to me:
in return I'll open mine, my heart of hearts, to her.
I'm not one to push a love so her back's to the wall,[423]
or hold out cupped hands, begging her to fill them.
Only men of accomplishment reach their aims;
if God permits, I will surpass them at their game,
Spurred on by an idea fit to clear any hurdle,
if one is determined to act on his intentions:
Formulate a view that rallies all and sundry,[424]
spend the night on guard against the enemy.

~ ٣٨ ~

وجِزاه عِنْد اقْفاه بالرِجْل مَكْثوح　　سَبْع كَثْحَاتٍ يِقْتِبِس مِن حَصاها

ما يَتْبَع المِقْفي حذا كِلّ يَنْبوح　　او ثَوَر هَورٍ ما يثَمِّن قِفاها

~ 38 ~

If she rebuffs me, she'll get kicked for her pains,
seven times, sparks flying from the hot pebbles.
Only dogs grovel before displays of contempt;
only oxen graze on without a care.

~ ٣٩ ~

يا وَنّتي وَنّـة طِـعـين الشِـطـيرِه   في ساعـةٍ يُوخَـذ طِمَعها عْشاوِه
خِلّي نَهار الكَون وَسْط الكِسيره   مـا لِه وَلَد عَـمٍّ ولا له دَناوِه
ولا يَعْرِف الطالع مِن ايّا عَشِيره   مِن كِلّ بَدْوٍ نَوّهـم بالعَتاوِه
عَلى عَشيرٍ ما لِقَينا نِظيره   بالحَضَر واللي مِعْتِنين البِداوِه
خِلٍّ بَرَى حالي سواة البِحيره   عِنْد السَتاد وصاحِبه قال ساوِه
الَى بغَيت ابْدي عَليه السِريره   صَدّتْ ولَدّتْ في نِظَرْها لَهاوِه
ما بَين تَرْبِيعِه وما بَين ذِيره   ولا مِن مِقاد ولا تبيّن عَداوِه
تَحْسِب تِغِلّيها لروحي بِريره   هو ما دَرَى انّه مِثْل حَبْس الاغاوِه
تِغِلّي الغالي للاقدام حِيره   تَمّم تِغِلّيها جِمال وحَلاوه
البِيض لَيل وزَينها زَمْهَريره   الَى اسْتِقَرّتْ بالسِما عِقْب ناوِه
عَذْرا بِقَلْبي واعْتِقادي خَشيره   عِنْدي جنَيه وغَيرها صَرْف ماوِه
ذا زَينها من يوم خِلْقَتْ صِغيره   ما هي من اللي زَينهن صِبْغ جاوِه
عندي وكِلّ مْوَلَّع في عَشيره   وراعى الوِطَن عِنْدي شَراية نِقاوِه
تِلِحّني لَحّة خَلوجٍ لِظيره   تِبيه يِتْبَع ساقِته بالتلاوه
اللي تعاف النَفْس عِدْوَى وطَيره   ولا يَرْكَب السَيل الوَعَر والنِباوِه

~ 39 ~

I groan like a warrior felled by a blade—[426] 39.1
prostrate while plunderers prowl,
Abandoned on a battlefield littered with corpses,
with no kin or relatives in sight, no help;
Without an inkling about that figure in the distance,
from the throngs of lawless Bedouin.[427]
This is how I feel about a love without peer,
either among settled folk or a nomadic crowd;
A lady who pared down my body like a piece of wood, 39.5
as does a carpenter who is told “Shave it!”[428]
When I am about to reveal to her my secret,
she bucks and bolts, gazes at me with a reckless glint;
In coquettish pause, or because thrown into a fright,
she’s not amenable to reason, though not unfriendly.
Haughty, the dame thinks her flirting is alms for me;
doesn’t she know it’s like suffering in a Turkish dungeon?
Her arrogance throws me into confusion:[429]
it’s conceit married to charm and loveliness.
The creamy girls are night; their beauty is the sun 39.10
when its blinding light breaks through a deck of clouds.
With all my heart, and firm conviction, I declare:
she is a gold pound—others are mere pennies—
Born as the natural beauty she is now,
unlike those who use makeup from Java.[430]
Like any lover who is in thrall to his amour,
I’d part with my wealth for my princess’s sake.
She nudges me, as a camel that has lost her young[431]
presses another calf to closely toe her steps.
A soul’s disgust is like consumption and paralysis: 39.15
insurmountable, like stony heights in a torrent’s path.[432]

العـارف العَـذّار مـا مِـنّه غِـيره　　اخاف مِن خَطْوا الهَـذور اللَعـاوِه
هـمَّاز لَمّـازٍ هـروجه كِثـيره　　عِنْد العَرَب كِنّه سِـلوقي ضَـراوه
راعى النِميـمه لا سَـعَتْ لِه بخِـيره　　حَلْقِـه لَعَـلّه للشِجَـر والدراوِه
عَسى عظـامه للشواغي الضِريـره　　واخَيضَـرٍ يُودِع عـيونه قراوِه

~ 39 ~

One needs friends who understand and forgive;
   one must be on guard against idle prattlers
Who whisper and wink and waffle:
   everywhere on people's heels like a hunter's salukis.
Let these muckrakers come to a nasty end, I pray:
   may their throats be eaten by syphilis and scrofula;
Let them be racked by severe pain in the bones,
   or an eye disease that leaves the sockets empty.[433]

~ ٤٠ ~

يومِ الرِّكايب عَـقّبن خشـمِ ابانات   ذِكَرْت مَـلْهوف الحَشا من عَـنايَه
لَيتِه رِديفٍ لي عَلى الهِجن هَيهات   امّا مِـعي والّا رِديف خْوِيايَه
اخَذْت لي مع طورِق الغيّ سَجّات   يومِ السَّعَد قايمِ وانا اتْبَع هَوايَه
يوم ان لي مَع تِلْع الارْقاب صِرْفات   ابيـع واشْـري بَيْـنهِن بالسَّعـايَه
الليـل نَجْدَع بِـه مَواعيد وضْوات   ولا خـاشَرِ الوَعّاد راعى الضَوايَه
واليَوم شِبْت وتِبْت عن كِلّ ما فات   وطوَيت عن كِلّ المَوارد رشايَه
الّا فـيوم اذْكِر خطات الخِونْدات   اللي مِـقاديمَه تَعَـدّى الحَـضايَه
تجازي الهَـرّاج بِغْضاي وِسْكات   ولا تبَـيِّن لِه سِـريـره وغـايَه
تِصِدّ عَمّا قال مِن غَير مجْفات   وِتعْـطيه خَـدٍ مِثْل شَمْس المِرايَه
مِن آن في قَـلْبي جروحٍ خَفِيات   وانا اخَبْـر مـا بي سِـببَها مِن آيَه
آيَة هَوى مـا هي بِطِبّ المـداوات   انا طِبيب الروح مـا بي غوايَه
يَطْري لي الهاجوس هاجوس الافات   وعَرَض لي المِبْعِد على كِلّ رايَه
مـا هيب بِدْعَه تَلْحَق النَفس شَرْهات   ناسٍ غَـدوا قِـدْمي وناسٍ وَرايَه
لولاي اوَسّع خاطِري بالتِنَهّات   وابْصِـر بحالي مِن خَلاي بْخَلايَه
لاغْدي كِما المِذْهِب وارَمّي بالاصْوات   خِـبْلٍ على مـا قال راعى الروايَه

~ 40 ~

As the camel train disappeared over the spur of Abānāt,[434] 40.1
I recalled and pined for my days with the wasp-waisted.
In my dreams, she rides with me on speedy mounts,
clasping my middle, or seated behind my companion.[435]
Traveling love's road became second nature;
Fortune's star rose and guided my steps.
Those days, I did brisk business with the slender-necked:
buying and selling, I used to hurry from one to the other.[436]
At night, we'd rendezvous and take walks in the dark, 40.5
alone, unobserved, away from the beaten track.[437]
Now I've gone gray and foresworn my old ways,
drawn up my frayed ropes from all watering holes—
Except when haunted by memories of a buxom beauty
whose tresses tumble down to her lap.
She meets a gossip with averted eyes and stony silence;
she will not betray her secrets and designs.
Not rude, she keeps his advances at arm's length
and turns a cheek like a shining mirror to him.
In my heart, my long-festering wounds lay hidden; 40.10
no one but me knows how they were inflicted.
Passion's symptoms can't be treated with medicine;[438]
I am loath to go and ask for a doctor's prescription.
Haunted by baleful thoughts, plagued by obsessions:
the target of the devil's whisperings at every turn.
That a soul is visited by desire is no novelty:
others were swept off their feet–I won't be the last.[439]
But for relief brought by sighing and sobbing,[440]
and times spent alone pondering deeply on my fate,
I'd go mad and start rambling in delirium; 40.15
a brainless dolt, as in all the old stories.[441]

باهْل الهَوى مِن شارِب الخَمْر شارات   وِبْهُم مِن اللي يَطْرِد الصَيد شايَه
شارات راعي الخَمْر فاقَه وسَكْرات   والصَيد وِلْعِه ما على الله كمايَه
ولو اتْمَنّى لي مِن المال غَلّات   وانَفِّد الغَلّه واحَصِّل منايَه
مَير المِقِلّ ضِعيف ما فيه نَوهات   وراعي التِمِنّي مِثْل زَرّاع طايَه

Passion's devotees share traits with wine bibbers,
resemble hunters in their dogged pursuit of game:
Wine drinkers get drunk and then they get sober;
as for the hunters—well, God only knows!
If I had my wish, I would ask for a fortune
and pay any price just to fulfill my desire.
But every poor soul must adjust his ambitions;[442]
mere wishful thinking is like sowing seeds on a bare rooftop.[443]

ياهَنّ مِمّا يِنْعِش الروح شِفْ سِـلي   ما دِمْت انا مـاجود والنَـفْس حَيّـه
انا وِجيع القَـلْب ما يِنْعَرِف سِـلي   ما نيب راعى العِـلّة الابْـرَحِيّه
يا رَبّي انّك قـادرٍ تِنْتِصِف سِـلي   مِن واحـدٍ ما غَيـر زَوله نِحْيّه
غِرْوٍ تِسَبَّب لي يِريد التَلَف سِـلي   بِجيـدِه ومَجْدولِه ونِجْـلِه وغَيّه
يِقْـفي ويِقْبِـل بين وِلْفٍ وجَفْـلي   ياعِـد ويِبْعِـد نِيّتِـه سَـذْوِرِيّه
والَى بَغَيت اعْطي طِريقٍ لِقَف سِـلي   وارْخى المَلَيثِم لَين تَبْدي شِفِيّه
هَرّج ودَرّج بالخَطَى وِانْعَطَف سِـلي   لَين اسْمَعِه لا سَمْع صَيحَـة نِبيّه
والَى بغَيت اتْـرِك مِجاله هَنَف سِـلي   وعَوّدْت لِه والقَلْب رِكْب ارْدِعيّه
عَزّ الله انّهِ ما مِشَى بِالنِصَف سِـلي   مَكّـار سَحّـارٍ عـقوده رِدِيّه
يَبْغي يعَسّفْني وهوما انْعَسَف سِـلي   خَـطِيّةٍ يا كِبْـرَهـا مِن خَـطِيّه
يَبْـغِيـني امْشي لِه طِلِي بِكَفْـلي   لا لي كَلام ولا مِـعي مَـقْـدِرِيّه
الَى شِكَيت الحال لِه ما صِحَف سِـلي   يَلْعَب بي الشِـطْرَنْج لا رِحْـم حَيّه
ما هوب مِثْلي يوم اسَجّم وغَفْـلي   يِفِـزّ قَلْبي يوم يِطْـرَى سِمِيّه
الَى بَغَيت اشْرب يِنِفّ العَذَف سِـلي   يِبيـني اشْـرب مِنه شَـرْبَة ضِحِيّه
حَرْفٍ وذَرْفٍ مِعْلِقٍ بالطَرَف سِـلي   والّا فـعَفّ وعـاف ذَبْحَـة خَوِيّه
يا لَيتني ما اعَرْف مِن لا وِلَف سِـلي   اللي سَـلَم مِن عِـرْفـهـم واهَـنِيّه

~ 41 ~

Hey what's-your-name, give me the stuff that revives me;[444] 41.1
for as long as I breathe and my heart still beats.[445]
I nurse my heart's grievous wound in silence;
it is not a disease that is plain for all to see.[446]
My Lord, it is in Your power to do me justice:
I yearn to catch a glimpse of her shape—[447]
A frisky girl who spells ruin to the infatuated,
with her neck, locks, wide eyes, and dalliance.
She wavers between affection and apprehension, 41.5
between promise and distance—adrift on whims.
If, at my wit's end, I go my way, she cuts in front of me,
lifts a tip of her veil, revealing her lips to me.
She chatters as she trips along, sidling up to me,
until I listen—may she miss the Prophet's shout![448]
If I try to escape her spell and she smiles at me,
I retrace my steps with wildly pounding heart.
God Almighty, she did not treat me fairly:
she schemes and bewitches with empty promises.
She wants to break me in, but won't be tamed herself:[449] 41.10
how wrong and unfair; what a flagrant injustice!
She wants me to submit like a lamb led by the neck,[450]
without having a say and in abject submission.
If I utter a complaint, she shows no sympathy:
she plays chess with me—may her kin be damned!
She's unlike me: if I am distracted and wander a bit,
my heart jumps at the very mention of her name.
When I want to drink, she blows foam at me across the pool:
the drink of a sheep before it is slaughtered.[451]
She is a deadly shot when she has lit her matchlock's fuse: 41.15
Or she may relent and be loath to take her companion's life.[452]
She who harbors no affection for me, how I wish I'd never met her;
lucky the man who is spared the torment of such affairs!

~ ٤٢ ~

يا وَنّتي وَنّة كِسير المِشانيط   يشوف مخّ الساق بين الجِباير ١،١،٤٢
قالوا تحِيط وقِلت والله ما احِيط   قالوا لي ابْشِر قِلت اسوق البِشاير
يا عيال اهَل رَكْبٍ من الرِدْف اماليط   مضَمَّرات وساسِهِنَّه حَراير
اسرُوا ليا مِنّه دِمَس عنكم الخَيط   يا هل النِضا لعَلّها إلكم سِفاير
والصِبحْ عند مْقَلِّط البِنّ تَقْليط   ابو خشَيم وبَلِّغوا بالسَراير ٥،١،٤٢
سَقْوى الى جَتّنا ركَابٍ قُواليط   جَونا قلوطٍ قِدم غازي وساير
وابن محَيّا والرِباعين والضِيط   واولاد رَوق متَيِّهين العَشاير
جرح الهوى ينماز يا ناس لو خِيط   لوكان حَطّوا به قِويّ المَراير

مطوّعٍ راحت علومه خَراميط   تِخّ العبيد اللي ثِمَنهم طراير ١،٢،٤٢
خيبة رجا لا هوب رِقْعه ولا خَيط   من مارثَة غَزْو الحكاك الذَخاير

~ 42~

Muṭawwaʿ Nifi

I moan like a man whose leg is tied with Mishānīṭ straps,[453] 42.1.1
the bone marrow visible through the splints.
"Can you hang on?" they said, "By God, I can't!" said I.[454]
"Chin up, we'll help!" they said; "I'll pay you!" was my reply.[455]
Listen, dashing riders of fleet bare-backed camels,
sleek, well-muscled, well-sired, pedigreed:
"Set off at night, in fading light, as soon as darkness falls;[456]
God speed, hardy cameleers, to your journey's end:
In the morning you'll meet Abū Khshēm, a man whose coffee's always fresh; 42.1.5
Tell him our news, what is secret and what isn't.
If all is well, mounted men will meet and guide you,
before raiding parties and other guests arrive.
Greet Ibn Mḥayya, and the Ribāʿīn, and al-Ḍīṭ,
all men from al-Rūgah who scatter tribes like chaff.
Too wide gape the gashes made by love's passion[457]
to be stitched by even the strongest threads."

Ibn Sbayyil

The Muṭawwaʿ is all fakery and tawdry nonsense:[458] 42.2.1
He's the pup of slaves bought and sold for pennies.[459]
He's no use, not even for patching or sewing,
a scrap from a slaves' raid scouring a pot.[460]

مبـدّلٍ طَوعـه بتيـطٍ وقِـرمـيط   ونطـاز وانْطِـزْ به بمِفْـرَق وعـايـر
يِمْـلك ولو ما جا شهود وتضابيـط   والَى تِكاثـر شَـرْطهـم مـا يخـايـر

بِـدَيت لي قـافٍ بنَيته على الطـا   حَيث انّ حَرْف الطا صِعيبٍ شِطيطِ ١،٣،٤٢
يا من لقَـلبٍ عَـطّه الوِدّ عَــطّـا   مِـتبْيّنٍ مـا عـاد هو بمْـغَــطوطِ
هَيّــض علـيّ جُوَيـدِلٍ مـا تَغَـطّى   رِيحـه زبادي بِمسْـك مْخَـلوطِ
يا شِـبْه غِـرْنوقٍ مَـعَ جَول بَطّـا   بَطّ البَحَر مـا هوب بَطّ الشـطوطِ
كِنّـه عـلى شَوكْ الهَـراس يتوَطّـا   والّا المـيابِـر يوم بالرِجْـل يُوطِي ٥،٣،٤٢
لَيـته يواجِـهـني وهو مـا تَغَــطّى   اشوفـــ مجـدولٍ زَهَتـه المشوطِ

مــطوّعٍ يا مـال كشْـف المـغَـطّى   ياخِـذ على رِقّي المَـنابـر شـروطِ ١،٤،٤٢
شَـرْهٍ عـلى وِرْعٍ وهو مـا تَغَــطّى   يلْعَب مع الوِرعـان بامّ الخَـطوطِ

لا يا عــبيله يا عَـريـض المبطـا   عَيـرٍ الَى مــنّي نَغَـزْته ضِـروطِ ١،٥،٤٢

His piety is baloney and empty prattle,[461]
and hopping and dancing in every part of town.[462]
He marries without witness or document:
whatever the bride-price, it's never too much for him.[463]

Muṭawwaʿ Nifī

I compose my verses to rhyme in *ṭāʾ* 42.3.1
since *ṭāʾ* makes for a difficult rhyme.[464]
Poor heart, fallen prey to love's vagaries:
clear and simple, no two ways about it.
A lovely young thing stirred my blood,
her uncovered plaits smelling of civet and musk.
She struts like a long-legged crane among ducks:
the ducks on the water, not those on shore.
She treads with care, as if on thorns, 42.3.5
or afraid to step on needles.
If only she would meet me unveiled,
my eyes would see her well-combed tresses.

Ibn Sbayyil

Muṭawwaʿ, may your deepest secret be exposed:[465] 42.4.1
you take money for ascending the pulpit.[466]
Shame on you for lusting after an unveiled girl
playing hopscotch with boys in the sand.[467]

Muṭawwaʿ Nifī

What now, little fat-assed ʿAbdallah, 42.5.1
donkey that farts when my stick pokes its hole.[468]

نِجْـر المـطَوّع يوم سـامه دغَيليب   هو يحْسِب انّي جـالبِـه للمِبيعِـه ١،٦،٤٢
صَكّوا بِي الاجناب هم والاصاحيب   قـالوا تبيعـه قِلْت واللّه ما ابِيعِـه
باغٍ الَى جَونا هـل الفِـطّر الشِـيب   اجواد مِـرْفِـقْـهم عَـدُوّ الشـرِيعِـه
اوّل قـراهـم دَلّتـينٍ وتَـرْحـيب   تَـرْحيبةٍ سَهْله ونَفْسٍ رفـيعـه
عَسَى صِبِيٍ ما يَعَـرْف المُواجـيب   تِجـيه لَيعـات اللِيـالي سِرِيعـه ٥،٦،٤٢
مِن شَبّ من صِغْره الى حِرْوة الشَيب   ما حاش من دَرْب المَراجل سِـبِيعـه
ما نيب احِبّ اللي بطَبْعِـه عَذاريب   عن الرِدي نِلْقَى فجُوجٍ وِسـيعـه
صَخَرْت عَسْر القِيل غَصْبٍ بلا طِيب   تِجِين عَسْرات القُوافي مـطِيعـه

اللي يجي يَمّـه هـل الفِطّـر الشِـيب   شَرْق الهيَيْشه من يِسـار الرِفيعـه ١،٧،٤٢
والّا المـطَوّع كِلّ هَـرْجِه تِكـاذيب   والَى بَغى مـا هـيب تَـرْفَه تِطِيعـه

لا ضاق صَدْري ,قُمْت اصوّت لنوره   هاتي حَطَب وارْمِيه للجار والضَـيف ١،٨،٤٢
من قَبْـل وِلْد اللاش يِبْـدي بشوره   حَمَسْت من بِنّ اليمَن غاية الكَيف

Muṭawwaʿ Nifī

Dghēlīb offered a price for Muṭawwaʿ's mortar,[469] 42.6.1
because he fancies I put it up for sale.
Strangers and my own kin all pressed me:
"Sell it!" and I said, "By God, I won't!"[470]
I need it for travelers on travel-worn mounts,[471]
honorable men, accompanied by Shariah's defiers.[472]
They are welcomed with two pots of coffee and warm greetings;
simple words, spoken with unaffected ease and sincerity.
A young man who does not honor hospitality's demands, 42.6.5
may quickly fall on evil days;
Men who spend a life from cradle to grave
without the most trivial manly deeds—
I feel revulsion at misfits of feeble character:
I give lowlifes like these the widest berth.
I subdue refractory verse one way or another,
until the hardest rhymes meekly obey my scheme.

Ibn Sbayyil

Riders on camels, gray from grueling marches,[473] 42.7.1
East of al-Hyiyshah, left of al-Rifīʿah:
Know that al-Muṭawwaʿ speaks nothing but lies!
When he wants it, his wife Tarfah doesn't put out.[474]

Muṭawwaʿ Nifī

When my mood is blue I call for Nūrah:[475] 42.8.1
"Quick, get firewood for neighbor and guest!"
Before the good-for-nothing has uttered a sound,
I've roasted a delicious brew from Yemeni beans.[476]

مطوّعٍ يا كِبر هَوله وجَوره   گَله على دَور السَنه مِدّ ونصَيف ١،٩،٤٢
ودلالهم دِبّ اللِيال مْهَجُوره   وخِطّارهم ما غَير ابو زَيد وحْنَيف

يا شِبْه ديكٍ قاصراتٍ شبوره   حِسّه صِليب وفِعْل يِمْناه ما شِيف ١،١٠،٤٢
وَين انت عنّا يا مبَقِّط بعوره   يوم الفضول يْحَتِّتون التِطاريف
لوانت عَذْرا كان اقول مْعَذوره   تْحَدِّرَت بالطَيز مال الزَعانيف
جازيتِني عِقْب الجماله بوَره   تَر ضَيعَتِك ما بين مَطْناي والخَيف

انا اشهد انّ الباب حَقّه علينا   والّا القلاقل والِمجاري قويه ١،١١،٤٢

فاتَتْ وَرى ما قام يَمّه حَدَينا   ثُم اغلَق المِجْرى بوَسط البِنيّه ١،١٢،٤٢

يا نوّ يا مامور ما احلاك من نَوّ   على ديار السِرّ نُوره تساوى ١،١٣،٤٢

~ 42~

Ibn Sbayyil

Muṭawwaʿ! What's all this sound and fury?[477] 42.9.1
Over a year, you spend a paltry seven pounds and some.
All night long, your coffeepots stand abandoned;
Your only customers are Abu Zēd and Ḥnēf.[478]

Muṭawwaʿ Nifī

Hey crowing cock! You're all bluff and bluster:[479] 42.10.1
loud bombast, but no deeds anywhere found.
Where were you? Busy shuffling your turds,
when we fought the fast-shooting al-Fuḍūl![480]
If you were a girl, I'd forgive you,
you saggy-assed lowlife![481]
You rewarded my favors with treachery:
I lost you between my tent and al-Khayf mosque.[482]

Muṭawwaʿ Nifī

I swear to God, we owe it to the door,[483] 42.11.1
the key and the lock's wooden teeth.[484]

Ibn Sbayyil

Too late! Why did one of us not get up 42.12.1
to close it? Lock and key are strong.

Muṭawwaʿ Nifī

What a wonderful rain cloud, at the Lord's command, 42.13.1
its lightning resplendent over the lands of al-Sirr.[485]

~ ٤٢ ~

هــذي بـروقـه تِشْـتِعِل كِنّها ضَوّ   مِن عِقْبه الوِدْيان صارت تَعاوَى ١،١٤،٤٢

~ 42~

Ibn Sbayyil

Those flashes of lightning have set the sky ablaze: 42.14.1
valleys will roar with thunderous torrents.

~ ٤٣ ~

يا ابنْ سبيّل ماش دايمٍ عوافي   سِمِعْت لي عِلْمٍ وَرا الضِلْع حدّه ١،١،٤٣
كانه وِكيد الشرْق ما هوب صافي   كم ذَود حربي يجيبه نِكِدّه
والحضر صابهم البَلا والخفافِ   جاهم علوم وبَدْوُهم مِسْتِرِدّه
هَيلا عليكم يا الحضير الضعافِ   كم ابنْ عمٍّ لك بِلحْيه نِشِدّه
ولّا انت يا عِيد الركاب الملافي   كافيك فِنجالٍ علينا تِمِدّه ٥،١،٤٣

يا سمير ما عندي لهرْجك مَلافي   دُوادي ما هي علومٍ مسِدّه ١،٢،٤٣
علوم الطَراقي يا العقول الخفافِ   لا تتْبِعه يا سمير تقلْعَك شدّه
كانه وِكيد العِلْم ليّه مكافي   عيال الرِشيد اللي خذوها بحدّه
بضياغِمٍ ما ثمّنوا لِلقُوافي   يتْلُون ابو مِتْعِب على وِرْث جدّه
كم طاح في رَوجاتِهن مِن سنافِ   عِقْب التّدجّر والطَنا ترْب خدّه ٥،٢،٤٣
كم ضاع بين قْيونها والخفافِ   من غيتْران ومجْهمٍ مِن يعِدّه
واتلا نقايصكم عذي الرَهافِ   ما له حلال و لا بعيرٍ يشِدّه
خلّي طريحٍ بالمعاره خلافِ   ابو دليقٍ فوق مَتْنه يكِدّه

~ 43 ~

Smēr of the ʿUtaybah tribe

Hey, Ibn Sbayyil, things are out of kilter: 43.1.1
unsettling news from the mountain's edge.[486]
If true, the East is heading for a rough time of it.[487]
Toiling at our wells were the enemy's camels;[488]
Villagers, hit hard, trembled in fear
when told to pay, but most Bedouin did well.[489]
Watch out, feckless sedentary weaklings:
we've pulled many of you by the beard![490]
Since you provide comfort to tired camel riders, 43.1.5
pass me a cup of coffee–that'll do![491]

Ibn Sbayyil

Smēr, I will provide no comfort for your ranting,[492] 43.2.1
empty chatter that serves no purpose;
Gossip carried by mindless travelers:
don't believe a word—the devil take you!
And if it's true, the loss will be made good
by al-Rashīd's men, victorious warriors
From al-Ḍayāghim, who attack without giving heed,
led by Abū Mitʿib, true scion of a noble house.[493]
When they charge, the field is littered with corpses: 43.2.5
fine men who paid for their bluster and swagger.
Countless animals, hooved or on pads, lost:[494]
magnificent herds of white and black camels.
One of the plundered is an exquisite woman:[495]
with nothing left, not even a riding camel,
Bewildered and cast out in the open,
her lovely hair draping her back.

ألا يا سِعْد عَيني ساعة انّ العِلْم لافاني وانا في بَيت ابِن هِنْدي على السَلم مْتَحِرٍّ لِه ١،٤٤
شَهَر مِن ماكَره ولا تَوانى طَير حَورانِ على بِعْد النَحايا واصْبحَن ذِرْوات يَبْرَن له
غَطا حَيد الرِدامَى مِن عَسام الخَيل عَكْنانِ واهَلْ جَوبَة وضاخ ارْجَف بهم قاع الوِطَى كِلّه
والَى واشَيب عيني يوم جا للمِلْحْ ربّانِ تَنا خوا بالطَنايا والجرَد بايمانهم سَلّه
تِقَنَّعت السِبايا بالطَنايا قصْر فَيحانِ واخَذ طَرْش الطلوح ووَرَّد البَيرَق على الحِلّه ٥،٤٤
تِهَزّا بالطَنايا ياسِيّ الكَلْب سِدْحانِ تِهَزّا بالطَنايا والطَنايا للعَدُو عِلّه
تَراكِم يا عتَيبه لابْو مِتْعِب وِرْث جِدّانِ تَحَت رِجْله ولا يِخْطيكِم البَيرق الى فَلّه
تَعَيّن يا عبَيله في مِفاصِخ نجْل الاعْيانِ الَى جَنّك فِصيحٍ يَمّ قَصْرِك وِزْبَن ظِلّه

~ 44 ~

Minī' al-Gi'ūd al-Ṣāni' [496]

What joy, this message that quickened my eye: 44.1
the news I awaited in Ibn Hindī's land! [497]
The Ḥawrān falcon soared from its nest, resolute,[498]
eyes trained on distant lands, camel troops in its wake.
Dust thrown up by horses enveloped al-Ridāmā's rocks;
at Jōbat Wḍākh the earth trembled under people's feet; [499]
Woe to the enemy when clouds of gunpowder drift;
Shammar with short swords shout battle cries with fury.[500]
Horsemen covered Fayḥān's homestead in swirling dust, 44.5
swept up Ṭalḥah's herds, and planted a banner in their camp.[501]
Lazy dog, you belittle the warriors of Shammar!
mocking those "swollen with fury," bane of the enemy.[502]
Listen, 'Utaybah, you are Abū Mit'ib's subjects of yore: [503]
his foot on your neck, his banner fluttering in your face.
Little 'Abdallah! [504] Look to the doe-eyed beauties fleeing,[505]
bereft of their robes, and to the safety of your town.

~ ٤٥ ~

عسى العِلّة تَحَدَّر عَنك يا مَرْموم الانهادِ   لعـلّه في نِفي والحَيـد والاثله مِـماسـيها ١،١،٤٥

علام الصانع اللي ما يميّز قِيله الغـادي   يعـرّضنا وِجع ظَيرٍ له اللي مِرْمِسٍ فـيها ١،٢،٤٥
هـلوانه هو تَعَوَّذ من ابليس وكَبّ الاجْوادِ   ولا ذِكْرَت لنا العِلّه ولا فَوَّه لنا فـيها
ولو هي بِنْت مِن يَثْني نَهار الكَون وطرادِ   صِبَرنا مَير بِنت اللاش ما نِصْبِر نجـازيها
كبيرٍ بَطْنها من كِثْر ما تاكِل من الزادِ   كِما خَطْو المِكون اللي ثْرِيد البَيض حاشيها
والى منها تَخَطّت مَشْيَها ما هوب مِتْقادي   كِما عَيرة فِريقٍ عَـضّ شـابيها عَـلابيـها ٥،٢،٤٥
والَى مِنها تَغَدّت واطْـلَعوها كَتّ الوادي   مجـادِلها تِطِبّ القـاع والرامي يسَوّيها

~ 45 ~

Rbayyiʿ al-ʿAbd[506]

May illness not touch you, full-bosomed beauty: 45.1.1
let it strike Nifī, al-Ḥēd, and al-Athlah and remain!

Ibn Sbayyil

Why does this dumb blacksmith, out of his depth,[507] 45.2.1
want to send his rotten old she-camel our way?
Seek refuge from Satan! Why insult honorable men?
We were not told about the illness and its causes.
If she were born to a knight who wards off the enemy,
we'd suffer it, but not the daughter of an oaf:
A paunchy bitch, busy stuffing herself with food:
dabb lizard, potbellied from porridge and eggs.[508]
If she gets to her feet, she staggers from side to side, 45.2.5
a neighborhood she-ass bitten in the neck by a horny male;[509]
After lunch, let loose, she runs free in the wadi:
her hair rubs the earth where she's thrown down and mounted.

~ ٤٦ ~

حِطّ الاخاوه يا غُمَيصاني   يا قايد البَقْرَه باذانيها ١،١،٤٦

اعْطيك شِلْوٍ مِثْل سِحْماني   تَنْبَح وَرَى القَرْيه واهاليها ١،٢،٤٦

~ 46 ~

Ibn Thaʿlī[510]

Pay the protection money, bleary-eyed villager[511] 46.1.1
pulling along a cow, holding it by the ears![512]

Ibn Sbayyil

I'll chuck you a bone, you mangy mutt:[513] 46.2.1
go bark outside the village to protect its people.

Notes

1 Q Anbiyā' 21:83–84, and Ṣād 38:41. The phrase, *yā-ṣabr Ayyūb*, is identical to the English expression, "to have the patience of Job." It is listed as an Arabic saying in al-Juhaymān, *Amthāl*, 9, 159. In this and other poems Ibn Sbayyil addresses himself directly to God with a request to lighten his burden, with reference to the Lord's servants who are named in the Qur'an as beneficiaries of His acts of mercy.

2 Similarly, the poet Muṭawwaʿ Nifī prays: "By the life of Him who dressed date palms in green and restored vision to blind Jacob." Al-Masridī, *Muṭawwaʿ Nifī*, 107.

3 Q Yūsuf 12. Patience of a different kind is advised by Mḥammad ibn Liʿbūn: "Riders, you are not on your way to bring Joseph to Jacob" (*yā-rakb ma sirtū bi-Yūsif li-Yaʿgūb*), i.e., "tarry for a moment until I have prepared my message for you to carry." Al-Faraj, *Dīwān al-Nabaṭ*, 109.

4 Cf. Q Ṭā Hā 20:11, Shuʿarā' 26:10, Naml 27:8, Qaṣaṣ 28:30, Nāziʿāt 79:16, where Moses observes a fire in the sacred valley of Ṭuwā and where God calls to him and instructs him to teach Pharaoh a lesson. In each case the verb "to call, cry" (*nādā*) is used, as in this verse. In the Qur'an it denotes the commencement of direct communication between God and one of the prophets, as when Job loudly calls God (Q Anbiyā' 21:83) or Jonah (Q Anbiyā' 21:87 and Qalam 68:48).

5 Q Anbiyā' 21:87, *Dhū l-Nūn*, lit. "the man of the whale," i.e., the prophet Jonah (Ar. Yūnus). The poet Muḥammad al-ʿAbd Allāh al-Qāḍī from ʿUnayzah makes a similar appeal with reference to the prophets: "I suffer the misery of Job and the tribulations of Jonah" (*w-bī ʿillat Ayyūbin w-ghirbāl Dhā n-Nūn*). Al-ʿUbayyid, *al-Najm al-lāmiʿ*, 78.

6 Q Naba' 78:80, "We taught him [David; Ar. Dāwūd] the making of coats of mail (*labūs*) for you to fortify you against your violence." In heroic Nabaṭī poetry the same root (*l-b-s, labisa* "to wear, dress") is used for a Bedouin knight dressed in a coat of mail: *malbūs*, pl. *malābīs*. Q Sabā' 34:10: "'We taught him [David] to forge iron'" (lit., as in this verse, "'to make it soft'"). It is already a common topos in pre-Islamic poetry, e.g., the line of Bashāmah ibn ʿAmr, "'And double mail coats of David's weaving–see how the sharp swords ring as they smite them!'" (*wa-min nasji Dā'uda mawḍūnatan / tarā li-l-qawāḍibi fihā ṣalīlā*). Lyall notes that the story "was widely spread in pre-Islamic Arabia, and 'mail-coats of David's weaving' is a stock phrase." *Al-Mufaḍḍaliyyāt*, 1, 89; 2, 27, 29.

7 David and his son Solomon (Ar. Sulaymān) are paired in the Qur'an, as here. God subjected (*sakhkhar*, in this Nabaṭī verse, *ṣakhkhar*) powerful winds to Solomon's command (Q Anbiyā' 21:81, Saba' 34:12, Ṣād 38:36).

8 This change to third person might be part of deliberate ambiguity about who is the subject of this poem, see next note.

9 'Urqūb was a man of the 'Amālīq (the Amalekites of the Bible, named as one of the early tribes to speak Arabic) in Yathrib, later Medina, who promised his brother a share of his date harvest, but kept postponing until the dates had reached the last stage of ripeness, *ruṭab*. He then cut off the date bunches and kept them for himself. Hence the saying *mawāʿīd ʿUrqūb*, "'Urqūb's promises," i.e., insincere promises made with the intention to string someone along; also, *akdhab min ʿUrqūb*, "more mendacious than 'Urqūb" (al-Maydānī, *Majmaʿ al-amthāl*, 1, 367–68); al-Juhaymān, *Amthāl*, 8, 260. The proverb occurs in a verse by 'Alqamah al-Faḥl (Jacobi, *Poetik*, 41); and in Ka'b ibn Zuhayr's "mantle" poem in praise of the Prophet Muḥammad: "She took the promises of 'Urqūb as a model: vaporous pledges without substance" (*kānat mawāʿīdu ʿUrqūbin lahā mathalan, wa-mā mawāʿīduhā illā l-abāṭīlū*). One interpretation is that in these verses Ibn Sbayyil expresses his fear of Muḥammad ibn Rashīd (see n. 249). The poet's prayers and dread of an unnamed companion (§1.10) conform to similar passages on the theme of the beloved's whims and vain promises that compound his anguish, as in the identical simile by Ka'b ibn Zuhayr (in Nabaṭī ghazals the male pronoun is used to denote the beloved). But these verses are atypical in Ibn Sbayyil's ghazals. Perhaps then, there is indeed a deliberate ambiguity that hints at the poet's apprehension about Ibn Rashīd's opinion of him. Muḥammad ibn Sbayyil comments that the poet was promised a loan for his work in agriculture but did not receive it (*Diwān*, 152).

10 In poetry the exclamation "what is the use of" (*wish khānat al-*), translated here as "why rejoice," accompanies grief at the beloved's departure with her tribe, or is an expression of general regret, as in Riḍā ibn Ṭārif al-Shammarī's verse, "Oh, so uncertain is fate (*wā khānt ad-dinyā*); many a camp has become deserted" (Sowayan, "A Poem and Its Narrative by Riḍa ibn Ṭārif al-Shammarī," 69). In poetry the words "nights" or "days" are often employed as synonyms for "inscrutable fate."

11 This verse resembles one by Fhēd al-Mijmāj: "My heart is perplexed by the Bedouin's departure; it squirms like a sick person when the hot branding iron touches his skin" (*yā-min li-galbin min shidīd al-ʿarab jāḍ / ćimā yijūḍ ilā awnas al-kayy mamrūḍ*)—referring to a common treatment in Arabia before the introduction of modern medicine (Ibn Junaydil, *Aʿlām*, 60). Also, this primeval scene of Arabic poetry could have been copied from 'Alqamah al-Faḥl's lines: "I was not aware of the coming separation until

they readied the camel train and the pack animals were strapped at dawn; / the tribe's slave girls piled the loads onto the couched animals, and the burden was fastened with red-striped cloth" (*lam adri bi-l-bayni ḥattā azmaʿū ẓaʿanan, kullu l-jimāli qubayla l-ṣubḥi mazmūmū / radda l-imāʾu jimāla l-ḥayyi fa-ḥtamalū, fa-kulluhā bi-l-tazīdiyyāti maʿkūmū*) (Jacobi, *Poetik*, 18–19).

12 Again, a noteworthy resemblance to the next verse in al-Mijmāj's poem: "By God, when the Bedouin made up their mind, and you see the small tent of the beloved struck down" (*lā w-allah illā ṣār li-l-badw niḍnāḍ, dūnik ḥajīr mghēzil al-ʿēn magḍūḍ*). And in another, well-known, poem by al-Mijmāj: "By God, when the Bedouin depart on their migrations, all strike tent and load up their pack camels" (*lā w-allh ilā shaddaw al-badw nijjāʿ, killin hadam mabnāh w-irtadd zamlih*) (Ibn Junaydil, *Aʿlām*, 60, 56). Muṭawwaʿ Nifī uses the same opening line: "By God, when the Bedouin depart and rush off, heading upcountry toward al-Difīnah" (*lā w-allah illa shaddaw al-badw ʿajlīn, ṭārīhum al-misnād yamm al-Difīnah*) (al-Masridī, *Muṭawwaʿ Nifī*, 98). But al-Mijmāj's appealing verses with scenes of Bedouin life, followed by verses extolling his beloved, do not reach the complexity, diversity, and finesse of layered construction of Ibn Sbayyil's work. In these examples, the introductory particles and asseverations—for emphasis, but also as a metrical expedient—are similar to CA *alā*. "Kneel their animals," lit. "to force the animal down and fetter its legs" (*ʿafat*, here in passive form, *ʿfit*, noun *ʿaft*; CA *ʿafata* "to bend"). When camels are thrown down (*yaʿaftūnah*) and fettered, they try to roll and kick wildly, stirring up clouds of dust on their resting place at the camp.

13 In these scenes, poets of the school of Ibn Sbayyil often use verbs with doubled roots in a way that reinforces the impression of urgency and speed, as in this verse the feminine plural *haddann* (the last consonant is doubled for metrical reason), "to strike down (the tent)," and *ṭawwan*, "to fold up (the tent)." Similarly, al-Mijmāj: "They folded up the tents and watered the animals and rushed off after their stay at the wells during the hot season" (*ṭawwaw w-rawwaw w-intawaw ʿigb migyāẓ*); "they ascended, plunged over the crest, and disappeared from view" (*shaffaw w-haffaw w-ittigaw ʿigb al-iʿrāḍ*) (Ibn Junaydil, *Aʿlām*, 61–62). Also, Burckhardt, *Notes*, 36: *shaddaw w-maddaw*, "they have broken up and are gone."

14 The same image in a line by the pre-Islamic poet Zuhayr ibn Abī Sulmā: "Slave girls fetch the tribe's camels and load them: it takes to midday amid the confusion" (*radda l-qiyānu jimāla l-ḥayyi fa-ḥtamalū / ilā l-ẓahīrati amrun baynahum labikū*) (*Sharḥ dīwān*, 164: the first hemistich is almost identical to a hemistich in ʿAlqamah's lines quoted in n. 11). Burckhardt notes the widespread presence of slaves among the Bedouin of the Syrian desert: "There are but few sheikhs or wealthy individuals who do not possess a

couple of them" (*Notes*, 356–57). And: "To every tent, or to every two or three tents, there is a shepherd, or person to attend the cattle, either a younger son, or a servant" (ibid., 181–83).

15 "Intrepid knight": *khayyāl min garribat bih*, lit. "a knight [who is lethal] to those who come close [in the attack]," a standard expression in Nabaṭī poetry.

16 A reference to the well-attested contrast between camel-raising Bedouin and (semi-) nomads who specialize in herding sheep (*shāwī*). The latter are considered less mobile and warlike than the camel nomads, and therefore inferior to them. This distinction has become a literary motif, as in the poems of ʿIdwān al-Hirbīd and their associated narratives, in a nineteenth-century setting in the Nafūd desert of northern Arabia among the tribes of the Shammar confederation. The inability of sheepherders to keep pace with their camel-raising colleagues on their migrations is a stock element of these tales, e.g., Sowayan, *Ayyām al-ʿarab al-awākhir*, 197, about al-Hirbīd's vain attempts to keep up with the camel nomads, a venture into which he is forced by his wife: "'Listen, my dear cousin, it is not that I do not want, but we cannot keep up with them; they are camel owners who go where fancy takes them, and they leave us far behind.' But she said: 'By God, I will no longer stay with you if you part ways with them.'" This was also the reason for his quarrel with other Bedouin poets that prompted the composition of his famous poem "al-Shēkhah." (*Ayyām al-ʿarab*, 215–20).

17 As in the saying "they are like Bedouin who break up camp" (*ćinnihum badwin shāddīn*), explained as "the hustle and bustle of the Bedouin's preparations for departure when their shouts mix with the noise made by the animals, creating a din that unsettles those not used to it"; it also has the general meaning of "pandemonium." The same meaning is conveyed by the expression "they are like Bedouin who water their herds at the well" (*ćinnihum badwin wārdīn*) (al-Juhaymān, *Amthāl*, 6, 175–76). Like much in this poetry, the motif's antecedents are old, e.g., it echoes the *muʿallaqah* poem of al-Ḥārith ibn Ḥillizah: "They collected their belongings in the evening, and next morning they awoke with a terrible din: people shouting and others calling back, horses neighing, and camels roaring" (*ajmaʿū amrahum ʿishā'an fa-lammā, aṣbaḥū aṣbaḥat lahum ḍawḍā'ū / min munādin wa-min mujībun wa-min taṣ, hāli khaylin khilāla dhāka rughā'ū*) (al-Zawzanī, *Sharḥ al-muʿallaqāt*, 158).

18 "Reports," lit. "it is mentioned, reported to them [by scouts or travelers] . . . with a precise description" (*yidhkar luhum . . . b-natbih*; the Najdī verb *nitab, nattab* means "to inquire about the origins, the conditions of someone or something"; *mnattabah* is said about a pedigreed horse or camel (CA *bannata*; the Najdī usage is a case of transposition of consonants). Al-ʿUbūdī, *Muʿjam al-uṣūl.*

19 Lit. "It [the eye] arrives at their lookout and surveys the scene." The plural pronoun refers to the departed tribe and may refer to the elevation's nearness to their camp, now abandoned, or it may be a synecdoche for the entire scene of separation from the beloved and her kin: the departure of the tribe, the deserted camp, the camel train disappearing over the horizon, the disconsolate poet watching from a lookout.

20 As in the saying: "One's feet walk according to the heart's inclinations" (*ʿalā naḥāyā al-galb yamshin al-agdām*), to express the driving force of inner motivation (al-Juhaymān, *Amthāl*, 4, 392). Al-ʿUbūdī, *Amthāl*, 852–53 points to a similar verse by al-ʿAbbās ibn al-Aḥnaf: "Your feet will try to run with you to the beloved, but only because it is ordered to do so by the heart" (*tarā al-rijlu qad tasʿā ilā man tuḥibbuhu, wa-mā l-rijlu illā ḥaythu yasʿā bi-hā al-qalbu*). And in the *muʿallaqah* poem of Imru' al-Qays: "You were emboldened by seeing me killed by love for you, and your belief that the heart will do whatever you order" (*agharraki minnī anna ḥubbaki qātilī / wa-annaki mahmā taʾmurī al-qalba yafʿalī*) (al-Zawzanī, *Sharḥ al-muʿallaqāt*, 15). Here the heart is merely an instrument for the beloved to exercise power over the poet-lover.

21 "Ordered [. . .] to give satisfaction (*mistaʿatbih*)," i.e., by the heart (CA *istaʿtabtuhu fa-aʿtabanī* "I asked him for satisfaction and he satisfied me").

22 Ibn Sbayyil ran a shop in the market street near his house that catered to the needs of the Bedouin.

23 This would be around four o'clock in the afternoon, when the social life resumes after a noon pause and the afternoon prayers.

24 See introduction, p. xxv, on the placid mind, *dilūh*. It has the general meaning of "mindless" in early classical poetry, e.g., in the *muʿallaqah* poem of al-Ḥārith ibn Ḥillizah: "Seeing the site empty of its former inhabitants, I cry all day with mindless abandon (*dalhan*), though crying does not bring her back" (*lā arā man ʿahidtu fa-abkī al-/yawma dalhan wa-mā yuḥīru l-bukāʾū*). Al-Zawzanī, *Sharḥ al-muʿallaqāt*, 155.

25 As in the Najdī saying: "He pulled him with all his power as a bucket is hoisted from a well" (*tallih tallat al-gharb li-rshāh*). Al-Juhaymān, *Amthāl*, 133–34.

26 Lit. "A she-camel that remained without young and therefore has a surplus of strength compared to camels with calves." In addition, it is unruly because it has not been trained for the grinding work as an animal used for traction at the well.

27 "They reckon it a hard lot to be a well-driver, and break the night's rest [. . .]. They are the poorest young men of the village, without inheritance, and often of the servile condition, that handle the well-ropes, and who have hired themselves to this painful trade." Doughty, *Travels in Arabia Deserta*, 1, 594; for similar citations, see Bräunlich, "The Well in Ancient Arabia," 515.

28 The verb *amras*, "to slip off," is used when the rope that holds the heavy bucket slips off the pulley sheave and the bucket plunges back into the well (CA *amrasa*). Al-ʿUbūdī, *Muʿjam al-uṣūl.*

29 In this verse the Arabic suddenly changes into second person address, lit. "it is as if you are urging him [the slave] and shouting to him to drive the camel as hard as possible." The poet has adopted this feature from "Bedouin" oral narrative style: this use of the second person suffix pronoun, "the -*k* of courtesy . . . projects the oral nature of the narrative performance" (Sowayan, *The Arabian Oral Historical Narrative*, 52). In the translation this idiosyncrasy has been omitted.

30 As in the early classical line: "The sides of the buckets knock against the sides of the shaft" (*taḍribu aqṭāru l-dilā jirābahā*). Bräunlich, "The Well in Ancient Arabia," 304, 505–6.

31 This line has become proverbial as an exclamation of regret and yearning for loved ones that have gone, perhaps forever (al-Juhaymān, *Amthāl*, 10, 371). Its repetitive phrasing in the Arabic—which translates literally as "loving loved ones"—reinforces the plaintive yet soothing harmony of long vowels and soft consonants that in English would sound: *yaa-ʿeen ween* ("ee" pronounced as a lengthened "ay-" in "lay") *aḥbābć illi tiwiddiin* ("ii" pronounced "ee" as in "see"). Remarkably, the lyrical note struck in the initial line is not further developed in the poem. Rather, it continues to elaborate on the second hemistich with images from the cycle of the Bedouin's seasonal migrations.

32 In al-Bulayhid, *Ṣaḥīḥ al-akhbār ʿammā fī bilād al-ʿArab min al-āthār*, 2, 203, the second hemistich reads: "Who wander to lush herbage on rain-fed pastures" (*illī ilā zāf al-ḥaya rabbaʿaw bih*).

33 A verse similar to one by Fhēd al-Mjimāj, see introduction, n. 1.

34 The space where the herds rest is covered with their droppings, which turn into dust that is scattered by the wind.

35 That is, early autumn before the last two of the seven stars of Ursa Major make their appearance.

36 The second hemistich is particularly dense in meaning. The pack camels (*zaml*) set out from Nifī to travel to lower country (*ḥaddar*), i.e., east or northeast toward al-Yamāmah and beyond toward al-Aḥsā' province and the Gulf, in order to stock up on dates and other staples, and possibly ropes and utensils. The caravan that carries the goods and chattels, women and children (*ẓaʿn*, similar in meaning to *al-ẓaʿīnah* of early classical poetry) is preceded by the armed men who lead their horses alongside their riding camels (*salaf*). This caravan heads west toward the higher ground (*sannad*) of their new camping ground on the pastures of High Najd, which usually receive a relatively greater

share of rainfall. The *ẓaʿn* is of special concern to the poet because it carries away his beloved on one of the camel chairs. He would stop her if he could, as ʿAmr ibn Kulthūm says in his *muʿallaqah* poem: "Stop the camel train before we separate, and give us a chance to speak our minds and know for sure; / stop and let me ask you if it was forced by your tribe's departure, or have you betrayed a trusting friend?" (*qifī qabla l-tafarruqi yā ẓaʿīnā / nukhabbirki l-yaqīna wa-tukhbirīnā; qifī nasʾalki hal aḥdathti ṣarman / li-washki l-bayni am khunti l-amīnā*). Al-Zawzanī, *Sharḥ al-muʿallaqāt*, 119.

37 Because the Bedouin, and with them the poet's beloved, migrated to the pastures as soon as they received these reports, leaving the bereaved village poet behind. Also, the shaykh does not tell anyone where they are headed for, see §24.27 and n. 288.

38 In this and the preceding three verses, the poet achieves the feat of squeezing in various types of rains, associated stars and seasons, and pastures. The stars mark the end of the hot season, spent at Nifī's wells, when the Bedouin set out for the pastures of early fall, *miṣfār*. They had been told that there was plenty of herbage left from the previous year's late-fall and winter rains; in that high country the moisture had been replenished by floods that occurred in late spring, close to the beginning of the hot season (*al-gēẓ*). Literally, the Arabic says "toward the end of the eclipse" (*al-kannah*), that is, the disappearance of the Pleiades from 28 April to 6 June, which traditionally signals the onset of the great summer heat (al-ʿUbūdī, *Muʿjam al-anwāʾ*, 248–50). In other words, the area had hardly been dry that year: the rains of winter were followed by the rains of late spring. The hyperbole is Ibn Sbayyil's, but the topos is also found in the work of other poets of his group. Al-Mijmāj, the poet stylistically closest to him, depicts Bedouin who at the end of summer set out in the direction where they espied distant lightning. He adds that the green in that area is mixed with plants that have held out since the rains of late spring, *ṣēf* (Ibn Junaydil, *Aʿlām*, 61).

39 Lit. "food from God's house," i.e., Mecca, for the rice is imported through the Red Sea harbors.

40 Either their calves are slaughtered for food, in which case the mother moans incessantly, or because they are not impregnated and are kept as riding camels. The incomprehensible grumblings refer to the language spoken by soldiers of a regular army, as in the line of Riḍā ibn Ṭārif, "Their grumblings resemble the speech of men wearing a red fez" (*yashdin riṭīn illī ʿalēhum ṭarābīsh*), i.e., Ottoman Turks. Sowayan, *al-Ṣaḥrāʾ*, 601, and "A Poem and Its Narrative."

41 Bedouin know the precise borders of their tribal homeland (*dīrah*), even without the use of maps. The borders of these ranges are specified in poems, together with various landmarks, often in conjunction with descriptions of thunderstorms and lands

showered with rains (as in the final verses of Imru' al-Qays's *muʿallaqah* poem), see the chapter "The Borders of the Tribal Land" in Kurpershoek, *Oral Poetry*, 4, 464–83. A horse, usually a mare, is a Bedouin warrior's most prized possession and fed with dainties (*mabrūrah*) and the best available food (see also §13.11). It is given precedence over the other members of the owner's household so that it is always in excellent shape for the hour of need, for example to overtake rustlers who drive away the camp's camels. Bedouin raiders would always try to capture the best animals on their raids, and therefore the milk of a stolen she-camel can be expected to be even more nutritious and tasty than that of other camels. Doughty notes: "They milk first for the mare and then (often in the same vessel) for the nomad household" (*Travels*, 1, 304). In early poetry the same point is made, e.g., the line of Jarīr (d. 110/729): "That is why we come well prepared: for such occasion we feed our horses milk and cover their backs" (*innā ka-dhāka li-mithli dhāka nuʿidduhā / tusqā l-ḥalība wa-tushʿaru l-ajlālā*) (Abū Tammām, *Naqāʾiḍ Jarīr wa-l-Akhṭal*, 96; Bakhouch, *La rivalité d'honneur*, 96). And the pre-Islamic poet Mutammim ibn Nuwayrah says: "He [the horse] gets the collected milk of many she-camels [. . .]" (*al-Mufaḍḍaliyyāt*, 2, 22).

42 The comparison of warhorses to birds of prey is a common one and derives from its movements, as explained in the verse by al-Dindān: "They [the horses] are like kites—pouncing, flying up, and pouncing again" (*mithil al-ḥadāyā b-mirkāḍin wa-misnādī*) (Kurpershoek, *Oral Poetry*, 1, 105); also in ancient poetry, e.g., al-Muzarrid, "When the horse is seen with the rider mounted, men say, 'A hunter's falcon!'" (*matā yura markūban yuqal bāzu qāniṣin*) (*al-Mufaḍḍaliyyāt*, 1, 165; 2, 58).

43 The horse's response to the pull of the reins is so eager that the reins seem to fold in two as its head rears and almost reaches the rider's shirt. In this position it resembles a pregnant camel's tail, which she raises to signal her unavailability to studs. The line is also a saying: "He holds his head high, like the raised tail of a pregnant she-camel" (*rāfiʿin rāsih mithl al-muʿashshir*), i.e., "he is arrogant, conceited" (al-Juhaymān, *Amthāl*, 3, 160). The same image is used for a spirited riding camel in the *muʿallaqah* poem of Ṭarafah: "And if you wish you can raise her head to the height of the saddle's pole" (*wa-in shiʾta sāmā wāsiṭa al-kūri raʾsuhā*), i.e., if he pulls the reins he makes her raise her head to the same height as the spot where the rider puts his feet on the saddle's cushion (al-Zawzanī, *Sharḥ al-muʿallaqāt*, 56; al-Tibrīzī, *Kitāb sharḥ al-qaṣāʾid al-ʿashr*, 39).

44 Cf. Ḥmēdān al-Shwēʿir's similar boast: "We dug up the well of revenge when it had over time become filled with the drifting sands of neglect. / We blew on its fire, well-nigh extinguished, until the tongues of flame shot up in a roaring blaze" (Kurpershoek, *Arabian Satire*, 117).

45 See n. 287. The image is akin to the one in which camels are shackled in battle, as in al-Dindān's line: "The camels are hobbled with iron chains and driven steadily" (*ṣikk al-jimal b-al-ḥadīd w-ʿajjalaw sōgih*), as a sign of the tribe's commitment not to yield. Kurpershoek, *Oral Poetry*, 1, 105; 4, 477n.

46 Battles are likened to markets where goods are bought and sold. In this case, brave warriors do not hesitate to risk their lives, i.e., offer them for sale, and take the life of others, i.e., buy them.

47 See nn. 179 and 417. In pitched battle, warriors would be whipped into a fighting frenzy by shouts of young women riding in an ornamental litter chair, occasionally baring their shoulders (Musil, *Rwala*, 214–15, 540–41; Hess, *Von den Beduinen des Innern Arabiens*, 53, 101). "If a girl or a woman wants to encourage her kinsmen to the greatest bravery in a dangerous fight, she does so not by words alone but also by significant deeds. So, for instance, she opens her dress on the breast as a sign of how she means to reward the bravest. Her lover then forgets everything else, only wishing not to perish in the fight, in order that he may enjoy the promised reward, Musil," *Rwala*, 223. The presence of women at the battle also encourages the tribe's warriors to do their utmost for fear the women will fall into enemy hands, as in early classical poetry, e.g., the *muʿallaqah* of ʿAmr ibn Kulthūm: "We prevent at all cost the humiliation of seeing the beautiful women at our side parceled out as booty" (*ʿalā āthārinā bīḍun ḥisānun / nuḥādhiru an tuqassama aw tahūnā*) (al-Zawzanī, *Sharḥ al-muʿallaqāt*, 132). Similarly, before Islam women would accompany warriors to battles to ensure they would fight to death rather than flee in ignominy. For the same reason some Bedouin tribes would drive their most prized herds into battle, see Kurpershoek, *Oral Poetry*, 1 n. 16.

48 In al-Faraj's edition, *Dīwān al-Nabaṭ*, 190, the next verse corresponds to this edition's §3.15.

49 The raiders would send scouts out to reconnoiter the terrain and presence of the enemy's herds. The scout would be entitled to an additional she-camel when the raid leader divided the plundered herd. Sowayan, *Ayyām al-ʿarab*, 610, about the poet Abū Zwayyid's role as a scout.

50 If their herds graze on a distant pasture, accompanied only by a few men (*ʿazīb*), the animals are under threat of being raided by enemies. In that case, they lose no time in rallying to their assistance, chasing away the raiders, and ensuring the safety of the herd. On the other hand, they invariably return with captured animals from their own marauding expeditions, and on the raid's eve tell their herdsmen to expect good tidings, i.e., captured animals, as additions to their herds.

51 In raiding lore, singing is usually reserved for the moment when the raiders and their booty have returned to the safety of their own tribal territory. For instance, Passage of Singers (*Rīʿ al-Mghannī*) in the northern area of the Nafūd desert, is so named because when raiders of the ʿAnizah or Shammar tribes would cross it into their own territory, they would feel safe and start singing. Sowayan, *The Arabian Oral Historical Narrative*, 163. Perhaps here it is meant to glorify this tribe's undisputable superiority.

52 Among Ibn Sbayyil's love lyrics, this is one of the simplest, more in the nature of a song. It is a convention to hide the identity of the beloved and to address her as "Miss X." In poetry, the most common name used for this purpose is Zēd (CA Zayd). It is another convention to use the masculine pronoun and suffix for the beloved.

53 When the beloved is not open to amatory advances by the lover-poet the verb *ṣadd*, "to rebuff," is used (as in classical poetry *ṣudūd* or *hajr*, Bauer, *Liebe und Liebesdichtung*, 354), frequently, as here, after she has shown herself receptive to being courted. In classical poetry, this coldness of the beloved came to substitute for the physical separation in earlier poetry, *firāq* or *bayn*, due to the different migratory paths of Bedouin groups—terms that are also used by Ibn Sbayyil and other Najdī poets in a context of scenes from Bedouin life. Instead of *ṣadd*, the poet also uses the verb *agfā* (CA *qafā*), "to turn one's back," here with the meaning "to give the cold shoulder." In the latter case, in the absence of any sign of reciprocity, Ibn Sbayyil's lover-poet desists from further attempts. See introduction, pp. xxv, xxviii.

54 See n. 80 to §6.13 on the runaway camel as a metaphor for the heart that absconds to escape the dictates of reason.

55 Lit. "an old man (*ʿōd*, CA *ʿawd*) who dotes (*mihrāʿ*, CA *muhraʿ* 'anxious, eager because of anger, fear, desire') on his grandson (*ṣīb*)."

56 See n. 68 to §6.3 on the topos of hiding one's feelings and n. 67 to §6.1 on the lover's ordeal and patience in suffering.

57 §8.11 is the same verse. The lover's foolishness versus good sense frequently occurs as a theme in early Arabic poetry, as in Abū Dhu'ayb's similar line: "If you call me foolish toward you, you made me buy good sense with my foolishness. / My friends said, 'You lost in the bargain,' while I thought the opposite; who is right?" (*fa-in tazʿumīnī kuntu ajhalu fīkumū, fa-innī sharaytu l-ḥilma baʿdaki bi-l-jahlī / wa-qāla ṣiḥābī qad ghubinta fa-khiltunī, ghabantu fa-mā adrī a-shakluhumū shaklī*). *Dīwān Abī Dhu'ayb*, 185, and Jacobi, "Die Anfänge," 240–41.

58 In early Arabic ghazal poetry this topos is already part of the inventory, as in this line by ʿUmar ibn Abī Rabīʿah: "When I tell my heart that she is not worth dying for from love,

it mutinies; censure only makes it worse" (*idhā qultu lā tahlik asan wa-ṣabābatan, ʿaṣānī wa-in ʿātabtuhū zidtuhū jiddā*). *Dīwān*, 104.

59 "White in the flanks," a camel epithet to denote a hardy mount whose flanks have gone white because of the constant rubbing of the rider's feet on long journeys. Muṭawwaʿ Nifī composed a poem on a similar occasion when tribesmen of al-Fuḍūl—according to another version, al-Bgūm—stole small cattle from the people of Nifī (al-ʿUmarī, *Dīwān Suʿaydān ibn Musāʿid Muṭawwaʿ Nifī*, 19, and Poem 42.10). It is Ibn Sbayyil's only poem composed in a meter of exclusively long syllables (see Kurpershoek, *Arabian Satire*, xxxiv); and with a strophic rhyme, AAAX, BBBX, and so on, called *mrawbaʿ*. See Sowayan, *Nabaṭi Poetry*, 174, and Kurpershoek, *Oral Poetry*, 1, 65–66.

60 The poet ʿAbd Allāh al-Luwayḥān, born in Nifī, dates this poem to 1899/1900, when a number of sheep owned by people of Nifī were stolen by Bjād al-Kharrāṣ of the ʿUtaybah tribe. At that time the town had an agreement with Ṣnētān al-Ḍīṭ, a chief of al-ʿIḍyān of ʿUtaybah, to provide protection against other ʿUtaybah tribesmen (see introduction, p. xxvi, and the section with invective poetry, Poems 42.1–46.2). By coincidence, four days before the event, six men of al-Ghanānīm of ʿUtaybah had stayed at the house of Ibn Sbayyil, who had entertained them as the town's headman. He had given them provisions for the road and they had drunk milk of his sheep and goats, which according to tribal custom would oblige them to intervene in his favor in case of any misdemeanor against him by their fellow tribesmen (§§5.31–32). Indeed, al-Ḍīṭ took action and succeeded in recovering most of the animals for the owners, but a few, including one held dear by Ibn Sbayyil (§5.41), were not among them. On that occasion, Ibn Sbayyil composed this poem and sent it to al-Ḍīṭ (al-Luwayḥān, *Rawāʾiʿ min al-shiʿr al-nabaṭī*, 152–55). The story and some of the verses are also found in the manuscript of al-ʿUbayyid, *al-Najm al-lāmiʿ*, 79, as an example of the payment of protection money (*khafārah*) and its connection with the honor of the protecting tribe. According to this version, the animals were returned and the perpetrator of this violation of custom, Bjād, was killed by tribesmen of al-Ghbayyāt of ʿUtaybah.

61 Lit. "it disappeared, was lost without compensation" (CA *ṭall* "blood spilled without compensation").

62 Lit. Ḥnēf and Nāyif, i.e., the common sort; men without distinction.

63 Mārig, one of al-ʿIḍyān to whom the poet's appeal was addressed in §5.7.

64 Humorously, the poet lets the sheep make the appeal, in §5.15, and here confirms that it is answered. The verb *nakhā* means "to invoke someone's honor in an appeal for assistance by shouting the person's battle cry, *nakhwah*." "Whoever hears his own war cry

uttered by an oppressed man feels ashamed and has to give help or else lose his reputation." Musil, *Rwala*, 503.

65 Shāliḥ al-Ḍīṭ, the shaykh of al-ʿIḍyān.

66 Possibly, the feat described in §§5.57–63 is the imagined result of the poet's appeal, which his messenger conveyed to al-ʿIḍyān. It is hard to determine whether the poet is entirely serious in his appeal. As often with Ibn Sbayyil, the poem has a certain tongue-in-cheek quality.

67 On the lover's ordeal as a test (*imtiḥān*) of his devotion and stamina in the pursuit of passion, see introduction, pp. xxii, xxviii and its n. 63. The topos is identical in classical poetry, as in the verse of Khālid ibn Yazīd, "Do not put my endurance to the test by turning away from me, because my capacity for enduring has reached its limit" (*lā tamtaḥin ṣabriya bi-l-hajri fa-innanī ṣifrun mina l-ṣabrī*). Bauer, *Liebe und Liebesdichtung*, 395. See also §13.5.

68 The lover-poet's struggle to hide his feelings is found in similar words in early poetry, as in this verse by al-Nābighah al-Dhubyānī: "I kept it a secret for you that I spent my night at Jamūmayn sleepless, that my grief is twofold, one hidden, the other known" (*katamtuka laylan bi-l-Jamūmayni sāhirā, wa-hammayni hamman mustakinnan wa-ẓāhirā*) (Jacobi, *Poetik*, 88; al-Nābighah al-Dhubyānī, *Dīwān*, 63). In early poetry it is also used for any secrets of a person who dissembles his true sentiments, as in the *muʿallaqah* poem of Zuhayr ibn Abī Sulmā: "He kept it a secret hidden inside, never showing his real intentions before he embarked on his plans" (*wa-kāna ṭawā kashḥan ʿalā mustakinnatin / fa-lā huwa abdāhā wa-lam yataqaddamī*) (al-Zawzanī, *Sharḥ al-muʿallaqāt*, 83). In §14.2.47, the same word, *mistikinnah*, is used for the poet's beloved, "well-hidden inside her tent."

69 See introduction, p. xxv, §§26.14 and 33.6, and nn. 133 and 346 on the poet's compulsive need to divulge his secret.

70 The metaphor of love as a disease of the heart is ubiquitous in early poetry, e.g., the line by ʿUmar ibn Abī Rabīʿah: "My love for you makes me sick at heart, and wildly roused at the dove's mournful cooing" (*wa-ḥubbuki dāʾun li-l-fuʾādi muhayyijun, safāhan idhā nāḥa l-ḥamāmu l-hawātifū*). *Dīwān*, 256.

71 That is, only reunion with his beloved can cure his illness, as in the saying: "My heart has a bleeding wound and can only be cured by the one whose arrow hit it" (*galbī ṣiwīb w-ad-dwā ʿind rāmīh*) (al-Juhaymān, *Amthāl*, 10, 259–60) and as in the poetry of the eighteenth-century Najdī poet Rumayzān ibn Ghashshām (see Kurpershoek, *Arabian Satire*, xiv): "She is my ailment, misery and disease, and she is the cure that revives the dead," Sowayan, *al-Shiʿr al-nabaṭī*, 458. See also n. 123 and §27.1.3 on the heart in

agony. An early example of this trope occurs in a poem by al-Marrār ibn Munqidh: "She is my malady and my healing rests with her; if she withholds the cure, it will be hard to overcome" (*wa-hya dāʾī wa-shifāʾī ʿindahā / manaʿathu fa-hwa malwiyyun ʿasir*) (*al-Mufaḍḍaliyyāt* 1, 159; 2, 54). Majnūn Laylā expresses it in a more direct way: "As remedy for my love of Laylā, I treat myself with Laylā, as the drinker of wine treats himself with wine" (*tadāwaytu min Laylā bi-Laylā ʿani l-hawā, kamā yatadāwā shāribu l-khamri bi-l-khamrī*) (al-Farrāj, *Dīwān Majnūn Laylā*, 160).

72 The beloved is referred to conventionally in the masculine form, but in the translation the feminine form is used.

73 Reading from the Qurʾan was commonly recommended as a treatment for the sick. The contrast with the preceding risqué line is amplified in the next verse. According to al-Faraj, *Dīwān al-Nabaṭ*, 204, the words *ḥarf al-Grān*, "letter of the Qurʾan," is a reference to the letter *nūn* and its likeness to the line of the beloved's eyebrows. The poet's choice of image may stem from a visual experience, i.e., an illiterate's fascination with a beautiful script, hence his comparison of the beloved's eyebrows to a line of elegant writing (communication from Saad Sowayan).

74 Lit. "Before it melts and meets its fate at the appointed time." Bauer, *Liebe und Liebesdichtung*, 373, mentions the topos of the lover's "melting away," *dhāba*, and his "rotting away," *baliya*.

75 A standard epithet of the beautiful lady without mercy: she is pitiless in letting the poet-lover yearn for more, as in the phrase of Abū Tammām: "You have no compassion for me" (*lasta tarḥamunī*). Bauer, *Liebe und Liebesdichtung*, 451.

76 On the parallels between §§6.10–12 and lines by ʿUmar ibn Abī Rabīʿah, see introduction, p. xxii, and nn. 82 and 129 below. See also his lines: "If you kill me for no reason, wrongly, as a desperate lover I tell you: / 'Enjoy murdering my pure affection, my fondness of you received a whipping with my own flesh and blood!'" (*fa-in taqtulī fī ghayri dhanbin aqul lakum, maqālata maẓlūmin mashūqin mutayyamī / hanīʾan lakum qatlī wa-ṣafwu mawaddatī, fa-qad sīṭa min laḥmī hawāki wa-min damī*) (*Dīwān*, 345). Or al-Walīd ibn Yazīd, "It is not fair to treat a lover cruelly" (*wa-laysa ḥaqqan jafāʾu man waṣalā*) (Jacobi, "Al-Walīd ibn Yazīd," 148). The line of Ibn Sbayyil is also a popular saying to describe the torments lovers inflict and suffer (al-Juhaymān, *Amthāl*, 7, 179–80).

77 The shape of a cross is used as a brand by the Mzēnah tribe of the Ḥarb confederation; the three vertical rings by al-Maghāybah tribe of the Ṭalḥah division of al-Rūgah of ʿUtaybah. This original simile is quoted as indicative of Ibn Sbayyil's deep and sympathetic knowledge of Bedouin life.

78 A well-known saying: "Wounds call for revenge" (*al-jrūḥ gṣāṣ*), i.e., "one should respond in kind" (al-Juhaymān, *Amthāl*, 2, 195). ʿUmar ibn Abī Rabīʿah lays down the same rule: "[Kill him without ado or torture] Or seek compensation by killing the killer, as detailed in the scripture, 'a life for a life'" (*aw aqīdī fa-innamā l-nafsu bi-l-nafsi qaḍāʾan mufaṣṣalan fī l-kitābī*) (*Dīwān*, 45); and: "Whoever slays a soul as you do is an oppressor and must pay for his injustice with his own life. / As revenge and redress, I only wish for you, so why not bestow that kindness on me?" (*man yaqtuli l-nafsa kadhā ẓāliman, wa-lam yuqidhā nafsahū yaẓlimī / w-anti thaʾrī fā-talāfay damī, thumm ijʿalīhi niʿmatan tunʿimī*) (*Dīwān*, 389).

79 Such condescending kindness shown by the beloved is the minimum ʿUmar ibn Abī Rabīʿah hoped for: "My darling, please be kind, don't you see how sadness floods my eyes with tears?" (*yā-khalīlu rbaʿan ʿalayya wa-ʿaynāya, min al-ḥuzni tahmulāni btidārā*). *Dīwān*, 161. Also in §19.10.

80 Lit. "she made my camel run away," also §4.6; i.e., instead of bestowing kindness on him, she keeps him in suspense. In ghazals the heart, or soul, is frequently compared to a runaway camel that escapes from the unpalatable commands of reason (*ʿagl*) and will only be retrieved by its owner if he shows understanding for its feelings and if the beloved has some compassion for the heart's predicament. See also §13.35 and §29.13. An early equivalent for it is the line by Ṭarafah: "Salmā ran away with all of your sound judgment, a prey that she ensnared in her nets" (*wa-qad dhahabat Salmā bi-ʿaqlika kullihī, fa-hal ghayru ṣaydin aḥrazathu ḥabāʾiluh*) (Jacobi, *Poetik*, 128). The idea of the heart as runaway camel is expressed in this verse of Abū Dhuʾayb, with *ʿāzib* in lieu of *dhihīb*: "The yearning cooing of the dove stirs my heart, and reawakens in me a distant love that lay dormant" (*tadʿū l-ḥamāmatu shajwahā fa-tahījunī, wa-yarūḥu ʿāzibu shawqiya l-mutaʾawwibū*) (*Dīwān Abī Dhuʾayb*, 23, and Jacobi, "Die Anfänge," 241–42). Here the meaning of *ʿāzib* is "distant, alone, and lonely." Also, "camels that pasture far away," as in al-Nābighah's similar verse, "the night brought back to me the distant herd of my sorrow, and from all sides increased its size twice" (*wa-ṣadrin arāḥa l-laylu ʿāziba hammihī / taḍāʿafa fīhi l-ḥuznu min kulli jānibī*) (*Dīwān al-Nābighah al-Dhubyānī*, 9). In contemporary Bedouin vocabulary an *ʿazīb* is a herd of camels that spends the night or several nights at pasture at a considerable distance from the camp before rejoining the main body of the group (see n. 50). In all cases the same notion is expressed: the poet-lover's heart, or memory of his beloved, disappears into the desert and he goes in search of it, or it is brought back to him (*ʿazaba ʿanhu ḥilmuhu*, "his common sense left him"; *kalaʾ ʿāzib*, "untrodden pasture"; *aʿzabu ʿan al-māʾ*, "far from water"; *ʿazabat al-ibl*, "the camels were far away in the pastures and did not return to camp at night,"

Ibn Manẓūr, *Lisān al-ʿArab*, 2923–24). The verb in Abū Dhu'ayb's line, "it stirred me," *tahījunī*, is common in *nasīb*-style opening lines. In Nabaṭī poetry the equivalent is the verb *hāḍ* or *hayyaḍ* (CA *hāḍa*, "to renew the pain," as in *hāḍa al-ḥuzn qalbah*, "his heart was afflicted by grief time and again; to be stirred; to bring someone in the mood for composing poetry," Hess, *Von den Beduinen*, 143); it refers to the cause of the poet's mental agony and indicates the onset of emotions that transport him into a mood conducive to the composition of poetry. See Kurpershoek, "Heartbeat," 42.

81 A variation on the saying "One's own life is of more immediate concern than even one's parents" (*al-rūḥ abdā min al-wālidēn*), used as an excuse for people's tendency to give priority to their personal interests. Al-Juhaymān, *Amthāl*, 3, 207.

82 The same image occurs in §35.11: the poet-lover as servant slave who likes to be ordered around. It is a common motif in the seventh-century ghazal poetry of ʿUmar ibn Abī Rabīʿah, e.g., in the verses: "Don't slay me; seeing me so devoted in my love for you, should convince you that killing me is wrong. / I said to her, 'By God, I am at your beck and call, obedient in word and deed'" (*fa-lā taqtulīnī in ra'ayti ṣabābatī, ilayki fa-innī lā yaḥillu lakum qatlī / wa-qultu la-hā wa-llāhi mā ziltu ṭā'iʿan, lakum sāmiʿan fī rajʿi qawlin wa-fī fiʿlī*) (*Dīwān*, 304). This is a measure of the poet-lover's *ṣabr*, "patience," but in ghazals it more often denotes his willingness, or even eagerness, to submit to his ordeal (*imtiḥān*), defined by Ibn Qayyim al-Jawziyyah as *ṣabr ʿalā ṭāʿatih*, "obedient and uncomplaining subservience to the beloved" (Kuntze, "Love and God," 164; Bauer, *Liebe und Liebesdichtung*, 397). Endurance and the condition of a slave are merged into absolute obedience in the literal sense, *al-samʿu w-al-ṭāʿatu*, as mentioned by Bauer, *Liebe*, 413, and in §§18.17–18 in the double sense of not obeying the censurers, *mā asmaʿ wlā aṭīʿ*, and complete obedience to the beloved, *li-mā yahwāh sammāʿ wi-mṭīʿ*. The same topos is found in two verses that end a poem by another member of Ibn Sbayyil's "school," ʿBēd ibn Hwēdī: "How I wish to be her slave, servant, and captive; a slave called Frēḥān, always at her beck and call. / My desire is to slave away for them, from 'good morning' to my last gracious bow, 'a pleasant evening.'" (*yā-lētinī b-al-milk lih khādimin w-asīr, w-abā ajhad luhum b-al-nōb w-ismī Frēḥān / abā ajhad luhum b-al-nōb w-aṣabbiḥih b-al-khēr, w-amassīh ʿafw rḍāh ilā jā massayān*) (Ibn Junaydil, *Aʿlām*, 153). In a related simile, the slave is the one who unjustly treats the camel used to draw water, while for the poet-lover this camel's plight symbolizes the pain inflicted on his heart, see §34.3 and n. 397.

83 This poem does not appear in any published collection.

84 In poetry the Arabic *hashīm* is used with the meaning of "dead wood, debris" that is carried by a torrent and swept on the sides of the torrent bed. Often, as in this verse, it is a metaphor for persons who meet a deadly fate, and not necessarily because of a flood.

85 "Go raving mad," lit. "to throw voices," i.e., "to speak in a loud voice and incoherently to oneself," also §§14.1.23 and 40.15.

86 A common image in ghazals, see also §§8.8 and 19.3.

87 In Najdī poetry the pigeon-toed walk is considered very becoming to a girl. Hence the saying "The person wanted to walk like a pigeon and then forgot how to walk" (*baghā mashy al-ḥamāmah w-ḍayyaʿ mashyitih*), i.e., unable to attain the best, he became also incapable of what he knew until then. Al-Juhaymān, *Amthāl*, 2, 43.

88 An ancient stereotype followed by these poets, as in this line on the delights of fatty calves by ʿBēd ibn Hwēdī: "If she lifts the hem of her robe you behold calves, like boiled white fat, cooked to perfection" (*w-al-sāg ćinnih yōm yarfaʿ l-al-aslāb, ʿaṣbin ghashāh al-fōḥ w-agfat niyātih*). Ibn Junaydil, *Aʿlām*, 168. See n. 89 below.

89 The same image in §§19.19, 20.4, 34.10, 36.17, and introduction, nn. 33 and 34; see also n. 295 to §26.6. As in classical poetry, the posterior and breasts are not considered taboo parts of the human body and are eulogized without inhibition. Ideally, the buttocks should slope and bulge like a sand hill and their soft, cushiony flesh should quiver when in motion. This imagery even occurs in relatively recent recorded oral narrative that accompanies late-nineteenth- and early-twentieth-century Bedouin poetry, as when the poet Abū Zwayyid flirts with Mikīdah, the daughter of Jamʿān al-Ghēthī of the Shammar tribe: she wades into a pool of water and pulls her dress up to the knees, and he follows her while she lowers her veil, as described by Ibn Sbayyil in §§26.8–9, and "watches her behind quiver like this [the narrator makes a hand gesture]," *w-yishūf rdūfahā tihtazz hā-l-lōn* (Sowayan, *Ayyām al-ʿarab*, 614); the same vocabulary is used in classical poetry for "to quiver" and "to sway gently," *irtajj* and *ihtazz* (Bauer, *Liebe und Liebesdichtung*, 311). Because of its size, a heavy behind is a source of female pride, but it comes at the price of discomfort while walking, because it weighs down on the beauty's gait and shifts the body's center of gravity toward the rear (in classical poetry *radāḥ*, "heavily laden, endowed with heavy behind and hips," ibid., 310). This somewhat impedes her forward motion, as graphically pictured in §26.6, and explained by the classical poet al-Mutanabbī: "They marched away with a delicious damsel, with a posterior so heavy that she had trouble getting to her feet" (*bānū bi-khurʿūbatin lahā kafalun, yakādu ʿinda l-qiyāmi yuqʿiduhā*) (*Dīwān Abī l-Ṭayyib al-Mutanabbī bi-sharḥ Abī l-Baqāʾ al-ʿUkbarī*, 1, 297). The bosom is not quite as voluminous and cannot serve as a counterweight. But buttocks and breasts do engage in a tug-of-war when the lady's movement stretches her skirt on both sides, with each part fighting for the scarce space left by their mass of flesh, see introduction, p. xix. In general, early classical ghazals, like Nabaṭī poetry, show a pronounced preference

for accumulation of fleshy tissue at the hind parts and the calves (§7.8) , as in the verse of ʿUmar ibn Abī Rabīʿah: "The brass rings that clasp her calves sink into the flesh, if she goes easy, and almost snap; / and if she gets up, with a lot of effort, her behind almost bursts through" (*wa-yakādu l-ḥijlu min ghaṣaṣin, ḥīna tastaʾnīhi yankasirū / wa-yakādu l-ʿajzu in nahaḍat, baʿda ṭūli l-buhri yanbatirū*) (*Dīwān*, 184); a similar verse, ibid. 254. Such a woman is called a *khadallajah* (ibid., 279, and *al-Aghānī*, 104) (*khaḍalat al-sāq* is "(a woman) with round, fleshy calves," *Dīwān*, 155). An extreme case is found in the *muʿallaqah* poem of ʿAmr ibn Kulthūm, where the beloved's hips are too broad for her to move through the doorposts, and whose voluminous haunches drive the poet crazy with desire (*wa-maʾkamatan yaḍīqu l-bābu ʿanhā / wa-kashḥan qad junintu bihī junūnā*) (al-Zawzanī, *Sharḥ al-muʿallaqāt*, 121). See also al-Marrār ibn Munqidh, "the flesh of her inner thighs on one side knocks against that on the other," "she has to keep her legs apart when she comes toward you, large in body, heavy in the hips, swaying hither and thither as she moves," a plumpness of her leg that bursts "seventy *mithqāl*s of silver molten for her anklets," (*al-Mufaḍḍaliyyāt*, 2, 53). It is clear from imagery and vocabulary that this physical ideal is derived from the Bedouin's delight in camels that fatten on lush spring pastures, which are a symbol of fertility as much as rain-laden clouds, which are also compared to fat and pregnant she-camels—in this *muʿallaqah* poem and in the verse of latter-day Bedouin poets like al-Dindān and Ibn Batlā, see Kurpershoek, *Oral Poetry*, vols. 1 and 3.

90 Elsewhere, Ibn Sbayyil contrasts the arrival of the Bedouin at the start of the hot season, when herbage has dried up, with the springtime of his heart when the sight of Bedouin belles makes the shoots of his heart burst into flower. See §§2.15, 24.3, and introduction, n. 29.

91 The word for "seductress" is *al-salhamah* (from CA *aslahamma*, n. *muslahimm*, which means "sickly and pallid, either from unknown disease or as if paralyzed because of a troubled mental condition"). It corresponds to classical poetry's beauty with sickly eyes, as in Ibn Khafājah's line, "because of sick-eyed gazelles sleeping at the Euphrates" (*li-marḍā jufūnin bi-l-Furāti niyāmī*), Schippers, "Nasīb and Ghazal in 11th and 12th Century Arabic and Hebrew Andalusian Poetry." The lowering of the eyelids gives the beloved a deceptive, languid look while she takes aim with the arrows of her glances. See details in Bauer, *Liebe und Liebesdichtung*, 283–96, and n. 143.

92 It is not clear in the Ibn Yaḥyā MS what the exact word is: *ṭalʿ* "fruit" is one guess.

93 A *khidhrūf* (CA *khudhrūf*) is a spinning top made of a piece of wood that produces a humming sound. Al-ʿUbūdī, *Muʿjam al-uṣūl*.

94 Lit. "Against me, he dresses in hide as if he dons his cloak." The image also occurs in other poetry, e.g. Ibn Shuraym, *Diwān Sulaymān ibn Shuraym*, 48. Here the enemy faces the poet-lover dressed in a skin or hide (*jild*), presumably of a wolf or other wild animal, i.e., he harbors evil intentions. The poet speaks about the backbiter and informer (*wāshī*) who seeks to expose the lovers' feelings and rouse public opinion against them with the aim of ruining their affair.

95 Lit. "circling (in the air) at a distance," as in the popular saying "I owe it to the beloved to keep her identity and whereabouts secret [to be seen circling at a different, distant place] when speaking to others" (*ḥaggih ʿalayy ilya harajt abʿid al-ḥōm*), in order not to provide ammunition to those who are lying in wait to expose them and create a scandal that will destroy their affair and reputation. In general, it refers to one's discretion and concern to protect the secrets of friends and loved ones (al-Juhaymān, *Amthāl*, 299–300). The topos is an ancient one, as in the line of ʿUmar ibn Abī Rabīʿah: "When I enter a quarter I look the other way, on purpose, so as not to give away my amatory purpose" (*lammā dakhaltu manaḥtu ṭarfī ghayrahā, ʿamdan makhāfata an yurā rayʿu l-hawā*) (*Dīwān*, 17); and "In love I cling to roundabout ways, wary of people's watchful eyes, staying far from her dwelling" (*wa-innī la-ahwāhā wa-uṣrafu jāhidan, ḥidhāra ʿuyūni l-nāsi ʿan baytihā ʿamdan*) (ibid., 104).

96 "Follies of love," whereas in CA *ʿajrafah* means "rudeness in speech." In this poetry the plural *ʿajārīf* also means "words exchanged among lovers" and "the incomprehensible but delightful babbling of a toddler"; and as in the saying "a little boy, but the time of his spontaneous, charming behavior has ended," i.e., "little boys grow up" (*ṣibayy w-zālat ʿajārīfih*). Al-Suwaydāʾ, *Faṣīḥ al-ʿāmmī fī shamāl Najd*, 2, 616; al-Juhaymān, *Amthāl*, 4, 128.

97 "When my mind is at rest (lit. broadens)."

98 Similar to a saying, "away with it, get it" (*riddih w-hātih*), in reference to someone who cannot make up his mind and gives contradictory signals. Al-Juhaymān, *Amthāl*, 3, 188.

99 The falcon has flown away and the desperate owner tries to lure it back by running in its direction, waving a cloth, and shouting. See §§37.5–6.

100 See §4.14, the same verse on the lover's foolishness.

101 It is a common topos in ghazals to curse the informer who spies on the lovers and the censurer. Often this miscreant earns no more than perfunctory mention, but occasionally poets compete to outdo others in the invention of a horrible fate for him, similar to the agonies suffered by the amorous heart in the similes employed in the *nasīb*, see introduction, p. xxii. For example, ʿBēd ibn Hwēdī's verses: "Let my censurer be struck by a lance with a long shaft and hooked blade, / the Najdī type, smooth and without blemish,

that plunges into the body and comes out at the other end" (*w-min lāminī fī ḥibbihum ji'l yihdaj, bi-mshalshilin 'ūdih ṭiwīlin rahāwī / bi-mshalshilin mā fīh tak'īb w-'ūj, samḥ al-ǵna ma' sāgat al-jibb hāwī*) (Ibn Junaydil, *A'lām*, 104; and as explained to me by Ibn Junaydil in our meetings). And Muṭawwa' Nifī: "May the children of one who blames me die from typhoid fever, or if they live, as poverty-stricken deniers of Muḥammad's prophethood" (*min lāminī bātū 'yālih ma'āwā, ḥayyin figīr w-jāḥidin li-l-nubuwwah*) (al-'Umarī, *Dīwān Muṭawwa' Nifī*, 4 and al-Masridī, *Muṭawwa' Nifī*, 78).

102 In poetry, a person in the throes of utter despair and grief is often likened to a *khalūj*, a mother camel that has been bereft of her young, and that in consequence refuses to eat, groans day and night, and behaves erratically (it has the same meaning in CA). In this verse, the poignancy is enhanced by the fact that the animal is not aware that within her sight the men are enjoying the calf's grilled entrails and liver, as a prelude to eating its roasted meat. In the *mu'allaqah* of 'Amr ibn Kulthūm the image occurs introduced by the formula of grief, *wajdī*, also common in this poetry, and the kindred agony felt by an older woman who lost her children: "My suffering is more cruel than the agony felt by a she-camel that lost her calf and keeps moaning day and night, / or the grief of a graying mother whose nine children lie buried in their graves" (*fa-mā wajadat ka-wajdī ummu saqbin, aḍallathu fa-rajja'ati l-ḥanīnā / wa-lā shamṭā'u lam yatruk shaqāhā, lahā min tis'atin illā janīnā*). Al-Zawzanī, *Sharḥ al-mu'allaqāt*, 122.

103 §§8.18–19 occur in somewhat different wording in al-Bulayhid, *Ṣaḥīḥ al-akhbār*, 2, 206.

104 This form of poetic dialogue occurs frequently in the work of the seventh-century ghazal poet 'Umar ibn Abī Rabī'ah, mostly between the poet-lover and his beloved, but also in other situations, as between the principal lady and her ladies-in-waiting (*atrāb*), with alternate lines starting with "she said," *fa-qālat*, "they said," *fa-qulna* (*Dīwān*, 265). The rhyme of this poem enhances its plaintive tone, with enough melodrama to give it a playful twist. In these verses of question and answer, the first hemistich rhyme, ending on a drawn-out, moaning *–āh*, is repeated in the poet's reply. The lengthening of vowels in such exclamations is common, as in al-Mijmāj's line, "Ah, my wound" (*wa-wā-jarḥī*), and "Ah, lovely young she-camel" (*wā-bakritāh*) (Ibn Junaydil, *A'lām*, 43, 57). Also, *gilt āh wā-waylāh min 'illati āh* and, in another verse, *āh wā-'azāh min wagtin shirīr* (al-Haṭlānī, *Dīwān ash'ār nabaṭiyyah min al-jazīrah al-'arabiyyah*, 114, 126; see next note).

105 "One like her," *ḥiliyyih* has become *ḥilyāh*. The poem echoes the *hā'iyyah* of Muḥammad ibn 'Abd al-Raḥīm al-Tamīmī, known by the sobriquet Muṭawwa' Ushayqir, a semi-legendary poet who is said to have died from lovesickness in 1601. For instance, the lines

"I bit the tops of my thumbs in despair [cf. §37.20] and said, 'Ah' from burning pain, 'Ah'; If by moaning 'Ah' my ailment were cured, I would intone 'Ah' in my mind forever" (*fa-ʿaḍḍēt min ḥirr ash-shikiyyih anāmilī / w-gilt āh min ḥirr al-mṣībah āh; w-law gōlat āh tibri mawājiʿī /ćaththart anā fī ḍāmirī gōl āh*) (Sowayan, *al-Shiʿr al-nabaṭī*, 387); and in somewhat different wording, Ibn ʿAqīl, *Kayfa yamūt al-ʿushshāq*, 394, 399, 446. The rhyme of this poem's first hemistich, *-āh*, corresponds to the classical *ḥarf al-nudbah*, the particle of lamentation, with *wā-* preceding the noun, generally with the termination *-ā* or in pause *-āh*, as here. This may correspond to the normal inflection of a verb, as *tansāh*, "you forget him/her," in line 11, or it might be slightly adapted for the purpose, as *wā-yāh*, for *wi-yyāh*, "with (regard) to him/her," in line 12, and *wa-hādhāh* for *wa-hādhā*, "and this person," in line 13. The plaintive *-āh* is amplified by the interjection *āh*, "oh!" in the second hemistich, where the poet-lover rebuts the critical observations of his self-appointed counselors. In line after line, the direct speech maintains the syntactic parallelism of *gālaw*, "they said," and *gilt*, "I said," to separate and contrast the voices of reason without discernment from the sentiment-driven logic of the poet, see introduction, n. 80 and §§4.14 and 8.11. The word for "beautiful women," *bīḍ*, lit. "white-colored, white of skin," is very common in ghazals. In this poetry it is clearly derived from *bīḍ*, the plural of *abyaḍ*, "white." But in early poetry the same meaning attaches to *bayḍah*, "egg," as a metaphor for a beautiful woman. In his commentary on Imru' al-Qays's *muʿallaqah* line, "the creamy beauty who is kept unassailable in her little tent's hiding place" (*wa-bayḍati khidrin lā yurām khibā'uhā*), al-Zawzanī gives three reasons for the comparison: it is kept safe and pure by the brooding birds; it is kept hidden from view under the parents' feathers; and its color is immaculate because it is not exposed to the elements, while its attractiveness is enhanced with a touch of a more creamy color (*Sharḥ al-muʿallaqāt*, 16–17); and a modern Bedouin poet, al-Dindān: "The white of her skin shades into olive" (*dāmlin ṣāfī ʿafārih bi-ṣ-ṣifārah*) (Kurpershoek, *Oral Poetry*, 1, 148–49).

106 "Close, amatory union with her," *lāmāh*. A proverbial saying is: "Forget her embrace with that of another" (*ins lāmah bi-lāmā*, CA *al-lā'm*, "meeting in agreement"). Al-Juhaymān, *Amthāl*, 1, 389.

107 "His beloved must resemble a banana branch, which grows from a strong stalk, is thin in the middle, but spreads out toward the top, where it bears the ripe or ripening fruit." Musil, *Rwala*, 323.

108 A much-cited popular saying about the fascination one's true love exercises on the imagination, even if one has married the maximum of four wives allowed by Islamic law (al-Juhaymān, *Amthāl*, 6, 301). The same notion is found in a poem by Nimr ibn ʿAdwān,

a poet from al-Balqā', now in Jordan, who became legendary for mourning his beloved wife, Waḍḥā, who died at a young age: "Even if the Bedouin girls were led to me in two long rows, O 'Iqāb [his son], my dear friend, I would take none but Waḍḥā alone" (*lō jann banāt al-baduw yā-'Gāb ṣaffēn, yā-khayy mā ākhidh ghēr Waḍḥā waḥadhā*); and in another poem, he swears that he would not exchange her for all girls between Najd, Tunis, and Sinjār: the girls of al-Ṣalab, the Bedouin, the settled people, the Turks, the infidels, and the Christians (Musil, *Rwala*, 193–96; see Sowayan, *al-Ṣaḥrā'*, 302–20, on the legendary nature of Nimr's poetry and narratives, discrepancies in transmission, and the literature about it).

109 It must be assumed that the poet speaks about a Bedouin beauty. Ibn Sbayyil and his neighbor Muṭawwaʿ Nifī frequently make the point that their love is doomed, if only because they are of a lower class than their beloved's Bedouin lineage, see introduction, pp. xii, xviii.

110 A frequently quoted saying, lit. "he carries his disease in the sleeve of his robe" (*nāǵlin dāh bi-rdāh*), used when speaking about someone whose pursuits or lifestyle impair his health and well-being, possibly resulting in death, but who persists in his self-destructive ways (al-Juhaymān, *Amthāl*, 2, 239, and 8, 301); also *dāhā fī rdāhā* (ibid., 3, 76), "she carries her illness in her sleeve," explained as: "she is threatened by a danger that comes from her closest relatives;" and " this district's problems are of its own making" (*dīrtin ṣār dāhā al-yōm b-rdāhā*) (ibid., 3, 114).

111 Both the words "dry riverbed, valley" (*wādī*), and "torrent(-bed)" (*sēl*), occur in versions of the poem. The hemistich is a well-known saying on the wisdom of abstaining from undue interference and allowing things to follow their natural course, especially if doing otherwise would be a vain effort (al-Juhaymān, *Aʿlām*, 9, 188). Al-'Ubūdī, gives the variant "each dry riverbed has its own torrent" (*mā yijīk min wādin illā sēlih*), and its CA equivalent "each twig has its own juice" (*li-kull 'ūdin 'uṣāraratuh*), i.e., "every bird sings its own song" (*Amthāl*, 1276).

112 A fictional name for the poet's beloved.

113 Here Bkhīt is a fictional name for the woman's servant girl.

114 The poet implies that he reaped the fruits of his carefully laid amatory designs.

115 The verb at the end of the first hemistich, *wi-rjahannēt*, is derived from the classical *arjahanna*, which among other things means "to be heavy, copious, abundant, multitudinous" (Ibn Manẓūr, *Lisān*, 1587). Here it means, "I quaffed from it to my heart's desire." See also §36.24. Her saliva is a potion with magical qualities, a point that is forcefully made in the line of 'Umar ibn Abī Rabīʿah: "If the dead were given a swig of her

spittle, after emptying the goblet of death, they would rise and walk" (*law suqī l-amwātu rīqatahā, baʿda kaʾsi l-mawti la-ntasharū*) (*Dīwān*, 184).

116 The comparison of the beloved's eyes to those of a falcon is standard in ghazal poetry. The falcon pictured here rampages with lethal effect among a flock of bustards, striking down more than one bird in his swoop: one is fatally hit (*ʿafat* "to twist, bend;" CA *ʿafata*) and another is already killed. Remarkably, the poet uses the same language to describe the beloved's onslaught as for the havoc wrought in battle by Ibn Rashīd, §23.19 ff.

117 This is one of two poems in the collection devoted to the subject of popular wisdom (the other is Poem 21). It is not typical for Ibn Sbayyil. It has only a single rhyme at the end of the line, and not a separate rhyme for both hemistichs (Poem 23, the ode to Ibn Rashīd, is the other exception), and the metrical pattern at the end of the first hemistich varies. This might point to a poem of an earlier date by another poet, but there is no evidence for it and the manuscripts ascribe it to Ibn Sbayyil.

118 "Labor and sweat" (*al-kidd w-al-kidā*), lit. "(a peasant's) toil and hardship (CA *al-kudyah, al-kudāh* 'hardship, a hard spot;' *akdā* 'to press, urge; to be hard up')."

119 As in al-Dindān's poem on drought and poverty suffered by the Bedouin: "When struck by misfortune, he endures, accepting God's decree and submitting himself to his fate" (*w-yiṣbir ʿalā mā jā min Allāh lyā ṣīb, w-yagnaʿ b-ḥukm Allāh wa-yarḍā al-migasīm*). Kurpershoek, *Oral Poetry*, 1, 141.

120 "Right, virtue" here means the duties imposed by the desert code of honor, including "meticulous adherence to the *lizūm* [lit. 'the necessary'], the obligations of hospitality and formal manners in the presence of guests and strangers." Webster, "Notes on the Dialect and the Way of Life of the Āl Wahība Bedouin of Oman," 482.

121 On the theme of the world's inequities, see Kurpershoek, *Arabian Satire*, 11, 111, 144 n. 82.

122 A bird's wing is a symbol for ambition and able resolve, as in Ḥmēdān al-Shwēʿir's verse: "He sat with folded wings, like a lice-ridden raptor" (Kurpershoek, *Arabian Satire*, 31, §11:13); and the opposite: "whoever had a wing to fly, took off" (Sowayan, *al-Ṣaḥrāʾ*, 350, 601, and "A Poem and Its Narrative," 69).

123 Sowayan interprets this verse as a metaphor for composing poetry. In this reading, "I am blown along with the winds" would mean that his words come like gusts of wind, as handfuls of seed sown by a farmer are carried by the wind (*al-Ṣaḥrāʾ*, 209). Indeed, one might see a parallel with the line of the pre-Islamic poet al-Musayyab ibn ʿAlas: "I shall send to him an ode carried by the winds" (*fa-la-uhdiyanna maʿa l-riyāḥi qaṣīdatan*) (Lyall, *al-Mufaḍḍaliyyāt*, i, 96–97). The "distressed heart" (*al-galb al-mashʿūf*) was already part of ghazal terminology in early classical poetry, as in the

line of Abū Ṣakhr al-Hudhalī: "She who made your heart suffer the agonies of passion has the power to free you from your load of troubles" (*bi-yadi lladhī sha'afa l-fu'āda bi-kum, faraju lladhī alqā mina l-hammī*) (Dmitriev, *Abū Ṣakhr*, 64). As a topos, it is akin to the lover's illness that can only be cured by the beloved who caused it in the first place, see §6.5.

124 "The burden of passion," is already mentioned in early ghazals, as in 'Umar ibn Abī Rabī'ah's verse: "Good Lord, you saddled me with a heavy load of love; good Lord, I don't have the patience and resolve to bear it!" (*rabba ḥammaltanī min al-ḥubbi thiqlan, rabba lā ṣabra lī wa-lā 'azma 'indī*). *Dīwān*, 111.

125 See §§29.1–4 for a more elaborate version of this simile.

126 "Her sweet conversation," as in the line of al-Muzarrid: "When I sported with Salmā, ah! sweet was her speech to him" (*wa-alhū bi-Salmā wa-hya ladhdhun ḥadīthuhā*) (*al-Mufaḍḍaliyyāt*, 1, 161; 2, 58). Here and in §36.22, Ibn Sbayyil gives a creative twist to the stereotyped comparison of the beloved's conversation (*ḥadīth*) to pearls or honey (Bauer, *Liebe und Liebesdichtung*, 330). The beloved is *shāḥḥ*, jealous of allowing anyone to partake of her honey.

127 The sting is the result of a poison called *dhirnāḥ*, a toxic blistering agent produced by the Spanish fly or *Cantharides* of the blister beetle family. See also n. 422.

128 This hemistich became a popular saying. It refers to the belief that the only chance of survival for a person bitten by an animal with rabies lies in keeping him awake all night. According to another version, this person was kept locked up in a dark room for forty days, the reason being that according to popular belief seeing the flicker of a distant lightning would cause him to die instantly. Given the small chance of recovering from rabies, especially after seeing lightning, the saying means that the person is virtually doomed. Al-Juhaymān, *Amthāl*, 4, 359–60. The Arabic *shāf lih*, lit. "he saw for himself," is another feature of the "Bedouin" oral narrative style, known as the "pseudo-dative," like the "*-k* of courtesy." (see n. 29, Sowayan, *The Arabian Oral Historical Narrative*, 55–57).

129 See introduction, n. 37 and nn. 76 and 78 above. 'Umar ibn Abī Rabī'ah uses the same expression: "She pierced my heart, slaying me without the use of weapon" (*aqṣadat qalbī wa-mā in aqṣadathu bi-silāḥi*) (*Dīwān*, 86). "You have killed me. How could you! I've committed no crime or sin. / Has not God, in the revelation he sent down, made very clear in a verse that leaves no doubt: / Whoever slays a soul as you do is an oppressor and must pay for his injustice with his own life. / As revenge and redress, I only wish for you, so why not bestow that kindness on me? / Appoint an honest person as an arbitrator between us, or make your own decision as to what to do. / Let's have

just one session together, in all probity, with no forbidden play. / Let me know how you feel about, by God, killing a good Muslim man." (*Qataltinā yā-ḥabbadhā antumū, fī ghayri mā jurmin wa-lā ma'thamī / w-allāhu qad anzala fī waḥyihī, mubayyinan fī āyihī l-muḥkamī / man yaqtuli l-nafsa kadhā ẓāliman, wa-lam yuqidhā nafsahū yaẓlimī / w-anti tha'rī fā-talāfay damī, thumm ij'alīhi ni'matan tun'imī / wa-ḥakkimī 'adlan yakun baynanā, aw anti fīmā baynanā fa-ḥkumī / wa-jālisīnī majlisan wāḥidan, min ghayri mā 'ārin wa-lā maḥramī / wa-khabbirīnī mā lladhī 'indakum, bi-llāhi fī qatli mri'in muslimī*) (*al-Aghānī*, 1, 205; *Dīwān*, 389–90. See also §§6.12, 28.15, and 36.10).

130 A similar line by 'Umar ibn Abī Rabī'ah: "I can't blame a soul after what happened" (*fa-lam ara lawma l-nafsi ba'da lladhī maḍā*). *Dīwān*, 356.

131 See §6.3 on the topos of hiding one's feelings, and §§15.1–5 on the subject of smoking. Here it alludes to the love hidden deeply in his chest—as deeply as a smoker desperately inhales after a long period of abstention.

132 The line has become a popular saying, meaning that it is impossible to hide one's infatuation, no matter how hard one tries (al-Juhaymān, *Amthāl*, 6, 296). "The wish to disclose is the distinguishing mark of the lover; but to protect his love he is sworn to secrecy;" he follows "an inner compulsion to reveal his secret" (Kuntz, "Love and God," 167).

133 This saying expresses the notion that there is a limit to one's endurance or patience with suffering (al-Juhaymān, *Amthāl*, 7, 254). In ghazals, the word *ṣabr* does not merely denote patience, but rather the poet-lover's resolution, stamina, discipline, and endurance in the face of pain and suffering (Bauer, *Liebe und Liebesdichtung*, 395) as part of the self-imposed ordeal caused by devotion to an unattainable ideal of passionate love, *ṭard al-hawā*. As here, the psychological anatomy of love in 'Umar ibn Abī Rabī'ah's poetry describes attempts to keep a passion secret as a cause of intolerable suffering: "I kept my passion hidden until I became worn out and ill: pity a heart that cannot endure and stand firm" (*katamtu l-hawā ḥattā baranī wa-shaffanī, wa-'azzaytu qalban lā ṣabūran wa-lā jaldā*) (*Dīwān*, 104).

134 These verses draw on the repertoire of stereotypical images that is routinely used as an introduction of polite flattering in the poet's address to an esteemed person, as here "love of (a woman) who loosens her hair." See also nn. 300 and 334 on such stereotyped noun combinations. It may refer to his wife or beautiful women in general who dream of being his wife. It simply means that he is a fine and attractive man, see also n. 154. It is a common form of address in poetic correspondence, see §§17.1.2, 17.2.13, 27.1.19, 27.2.22. This verse praises the addressee's courage and power in halting the enemy's onslaught and thereby providing gallant reassurance to the tribe's women, who shout

to the warriors and are so distraught by the fray that they forget about their veils and inadvertently let them slip. In this case, however, the addressee, Ibn Zirībān, was exactly such a tribal knight who died while fighting on horseback: see glossary.

135 See n. 41 on the custom of feeding one's horse the milk of one's best she-camels.

136 These two verses picture the terrifying onslaught of the enemy's champion knight who routs the horsemen of the opposite side—until an even greater hero, namely, the poem's addressee, bursts onto the stage to snatch victory from the jaws of defeat. See the similar verse in his next poem, §14.2.28.

137 "Shelter," lit. "center, fixed abode."

138 See §6.5, §9.14, and n. 123.

139 This extended simile is built on the way travelers in the desert would draw water from wells—not oasis wells for irrigation that are operated on a larger and more organized scale: large and heavy buckets, fixed wooden and stone structures over the well for hoisting the buckets up, teams of specially trained camels that pull the ropes as they walk up and down a path of a fixed length, and with clear markings where the animals had to turn. Travelers carried their own well equipment—principally a bucket and a beam with a wooden sheave over which to run the rope. They would use one of their own mounts to assist in pulling up the bucket, an animal not trained for this purpose. When the bucket had been hoisted up, they would shout to the man leading the camel to halt and return. In this case, the camel took the shouts and pulls as a sign to pick up the pace, wreaking havoc with equipment on which the men's life depended.

140 A popular saying in almost the same wording is *lā hūb rāyidni wlā aḥrazt arūdih,* here in reference to unrequited love. Al-Juhaymān, *Amthāl,* 6, 254.

141 See n. 78 above.

142 See introduction, p. xxii.

143 This line is quoted as a popular saying. The literal meaning is "whoever had a taste of love with a sultry, sleepy-eyed look (*al-salhamah*) will not forget," i.e., the seductive magic of the deceptive, sleepy look with lowered eyelids that has the lover spellbound (al-Juhaymān, *Amthāl,* 8, 167; see also n. 91). Obviously, never forgetting one's sweetheart is a lover's standard assertion, put succinctly by the early poet al-Marrār ibn Munqidh: "Never in all time will I forget her (*mā anā l-dahra bi-nāsin dhikrahā*), so long as a turtledove calls upon her mate!" (*al-Mufaḍḍaliyyāt,* 1, 159; 2, 54).

144 A popular saying: "Not every piece of wood lends itself to being carved into the kind of walking cane that I am looking for" (*sharhah yidī mā kill ʿūdin taʿaṣṣāh*). It denotes pickiness and a refusal to content oneself with less than the very best (al-Juhaymān, *Amthāl,* 4, 53). Its opposite is: "Any piece of wood from him will do for me as a stick" (*kill ʿaṣan*

minh tʿaṣṣī), said of an influential person whose every action or word in one's favor will be welcomed (ibid., 6, 106).

145 Lit. "my soul is hard to catch," i.e., "hard to please" (*nafsī shirūdih*).

146 See introduction, p. xxv and §38.1.

147 In a note, al-Faraj explains that *ḍimān* here means "ripe ulcers that are about to burst open" (the CA meaning of *ḍamān, ḍamānah* is "chronic disease, ailment") (*Dīwān al-Nabaṭ*, 170). The *lhūd* are ulcers caused by friction of the wooden pack saddle on the animal's skin.

148 The poem is found in the al-Rabīʿī manuscript on unnumbered pages, wedged between verses of Ibn Sbayyil's reply to this poem, pp. 106–7 of the MS.

149 Possibly, the Arabic *ḥamād*, "gravel plain," refers to al-Ḥamādah, a location in the western uplands around ʿAfīf in the tribal area of ʿUtaybah.

150 The same meaning is expressed in Ibn Sbayyil's §14.2.10: the she-camels are fully rested and have been pampered, therefore the moment has come to draw on their reserves for grueling desert marches. On the significance of the appearance of the star Canopus, see introduction pp. xviii–xix, and nn. 173 and 374.

151 Ibn Sbayyil is praised for being a *rīf*, which in Nabaṭī poetry does not mean "rural area," but "lush pasture, a pleasant place of repose and recovery" (as in §32.4); it occurs with the same meaning in Ḥmēdān al-Shwēʿir (Kurpershoek, *Arabian Satire*, 93, §22.36).

152 In his reply, Ibn Sbayyil echoes this line by using the same expression, "barebacked camels," §14.2.29.

153 Again, Ibn Sbayyil repeats this verse when he affirms that he has fitted out the camels according to these precise instructions, §14.2.30.

154 The description of Ibn Sbayyil, a peaceable villager, as a bloodthirsty desert knight shows that these chivalrous epithets are routinely used as flattering and somewhat bantering forms of address, without any relation to their original meaning. It simply means: "You are a fine and respectable fellow," see also n. 134.

155 That is, he is not interested in any other subject and is only looking for her.

156 The camels set out from Ibn Zirībān's, who set up camp in the eastern sands of the peninsula, toward the west, in the direction of Mecca, on their way to Ibn Sbayyil in Nifī. Ibn Hādi may refer to the famous chief of the Qaḥṭān (Ghaṭān) tribe. Al-Shunbul is a place in northern Syria. Like the description of Ibn Sbayyil as a redoubtable knight, the places named are routine exaggeration (*mubālaghah*). The message is: look for her in every nook and corner within the confines of the far-flung tribal world, from Yemen and Oman in the south (see §27.1.26, where Ibn Zirībān lists Najrān) to the northern fringes

of the Syrian desert, where the Arab tribal world shades off into Kurdish, Turkish, or Iranian lands.

157 Lit. "the district of Ḥusayn (Ḥsēn) and the land of the Agas," a reference to the Ottoman Turks in the Hijaz. Ḥusayn may refer to one of the Sharifs who ruled Mecca under Ottoman sovereignty. Their relatively civilized circumstances are implictily contrasted with the ways of the tribal interior.

158 The Arabic *mārtiyyāt* probably refers to a rifle of the Martini type, as in one version of the corresponding verse in Ibn Sbayyil's poem in reply, §14.2.34. In al-Luwayḥān's edition the word is *māṭliyyāt*, which was explained to me as "an Italian rifle that fires just one big bullet." It is not known who is meant by al-Ṣulṭān.

159 Bedouin and townfolk in Najd, i.e., all its inhabitants. See n. 330: its general sense is: "everywhere and with everyone in the world as we know it."

160 One raises a white flag for his benefactor. Its opposite is *sawwid allah wajhik* "may God blacken your face," said to a person who has refused to render assistance.

161 Musil, *Rwala*, 182, explains that with many tribes "it is customary to pick up a pebble from the grave of a friend and to throw it aside so as to lighten the burden. On the grave of a girl or woman they also lay the three stones, that held the kettle in which the deceased cooked in her last days." Here these stones, *huwādi*, may also simply denote gravestones.

162 *mkhaḍḍibīn al-hanādi* "Indian blades dyed, smeared with red," i.e., those whose swords drip with the enemy's blood.

163 This line is echoed by Ibn Sbayyil in his reply at §14.2.31, where he asserts that the addressee did indeed put him in a tight spot, contrary to what Ibn Zirībān claimed in this verse.

164 Lit. "to make distant the *ḥirwah*: what is expected; place where a person or animal is expected to be found" (CA *taḥarrā* "to pause in expectation, try to decide the most suitable course"); and "to throw voices," i.e., to talk as if one speaks to himself, is confused, and not in his right mind. See also §8.8.

165 An Arabic text and translation of this poem was published by me in *Arabian Humanities*, see bibliography. A pure breed for a long time, as in: "For generations (*tilādan*) they had been shot at and preyed upon at that place" (*tilādan ʿalayhā ramyuhā wa-ḥtibāluhā*) (*Dīwān Dhī l-Rummah*, 1, 538–39). The word *tilād* also occurs in the *muʿallaqah* poem of Zuhayr ibn Abī Sulmā in relation to camels given as blood money, with the meaning of "old, inherited wealth" (*tilād, talīd*) (al-Zawzanī, *Sharḥ al-muʿallaqāt*, 80). The commentary of al-Tibrīzī clarifies that the original meaning is "original, from the place where it was born" (*Kitāb al-sharḥ*, 58). Here the original meaning is intended.

166 In these two opening verses, the poet traces the swift mounts' pedigrees to famous camel breeds of two tribes at opposite ends of the Arabian interior: Ṣayʿar, a tribe at the southern extremity of the Empty Quarter on the confines of Yemen, and al-Sharārāt to the north of al-Jawf in Wādī Sirḥān, a depression that leads toward Syria.

167 Tribes from far and wide take their mounts to be sired by this thoroughbred stud.

168 They are gray because of the continuous rubbing on long trips. "The shoulder blades rub against the cushion on which the rider rests one foot while the other foot touches the spot covered by the breast girth, which holds the saddle behind the forelegs on the breastbone." Musil, *Rwala*, 298.

169 Lit. "they were never impregnated and their teats were never closed with sharp clamps to prevent their young from suckling at will." These riding camels have more strength because they have never given birth and never produced milk for calves. The teats of camels with calves are closed with sharp clamps in order to prevent their calves from suckling at will.

170 Musil, *Rwala*, 298, comments: "A good camel will utter no sound when being saddled; this is very important at night or in a dangerous territory. On forced marches, a camel is expected to listen well and to observe the country in all directions so that she can, by quick breathing, arching her spine, or by a motion of the neck, call the rider's attention to any possible danger." The same observation is made in the *muʿallaqah* poem by Ṭarafah ibn al-ʿAbd. Geiger, "Die Mu'allaqa des Ṭarafa," 367–69.

171 In the traditional division of seasons, *ṣēf* (CA *ṣayf*, "summer") and its pastures, *miṣyāf*, follow winter, and therefore coincide with what is now considered the season of spring, while *ribīʿ* (CA *rabīʿ*), "springtime," comes before the *miṣyāf*. In early June, it is followed by the onset of the hot season, *al-gēẓ* (CA *al-qayẓ*). Al-ʿUbūdī, *Muʿjam al-anwāʾ*, 166.

172 The popular saying is: "When it interlocks on the eleventh, the cold season begins" (*grān ḥādī bardin bādī*), i.e., when the Pleiades come close to the moon on the eleventh day of the Arabic month. Al-ʿUbūdī, *Amthāl*, 974.

173 The appearance of the seventh and last star of Ursa Major in early October is considered the beginning of the *wasmī* season when Najdī people pin their hopes on plentiful autumnal rains of the stars Canopus, the Pleiades, and Gemini (CA *wasmī*, "the rains of early spring," so-called because in its traces, *wasm*, the annuals shoot up later in the season). See n. 374.

174 The camel description of pre-Islamic poet Bashāmah ibn ʿAmr makes the same point: "I brought up to the saddle a camel hard as a wild ass [. . .]. She has been wandering at large in a year of good pasturage, and no slave has ever called a youngling to suck her teats" (*fa-qarrabtu li-l-raḥli ʿayrānatan [. . .] taṭarradu aṭrāfa ʿāmin khaṣībin / wa-lam*

yushli ʿabdun ilayhā faṣīlā) (*al-Mufaḍḍaliyyāt* 1, 82–83; 2, 26). And al-Marrār ibn Munqidh combines Ibn Sbayyil's verse 3–11 in two lines, for his camel "is ready to face anything" after being "trained, then allowed a period of idleness and grazing in preparation for the hour of need; nine years old or a bit more, never impregnated—not a drop was milked from her" (*rāḍahā al-rāʾiḍu thumma stuʿfiyat, li-qirā l-hammi idhā mā yaḥtadhir / bāzilun aw akhlafat bāzilahā, ʿāqirun lam yuḥtalab minhā fuṭur*), (*al-Mufaḍḍaliyyāt* 1, 149; 2, 51).

175 ʿAbdallah ibn Ḥasan ibn ʿAskar, the headman of al-Majmaʿah, well known for his hospitality. As Musil, *Rwala*, 299, explains: "Bedouin she-camels are easily scared by the shade and the rustling of palm groves, as well as by the high walls enclosing them."

176 The expression *mkhallātin luh ṭurguh* means: "he is peerless, unique in a certain pursuit." A popular saying is: "The roads traveled by so-and-so are left alone," i.e., he is so redoubtable that no one dares to waylay him. Al-Juhaymān, *Amthāl*, 5, 162.

177 Lit. "well-constructed," as in the verse of Mbārak ibn ʿAbīćih (ʿAbīkah), the headman of Gnā, a village at the southern edge of the Nafūd sands: "I built a fine house for you, strong like a fortress (*ḥaliyy al-ʿǵādi*, sg. *ʿigdah*, 'an impregnable construction') for you." Sowayan, *al-Ṣaḥrāʾ*, 430.

178 See n. 175.

179 Lit. "thrones" (CA *takht* pl. *tukhūt*), i.e., the strongest camels that carry the tribe's most precious possessions into pitched battle: the litter chairs of its nobles, maidens, and other tribal emblems. See nn. 47 and 417. Al-Rikhmān is the addressee's section of ʿIlwā.

180 He does not sleep but stays awake most of the night at the fire, ready to serve any guest who may show up.

181 §§13.11–12.

182 Lit. "You put me between the letters *qāf* and *ṣād*," for the noun *al-giṣā*, "difficult, embarrassing position" (CA *qaṣā* "distance, remoteness"). Al-Faraj, *Dīwān al-Nabaṭ*, 176.

183 The second hemistich is a proverbial saying, lit. "The leather is well-stitched and the strands of wool are stretched out and ready to be spun" (*kharzin bi-tarzin w-rāʿī al-ṣūf sādī*), i.e., everything is in tip-top shape and ready to go. Al-Juhaymān, *Amthāl*, 3, 28; al-ʿUbūdī, *Amthāl*, 461–62.

184 Lit. "products crafted by the Christians" (*shughl al-niṣārā*), i.e., firearms. In the edition of Ibn Sbayyil's grandson, this has been replaced by *mārtiyyāt*, "Martini rifles."

185 The saying is "at hand, within reach of hand" (*gaḍbin b-al-yad*), i.e., the matter is almost settled, no further difficulties are expected. Al-Juhaymān, *Amthāl*, 5, 295–96.

186 The common Najdī term for adherents of the Twelver Shiʿah Islam, *al-arfāḍ*, "the refusers," usually in a pejorative sense, as in al-Mijmāj's line, "I felt as if I had been jailed in a prison of the *arfāḍ*." Ibn Junaydil, *Aʿlām*, 62.

187 The Ottoman telegraph line reached Basra from Baghdad in 1865.

188 An expression *mʿazzī salāmāt*, used to congratulate someone, not so much for a gain but for emerging unscathed from a hazardous undertaking (al-Juhaymān, *Amthāl*, 8, 82–83). It seems the reference is to Ibn Zirībān's promise not to burden Ibn Sbayyil unduly, cf. verse 22 of Ibn Zirībān's poem. The expression "lies" should not be taken literally: the intended meaning is "your teasing," a friendly, playful reproach. "You made me haggard," in the preceding verse, is an expression already encountered in seventeenth- and eighteenth-century Najdī poetic correspondence, e.g., Khalīl ibn ʿĀyiḍ, dubbed "Muṭawwaʿ al-Maskūf" (see Kurpershoek, *Arabian Satire*, xiv): "You tired me and you have worn me out with excuses" (*atʿabtinī w-ardhētinī b-al-maʿādhīr*), Sowayan, *al-Shiʿr al-Nabaṭī*, 494.

189 Lit. a lover lies (when he says that he has repented from love) and the devil has not died (i.e., he must be on his guard against ill-intentioned meddlers).

190 Here "kin" denotes the Bedouin's "household complex" (Webster, "Notes," 478), the small group of kinsmen that migrates and camps together, called *firīǵ* (CA *farīq*).

191 Bedouin women take care of the sheep and goats and milk them. They cook behind a partition that protects the hearth from the wind, with three stones to hold the kettle over the fire.

192 At this stage of the search for the beloved, often compared to the search for a runaway young she-camel (see n. 80), more or less educated guesses are made as to her whereabouts, expressed by the word *hagwah*, "I think that, probably, most likely," as in al-Mijmāj's line about this she-camel, "My guess would be that she is at [. . .], *al-hagwat innih* [. . .]." Ibn Junaydil, *Aʿlām*, 57.

193 See Ibn Zirībān's verses §14.1.19–20, where he asks Ibn Sbayyil to report whether she is still alive. The "reward" seems to refer to the *bshārah* (CA *bishārah* pl. *bashāʾir*), "a reward given to him who announces a joyful event." An alternative reading is that the one still alive is the poet, in which case the translation is: "I am doing well and am not in need of reward from you."

194 Dūshān, singular, Duwīsh, are the shaykhs of ʿIlwā–a name that inspires fear because of their fierce, warlike reputation. One of them, Fayṣal al-Duwīsh, the indomitable chief of the religious settlement of Bedouin of the Muṭayr tribe, al-Arṭawiyyah, was the leader of the fanatical *ikhwān* when they rebelled against the later king ʿAbd al-Azīz. The second

hemistich is a popular saying. It means that one will attain his objective by any means, if possible by peaceful means, if not by force. Al-Juhaymān, *Amthāl*, 4, 389.

195 "Between them, nothing but cavalry clashes" (*mā bēnhum ġēr iṣṭfāg al-ʿawādī*), an expression used in reference to neighboring groups or nations that are in a perpetual state of enmity and warfare (al-Juhaymān, *Amthāl*, 10, 286). In a comment on this verse, al-ʿUbayyid explains that the poet advises his friend to seek refuge with al-Jiblān, another tribe of Muṭayr, who were originally a branch of the Tamīm tribe and whose battle cry was "O rider of Ṣabḥā Mountain" (*khayyāl Ṣabḥā jbilī*), hence their tribal name, which refers to a mountain (*jibal*) (*al-Najm al-lāmiʿ*, 309). There are also British reports on armed encounters between Fayṣal al-Duwīsh and Ṣāhūd ibn Lāmī, the chief of al-Jiblān, of Muṭayr in 1926, under the heading "internal Muṭayr feuds" (Trench (ed.), *Gazetteer of Arabian Tribes*, vol. 10 (Muṭayr-Qumarah), 93).

196 Lit. "Hew out a step for your feet," a popular proverbial expression (*ḥaffir li-rijlēk marāġī*) (al-Juhaymān, *Amthāl*, 2, 294–95). Climbing down and up again in the shaft of a deep well—in order to clean the bottom, fetch things that fell into it, or scoop up water if there was only a little—was a dangerous task. The stone casing was laid in such a way as to leave protrusions on which the climber could put his feet. Nevertheless, falling into a well was a frequent cause of death.

197 This second hemistich of al-Bulayhid's version of the verse reads: "Before an envious, waffling fool gets in your way." *Ṣaḥīḥ al-akhbār*, 2, 202.

198 A well-known popular saying: "Do not act on basis of surmise and guess." Al-Juhaymān, *Amthāl*, 6, 225.

199 This saying is advice to take precautions in case one encounters unforeseen circumstances, such as carrying a waterskin even if cool weather prevails. Al-Juhaymān, *Amthāl*, 9, 301.

200 A popular saying, with a different noun but the same meaning, *lik hagwitin waḥdah w-l-al-nās hagwāt*, i.e., one should take the possibility of other people having different opinions, and plans that may thwart yours, into account. Al-Juhaymān, *Amthāl*, 6, 291–92.

201 An alternative reading: "A man in distress will find no relief in groans."

202 This line is a popular saying, similar in meaning to "a host's excuses do not serve a guest as supper" (§29.23), with the added twist that the thirsty beings at the rim of the well can actually hear the water as it is stirred by the movement of the bucket at the end of the rope (al-Juhaymān, *Amthāl*, 7, 213). Also: "A thirsty person easily imagines that he hears water sloshing in a large skin" (*ywarrā l-aẓ-ẓamyān khaḍḍ al-rāwyah*) (al-Juhaymān, *Amthāl*, 9, 308).

203 Here "to drink" may refer to drinking coffee and smoking a pipe. Both are conducive to reaching the state of *kēf*, here translated as "to lift the spirits," which Richard Burton describes as "the passive enjoyment of mere sense; the pleasant languor, the dreamy tranquility." *Personal Narrative of a Pilgrimage to al-Madinah and Mecca*, 1, 9.

204 In Nabaṭī poetry, poetry about coffee constitutes a genre in its own right. As in this piece, the description of the coffee ceremony is often followed by a set of moral prescriptions, an exposé on chivalrous virtue or the lack of it, and other conventional wisdom.

205 The craving: lit. "burning sensation," as in §13.3, and in a verse by Rmēḥ al-Khamshī: "When you arrive at his place, he will lift your spirits, knowing that you crave well-spiced coffee" (*lazman ilā jītūh yiṭrib lukum kēf / w-antum ʿalā l-binn al-mubahhar miḍārīm*). Sowayan, *al-Ṣaḥrāʾ*, 414.

206 The *ʿushar* shrub, "giant milkweed" also known as "sodom apple," can reach a height of five meters, but its milky sap is considered poisonous.

207 Her pace is agitated because of her strength and energy, as in the camel description of Ṭarafah ibn al-ʿAbd's *muʿallaqah* poem, "veering from side to side she rushes forth" (*janūḥun difāqun*). Al-Zawzanī, *Sharḥ al-muʿallaqāt*, 53.

208 That is, torrents that rush down narrow wadis to devastating effect. This and other lines parody images and turns of phrase that are commonplace in poetry on themes of popular wisdom and ghazals—in fact, as much of Ibn Sbayyil's own work—but here it is done purely in a spirit of fun and jest, following the lead given by his poetical correspondent, Ibn Zirībān. Language and sound play a big part in it, and meaning is secondary. For example, the rhyme is almost identical for both hemistichs: *-āshī* and *-āsh*. The fourth line's hemistichs end with the words that have the same meaning, *balā shī* and *ʿalā māsh*, "for nothing," which could be taken as the motto of the piece. Some words are slightly transformed for the sake of rhyme, for instance the final *-ī* of the last word, *māsh*, "nothing"; the rhyme word of the next line's first hemistich, however, is correct: *māshī*, which means "walking." In the sixth line, the first rhyme word is *ḥāshī*, which means "young camel," while the rhyme word at the end of the line is *inḥāshī*, where again the final *-ī* is added to *inḥāsh*, which means "to scram, run away." The comic effect of the melodramatic lines 6 and 7 is reinforced by an alliterative repetition of the rhyme's consonant, *shīn*: *ḥāshī, ḥarbash, ḥāshī, inḥāshī, kharfash, ḥāshī, khrāshī, ʿakkāshī*.

209 Lit. "beauty" (*zēn*), as in the expression, "I swear that everyone loves a thing of beauty" (*anā ashhad in al-zēn killin yiḥibbih*). Al-Juhaymān, *Amthāl*, 10, 52–53.

210 Grass cutters were among the poorest in Najdī society, see Kurpershoek, *Arabian Satire*, xv, 61, §18.2.

211 The etiquette of hospitality requires the host to let his eyebrows jump from joy at the unexpected arrival of guests.

212 In a poem's initial lines, the camel rider, generally the poet's messenger, is often accompanied by a troop of riding animals, see §14.1.1 for a humorous exaggeration of the number. The swift mount is contrasted with a camel that toils all night drawing water from a well for the irrigation of date palms or other crops, driven up and down the walkway by a slave—an image of degrading humiliation in the view of the Bedouin, see §2.20 and §34.2. In this piece the "message" is no more than an appendix to the camel description. In fact, the verses as such are the message: an acknowledgment of lines sent to Ibn Sbayyil by the addressee.

213 The names of male camels often end on *-ān*, e.g., Ḍabyān. Hess, "Beduinennamen aus Zentralarabien," 6.

214 They were sired by a famous stallion whose owner demanded a stiff price. They were spared from being impregnated and bearing young: their strength was reserved for arduous desert travel.

215 Al-Hīsh, possibly Wādī al-Hīshah is meant, a torrent bed that runs into Wādī al-Sirdāḥ in the province of al-Quwayʿiyyah in the tribal land of Bargā of ʿUtaybah.

216 See n. 168.

217 It was explained to me that the shadow is cast by Thahlān Mountain, which towers over the town; see further al-Shaʿrāʾ in the glossary of names and places.

218 The topos of a camel herd driven away by raiders riding their hardest, as a simile for the lover's stress and spleen, is developed into an extended simile in Poem 33. It is also the opening line of Poem 34. The same image is found in three verses by ʿBēd ibn Hwēdī, followed by the marker *ʿalēk*, "because of you," and a description of the beloved: "My heart is being torn as plundered camels are driven away, a herd of fine animals divided among the rustlers, / The pride of tribesmen who came in pursuit with flying banners, and when they caught them all hell broke loose: / Amid war cries the raiders threw down all they carried, and blindly fled into the wilderness" (*yā-tall galbī tall khaṭw al-wisāyiǵ, shimlūl dhōd w-shaʿtharōh al-mishāfīǵ / fīhum shifāḥah w-igtifōhum biyāriǵ, w-laḥǵ aṭ-ṭalab wi-ḥẓūẓihum b-at-tuwāfīǵ / ṣāḥaw ʿalēhum naṭṭalaw b-al-ʿalāyiǵ, w-min ghēr biṣrin jannibōh aṭ-ṭuwārīǵ*) (Ibn Junaydil, *Aʿlām*, 164–65). His son Ibrāhīm ibn ʿBēd ibn Hwēdī no longer bothered with the details of the extended simile and abbreviated the image by turning the beloved herself into a raider, that is, the raider of the poet's heart: "A pristine maiden who surprised my unsuspecting heart with a raid" (*ghirwin dahaj ghirrāt galbī bi-ghārih*) (ibid., 180).

219 In the second hemistich the Arabic *yilūʿūnih... talwīʿ* is an example of the use of the absolute accusative (*mafʿūl muṭlaq*) that is a manifestation of narrative techniques, in this case the use of "morphological echo and rhyme" (Clive Holes, *Dialect, Culture, & Society in Eastern Arabia*, 3:453–54). The frequent use of such devices is in itself testimony to Ibn Sbayyil's easy-flowing, narrative style of poetry.

220 "Miserably," lit. *ʿalā fālihum*, means "as destiny would lead them" (CA *faʾl*, "a good omen," but here it obviously has the sense of "they are on their own without any help in sight").

221 "The valley of seduction," *wādī al-ghayy*, see introduction, p. xxi. In Nabaṭī poetry *ghayy* is related to *hawā*, "love," mostly as an imaginary affair and a game pursued through poetry. In a playful manner, *ghayy* has the connotation of "seduction, rapture," but the connotation of "sinful" is added to spice up the game, not in the condemnatory fashion of the pre-Islamic poet al-Ḥādirah's line: "You are the sons of a woman given to sinful lust (*ghayy*), as people maintain" (*antum banū l-marʾati llatī zaʿama l-nāsu ʿalayhā fī l-ghayyi mā zaʿamū*). *Al-Mufaḍḍaliyyāt*, 1, 48.

222 A well-known expression: "He twists the rope and loosens the knot" (*yaftil w-yingiḍ*), here used in reference to one's unpredictable, arbitrary behavior; or to someone who twists his own plans while untwisting the plans of others, shrewd and resourceful (al-Juhaymān, *Amthāl*, 9, 283). It is also a quality of a mighty shaykh or despot, as in §23.12.

223 On the subject of complete subservience to the beloved and "religious" expressions of obedience, see §6.14 and n. 82.

224 Markets and prices are common metaphors for the poet to elaborate on the store he sets by his beloved, as in ʿBēd ibn Hwēdī's verse, "They said, 'Sell your love!' but I cling to it: if love were for sale at the market, I'd buy it," (*gālaw tibīʿ al-ḥibb w-anā ghalāwī, al-ḥibb law yijlab bi-sūgin sharētih*) (Ibn Junaydil, *Aʿlām*, 133). "From Cairo's gates to Mecca (*al-rīʿ*)": the poet's grandson who published this poem in the *dīwān* explained to me that the rhyme word *al-rīʿ*, "narrow passage, defile," refers to Mecca. "The plural of *rīʿ* is *rīʿān*, and 'the people of the defiles' (*ahl al-rīʿān*) from the Bedouin tribes were feared by pilgrims. When the pilgrims reached the narrow mountain passes (*al-fijāj*) after al-Ṭāʾif they would rob and plunder the pilgrims on their way to Mecca" (al-ʿUbūdī, *Muʿjam al-uṣūl*, 399).

225 The Arabic root *r-w-m* emphasizes the strength of feeling. The verb *rām, yirūm*, "to be strongly attached," refers to the emotional attachment to a child or young that comes with suckling it. If the calf is not taken away from the cow immediately after birth, the cow will withhold its milk unless approached by the calf. A she-camel that is separated from her young after she has smelled it will become unmanageable. Therefore, it also

denotes a desperate feeling of bereavement, and, as in this verse, an unbearable longing after separation from a beloved being. Al-ʿUbūdī, *Muʿjam al-azwāj fī al-turāth*, 140.

226 Lit. "someone who is broad-bellied (*kbārin dfūfih*, in reference to a big, older camel)." "Strong enough to endure," lit. "to have the strength" (*gawā*).

227 The rhyme makes use of a feature proper to the Najdī vernacular: the "*ghawa* syndrome," that is, the rearrangement of syllables when the second consonant is a guttural (*ḥ*, *ʿ*, *kh*, *gh*, *h*), so that *gahwah*, "coffee," is pronounced *ghawah* (Clive Holes, "The Language of Nabaṭi Poetry," 3.3.1; see also Sowayan, *Nabaṭi Poetry*, 150, for its effect on scansion). In this poem it is used for the end rhyme of §§19.2 (*mḥadhūfih*), 19.4 (*mkhaṭūfih*), 19.8 (*mʿarūfih*), and 19.13 (*mkhalūfih*). The feature is also used for metrical purposes in Poems 3, 7, 13, 25, 42.3, 42.9, and 42.10.

228 A proverbial saying: "I cry like a toddler who has just been weaned (*abćī bćā wirʿin ʿan al-dēd maftṭūm*)" (al-Juhaymān, *Amthāl*, 1, 33 and 9, 198). The infant's mother has died and it has been given to a foster mother (the verb *ʿājā*, noun *mʿājāh*, the infant is an *ʿajī*; CA *ʿājā*).

229 A saying: "He behaves like someone who lost his way during night travel because he cannot find the right star; someone who has lost his bearings, is confused, goes about things in a haphazard, inconsistent way" (*sarā sary manjūm*). Al-Juhaymān, *Amthāl*, 3, 260; al-ʿUbūdī, *Muʿjam al-anwāʾ*, 272–73.

230 ʿUmar ibn Abī Rabīʿah presents a similar image of indifference: "She said, 'Die from your disease or spend your life seeking remedy; we have nothing to offer to you'" (*qālat bi-dāʾika mut aw ʿish tuʿālijuhū, fa-mā narā laka fīmā ʿindanā farajā*). *Al-Aghānī*, 1, 202; *Dīwān*, 81.

231 See §7.12; introduction, p. xix and nn. 33, 34, 62; translation, nn. 89, 295, 413.

232 See §7.12; introduction, p. xix and nn. 33, 34, 62; translation, nn. 89, 295, 413.

233 "Gentleness is needed to make love work" (*mā yistuwī ḥibbin b-layyā libāgah*) is a Najdī saying (al-Juhaymān, *Amthāl*, 7, 214) (CA *labaq*, *labāqah*, "elegant apparel; gentle, refined, friendly conduct").

234 This hemistich is a version of the saying: "Love reveals itself in telltale signs" (*al-ḥibb bayyinātin muwārīh*) (al-Juhaymān, *Amthāl*, 2, 242). The hemistich is also listed as a proverbial expression (ibid., 245–46).

235 The Arabic *yālih*, *tālih*, are conjugations of the verb *walah*, "to yearn, desire" (CA *walaha* "to hanker, long for").

236 "Aficionado," *ʿīdī*, "used to doing something repeatedly, experienced."

237 These verses are adduced as illustration for the proverb "if a camel sheds wool [if it is in bad condition], it grows anew" (*al-ḥalāl wubrah, tiḥitt w-tiṭlaʿ* [or *tinbit min jidīd*]), used

to console someone who lost his possessions, i.e., one day you may be down on your luck and some other time things will go your way. Al-Juhaymān, *Amthāl*, 2, 307.

238 This is a standard topic in "wisdom poems," and therefore more common in the work of a poet primarily concerned with society and morality, like Ḥmēdān al-Shwēʿir, e.g., in his verse "I swear to God, it was Mnīf who said to me: You are only appreciated in your prime" (Kurpershoek, *Arabian Satire*, 15, §5.1).

239 A *ṣāʿ* is a measure variously given as nine liters or three kilos, or three *midd* of wheat. A *thimīn* is a small measure: one-eighth of a *midd*. As such it is used metaphorically in ghazals, e.g., "compared to my misery, the suffering of Job is no more than a quarter of a *thīmīn*," i.e., practically nothing. Al-ʿUbūdī, *Muʿjam al-tijārah wa-l-māl wa-l-faqr wa-l-ghinā*, 60. See also §34.7.

240 A similar meaning is conveyed in the saying: "From the head [i.e., by meeting face to face] and not in writing on paper" (*min al-rās walā l-girṭās*), on the time-honored wisdom of meeting in person as the most reliable way to bring clarity in a matter. Al-Juhaymān, *Amthāl*, 8, 169.

241 A generally accepted notion, e.g., the poet and chief of al-ʿIjmān tribe, Rākān ibn Ḥithlēn (1814–92), "after such treatment one cannot stay" (*min ʿigb dhōlā ma bhā lī gaʿādī*). Ibn ʿĀqīl, *al-ʿIjmān wa-zaʿīmuhum Rākān ibn Ḥithlēn*, 135.

242 The Bedouin used a torch to follow the traces of rustlers at night. It consisted of a kettle filled with firewood carried by two men holding the chains fastened to the kettle's handles, while the fire was kept burning by a third man who picked up dead wood on the way (Hess, *Von den Beduinen*, 102). In his explanation of the verse, al-Faraj comments: "If camels were stolen at night, the pursuing party would light a torch and carry it in a big pot attached with ropes to two camels in order to follow the traces of the raiders; this was called 'the torch of the shaykh.'" (al-Faraj, *Dīwān al-Nabaṭ*, 198).

243 Hunters would approach game in the late afternoon, with the sun at their backs, and the ostriches would flee in the other direction, casting shadows so long that one ostrich would seem to run in the shadow of the ostrich behind it. The same motif is common in ancient poetry, e.g., in the *muʿallaqah* poem of Ḥārith ibn Hillizah: "[the ostrich] heard a faint sound and ran from fear of a hunter approaching in late afternoon, not long before sunset" (*ānasat nabʾatan wa-afzaʿahā al-qun / nāṣu ʿaṣran wa-qad danā l-imsāʾu*). Al-Zawzanī, *Sharḥ al-muʿallaqāt*, 156.

244 Camels easily shy at dark objects that unexpectedly come close to them, such as trees, walls, and shadows, see n. 175. In this case, rags are thrown at them to scare them.

245 For scenes at the well, see also introduction, nn. 31, 32, and translation nn. 27, 139, 212. This image is very popular with poets of High Najd. For instance, Fhēd al-Mijmāj opens a

poem: "My heart is tugged at like a heavy bucket from a well, when some men pull it up and others catch it" (*ya-jarr galbī jarr dalw ilā mīl, dhōlā yijirrūnih wa-hādhāk yalgāh*). Ibn Junaydil, *Aʿlām*, 47.

246 On a major expedition, raiders would make their final attack on horses, drive away the camels stolen from the enemy, and then count on a train of pack camels (*zaml*, led by camel drivers, *zimāmīl*, sg. *zammāl*) to meet at an appointed time and place in the desert to supply them with water and other needs. In this case, one or both of the groups went astray and the appointment was missed. The raiders knew that the enemy was at the nearest well and that if they wanted to avoid falling into their hands they had to make a long march with hardly any water left in their skins—an ordeal that the exhausted horses and the weaker camels would not survive; and losing water on them would cause the entire group to perish. Therefore, their only chance of survival was the one depicted here: leaving behind anything that would encumber their all-or-nothing dash through the waterless desert, in the blistering heat of midsummer, symbolized by the stars that "spark summer's fire" (see n. 38), to the faraway well. Only the strongest of the stolen camels would serve their purpose—the other animals were left to their cruel fate, standing motionless in the quivering heat, like "scarecrows."

247 The Arabic word for "curly tresses" (*ʿathākīl*, "tangled") originally denotes the date bunches of a palm tree: their profusion and density are likened to the wild tumble of a girl's hair, as in the *muʿallaqah* poem of Imru' al-Qays: "Her pitch-black tresses stream down her back, in a profusion as dense as the tangled growth of a date palm's bunches" (*wa-farʿin yazīnu l-matna aswada fāḥimin / athīthin ka-qinwi l-nakhlati l-mutaʿathkilī*). Al-Zawzani, *Sharḥ al-muʿallaqāt*, 22; al-Tibrīzī, *Kitāb al-sharḥ*, 17.

248 In the version of al-Bulayhid, *Ṣaḥīḥ al-akhbār*, 2, 204, the verse reads: "Either I wait for them in vain, year after year, or I go in search of them, or their camels suddenly appear."

249 Though it is beyond dispute that this poem in praise of Muḥammad ibn Rashīd, the emir of Ḥā'il and the most powerful ruler in Najd in the second half of the nineteenth century, was composed by Ibn Sbayyil, the circumstances are not clear. It represents a major effort in a style and on a theme that are rather uncharacteristic in his oeuvre. What prompted him to do so—desire or fear—is hard to tell. Admiration pure and simple is the least likely explanation. The poem itself is perhaps the most reliable source, and in §23.43 the poet makes a pitch for being rewarded generously by the prince. On the other hand, Ibn Sbayyil was not known for soliciting financial rewards and may have included the verse because the prince would expect it and not doing so might be considered arrogant (a similar question arises with regard to the poet Ḥmēdān al-Shwēʿir: see Kurpershoek, *Arabian Satire*, xix, 138 n. 10). According to one story, one of the lieutenants of Ibn

Rashīd had threatened him and beaten him so severely that one of his hands remained paralyzed for the rest of his life, forcing him to compose this ode, as Ibn Junaydil maintains in his introduction to Muḥammad ibn Sbayyil, *Dīwān*, 15. In a later piece, not included in a published collection, Ibn Sbayyil speaks well of Muḥammad ibn Rashīd's successor (Poem 43.2 and n. 493). It is also said that when a delegation from Nifī visited the court in Ḥā'il, the prince sarcastically asked about the whereabouts of Ibn Sbayyil and why he had not joined the group to pay his respects. The prince's choice of words was derogatory: "How are things with your poet, the ladies' man" (*wish lōn shā'irkum, abā l-ḥrayyim*)? When his words were reported to Ibn Sbayyil, he realized that the ruler was not well disposed toward him and that it would be advisable to humor him with a poem in praise of his achievements. Another insulting nickname given to Ibn Sbayyil was 'Bēlah, "Little 'Abdallah," see §§42.5.1 and 44.8.

250 See introduction, n. 8.

251 These five are enumerated in the closing verse of Q Luqman 31: knowledge of the time of resurrection, the arrival of rains and sustenance, what is in the wombs, what a soul will acquire tomorrow, and where a person will die. The seventeenth-century Najdī poet Jabr ibn Sayyār (see Kurpershoek, *Arabian Satire*, xiv), employs the same language and image as Ibn Sbayyil in his next line: "A man whose intelligence penetrates what remains invisible" (lit. "the haunches of affairs"; *w-min lih bi-a'yāz al-ma'ānī biṣīrih*), Sowayan, *al-Shi'r al-nabaṭī*, 489.

252 Cf. §14.2.39 by Ibn Sbayyil on the use of the telegraph in his time.

253 For the Najdi saying *yaftil wa-yingidh*, see also n. 222. "He twists a rope and then unknots it again," i.e., someone who keeps changing tack, undoing his own earlier work (al-Juhaymān, *Amthāl*, 9, 283). Here it does not denote arbitrary and capricious behavior, as in §18.12, but the cunning and power that enable the ruler to carry out his own schemes while undoing plans laid by the enemy.

254 Lit. he gallops like an intractable camel that runs away with the loads on its back (*rithū'*) if it senses that the load is sliding and is getting out of balance—a common metaphor for a situation that becomes unsettled and deteriorates.

255 Al-Qaṣīm is an important province of Najd, a few hundred kilometers to the north of Riyadh, with major towns like 'Unayzah and Buraydah.

256 In Arabic there is a play of words: he conquered their homeland (*dārhum*) and the place where they sought refuge (*midārhum*), when he routed them (*dārhum*, CA *adār*).

257 A powerful tribe in the eastern part of Central Najd and a frequent target of Ibn Rashīd's raiding expeditions, as described in travel diaries, e.g., those of Charles Huber, *Journal*

d'un voyage en Arabie, 1883–1884 (*Journal of a Voyage in Arabia*) and Julius Euting, *Tagebuch einer Reise in Inner-Arabien* (*Diaries of a Journey inside Arabia*).

258 Thirb is a well where Ibn Rashīd surprised Muṭayr and took three hundred of their camels in 1894/95. The Ottoman governor of the Hijaz province suggested launching a military expedition against Ibn Rashīd, who refused to return his booty to Muṭayr, but Sultan Abdalhamid was on cordial terms with Ibn Rashīd and merely advised him to abstain from such depredations in the future (al-Haftā' and al-Shāṭirī, *Ta'rīkh qabīlat Muṭayr*, 183–87, which quotes these verses by Ibn Sbayyil). The episode is also told in the manuscript of al-ʿUbayyid, *al-Najm al-lāmiʿ*, 1, 130–31, who writes that the delegation of Muṭayr was fobbed off by the Ottoman governor of Medina, with the argument that the attack took place close to the borders of Ibn Rashīd and therefore outside his jurisdiction.

259 The despoiled Bedouin asked him for some of their camels to transport their women, children, and other dependents.

260 Here Ibn Sbayyil echoes the sentiment of another sedentary poet, Ḥmēdān al-Shwēʿir, when he says about the Bedouin: "A dog that scampers when you throw a stone at it, but if you throw a bone it will follow you forever" (Kurpershoek, *Arabian Satire*, 125, §30.19).

261 "Swollen with fury" (*ṭanā*): there might be an allusion here to a nom de guerre of the Shammar tribe, to which Ibn Rashīd belonged, "those swollen with fury" (*al-ṭanāyā*); see also n. 500 and §44.6.

262 This boasting of the horrors inflicted on the enemy's womenfolk echoes the line of the seventh- and eighth-century poet Jarīr in his duels with al-Akhṭal: "The war waged against you by our Qays tribe made your women lose their fetus, either because they were disemboweled or they miscarried from terror" (*wa-qad qadhafat min ḥarbi Qaysin nisā'ukum / bi-awlādihā minhā baqīrun wa-muʿjalū*). Abū Tammām, *Naqā'iḍ*, 67; Bakhouch, *La rivalité d'honneur*, 74.

263 In early Arabic poetry the same image is used to express the absolute power of the victor, as in al-Nābighah al-Dhubyānī's line: "So many wives lost their husbands, and so many children became orphans" (*yā-rubba dhāti ḥalīlin qad fajaʿna bihī, wa-mu'tamīna wa-kānū ghayra aytāmī*). Jacobi, *Poetik*, 78; al-Nābighah al-Dhubyānī, *Dīwān*, 106.

264 For the eventuality that they have to plead with him for their lives and possessions, they try to think of anything they did or said that might incline him to relent.

265 This time-honored method of inspiring fear and obedience through wanton and unpredictable violence (the *baṭsh* of modern Arab dictators) is succinctly expressed in the *muʿallaqah* poem of Zuhayr ibn Abī Sulmā: "Defiant when wronged, he promptly retaliates with his own violence; and he will wrong others even if he is not oppressed

by anyone" (*jarī'in matā yuẓlam yu'āqib bi-ẓulmihi / sarī'an wa-illa yubda bi-l-ẓulmi yaẓlimī*). Al-Zawzanī, *Sharḥ al-mu'allaqāt*, 84.

266 Lit. "through his stamp" (*mihir*, CA *muhr*). He decides on reward and punishment himself, not on basis of what he is told by courtiers; that is, he is a true ruler, not one who exercises power through the manipulation of confidants and is manipulated by them.

267 See the comment in n. 249 on the reasons that might have impelled the poet to include this heavy hint at a reward for his poem.

268 It is a common topos to compare a ruler's generosity to rich pastures, e.g., Ḥmēdān al-Shwē'ir in his poem of apology to Ibn Mu'ammar: "For pasture I would migrate to Muḥammad ibn Mu'ammar and not bother to go in search of grassy plains" (Kurpershoek, *Arabian Satire*, 93, §22.36). See also §27.1.18 and n. 151.

269 Lit. "only a little remained of it," similar to the phrase in Abū Nuwās: "Passion of love wasted him away and left almost nothing" (*lam yubqi l-hawā illā aqallī*), Bauer, *Liebe und Liebesdichtung*, 375; and Bashāmah ibn 'Amr: "whom death has all but overtaken" (*qad adrakahu l-mawtu illā qalīlan*), *al-Mufaḍḍaliyyāt*, 1, 87; 2, 27. Dh'ār ibn Mishārī ibn Rbē'ān (Rubay'ān) was a member of the family of shaykhs of al-Rūgah division of the 'Utaybah confederation in whose tribal land Nifī is situated. As a poet he was principally known for his verses on the coffee ceremony and its related social values, as was his father Mishārī.

270 Cf. the verse by 'Bēd ibn Hwēdī al-Dōsirī, "My heart is like a wadi struck by drought, because of them—dead wood without any green" (*galbī 'alēhum lōn wādin sanāwī, hamīd ma talgā al-khaḍar fī nbētih*) (Ibn Junaydil, *A'lām*, 133). The bitter apple, or colocynth, is one of the plants with the greatest resistance to drought.

271 See also §§2.15–17, 7.18, 32.6. In early classical poetry the same metaphor of the heart's drought is used, as in Abū Dhu'ayb al-Hudhalī's verse: "After you went to live elsewhere, the land where you left me is ravaged by drought, its moisture and fertility gone." *Dīwān Abī Dhu'ayb*, 23.

272 One might think of the strands of wool in different colors that are woven into the tent's inner sides.

273 A common phrasing in poetry, as in §14.2.14, "Some . . . and others" (*dhōla . . . w-dhōla*); "This one . . . that one . . ." (Kurpershoek, *Arabian Satire*, 105, §26:10–11). And Muṭawwa' Nifī, when asked to compose a poem by five women huddling around a fire, three girls and two older women: "Let it be this one here, together with that one; the one there give her respite [from the fire of Hell], and that one, as well as that one," (*la'all hādhī hī w-hādhī bi-hādhī, w-hādhā timahhal hī w-hādhī w-hādhīk*) (Ibn 'Aqīl, *Ḥadīth al-shahr*, 199).

274 See §2.1 and n. 10 for the expression "what is the use of" (*wish khānat al-*), rendered here as "Alas."

275 In the Bedouin division of the seasons, springtime (*ribīʿ*) refers to the first rains after the hot season, also called *wasmī*, see n. 173.

276 Similar scenes are described in relatively recent Bedouin poetry, such as the conversation between a wayfarer who reports on the places irrigated by rains and the poet Ibn Batlā, followed by the poet's instructions: "First thing in the morning, dear fellows, water your animals! As we are going to migrate, ready your pack camels!"; and in another poem: "I have seen it for myself: If you want to migrate to Najd, now is the time! Najd has wrapped itself in a cloak of flowering herbage." Kurpershoek, *Oral Poetry*, 3, 143–61.

277 The tribe's men ride ahead on their camel mounts, while their mares trot alongside. The mares are only ridden on short stretches, as when they charge or chase the enemy, so as to keep them fresh and not to wear them down.

278 Lit. "the drinker of the grasses." In Arabic, the same verb is used for drinking and smoking. This detail is a sure sign that the poem predates the Wahhābī rule of the *ikhwān* (see introduction, n. 8), who prohibited smoking, as happened in earlier phases of the Wahhābī movement: "The atrocities which the Ikhwan committed against innocent people who were merely 'guilty' of smoking tobacco [. . .]" (Habib, *Ibn Saʿud's Warriors of Islam*, 37). The Wahhābīs called tobacco (the Turkish word *titin*) "the urine of Satan" (Hess, *Von den Beduinen*, 112). Doughty says: "The Bedouins love well to 'drink' the fume of a strong leaf till the world turn round, yet will they say, after the Wahaby doctrine, 'Tobacco is *bawl iblīs*, the devil's water.'" And, "they all dote, men and women, upon *tittun*, tobacco. [. . .] Bedouins will abjectly beg tobacco even of their poor tribeswomen. [. . .] Tobacco is this world's bliss of many in the idle desert [. . .]" (*Travels*, 1, 289, 356).

279 When there is sufficient herbage and the heat is not too severe, the camels stay at their pastures (*ʿazīb*), returning every five days or so to the camp and the wells to be watered. Guarded only by a few shepherds, these herds are at a far remove from the camp and therefore vulnerable to raids, see n. 50.

280 I was given different interpretations of this line by Saudi informants, but the general notion is that of freedom amid plenty: the horses are left to trot around without any inhibition.

281 Lit. "the news report reached its full length," i.e., " a crisis, when friend becomes enemy, things threaten to get out of hand" (Sowayan, *al-Ṣaḥrāʾ*, 439). It is also a proverbial saying (*waggaf al-ʿilm ṭūlih*) "when push comes to shove, a crisis point is reached, the true state of affairs comes out under pressure, and no aspect remains hidden" (al-Juhaymān, *Amthāl*, 9, 51).

282 Similar in meaning to the saying "When all cut off their business relationships" (*yōm inn killin min ʿamīlih tibarrā*), i.e., when the relations between two or more groups have reached such a state of tension that even old and trusted partners can no longer deal with each other to service the needs of customers in their respective groups as before (al-Juhaymān, *Amthāl*, 9, 314). In the hemistich, the translation "old friends" refers to "men who belong to different tribes or groups and have a customary relationship of trust that enables them to do business in a friendly way." Usually, this is a relationship (called *ʿimlah*) between a Bedouin and a farmer or sedentary trader, as between Ibn Sbayyil and his Bedouin customers, who were each other's *ʿamīl*. For instance, the Bedouin and the farmer would exchange their produce, such as dates and wheat for butter (as in §32.1), or camels used for traction at the well for irrigation (Sowayan, *al-Ṣaḥrāʾ*, 363). A popular saying is: "Everyone transfers money through his agent" (*killin ynāgil b-ad-darāhim ʿamīlih*), in reference to the practice of paying someone to write to his counterpart in another town to pay a certain amount of money to someone there, because of the insecurity of the desert roads and the risk of the money being stolen if transferred in cash (al-Juhaymān, *Amthāl*, 6, 145–46). In a more general sense *ʿamīl* means a trader who provides credit to a farmer until harvest time—a period of anxiety for the peasant, whose labor may be in vain for many reasons beyond his control, as graphically illustrated in poetry (Ibn Junaydil, *al-Sānī wa-l-sāniyah*, 19; and Kurpershoek, *Arabian Satire*, 133).

283 It was explained to me that the chief, mounted on his horse, moves the hem of his shirt as a sign to attack. Normally, mounted warriors would attack the enemy in a coordinated manner: the function of *al-middib* (from CA *muʾaddib*) was to keep them in line and not allow anyone to rush off before all were ready. But if some wavered, an impatient and daring warrior might give his animals the spurs, and thereby force the others to follow (Sowayan, *al-Ṣaḥrāʾ*, 344 and 422). Waving the hem of one's shirt is also an urgent distress call in the desert and a request for assistance to people seen in the distance, if one is alone and cannot count on his tribe's rescue team (*al-fazʿah*, as in the expression "there is no one for him to wave to as a sign to come to his rescue," *mā lih min al-fazʿāt mūmī shilīlih*) (al-Juhaymān, *Amthāl*, 7, 156). Related sayings are: "Just waving your shirt's hem at him will see him off" (*yakfīh nafḍ al-shilīl*); and al-ʿUbūdī adds that in a general sense it may mean: "there is no one who waves his shirt's hem," *mā fihā mūmī shilīlih*, i.e., "there is no one at all" (*Amthāl*, 1230, 1775).

284 The language conveys the sense of action and excitement: *ḥawwaw w-raddaw b-awwalih wi-gharō lih*, see n. 13.

285 I.e., the herds were not accompanied by armed men who could offer resistance, but were only guarded by defenseless shepherds.

286 The shaykh or leader of the raid is entitled to a share of the booty taken by each of the participating groups in the raid, *ʿazil al-shēkh* (Hess, *Von den Beduinen*, 101).

287 When the Bedouin trek to the markets in fall to stock up and the wares are cheap, they buy as much as their pack camels can carry and more. The implied meaning is that they have no fear of any enemy and march at a leisurely pace. See also n. 45.

288 The chief is so powerful and self-assured that no one is bold enough to ask him about the destination or what he is up to: he expects unconditional obedience. This poem's adulation of unquestioned authority is akin to the characteristics ascribed to Ibn Rashīd in Poem 23. The combination of ferocious fighting and pastoral idyll in this poem is caught in a single verse in the *muʿallaqah* poem of Zuhayr ibn Abī Sulmā: "They met in fateful deadly encounter, then trekked again / toward the herbage of unsavory pasture grounds" (i.e., in preparation for the next round of warfare, *fa-qaḍḍaw manāyā bay-nahum thumma aṣdarū, ilā kalaʾin mustawbalin mutawakhkhamī*) (*Sharḥ al-muʿallaqāt*, 84).

289 The only source for these verses is the edition published by Muḥammad ibn ʿAbd al-ʿAzīz ibn Sbayyil, the poet's grandson, where this poem opens the collection. Remarkably, the long ode to Ibn Rashīd is not included in that collection.

290 In that period the Ibn Bassām merchant family in ʿUnayzah, an important town in the al-Qaṣīm region, was on the side of Ibn Rashīd, also because they depended on him for their trade routes.

291 Lit. "the highest mud layer of a house where the pigeons are kept" (*ʿirǵ al-ḥamām*; *ʿirǵ* is a layer of clay that is left to dry before the next layer is laid on it when an adobe house is built).

292 See introduction, n. 8. Toward the end of 1904, when ʿAbd al-ʿAzīz ibn Rashīd returned to Ḥāʾil, and from there continued to Iraq, he left a garrison of about three hundred men from the Shammar tribe in the al-Sirr region, south of al-Qaṣīm, under the command of Ḥsēn (Ḥusayn) ibn Jarād al-Nāṣirī. ʿAbd al-ʿAzīz ibn Saʿūd surprised twelve of them, including Ḥsēn, in the town of al-Fēḍah, also called Fēḍat al-Sirr. They were killed, and their bodies were left lying outside the walls of the town, as described in §25.9, before being buried. Ibn Junaydil, *ʿĀliyat Najd*, 3, 1044–49; Ibn Hadhlūl, *Taʾrīkh mulūk Āl Saʿūd*, 1, 61; al-Ziriklī, *Shibh al-jazīrat fī ʿahd al-malik ʿAbd al-ʿAzīz*, 1, 145.

293 The image of the beloved's camel train ascending the incline of an elevation, and thus for an instant clearly visible to the lovesick poet who has stayed behind, or speeding downward from the crest of a line of low desert hills, is a standard topos, e.g., Swēlim al-Suhalī: "The loaded camel train sped away, ascending an incline, then it plunged

down and disappeared among the stony hills" (*shālaw w-gaffann aẓ-ẓaʿāyin zaʿājīl, shaffaw w-haffaw w-ittigaw b-al-ḥzūmi*). Sowayan, *al-Ṣaḥrā'*, 447.

294 It is a common simile to liken camel trains in the distance to clouds, e.g., al-Mijmāj: "They sped away as a cloud sails away after it rained, its cumulus flashing with lightning" (*agfaw ćimā nawwin nithar māh w-inzāʿ, bargih yrafrif w-as-sidā yirtidim lih*). Ibn Junaydil, *Aʿlām*, 57; Sowayan, *al-Ṣaḥrā'*, 443.

295 The beloved's ponderous gait is part of her coquetry, but it is primarily caused by the weight of her voluminous behind, as explained in n. 89. This is clear from ʿUmar ibn Abī Rabīʿah's line on the same topos: "[with her heavy behind] she walks at a calm pace, excruciatingly slow, keeping her thighs apart" (*wa-tamshī fī ta'awuddihā, huwaynā l-mashyi fī badadī*); and: "She walks slowly, in her one-piece robe, unsteady like a drunk struggling uphill" (*tamshī l-huwaynā idhā mashat fuḍulan, mashya l-nazīfi l-makhmūri fī l-ṣaʿadī*) (*Dīwān*, 110, 118). The same comparison, and combination of heavy behind and "drunken" walk, is made in the *muʿallaqah* poem of ʿAmr ibn Kulthūm: "They amble with a very slow gait, quivering at the back like the walk of a drunk" (*idhā mā ruḥna yamshīna al-huwaynā / ka-mā ḍṭarabat mutūnu al-shāribīnā*) (al-Zawzanī, *Sharḥ al-muʿallaqāt*, 133).

296 "Groaning" (*mirzimāt*), i.e., the grumbling sound made by a she-camel that groans yearningly toward her calf (CA *arzamat al-nāqah*). Such a she-camel in milk would have a big and full udder.

297 The same excuse was adduced by the seventh-century ghazal poet ʿUmar ibn Abī Rabīʿah: "First I felt sorry for myself, then love's passion took hold of me: it's not just me; before me other men were afflicted by love's disease" (*fa-ʿazzaytu nafsī thumma māla biya l-hawā, wa-qabliya qāda l-ḥubbu man kāna dhā tablī*). *Dīwān*, 304.

298 See introduction, n. 52 and n. 439 below. It is a common excuse in poetry to hide behind predecessors with more social status than oneself, e.g., Saʿd ibn ʿAbdallah al-ʿAtānī from al-Shaʿrā': "They haunted scores of wonderful lads; / Before me the creamy beauties harrowed the heart of the Sudayrī chiefs [the principal family of al-Ghāṭ in Sudayr who are parented to the Saʿūd dynasty]" (*ćam min w-ćam snāfiyyin wahhagannih / w-al-bīḍ galbī ʿadhdhabann as-Sidārā*). Ibn Junaydil, *Khawāṭir*, 162.

299 See nn. 472 and 510.

300 "Sharp-pointed spears," *mdhalligāt al-ʿrēnī*: from CA *mudhallaq*, "sharp-pointed," and *ʿrēnī* from *ʿirn*, "tan wood" (CA *ʿirn*, "a species of thorn tree"). The *ʿrēnī*, or *ʿrēniyyāt*, "the narrow blade of a spear, which is manufactured chiefly in the town of ad-Dēr on the right bank of the Euphrates" (Musil, *Rwala*, 133). Here it is a stereotyped noun combination in the construct state, like in §27.1.5, and Ibn Sbayyil's reply to it, §27.2.36,

zōghāt al-adhhān, "(days when) men's minds run wild with fear," i.e., "bloody battle." See Kurpershoek, *Oral Poetry*, 2, 128–29.

301 The poem is found in the al-Rabīʿī manuscript on unnumbered pages, between a section of Ibn Sbayyil's Poem 14.2 and the poem numbered 14.1 in this edition, pp. 106–7 of the MS; and the Ibn Yaḥyā MS, 668–69.

302 See nn. 71 and 123.

303 See n. 295 on the beloved's "drunk" gait.

304 The name of a stud camel; see n. 213.

305 See n. 243.

306 "The callosities of the joints of the fore and hind legs and the breast of the camel are called her *thafināt* [or *athfān*, as here]: when they make but small hollows in the sand when she is couched, it is a sign of her being of good breed." *Al-Mufaḍḍaliyyāt*, 2, 20.

307 In its essentials, this camel description does not differ from the pre-Islamic *muʿallaqah* poem of Ṭarafah ibn al-ʿAbd. In the first hemistich the verb *shabhar* means "to look sharply, with an intense gaze."

308 Lit. "as if they were irritated by worms (*dīdān*)." As explained to me, the Bedouin believed that such camels were plagued by worms on the insides of their ribs, which made them run at a maniacal pace. Early classical poetry also mentions the apparent paradox of increasingly fast pace the longer the distance covered (because it shed fat), as in the *muʿallaqah* poem of ʿAntarah: "Will I be brought home by a pedigree she-camel that was denied the pleasures of suckling a calf; / that raises her tail as she picks up the pace after running all night and hammers the stony hills with her hoofs" (*hal tublighannī dārahā shadaniyyatun / luʿinat bi-maḥrūmi l-sharābi muṣarramī / khaṭṭāratun ghibba l-surā zayyāfatun / taṭisu l-ikāma bi-wakhdi khuffin mīthamī*) (al-Zawzanī, *Sharḥ al-muʿallaqāt*, 142). And Jarīr: "Each of the camels ran even faster at the time of the midday heat, as if their spirits and endurance increased with the distances crossed" (*min kulli ʿayhamati l-hawājiri zādahā / ṭūl al-mafāwizi jurʾatan wa-ḍarīrā*) (Abū Tammām, *Naqāʾiḍ*, 120; Bakhouch, *La rivalité d'honneur*, 140). These and many other instances show that the classical images and topoi were still common in the composition of Najdī poetry until well into the twentieth century.

309 I have not been able to locate this place.

310 See n. 154 on this somewhat laughable hyperbole.

311 See n. 80 on the runaway heart.

312 On account of its straight growth, tenderness, and the fragrance of its oil, poets since antiquity have likened beautiful girls to the ben tree (Arabic: *bān*). To compare a man

to such a tree is to belittle him: "a lad, like the branch of a ben tree, soft and pliable" (*ghulāman ka-ghuṣni l-bānati l-mutaghāyidī*) (*al-Mufaḍḍaliyyāt*, 1, 135; 2, 45).

313 Qaṣr Barzān was the palace of the Ibn Rashīd dynasty in Ḥā'il.

314 See n. 156.

315 See §14.1.1. The messenger is often said to ride at the head of a group of fast camels.

316 At this age, when it has grown its teeth called *sidāsiyyāt*, a riding camel is at the peak of its strength.

317 The Sharārāt tribe is famous for breeding the best camels in northern Arabia. These camels are frequently mentioned in poetry. There is a further twist because it is suggested that the Sharārāt had been remiss in paying their tithe to the "ruler," who can be none other than Ibn Rashīd, the emir of Ḥā'il. In this case they were intimidated into grudgingly paying up and Ibn Rashīd would have accepted no less than their best camels. In the poet's fantasy, these animals found their way into the messenger's escort. Though the rulers of the Ibn Rashīd lineage were tribal princes of Shammar, not formally independent sovereigns, and paid nominal allegiance to the Ottoman Sultan or, as circumstances demanded, to the Wahhābī rulers of the Ibn Sa'ūd dynasty in the south, they were more than mere tribal chiefs in the view of the Bedouin. After the battle of Thirb (see n. 258), Muḥammad ibn Rashīd taunted visitors of Muṭayr with the words: "You have sworn that no one would ever wrest your horses from you, but we did!" The Muṭayr tribesmen answered: "Our oath was meant for tribes like ours. But you are a ruler (*ḥākim*; the same term is used in this verse)." Al-Haftā' and al-Shāṭirī, *Ta'rīkh qabīlat Muṭayr*, 187.

318 The rhyme word *mishtān* was explained to me as "preoccupied, mentally agitated" (from CA *sha'n* "affair"), i.e., " his mind is busy with many affairs, plans."

319 I.e., not stopping off for refreshments and conversation.

320 A stereotyped description, in the nature of an epithet. While stingy people hide their tents in a dip in the terrain, generous men who care about their reputation put them up on high ground where they are conspicuous: they aim to attract guests, even in times of want, and spend without heed.

321 The Najdī sheep's tail is considered a delicacy and is eaten as unadulterated fat in Bedouin meals.

322 This verse is often cited as a hyperbolic description of the virtue of hospitality. The big leather bags in which water is carried on camelback from the well to the camp are smeared with fat on the inside for protection. When guests get up from their places around the tray and leave, they wipe the fat off their hands on the tent's front flap. As a result the woolen tent cloth becomes shiny with grease. This is taken as a sign of their

owners' hospitality. Al-ʿUbayyid, *al-Najm al-lāmiʿ*, gives this description of the tent of Hadhdhāl ibn Fhēd al-Shībānī: "I saw the front flap of his tent dripping with fat, as it is customary for guests after they finished eating to wipe their hands on it until a ropelike trail of fat runs under it" (quoted in Sowayan, *al-Ṣaḥrāʾ*, 414). Similarly, guests used to daub their riding camels' necks with the blood of animals slaughtered in their honor—a telltale signal when on their onward journey they would be asked about the identity of the hosts who had entertained them so generously.

323 Day and night, the hospitable owner of the tents pounds coffee beans and spices in the mortar and therefore "fights off sleep like a fiend" (§14.2.26). The loud rings of the pestle against the mortar's rim are heard far into the desert and are an open invitation to all and sundry to join the coffee maker for a cup.

324 Men of the highest social rank and those more advanced in age sit closest to the tent owner. But even men at the far end of the circle are served as much coffee as they wish.

325 In the heat of battle, women loosen their hair, bare their breasts, and cry out to embolden their tribe's fighters. See nn. 47, 179, and 417.

326 Another stock character: a woman who has not yet been divorced, but lives separated from her husband; or a married woman who is dissatisfied with her husband and longs for a better and braver man.

327 Upon reaching his destination, the messenger begins his direct address in which he repeats the words entrusted to him by the poet. In the course of his delivery, he quotes directly from the poet's discussions with other men. The end of direct speech is not clearly marked.

328 The mise-en-scène of a purported search for a beloved often involves a runaway young she-camel. It pictures the poet making the rounds to question people as to the whereabouts of an animal of his description (see also nn. 80 and 192). The owner of a real camel would, of course, mention the shape of its brand, but in this metaphorical sense it is expressly omitted, as al-Mijmāj makes clear in his more precise description of the animal: "She is not a young calf, nor an animal used for traction at the well, but a young white she-camel, not branded with a mark by its owner" (*lā hīb lā ḥāshī walā hīb mirjāʿ / ʿafran fitāt w-rāʿiyah mā wisam lah*) (Ibn Junaydil, *Aʿlām*, 57). Burckhardt describes how young Bedouin men would address dancing girls as they would "order camels to halt, to walk, and trot, to drink, and eat, to stop, and to lie down." Since addressing them by name would be a breach of custom, they would style her "camel": "This fiction is continued during the whole dance. 'Get up, O camel [the word used would be for a young she-camel, *ḥāshī*]'" (*Notes*, 253–56).

329 I.e., the settled inhabitants of the villages, the *ḥaḍar*, who are more punctual about religious obligations than the Bedouin.

330 See n. 159. "Villagers and Bedouin" is a time-honored way of saying "everyone," as in the verse, "She is superior to the women of settled folks and the Bedouin" (*rāqat ʿalā ḥāḍiri l-niswāni wa-l-bādī*) (Dmitriev, *Abū Ṣakhr*, 195). And ʿUmar ibn Abī Rabīʿah: "Then say, 'Bastard, you are the biggest liar of all people, the settled folks and the Bedouin'" (*thumma qūlī kafarta yā-akdhabi l-nāsi jamīʿan min ḥāḍirīna wa-bādī*) (*Dīwān*, 95); and "stories from Bedouin and villagers" (*aḥādītha man yabdū wa-man huwa ḥāḍirū*) (*Dīwān*, 133; *al-Aghānī*, 123).

331 Dhuwī ʿAṭiyyah and Kirzān are sections of the ʿUtaybah confederation.

332 The chief of al-Daʿājīn of ʿUtaybah.

333 The popular saying differs in a few details of wording (*mā sharṭin ʿalā ghēr burhān*), i.e., the customary reward (*sharṭ* has the general meaning of financial compensation for services, as in the exchange of barbs between Ibn Sbayyil and Muṭawwaʿ Nifī, see n. 463; and Kurpershoek, *Arabian Satire*, 27, §10:12, 140 n. 30) for the bringer of good tidings or other important news is only given if the report is underpinned by credible evidence (al-Juhaymān, *Amthāl*, 7, 76).

334 The poet seems to echo, playfully or ironically, Ibn Zirībān's *zōghāt al-adhhān*, "(battles, horrors) that drive men beside themselves with fear." See nn. 134 and 300 on noun combinations such as these, a characteristic feature of this poetry's style.

335 Lit. Zanātī, i.e., the courageous hero of the Banū Hilāl epic. Fayḥān ibn Gāʿid is the poem's addressee. The poet's search leads back to his friend who commissioned it, that is, the most beautiful woman is in his household or close to him.

336 The proverb is: "The flat, hard desert tract is the arena and the horses are ready for battle [lit. have reached their sixth year, are at their best age]" (*al-khadd mēdānin w-al-khēl girraḥ*, as in this verse, *al-khēl girraḥ w-ajrad al-khadd mēdān*). Al-Juhaymān, *Amthāl*, 3, 12–13, 65; Musil, *Rwala*, 375.

337 The poet uses the demeaning diminutive *ḥḍērī* for *ḥaḍarī*, "a person from the sedentary classes, a villager."

338 See §§35.11, 36.10, and introduction, n. 64 on the beloved's tyranny.

339 See introduction, p. xxii. Insofar as the poet's desire remains unfulfilled and he suffers excruciating pain on account of unrequited love, the beloved appears as a beautiful lady without mercy. The characteristics that attracted him to her in the first place are quite different, however. Apart from stunning looks, a woman's intelligence and charming conversation are indispensable parts of the poet's ideal of beauty. In the same vein, ʿAbdallah ibn ʿWēwīd says of his beloved: "My beloved is intelligent and not a teasing

flirt; she is not everyone's friend, and not easy with her favors" (*anā ṣāḥibī ʿāgil wlā hūb mazzāḥ, wlā hū min illī kill zōlin yʿashginnih*). Ibn Junaydil, *Aʿlām*, 80.

340 Lit. "we owe you no debt, nor do you have a guarantee (*ḍimān*) from a guarantor of the loan."

341 This trope goes back to the early days of Arabic poetry, as in the line of al-Marrār ibn Munqidh: "If my brothers were to slay her in retaliation, they would have avenged my death at her hands" (*wa-hya law yaqtuluhā bī ikhwatī, adraka l-ṭālibu minhum wa-ẓafir*). *Al-Mufaḍḍaliyyāt*, 1, 159.

342 A common topic in ghazals or other poems on partnering, such as Ḥmēdān al-Shwēʿir's observation: "I myself, son, am perplexed by maidens; I ended up going from one to the other: This one doesn't want me, that one I don't want— Either we can't agree or she is not right for me" (Kurpershoek, *Arabian Satire*, 105, §§26:10–11). The topic also occurs as a popular saying: "Fortune would not bring me the one I had chosen" (*illī nibī ʿayyā al-bakhat la yijībih*) (al-Juhaymān, *Amthāl*, 1, 339).

343 "Manly vigor" is a translation of the Arabic word *zʿētmānih*, which is the name of an aromatic plant to which various health benefits are ascribed (the Arabic name is used for desert thyme or white-leaved savory). Here it can be considered synonymous with the expression "in the flower of youth, in the prime of his life" (*fī ʿunfuwān shabābih*). The notion conveyed is that the heart suffers to an extreme degree, like wood that is being worked with the utmost force. In early Arabic the same image and terminology was used: "I will plane you down like a piece of wood," e.g., in threats uttered by al-Ḥajjāj against the people of Iraq, as explained in a comment to a poem of al-Ḥādirah, *Al-Mufaḍḍaliyyāt*, 1, 50.

344 The tool mentioned in the first hemistich is a *ǵaddūm*, an adze, a small one-headed ax used for the finer woodwork.

345 A saying: "lucky breezes blow in its direction" (*dhaʿdhaʿ hawāh*); "a person born under a lucky star who is generally liked and respected." Al-Juhaymān, *Amthāl*, 3, 129.

346 As Nöldeke notes, even in ancient times it was not regarded as contradictory "that the poet let it be known that passion of love was a deep secret." "Dhurumma," 189.

347 The line is similar to the proverb "a stick that is not flexible will break," or "better bend than break" (*al-ʿūd illī mā yilīn yinkisir*), meaning that it is advisable to go with the flow to a certain degree. Al-Juhaymān, *Amthāl*, 4, 434.

348 See §6.13 and n. 80.

349 The toy is a small tin, painted in bright colors, filled with pebbles, that produces a rattling sound when a child shakes it. In the popular saying, it refers to a man of no substance who can be easily swayed and whose words are without substance (al-Juhaymān,

Amthāl, 5, 135, and 8, 108). "In the Gulf, it is also, by transfer, the name of custom in the middle of Ramadan when children go round to neighbors' houses rattling pots, pans, and drums–anything that makes a rattling sound, *garga'ān*–and begging for treats, as in Halloween's 'trick or treating'" (communication from Prof. Clive Holes).

350 The hemistich has acquired the status of popular saying: "My cord cannot be detached from hers." Al-Juhaymān, *Amthāl*, 4, 460.

351 This line has become a popular saying. It asserts that infatuated lovers never tire of pursuits for which others would have no taste (al-Juhaymān, *Amthāl*, 8, 272); al-'Ubūdī gives the variant: "Hunting is his passion and the only thing he cares about" (*mā lih hamm illā aṭ-ṭrād*) (*Amthāl*, 1252).

352 That is, they do not feel the pain of walking barefoot on stony ground.

353 The first hemistich has achieved proverbial status in these exact words. It means that things tend to follow their natural course. For instance, if someone has fallen in love, he will follow his heart and will not be dissuaded by censurers. Al-Juhaymān, *Amthāl*, 3, 291–92.

354 This proverb teaches that a successful outcome depends on a number of interrelated factors; if one of them does not hit the target, neither will the other. Al-Juhaymān, *Amthāl*, 7, 79.

355 A popular saying in exactly these words, also used in the general sense that deeds count for more than words (al-Juhaymān, *Amthāl*, 4, 205–6). Evasiveness and attempts to wriggle out from the demands of hospitality were seen as indelible stains on one's honor from the earliest times, as in the deadly line of Jarīr (d. 110/729): "If the Taghlibite is faced with the demand to provide for a guest, he scratches his ass and utters a litany of excuses" (*wa-l-Taghlibiyyu idhā tanaḥnaḥa li-l-qirā / ḥakka stahū wa-tamaththala l-amthālā*) (Abū Tammām, *Naqā'iḍ*, 89; Bakhouch, *La rivalité d'honneur*, 92).

356 A well-known proverbial saying, "consent is the best rule" (*ar-rḍā sīd al-aḥkām*), meaning that the best way to rule or solve disputes is to do so with the consent of all concerned (al-Juhaymān, *Amthāl*, 3, 195). Al-'Ubūdī quotes the expression "peace is the best thing to agree upon" (*aṣ-ṣulḥ sīd al-aḥkām*) in a letter from Sa'ūd ibn 'Abd al-'Azīz ibn Muḥammad to an Ottoman governor; and in a poem by the sixteenth-century Nabaṭī poet Rāshid al-Khalāwī: "A dispute's best outcome is what both parties can accept; whoever declares himself sincerely satisfied will gain" (*tarā sīd al-aḥkām mā kān mirtiḍā, w-min yirtiḍī shayyin w-yahwāh fāz bih*) (*Amthāl*, 594–95).

357 In similar words, 'Umar ibn Abī Rabī'ah's verse: "I do whatever I can to please you, and I upbraid those who censure you" (*wa-abdhulu nafsī li-marḍātikum, wa-u'tibu man jā'akum 'ātibā*). *Al-Aghānī*, 162; *Dīwān*, 66.

358 The same meaning, without the metaphors, is expressed by ʿUmar ibn Abī Rabīʿah: "We talked to our hearts' content, and we enjoyed as much as we desired [. . .] ten nights in that place, settled our debts, and were done" (*wa-ḍarabnā l-ḥadītha ẓahran li-baṭnin, wa-ataynā min amrinā mā shtahaynā* [. . .] *fa-labathnā bi-dhāka ʿashran tibāʿan, fa-qaḍaynā duyūnanā wa-qtaḍaynā*). *Al-Aghānī*, 1, 143; *Dīwān*, 430.

359 This piece is only found in a book by Ibn Junaydil, *al-Sānī wa-l-sāniyah*, on the subject of oasis agriculture. Sinʿūs is a generic name for a member of Shammar, a tribe called Sanāʿīs in one of its battle cries. This Bedouin was hired by Ibn Sbayyil to do the hard work of guiding camels used for well traction up and down the walkway during the greater part of the night and parts of the day in the hot season, when the palm trees are in the greatest need of water. See nn. 212 and 397. Earlier, the hired hand had blamed the weak condition of the camel, but this time the animal had recovered and was in good shape. Therefore, Ibn Sbayyil says, he no longer has an excuse for his sluggishness. In the final line, he admonishes him to go about his work with fresh energy because otherwise no one will hire him next season; and if he makes a good impression he may even get hired with a pay raise. The poet is all the more anxious to see the harvest succeed because he is in debt to a trader—an element that reminds us of one of the poems by Ḥmēdān al-Shwēʿir (Kurpershoek, *Arabian Satire*, 133).

360 When the bucket has been hoisted up and emptied into the basin, the driver leads the camel back to the well up the walkway. After the effort of pulling up the heavy bucket on the way down the path, the animal should be allowed to recover—chasing the animal on the way up is condemned, see §§34.2–3. Also, when back at the well, the camel must be calm to allow the workers to shake the ropes so as to move the buckets in the well to fill with water for the next haul.

361 One is reminded of ʿUmar ibn Abī Rabīʿah's line that starts with a similar threefold repetition of an exclamation: "How nice, how nice, how nice! A sweetheart whose every whim I braved!" (*alā ḥabbadhā ḥabbadhā ḥabbadhā, ḥabībun taḥammaltu minhi l-adhā*). *Dīwān*, 119.

362 In the diwan compiled by Muḥammad ibn Sbayyil, this piece is attributed to Muṭawwaʿ Nifī (and he is followed in this by al-Masridī, *Muṭawwaʿ Nifī*, 86–87), but the manuscript versions include it in the work of Ibn Sbayyil. It is true, though, that the jesting tone is more characteristic of Muṭawwaʿ Nifī, who might be expected to pull his neighbor's leg on a theme so dear to his heart.

363 A variation on the motif of the silly graybeard, as in the *muʿallaqah* poem of Zuhayr ibn Abī Sulmā: "If an old man is a fool he will never see reason, while rash youngsters may still hope to attain wisdom" (*wa-inna safāha l-shaykhi lā ḥilma baʿdahū / wa-inna*

l-fatā baʿda l-safāhati yaḥlumī) (al-Zawzanī, *Sharḥ al-muʿallaqāt*, 89). And Hmēdān al-Shwēʿir's line: "I ask you, Māniʿ, what kind of folk are these, whose elders are as foolish as their youngsters?" (Kurpershoek, *Arabian Satire*, 13, §4.19).

364 Lit. "Nights that are short, that pass quickly," as in ʿUmar ibn Abī Rabīʿah's verse: "When you are distant the nights are long, but they feel short when you are around" (*fa-l-layālī idhā na'ayti ṭiwālun, wa-arāhā idhā qarubti qiṣārā*) (*Dīwān*, 156; *al-Aghānī*, 1, 136). In the chapter "Settlers and Nomads," Sowayan translated this poem as a particularly apt illustration of the subject (*Nabaṭi Poetry*, 24–27). At the end of the hot season the Bedouin are in a rush to leave the wells of the village where they spent the hot season, settle debts and get paid what is owed to them, and prepare for their migration into the desert, each of them bent on getting ahead of the others in a race for the best pastures (Sowayan, *al-Ṣaḥrā'*, 440). The rhyme word of the first hemistich, *shifāshīf*, is explained by al-ʿUbūdī as "little, paltry, less than what is needed." Many times he heard migrating Bedouin say: "There is little water in the wells at the moment" (*al-ma ha-l-ḥīn shifāshīf*), that is, insufficient for them and their herds (*Muʿjam al-uṣūl*, 7, 206). Among others, he quotes Ibn Sbayyil with this verse to illustrate his point.

365 Burckhardt observes that the Bedouin kept a certain amount of butter for themselves and that "the rest is sold to peasants and townspeople." "From one hundred ewes or goats (the milk of which is always mixed together) the Arabs expect, in common years, about eight pounds of butter per day." *Notes*, 201–2.

366 Normally, the herdsmen would have little to do and plenty of time. Now, even they are busy.

367 Also, al-Mijmāj: "Each of them follows his own track, veering away from the others" (*w-illi nawā darbin ʿazal w-ingisam lih*). Ibn Junaydil, *Aʿlām*, 56; Sowayan, *al-Ṣaḥrā'*, 443.

368 Lit. "The sudden end of *al-jizuw* (CA *al-jazw*)," the period in which camels and animals like gazelle can do without water because they absorb enough moisture from the grasses and plants that shoot up in the wake of plentiful rains. The Bedouin dig in the sand to see at what depth the earth has retained moisture and thereby measure what remains of this season. In al-Zawzanī's commentary to Labīd's *muʿallaqah* poem, the wild cow's abstention of water, *jaza'a al-waḥsh*, is explained as "the oryx found sufficient moisture in its grazing to be able to do without water": "During the long period of the cold and cool seasons, six months, they did not go in search of water" (*ḥattā idhā salakhā jumādā sittatan / jaza'ā fa-ṭāla ṣiyāmuhū wa-ṣiyāmuhā*) (al-Zawzanī, *Sharḥ al-muʿallaqāt*, 100); the verse is discussed more in depth in al-Tibrīzī's commentary, *Kitāb al-sharḥ*, 73.

369 In his note on §§32.6–7, Sowayan comments that herders of small livestock such as goats and sheep can no longer replenish their skin (the word *saʿn* denotes a small version of the bigger milk skin, *ṣimīl*) with milk because the animals' production of milk dries up in the heat. *Al-Ṣaḥrāʾ*, 93.

370 It seems the word for "elevations" (*mishārīf*) is also the name of some low ridges within view of al-Athlah (Ibn Junaydil, *Aʿlām*, 61). The hemistich is listed as a proverbial saying, with a verb that indicates departure instead of arrival, in reference to the spleen and uncertainties felt by lovers on their separation (al-Juhaymān, *Amthāl*, 10, 141). This verse explains the poet's exhilaration at the onset of the dry and hot season, which for the Bedouin means the end of their celebration of the spring season that gave new strength to face the hardships ahead: what counts for the poet-lover is the chance to be in the proximity of Bedouin beauties.

371 They show little consideration for herders of sheep and goats (*shāwī*) who are seen as less prestigious than camel nomads. See n. 16.

372 This hemistich has entered the collection of proverbial sayings. It refers to the notion that there is power in numbers and that a multitude of tribesmen and their animals makes an impression on others. Al-Juhaymān, *Amthāl*, 4, 311–12.

373 Ibn Junaydil, who is from High Najd and is considered one of the foremost experts on the area, writes that the villagers benefited from the fertilizing effect of the dung produced by the Bedouin herds. One year, tribes of the Ḥarb confederation spent the ninety days of the hot season at Nifī's wells and for some reason prolonged their stay beyond the customary period. Then one of the farmers composed some lines of verse in which he asked their shaykh to evacuate the land since it was time for the farmers to prepare it for sowing a new harvest—a request that was immediately followed by the Bedouin's departure. Those who tarried were admonished by the others: "Ibn aṭ-Ṭrēs [the shaykh] has already struck tent" (*gaddahā ibn aṭ-Ṭrēs*), which gained proverbial status, meaning that the matter is decided and that it is no use second-guessing him. *Khawāṭir*, 59–61.

374 On Canopus (Shel, CA Suhayl), and its significance in the cycle of seasons in the Arabian desert, see introduction, pp. xviii–xix, §14.1.3, and n. 173. It signals that it is time for the Bedouin to break up their encampment at the wells after the ninety days of the hot season. Before leaving, they stock up on dates, because it is also the time of the date harvest, as expressed in the verse of Zēd al-Khshēm from the village of Gfār, in the area of Ḥā'il near the Nifūd desert: "When Canopus makes its appearance, the Bedouin arrive in droves (to buy dates)" (Sowayan, *al-Ṣaḥrāʾ*, 425). Its proverbial status speaks from this saying: "Suhayl gives the lie to the prognosticators" (*shēl mćadhdhib al-ʿaddād*), i.e., the appearance of the star Canopus itself will put an end to the surmises of those who

pretend that they can predict the day. In other words, what counts is reality, not guesses and speculation (al-Juhaymān, *Amthāl*, 3, 287). Similarly, in a comment on a poem by Salamah ibn al-Khurshub, it is explained that people used to swear that a certain star that appears immediately before Canopus was indeed Canopus, though they were wrong, *al-Mufaḍḍaliyyāt*, 1, 43.

375 Though not made explicit, it is understood that these men brought reports about the state of the pastures. Their approach is from the southwest, that is, the higher grounds of High Najd and the direction of their customary migration. See n. 36.

376 This season is reflected in the Najdī saying: "At the time of the date harvest, everyone is generous" (*yōm al-ṣarām killin ćrām*); and in a poem by Mḥammad ibn Liʿbūn, "like a poor man's belly that is full at the time of the date harvest" (*shabʿat al-miskīn b-ayyām al-ṣarām*). Al-ʿUbūdī, *Amthāl*, 1797.

377 "The mejlis forecast the next journeys of the tribe, whereof a kind of running advice remains in all their minds, which they call es-shor; this is often made known to their allies, and is very necessary to any of themselves that are about to take a journey" (Doughty, *Travels*, 1, 290). Burckhardt avers that "the opinion of every distinguished individual in the tribe must be ascertained, and his consent obtained, when matters of general interest, or of public importance, are to be discussed" (*Notes*, 284–85).

378 Al-Mijmāj writes: "Neighbors like these are a pleasure to have [lit. pleasing to one's liver/spleen]" (*awayy jīrānin ʿalā l-ćabd ḥilwīn*), Ibn Junaydil, *Aʿlām*, 53.

379 Similarly, al-Mijmāj says: "They follow Abū Khālid, who protects the laggards on the field of battle" (*yatlūn ibū Khālid zibūn al-mitallīn*) (Ibn Junaydil, *Aʿlām*, 53). In one of his humorous poems, Muṭawwaʿ Nifī says that the shaykh listens to the advice of fellow tribesmen and then makes his own decision, but only after consulting his wife (al-Masridī, *Muṭawwaʿ Nifī*, 99).

380 As a popular saying, this line about the Bedouin's seasonal migrations acquired the more general meaning of people's search for means of subsistence or a better life, no matter how much exertion it takes (al-Juhaymān, *Amthāl*, 8, 118). It is found in almost the same words in common speech, as in this recording from Bedouin in Oman: "Wherever the rain has fallen they go to seek pasture" (*minēn yam ṭāḥ al-ḥayā ham yinayʿō lah*) (Webster, "Notes," 481).

381 See n. 218. The raiders collected a small group of camels (*shirshūḥ*) from a big herd that was spread out in pasture. They drove away the camels that grazed on the herd's far side so as to lose as little time as possible and not get bogged down by moving into the center of the herd and out again.

382 See n. 242 on the use of a torch to chase after rustlers at night.

383 See n. 417. Raiders, or men riding to war, would often be accompanied by a gunbearer seated behind them on the camel, a *ridīf*. If pursued by the enemy, the *ridīf* would slide off the camel and take aim at the pursuers with his rifle. The big camels of the small, fast-moving band of mounted rustlers are compared to *dōḥ* (CA *dawḥ*), "any kind of trees with spreading branches." "They tore off," the verb *shall, yishill*, "to go at great speed, to snatch something and rapidly take it far away" (CA *shalla* "to urge on, drive").

384 A camel brand identifies the tribal affiliation of its owner: in this case a tribe known for its ferocious fighters.

385 Also §41.9 and n. 401. The beloved's eyes are invested with the power to put the poet-lover under a spell by hitting his heart with the arrows of her glances, as in Abū Nuwās, "Your kohl-lined eyes have smitten my heart through sorcery and there became your hostages" (*wa-ramā ṭarfuka l-mukaḥḥalu bi-l-siḥri fu'ādī fa-ṣāra rahnan ladaykā*) (Bauer, *Liebe und Liebesdichtung*, 215 and 283 ff). An anecdote in *al-Aghānī*, 1, 76–78, tells about the reverse: ʿUmar ibn Abī Rabīʿah's poetry is said to bewitch women and he is reported as saying that women fell in love with him rather than the other way around.

386 This is a recurrent image in ghazals old and new: the enchanting grace of the way a startled gazelle holds its neck.

387 A saying to express one's unwillingness to continue a one-sided relationship without give and take. Al-Juhaymān, *Amthāl*, 8, 106.

388 Lit. "I turn away if the other does so, no matter how pretty she is," a saying in al-Juhaymān, *Amthāl*, 8, 96; also in §38.17. Similarly, Swēlim al-Suhalī: "I let go of the rope when I am rebuffed—when a sneak secretly poisons the drink" (*Majmūʿat ashʿār*, 213). An early classical example is Imru' al-Qays: "I cut off relations with those who cut me off, and I draw closer to those who seek my friendship" (*innī la-aṣrimu man yuṣārimunī, wa-ujiddu waṣla mani btaghā waṣlī*) (Jacobi, *Poetik*, 192). And the pre-Islamic poet Ta'abbaṭa Sharran says: "Nay, I say not, when a friend cuts short the bond and departs, 'Alas, my soul!' out of longing and soft self-pitying tears" (*wa-lā aqūlu idhā mā khullatun ṣaramat / yā-wayḥa nafsiya min shawqin wa-ishfāqī*); and if a mistress does not accede to his desire, "I fly from her straight" (*najawtu minhā najā'ī*) (*al-Mufaḍḍaliyyāt*, vol. 1, pp. 6–11; vol. 2, p. 3). Lyall comments in a note that "the ideal lover of old Arabian poetry is always ready to fling off a love that begins to grow cold" (*al-Mufaḍḍaliyyāt*, vol. 2, p. 5). A similar sentiment is expressed by ʿUmar ibn Abī Rabīʿah in the line "I will cut loose from your rope if you cut it, since I was told that you fell in love with someone else" (*wa-ṣaramtu ḥablaka idh ṣaramta li-annanī, ukhbirtu innaka qad hawīta siwānā*) (*Dīwān*, 401).

389 The line is a popular saying, meaning that one should reciprocate if the other person is forthcoming. Al-Juhaymān, *Amthāl,* 8, 92.

390 It is a saying that expresses distaste for the crowds around easily accessible, popular destinations or persons: if it becomes impossible to distinguish visitors from those who are on a prolonged stay, one's presence or absence will also be little noted (al-Juhaymān, *Amthāl,* 7, 251). It is a prelude to the poet's preference for more exquisite, discreet excursions into his "valley of temptation."

391 Sowayan reads: "A well of which the dregs fill a wide circle around it" (replacing *giṭīnih* with *nithīlih*). *Al-Ṣaḥrā',* 209.

392 Lit. "In the morning, when herds have been watered and driven to pasture (*miṣādīr*)." The well is dry because the herds are so big and have consumed all water. Those who wait until the herds are gone find nothing but the dregs.

393 In more straightforward manner, the same metaphor is used in the *mu'allaqah* poem of 'Amr ibn Kulthūm: "We drink water from a well with pure water, while the others must do with foul water and dirt" (*wa-nashrabu in waradnā al-mā'a ṣafwan / wa-yashrabu ghayrunā kadaran wa-ṭīnā*) (al-Zawzanī, *Sharḥ al-mu'allaqāt,* 134). Ibn Sbayyil uses the same metaphor, not for tribal boasting, but for his ghazal purposes. See n. 437.

394 This explains the meaning of the less explicit second hemistich of §2.12.

395 Lit. "A load of worries is discarded," i.e., the poet-lover is happy that he has achieved his *wiṣāl,* "union with the beloved."

396 See n. 218. The al-Da'ājīn of 'Utaybah were notorious for their extensive raiding, see glossary of names and places. This poem is attributed to 'Bēd ibn Hwēdī al-Dōsirī in Ibn Junaydil, *A'lām,* 143–44, and Sowayan, *al-Ṣaḥrā',* 347. Ibn Junaydil dates the poem to 1907, a year of plentiful rains and therefore called "the fair year," al-Msāwī, because it allowed all people to share in its blessings (Ibn Junaydil, *A'lām,* 117). In the manuscripts of al-Rabī'ī and Ibn Yaḥyā it is included in the work of Ibn Sbayyil (see index of poems). The latter view might find support in the fact that 'Bēd ibn Hwēdī composed a poem that employs the same rhyme in its end rhyme as in this poem's first hemistich, and with a first-hemistich rhyme that is closely related to this poem's end rhyme (*-ānih* instead of this poem's *-īnih*). Even the word of the end rhyme of Ibn Hwēdī's second line is identical to the rhyme word of the first hemistich of this poem's first line: "The yearlings and young calves of my soul are groaning: at the end of night their mothers were taken by a thief" (*tirazzam mifārīd aḍ-ḍimāyir w-ḥīrānih, khadh immātihin min tālī al-lēl sarrāg*) (ibid., 157).

397 The hard-driven camel used for traction at the well is a popular and ancient topos in the similes of *nasīb*-style poetry. Poets of the "romantic school" (see introduction) often

add to the drama by picturing the camel's driver as a slave who is pitiless and indifferent to the animal's suffering. Since the poet identifies with the camel that hoists the heavy buckets from the well, the *sānyah*, and likens his agony of love to its ordeal, he defends its rights and blames the slave for violating religious injunctions that call for a lenient treatment of animals. In the dispute between a father, Mubārak ibn ʿAbīćih, the owner of palm groves and the head of the village of Gnā on the southern edge of the Nafūd desert, and his son who wanted to switch to a Bedouin life, the son accuses the "key-bearing villagers" (*nāǵlīn al-mifātīḥ*) of cruelty and pities camels on the well's walkway after a desert life of freedom and dignity, while his father objects that camels are there to be driven without consideration or sympathy in the interest of the date harvest and their visitors (Sowayan, *al-Ṣaḥrāʾ*, 429–30). Typically, the villager Ibn Sbayyil and his fellow poets take the side of the Bedouin voice in this dispute–admittedly of a literary nature, but also illustrative for perceptions of a cultural and economical dichotomy. In a similar vein, a famous poem by Mashʿān al-Htēmī opens with this scene: "In these eloquent verses Mashʿān al-Htēmī made rhyme and meter dance inside his chest. / I cry and moan like three worn-out camels that hoist the greenish water from a gushing well, / driven by a slave who beats them all night and lacerates their tender parts with the tips of his rods" (*yigūl Mashʿān al-Htēmī tifalham, gāfin rijas bēn aḍ-ḍlūʿ al-maghālīǵ / yā-wannitī wannat thalāthin halāyim, min nisafhin khiḍr al-jmām al-daghārīǵ / sawwāgihin ʿabdin maʿ al-lēl yajham, w-anjaḥ miṣākhifhin bi-rūs al-misāwīǵ*) (Ibn Junaydil, *Aʿlām*, 105). And by the same poet: "My heart whines like a pulley wheel running over a well, the ropes pulled by three bulky camels going back and forth, / chased down the slope by a slave without feeling for his master's animals." (*lajjat maḥāl al-bīr yōm ytidāraj, tiǵbil w-tiǵfī bih thalāthin ʿadāwī / sawwāgahā ʿabdin lyā gām yanhaj, ʿabdin ḥalāl al-gōm mā hūb yāwī*) (ibid., 100). In his seven verses on the motif, the ancient poet Zuhayr ibn Abī Sulmā's pictures it in a touching image: "(A camel) fearful of the man who drives her down the path, stretching its back and neck in terror at his stick" (*wa-khalfahā sāʾiqun yaḥdū idhā khashiyat, minhu l-ʿadhāba tamuddu l-ṣulba wa-l-ʿunuqā*) (*Sharḥ dīwān*, 39). Because the lowest of the low toil on the walkway, the path itself is used as a metaphor for utter degradation in the invective of the early poet Jarīr (d. 110/729): "Little al-Akhṭal left his mother downtrodden like a walkway where a camel hurries up and down drawing water" (*taraka al-Ukhayṭilu ummahū wa-kaʾannahā / manḥātu sāniyatin tudīru maḥālā*) (Abū Tammām, *Naqāʾiḍ*, 90; Bakhouch, *La rivalité d'honneur*, 94). For the same reason, the walkway (*manḥāh*) is called "the world's graveyard" (*magbarat ad-dinyā*) (Sowayan, *al-Ṣaḥrāʾ*, 392).

398 Lit. "one-eighth of a *midd*" (*thimīn*), a very small amount, see §21.19.

399 Similar to ʿAbdallah ibn ʿWēwīd's verse: "I will testify, my heart's love, that you are the one who slays it, but whoever faces his destiny because of his sweetheart [here the generic name for an unidentified love, 'Zēd,' is used] is sure to be granted Paradise" (*anā b-ashhad innik yā-hawā al-galb dhabbāḥ, w-min adrak niṣībih Zēd tiḍman lih al-jannah*). Ibn Junaydil, *Aʿlām*, 82.

400 The same expression occurs in a verse by a poet known as Ibn al-Muṭawwaʿ of the al-ʿIjmān tribe: "I have a she-camel that always groans with yearning" (*lī fāṭirin ḥanīnahā lih tihijrāʿ*). Ibn Junaydil, *Khawāṭir*, 111.

401 The heart is "seduced," *maftūn*, and the poet knows that the beloved's guileless appearance conceals deceit, aimed at ensnaring him (§35.8), but he willingly plays the game. He is spellbound by her glances, which paralyze his normal faculties and blind him to the danger of his losing control (see §33.9). This is the *fitnah* brought about by the beloved's beauty, a personalized version of actions that risk loss of control over the social, political, and religious order. Bauer, *Liebe und Liebesdichtung*, 214.

402 See §9.11. Her answer is not mentioned, but presumably it is along the lines of §§28.11–12.

403 See n. 82 on the topos of the poet-lover's subservience and obedience.

404 This line is a proverbial saying. If someone settles in the beloved's land, far from his own kin, for the sole reason that she lives there, it demonstrates how infatuation has the power to bring about changes in one's life (al-Juhaymān, *Amthāl*, 6, 311–12). In modern standard Arabic, *waṭan* means "fatherland, one's home country," but among the Bedouin it refers to the area where they usually roam: "A vacated site is termed *dār*, pl. *dīrān*, and the general locality containing a number of such semi-permanent habitations is a *waṭan*" (Webster, "Notes," 479). Here it is used as a synonym of *dīrah*: the district where one lives or the land a Bedouin tribe considers its own; also, *bilād*, "country, land," as in the verse of Abū Dhu'ayb al-Hudhalī cited in n. 271. The verse is discussed in detail in Jacobi, "Time and Reality," 8, especially the poet's subjective point of view as contrasted with the "objectivity" of the pre-Islamic and other earlier poetry. Of course, in this respect Ibn Sbayyil follows in Abū Dhu'ayb's steps rather than in those of the poets who preceded him.

405 Here the Arabic word used for "man" is derived from Adam, *ādam*, and adapted for the rhyme, *mūdimānī*. It occurs in the same rhyming position in a verse by another poet from High Najd, Mḥammad ibn ʿAbdallah ibn Manṣūr, who worked in camel transport and agriculture: "By your life, my palm trees, I would not part with you, but lack of help may force a man's hand" (*ḥalaft yā-gharsin lanā mā nkhallīh, w-ithr al-waḥādah tikhlif al-mūdimānī*) (Ibn Junaydil, *Khawāṭir*, 70). The opening line is a common one in Nabaṭī poetry, as in this anonymous poem, *yā-llāh ya-llī ʿālim mā nikhfī* (al-Haṭlānī,

Dīwān ashʿār, 95); an identical first hemistich and a very similar second hemistich occur in a poem by Khalaf Abū Zwayyid (Sowayan, *Ayyām al-ʿarab*, 596).

406 As in the first verse, the final word in Arabic is made to fit the rhyme: *al-miʿribānī* is derived from *ʿarab* and *ʿirbān*, "Bedouin tribesmen," also used as general term for "men, people." Similarly, ʿBēd ibn Hwēdī: "O Lord who kindly looks after the needs of common people and the nomads" (*liṭīfin bi-khaṣṣāt al-malā w-al-ʿrēbānī*). Ibn Junaydil, *Aʿlām*, 151.

407 The court of love is already present in the ghazal of ʿUmar ibn Abī Rabīʿah: see n. 129.

408 See introduction, pp. xxviii–xxix. Ironically, the poet, in pursuit of his sinful dalliance, positions himself on the side of law and order, represented by Islamic law, and accuses his beloved of literally playing with fire: in Najdī tradition, Ibn ʿAmmār is associated with *al-ṭāghūt* (a tribal judge as opposed to a Shariah judge). The ordeal itself, of course, is part of the cruel treatment (repeatedly expressed by the noun *imtiḥān*, "test, ordeal," and its verb) the lover-poet receives at the hands of his beloved. The first hemistich is listed as a proverbial saying. Ibn ʿAmmār, a Bedouin of the Ḥarb tribe between al-Qaṣīm and Medina, was known for adjudicating according to Bedouin customary law (*ʿurf*) in disputes submitted to him by litigants. The opposition in this verse is between someone who wishes to arrive at a correct and civilized solution, in accordance with the law of Islam, and a person who insists on using uncivilized Bedouin means (al-Juhaymān, *Amthāl*, 5, 314). Implicit is also the claim to a higher level of "civilization," based on Islamic precepts, boasted by townspeople, while the "uneducated" Bedouin of the beloved's group often had recourse to customary law. Until recent times, these methods were used as a kind of lie detector: if the accused denied guilt, he was asked to lick a red-hot iron. If his tongue survived the test unscathed, this was assumed to be proof of his innocence. Layish has recorded this ordeal of fire-licking (*laḥs al-nār*) in 1976, *Legal Documents from the Judean Desert*, 118. If the evidence is contradictory, the judge may decide to send the litigating parties to a *mubashshiʿ*, the person who administers the fire-licking ordeal, as described in historical detail by Burckhardt, *Notes*, 121–23.

409 One's guardian angel on the left shoulder keeps a record of a person's sins and missteps; the one on the right records the good deeds. As the angel on the left shows no sign of relenting, the lover turns to the one on the right in the hope of finding a more willing ear.

410 This hemistich is quoted in explanation of the irrational behavior of a lover who remains obstinately devoted to his attachment, even in the absence of any chance of fulfillment (al-Juhaymān, *Amthāl*, 10, 340–41). It is a stereotype of ghazals, as in Abū Dhuʾayb al-Hudhalī: "My heart revolted and I surrendered, no stranger myself to the pains it suffered" (*ʿaṣānī l-fuʾādu fa-aslamtuhū, wa-lam aku mimmā ʿanāhu ḍārīḥā*); and "My heart disobeyed and sided with her; and I complied, though unsure about the wisdom

of pursuing her" (*ʿaṣānī ilayhā l-qalbu innī li-amrihī, samīʿun fa-mā adrī a-rushdun ṭilābuhā*) (*Dīwān Abī Dhuʾayb*, 57, 30); and ʿUmar ibn Abī Rabīʿah, "I told my heart to stop its pursuit, but it tricked me and found ways to follow its desire" (*la-qad nahaytu fuʾādī ʿan taṭallubihā, fa-ghtashshanī wa-atā mā shāʾa muʿtamidā*) (*Dīwān*, 109).

411 See also §10.14. The pre-Islamic poet al-Ḥādirah introduces an extended metaphor on this topos with the verse: "And when she bandies speech with you, you see that she has a lovely smile and lips most sweet to kiss, as though one drank of fresh-fallen rain [. . .]" (*wa-idhā tunāziʿuka l-ḥadītha raʾaytahā, ḥasanan tabassumuhā ladhīdha l-makraʿī / bi-gharīḍi sāriyatin* [. . .]). *Al-Mufaḍḍaliyyāt*, 1, 53–54; 2, 17.

412 The word for "devious idler," *misniḥānī*, occurs in this line of Muṭawwaʿ Nifī: "Hordes of lethargic idlers are afraid to perform noble deeds" (*kam misniḥāniyyin ʿan al-marjilah dhall*). Al-Masridī, *Muṭawwaʿ Nifī*, 94.

413 The poet-lover watches from a rocky outcrop or other elevation as the beloved's camel train departs, or he climbs a lonely mountain where he vents his spleen and composes poetry. These images are ubiquitous in love poetry or any amatory prologue, e.g., Swēlim al-Suhalī: "As I stood watching on my peak of suffering, my eyes trained on a distant scene from the high ledge where I stood" (Sowayan, *al-Ṣaḥrāʾ*, 447). Therefore, the peak itself became a symbol of grief that might better be avoided, as in these verses by Zāmil ibn ʿIḍyān from al-Rass: "O heart, stay away from the lookout, do not go for it; O heart, avoid the agonies of its slopes; / her bulging behind is the cheerful sight of the neighborhood, how fortunate the man who kneads her luscious curves" (*yā-l-galb ṣāfiḥ margibin mā tnūlih, jannib ʿanih yā-l-galb ʿasrih marāǵīh / nāb ar-ridāyif gablat al-ḥayy zōlih, haniyy min farrak maḥānīṭ nāmīh*) (al-ʿUbayyid, *al-Najm al-lāmiʿ*, 77–78). For its broader context, see Kurpershoek, *Oral Poetry*, 1, the chapter "Parts of the Nasīb: The Lonely Mountain Scene; The Inspirational Process; The Suffering of the Heart," and the article "Heartbeat: Conventionality and Originality in Najdi Poetry."

414 That is, the wadi where Nifī is situated.

415 Lit. "It overtakes but no one can catch up with it" (*talḥag wa-lā tilḥag*); it is a set expression for "a fast horse," as in "give me my sword and ʿUbayyah, because it is a champion racer" (*faras talḥaq wa-lā tulḥaq*). Al-Bulayhid, *Ṣaḥīḥ al-akhbār*, 2, 123.

416 Lit. "all were involved in blood feuds" with the other party. Therefore, it is not just a matter of being robbed and retrieving one's possessions–there are scores to settle and lives to be paid, and they are ready for a bitter and bloody fight.

417 Bedouin warriors would be driven to displays of bravery by shouts and gestures of the tribe's young women who followed the skirmishes from their camel seats, see nn. 47 and 179. In this case, their presence is imaginary—the camels bearing the women's heavy

litter chairs could not possibly have caught up with the raiders—and part of this poetry's formulaic phrasing. The second hemistich refers to the gunman's camel-mounted kinsmen, who encourage him by shouting battle cries.

418 Biting one's thumbs in such a situation is a sign of utter helplessness, distress, and perplexity, as in "I bite the top of my fingers (in regret and despair)" (*aʿiḍḍ aṭrāf al-banān b-nājidhī*), Sowayan, *al-Shiʿr al-nabaṭī*, 457. The crestfallen warrior is at his enemy's mercy, and verse 15 mentions that there was blood between pursuers and pursued. Nevertheless, his enemies thought better of killing him (*ṣabr*, here with the meaning of finishing off an incapacitated enemy, as CA *ṣabara*, "to bind, hold someone, and then to kill him deliberately"). The reason given is that they did not want to be responsible for the misery awaiting his children if they became orphans. The fact that the pursuing tribesman had already lost his camels, and now in addition his reputed horse, may have been an additional consideration.

419 See introduction, p. xxv. The poet's contempt for thoughtless consumerism is reflected in the popular saying "happy is an idle mind" (*al-mistirīḥ illī min al-ʿagl khālī*), which al-ʿUbūdī (*Amthāl*, 1348–49) traces to similar words of ʿAmr ibn al-ʿĀṣ, and the old saying "No intelligent person can be happy and contented" (*mā surra ʿāqilun qaṭṭ*); and on the same note al-Mutanabbī's verse: "If all is well, an intelligent person suffers nevertheless, and if things are bad a dimwit is still at ease" (*dhū l-ʿaqli yashqā fī al-naʿīmi bi-ʿaqlihī, wa-akhū al-jahālati bi-l-shaqāwati yanʿamū*).

420 The hemistich has been adopted as a popular saying, meaning that one's heart is devastated by love, as swarms of locusts devour all green where they descend (al-Juhaymān, *Amthāl*, 5, 312–13). In a poem's prologue (*nasīb*), the heart is compared to a shrub that sprouts branches. In healthy condition, these are juicy and green. But if the heart sinks into melancholy, these sprouts wither—a situation compared to the damage wrought by locusts, as in the verse by the poet al-Dindān: "Woe unto a heart swarmed over by creeping young locusts, wave after wave alighting on the heart's branches at dusk" (*fa-yā mill galbin ḥall fīh al-dibā l-ḥannān, jithīlih ʿalā galbī taʿāgab maʿāshiyyah*) (Kurpershoek, *Oral Poetry*, 1, 127). In this example, the swarms of locusts metaphorically express the poet's feeling of being assailed by the onslaught of inspiration: bits and pieces of verse swarm over him and the poet frantically tries to gather as many of them as possible and to mold them to fit his prosodic and thematic scheme. A similar image occurs in early Arabic poetry, as in the line of Imruʾ al-Qays: "I drive the verses in swarms, as a strong youngster drives swarms of locusts" (*adhūdu l-qawāfiya ʿannī dhiyādā, dhiyāda ghulāmin jarīʾin jarādā*) (Jacobi, *Poetik*, 127). In Ibn Sbayyil's verse the word for locusts is *jind*, lit. "soldiers," a synonym for *jarād*, "locusts," (al-ʿUbūdī, *Muʿjam al-ḥayawān ʿind*

al-ʿāmmah, 1, 196–97), whereas *al-dibā* means "young locusts," but is also used to mean simply "locusts."

421 This line is listed as a popular saying about someone who is tossed about by conflicting thoughts and at a loss as to how to deal with his predicament. Al-Juhaymān, *Amthāl*, 6, 163.

422 Lit. "in whose eyes people are like *dhurnūḥ*, the venom of the blister beetle"; see also n. 127. It is a hyperbole for the girl's shyness and chastity: she stays out of people's view as much as possible, well aware of her attractions.

423 "I push him to the wall" (*arkāh ʿalā aṣ-ṣōḥ*). Al-Juhaymān, *Amthāl*, 1, 131; al-ʿUbūdī, *Amthāl*, 86–87; and 776 (*ṭaggih ṣōḥ*).

424 Lit. "Herds that stay far away from the camp on pasture and (sheep and goats) that are driven from the camp in the morning to graze in the surroundings."

425 "I warn you not to run after someone who turns his back to you" (al-Juhaymān, *Amthāl*, 1, 65) and, with the same meaning in different words, *lā taṭrid al-miġfī* (ibid., 6, 208).

426 A frequent opening marker of the *nasīb*, as Muṭawwaʿ Nifī in §42.1.1. Al-Masridī, *Muṭawwaʿ Nifī*, 85 (*ya-wanniti wannat kisīr al-mishāniṭ*). In his comment al-Faraj notes that the raiders are robbed of their booty by a stronger party of plunderers. *Dīwān al-Nabaṭ*, 182.

427 Left alone on the battlefield, grievously wounded, and unable to get up and walk, he is at the mercy of anyone coming. Bedouin loyalties are determined by tribal affiliation, and if a figure appears in the distance, he must fear the worst if the man approaching him belongs to an enemy tribe.

428 Similarly, on the carpenter's metaphor, §§29.1–3.

429 As in the saying "if someone acts arrogantly, don't bother with him; let him stew in his own juice" (*lā taghallā f-takhallā*). Al-Juhaymān, *Amthāl*, 6, 205.

430 This used to be a popular saying: "She made herself attractive with makeup imported from Java" (*zēnhā ṣibgh jāwah*), which means that it is not a natural beauty. The saying is also used as a warning against deceptive appearances in general (al-Juhaymān, *Amthāl*, 3, 238, and 7, 183). According to al-ʿUbūdī, it refers to a cheap red dye for clothes that fades after washing, but that interpretation sounds less convincing in this context.

431 According to another reading: "She nudges another she-camel, *ḍīr*, that shares her calf with the she-camel whose young was killed (*khalūj*) for the purpose of suckling it."

432 See §29.20 for the same proverb. It is used to affirm that a person who is in love cannot be made to go against his inclinations and will remain deaf to advice given by his well-wishers.

433 In these verses the poet gives a catalogue of gruesome diseases that, he prays, will befall his ill-wishers: ulcers in the throat caused by veneral disease, *shijar*; swellings, scrofula, in the glands of joints, ears, and throat, *drāwih* (CA *duruw*); severe pains in the bones, *shawāghi*; a particularly virulent ophthalmia, *akhēḍir*. The vocabulary of these diseases is explained in al-ʿUbūdī, *Muʿjam alfāẓ al-maraḍ wa-l-ṣiḥḥah*, 113–14, 134–35, 22–23, 235.

434 A famous landmark already mentioned in ancient poetry, e.g., Bloch, "Qaṣīda," 126; and in almost the same words by Zuhayr ibn Abī Sulmā: "Look, my friend, do you see the tails of camel trains where the wadi curves, a little beyond Abān?" (*tabayyan khalīlī hal tarā min ẓaʿāʾinin, bi-munʿaraji l-wādī fuwayqa Abānī*) (*Sharḥ dīwān*, 358); and Muzarrid ibn Ḍirār: "And Khālid, though he lives with you at the two Abāns, is not remote from us or far away" (*wa-mā Khālidun minnā wa-in ḥalla fīkumū, Abānayni bi-l-nāʾī wa-lā l-mutabāʿidī*) (*al-Mufaḍḍaliyyāt*, 1, 135; 2, 45).

435 The second option is less attractive, but it has the advantage of giving the lover-poet a good view of her. In this verse, the poet indulges unabashedly in a Bedouin dream, not unlike the firmly sedentary poet, Ibrāhīm, the son of the famous poet of ʿUnayzah, Muḥammad al-Qāḍī, in a poem to Muṭawwaʿ Nifī: "I wish to God that I may quaff from her lips, to cool my heart's flames and recover. / And I wish that I and my sweetheart would become Bedouin, so that we'd ride together through the wilderness, / and spend spring and the hot season in the land of the ʿIlwā tribe, then in winter go upcountry to the highlands of al-Shalāwā tribe" (*yā-lēt w-allah min thanāyāh arwī, abrid lahab galbī ʿasāy ātishāwa / w-yā-lēt ana w-iyyā al-wilīf ntibadwa, anā wu-hū fī kill daww ntakhāwa / miṣyāfinā w-al-gēẓ fī dyār ʿIlwā, w-misnādnā b-al-shibṭ ʿind ash-Shalāwā*). Al-Masridī, *Muṭawwaʿ Nifī*, 35–36.

436 References to an imaginary marriage market are a common topos: see n. 224.

437 This explains the intended meaning of §33.16. "Far from the track," lit. "a person who is on the move after dark (*rāʿ aḍ-ḍwāyah*, from the root *ḍ-w-y* 'to walk, ride at night, in the dark') does not have a share (*khāshar*) in our rendezvous;" i.e., the lovers make sure not to have their rendezvous close to a track such as the one to a well that might be used by people who after dark leave the camp to fetch water.

438 Passion's symptom (*āyat hawā*) has the double meaning of "sign, mark of passion" and the beauty queen herself, as in the verse of ʿAbbās ibn al-Aḥnaf, "you have come to mankind as a miracle (*āyah*) and a reminder" (*fa-jiʾti l-nāsi li-l-āyāti wa-l-ʿibarī*). Bürgel, "The Mighty Beloved," 289.

439 See introduction, n. 52 and translation, n. 298. More than a thousand years before Ibn Sbayyil, the ghazal poet ʿUmar ibn Abī Rabīʿah excused himself in similar manner by pointing to his ancestors in forgivable sin and, like Ibn Sbayyil, maintained that he had

not committed heresy, *bidʿah*: "My infatuation with her is nothing new: men before me pursued affairs and after me men will do the same" (*laysa bi-bidʿati amrin, qad aḥabba l-rijālu qablī wa-baʿdī*). *Dīwān*, 111.

440 On the topos of poetry as a release valve for pent-up emotion, see introduction, n. 11. Similarly, ʿBēd ibn Hwēdī expresses this need to broaden the mind and air one's feelings: "If things get hard I compose my lines of verse, as relief for what I kept in my breast and to comfort the mind" (*ilā ćithir hū ǵāsī timaththalt b-al-ǵīfān, awassiʿ baha ṣadrī ʿasā al-bāl yinsāḥ*), Ibn Junaydil, *Aʿlām*, 162.

441 In his comment on the first hemistich, al-Faraj traces the origin of the expression to a hunter whose falcon flew away (*al-midhhib*, see n. 80), and who tries to coax it back by calling (lit. "throwing voices," see nn. 85 and 164) (*Dīwān al-Nabaṭ*, 187). The reference is to the well-known stories of "martyrs of passion," such as Majnūn Laylā, who went insane. There are many similar stories and poems that circulated in Najdī lore at the time of Ibn Sbayyil. In two single verses attributed to him he refers to one of these, the tale of Ibn Dujaymā: "If green twigs of a tree suffered my grief, they would turn white like the rising sun. / But I fear dying a useless death, like al-Dujaymā, without revenge or paid settlement" (*law inn mā bī b-al-ghṣūn al-wirīgah / ghadann bīḍin ćannihinn al-mishārīǵ; akhāf min mōtin blayyā ḥagīgah / mithl ad-Dujaymā la ṭirid bih walā sīǵ*) (Muḥammad ibn Sbayyil, *Dīwān*, 176). Because Ibn Dujaymā died as a "martyr of love," and not in defense of his kin or in another honorable fashion, his death had no value according to the criteria of tribal society, and therefore there was no price put on it, either by exacting a life for a life or a settlement in goods or money. His name was Dikhīlallah ibn Nāshī, nicknamed al-Dujaymā, of the al-ʿIḍyān tribe of ʿUtaybah. He fell in love with a girl of Binī ʿAṭiyyah of ʿUtaybah–a tribe known for the beauty of its females. He collected the exorbitant bride-price they demanded, but was refused because he sang her praises in verse, which was regarded as dishonorable. He kept singing "his Laylā," and described how he watched the departure of the beloved's caravan (*aẓʿān*) from the top of an elevation, and is said to have died of grief (Ibn ʿAqīl, *Kayfa yamūt al-ʿushshāq*, 471–96). He was probably a contemporary of Ibn Sbayyil; and his tribe, al-ʿIḍyān, at one time inhabited Nifī and maintained close relations with the town, see nn. 60 and 510. Another cycle of stories and verse of that period and on this theme is connected with Khalaf ibn Dʿējā of al-Sharārāt and Mhēsin al-Ribshāni of al-Rwalah (Sowayan, *al-Ṣaḥrā'*, 434–37). This verse of Ibn Sbayyil is also part of the poet-lover's argument with the voices of reason—friends, members of his family, his own good sense—as in early Arabic poetry. ʿUmar ibn Abī Rabīʿah boasts how he refused such counsel: "At last they said, in one of our sessions, 'Have you turned insane or are you under a spell of sorcery?'" (*ḥattā maqāluhumū*

idh ijtamaʿū, a-juninta am dhā dākhilu l-siḥri) (*Dīwān*, 180); and "I followed them with my gaze, lovesick, as if a jinni had snatched up my mind" (*fa-atbaʿtuhunna l-ṭarfa muttabila l-hawā, kaʾannī yuʿānīnī mina l-jinni khāṭifī*) (ibid. 255). See also §33.9.

442 As in the Najdī saying: "If your means are limited, you must adjust your level of ambition" (*tarā ḍiʿīf al-ḥāl mā fīh nōhāt*). Al-Juhaymān, *Amthāl*, 2, 100–1.

443 This line is cited as a popular saying that derides wishful thinking and warns that unrealistic expectations come to haunt those who entertain them. Al-Juhaymān, *Amthāl*, 6, 24.

444 In address to a person whose name one does not know, or does not wish to identify, the word *hann* is used, as in the saying, "so-and-so the son of so-and-so," *hann ibn hann*, i.e., one does not know anything about a certain person or thing, as in the CA saying, *ghāṭ ibn bāṭ*. Al-Juhaymān, *Amthāl*, 9, 108.

445 ʿBēd ibn Hwēdī accords these powers to his beloved in similar terms: "Her words revive the lovesick heart" (*harjitih tinʿish al-galb al-mshaggā al-ʿalīl*). Ibn Junaydil, *Aʿlām*, 160.

446 The contrast is between a wound that is inflicted on the heart, and therefore invisible, and diseases that are plain to see. The rhyme word *abraḥiyyih* is related to *barāḥ*: "a flat and bare stretch of land without elevations or dips where people or animals could hide from view"; *abraḥiyy* means "clear, in the open, in good faith" (communication from Dr. Sowayan). Metaphorically, it means "plain speech, straightforward," as in the line *ṭawārīgī maʿ an-nās abraḥiyyih*, "I deal with people in a straightforward manner."

447 Lit. "her shape is distant" (*zōlih nḥiyyih*).

448 The Prophet's call on the Day of Judgment: "This goes together with the firm belief in the Prophet's intercession (*shafāʿah*), a privilege granted to him during his heavenly journey when he was promised in the Divine Presence that he would be allowed to intercede for his community. Therefore it is often told that Muḥammad will appear on Doomsday with his green flag (the *liwāʾ al-ḥamd*, 'flag of praise') and call out *ummatī ummatī* 'My community!' while all other humans ask only help for themselves. Descriptions of this scene are frequent in popular ballads from early times." Annemarie Schimmel, "The Prophet in Popular Muslim Piety," in the article "Muḥammad," *EI* 2nd ed.

449 The hemistich is a proverbial saying about a relationship without any reciprocity in sentiment, expression, or otherwise (al-Juhaymān, *Amthāl*, 9, 197–98). Lit. "She wants to tame and train me, but she does not act according to my wishes."

450 Lit. "She thinks I'm a lamb that follows the ewe's tail." The saying "he is like a child with tail fat" or "like a fat-tailed lamb" is explained by al-Juhaymān, *Amthāl*, 5, 120–21, as someone who leaves it to others to do the heavy lifting in life.

451 Al-Juhaymān, *Amthāl*, 1, 146, "I administer the drink given to a sacrificial sheep" (*asgāh sharbat ḍiḥiyyah*), meaning the last draft of water given to a sheep before it is slaughtered.

452 In this alliterative *willa f-ʿaff w-ʿāf* the verbs are *ʿaff* "to forgive" and *ʿāf* "to loathe." The beloved takes the shape of a marksman–professional and sharp (*ḥarf*), and dexterous (*dharf*)–who has lit the tip (*ṭaraf*) of her matchlock's fuse (*fitīl*) and is sure to hit the target with lethal effect. Or (*willa*), she may show leniency and be loath to kill her devoted admirer (the word "companion," *khawiy*, fits the rhyme but the intended meaning is "lover").

453 Al-ʿUmarī, *Dīwān Suʿaydān ibn Musāʿid Muṭawwaʿ Nifī*, 14 (hereafter: *Dīwān*). Al-Mishānīṭ is a section of the al-ʿIḍyān tribe of ʿUtaybah who have a reputation for inflicting incurable wounds in battle (in poetic lore, at least). Al-Masridī, *Muṭawwaʿ Nifī*, 85.

454 His companions ask the wounded man if he is still conscious and can hang on, *tiḥīṭ* (CA *aḥāṭa*, "to grasp, fully understand").

455 An ironic pun is intended: the wounded man knows these words of encouragement (*ibshir*, "chin up") will not help him, and therefore offers *bishāyir* "the customary reward for someone who brings good news."

456 Lit. when it has become hard to distinguish a thread in the dark.

457 The wound is too wide (*yinmāz* "it gapes, opens up, cannot be stitched," CA *inmāza* "to be separate, apart") to be held together by stitches, as explained in the next hemistich: even strong, tightly twisted thread (*mirīrah*), such as the one used to fasten leather loops on a falcon's foot (*sbūg*), will not do.

458 *Dīwān*, 15. The Arabic for "tawdry nonsense," *kharāmīṭ*, is a synonym of *kharābīṭ* (CA *kharbaṭa* "to throw into disorder, confuse"). In the tribal poetry war between Shammar and ʿAnizah from 1978 to 1985, the Shammar poet ʿĀyid Fahad al-Ribūḍ shot back to the ʿAnizah poet ʿAbdallah ibn Msayyib al-Ḥirwān al-Jaʿfarī a long poem with the line: "Ibn Msayyib, we easily solve your riddle; leave it, it is just a joke everywhere [. . .] We heard your tawdry nonsense so many times before, this kind of balderdash has become tedious" (*yā-bin Msayyib ghaṭuwkum ʿārifīnih, khallih yā-ʿallih ṣār b-ad-dār malhā* [. . .] *khīṭī w-bīṭī gablikum ʿārifīnih / khurbuṭ w-burbuṭ gablikum min ʿamalhā*). See also n. 461.

459 The word for "offspring" is *tikhkh*, explained to me by an informant as "lineage" (*nasab*). Al-ʿUbūdī quotes this verse and gives the meaning "essence, gist" (*Muʿjam al-kalimāt al-dakhīlah fī lughatinā al-dārijah*, 1, 146–47). "Bought and sold," lit. "who are given away for alms, a paltry sum" (*ṭarāyir*, "pennies given to a mendicant").

460 That is, he is of no use for anything at all: a worthless thing bequeathed by worthless people. Lit. "stemming, inherited from a raid, *mārthat ghazuw* (CA *mīrāth*) of the scrapings (*ḥkāk*, CA *ḥakk* 'scraping, scratching') from the remainders of food at the bottom

of the cooking pot (*adh-dhakhāyir*, CA *dhakhīrah* 'provisions, food, what is stored')." The story is that a group of slaves went raiding but had forgotten to bring a cooking pot. To make their gruel, they scattered their wheat in a well. One of them went looking for the result and drowned, but the other slaves suspected him of diving to the bottom to eat the last scrapings. They went looking for him and suffered the same fate. Similarly, a Najdī saying is: "Three slaves went raiding and the three returned," said about a futile or imaginary enterprise. Al-Juhaymān, *Amthāl*, 5, 26–27.

461 The Arabic is an alliterative expression of the *itbāʿ* type. Lit. "He has turned his devotion to religion (*mbaddilin ṭōʿih*) into empty prattle (*bi-tīṭin w-girmīṭ*)." This type of nonsensical *itbāʿ* is popular in jocular poetry, e.g., the poet of the Shammar tribe who styles himself Skrūb ʿAkif ("Bent Screw") in the line: "If you are love-drunk with me, darling, then I am blotto because of you, my sweetheart" (*kān ant ʿaliyy ya-shōg tinbiṭ nibīṭī / tara anā ʿalēk yā-shōg khāqā bāqā*; and in a repetition: *w-kān ant ʿaliyy yā-shōg khīṭī bīṭī / anā ʿalēk yā-shōg ṭāgā ṭāgā*).

462 "His hopping, dancing on one foot," explained as the meaning of *nṭāz*.

463 See n. 466. As the town's religious man, he marries people but he does so without any scruple as long as they pay him his fee. For instance, if the bride-price is exorbitant he makes no effort to convince them to moderate their demands, as would be expected from a conscientious practitioner of Islamic law. In fact, therefore, he is accused of being corrupt. A Najdī saying is: "He is a man of religion (*muṭawwaʿ*), but when given a chance he filches whatever he fancies and tucks it away" (*mṭawwaʿ w-b-al-khafā in shāf shin lashshih*). Al-Juhaymān, *Amthāl*, 8, 76.

464 *Dīwān*, 16.

465 *Dīwān*, 16–17. For the story behind this exchange, introduction, n. 86.

466 A saying used to taunt those who pretend to have high morals but whose actual conduct suggests otherwise. Al-Juhaymān, *Amthāl*, 8, 73–74; and n. 463.

467 The game "mother of the lines" (*umm al-khuṭūṭ*), also known as *al-ʿatbah* and by other names, is played by boys and girls, though it is more commonly associated with girls. A long rectangle is drawn in the sand, which is then divided into squares; one of the players throws a bone or some other object into one of the marked spaces and, hopping on one leg, tries to move it forward with his or her foot to the next square, and so on, without stepping on one of the lines (*khuṭūṭ*) drawn in the sand. Sowayan, *al-Thaqāfah al-taqlīdiyyah fī al-mamlakah al-ʿarabiyyah al-suʿūdiyyah*, 12 (*al-alʿāb*), 98–101.

468 *Dīwān*, 17. He crows that he successfully provoked Ibn Sbayyil into launching his tirade and making a fool of himself.

469 *Dīwān*, 10.

470 See introduction, pp. xv–xvi and n. 19. The poet addresses himself to Dghaylīb ibn Khnēṣir al-Asʿadī of ʿUtaybah, who joined the game of tempting the poet to sell his mortar (Ibn Junaydil, *Khawāṭir*, 135).

471 Lit. "men riding mature she-camels" (CA *fāṭir*, camel whose eyetooth breaks through) with gray sides from incessant rubbing of the rider's feet on the fur. It is a stereotyped noun-adjective combination that simply means "excellent riding camels," see Kurpershoek, *Oral Poetry*, 2, 125–31.

472 There is some debate on the meaning of the expression "enemy of the Islamic law (Shariah)" in this verse; see Sowayan, *al-Ṣaḥrāʾ*, 419, where "enemy of the Shariah" is explained as "starvation, as it forces people to rob and steal or in other ways to contravene Shariah law" (Ibn Khamīs, *al-Adab al-shaʿbī fī al-jazīrat al-ʿarabiyyah*, 466). Ibn Junaydil comments that it refers to the Bedouin, who waylay and rob travelers and demand a tribute in exchange for "protection" ("token of brotherhood," *khuwwah*, CA *akhāwah*, see nn. 60 and 510) (*Khawāṭir*, 136–37). As the verses are clearly jocular—the mortar of the Muṭawwaʿ is a running gag in a number of poems and narratives—it seems that the reference might be to Bedouin "companions" who would accompany travelers for safety through their tribe's territory. This custom was in violation of the Shariah, which would not allow travelers to be plundered or molested on any account. Therefore, such a Bedouin escort could be called "enemy of the Shariah." The word used for the escort, *mirfig*, occurs in a similar context in a poem by ʿBēd ibn Hwēdī, where he compares his love to the camel carrying the embroidered palanquin from Damascus to Mecca, accompanied by Turkish soldiers who are not in need of a Bedouin escort (*maʿ adwāl Tirkin mā khadhaw maʿhum arfāg*) (Ibn Junaydil, *Aʿlām*, 158). See also Kurpershoek, *Oral Poetry*, 4, 453, where the narrator tells how he had to accompany a friend from another tribe through his tribe's territory even after the establishment of Saudi rule because of a blood feud.

473 Al-Masridī, *Muṭawwaʿ Nifī*, 54–55.

474 Tarfah was the second wife of Muṭawwaʿ Nifī. His first wife was Nūrah, about whom Ibn Sbayyil said: "How delightful, the lightning over Nūrah's land, but her light shines many times brighter [the name Nūrah is related to the word for 'light,' *nūr*]. / More luminous than the sun, the full moon, or a gracious holder scented with delicious perfume" (*yā-zēn barrāgin ʿalā dār Nūrah, nūrāt wājid mēr fī nūraha zōd / lā shams lā nisf ash-shahar min bdūrih, lā ḥiggitin fīhā min al-wizn ʿangūd*). Al-Masridī, *Muṭawwaʿ Nifī*, 79.

475 *Dīwān*, 18. It is said that here Nūrah is his daughter, not his wife, also called Nūrah, see n. 474, al-Masridī, *Muṭawwaʿ Nifī*, 53.

476 Al-Masridī, *Muṭawwaʿ Nifī*, 55–56. Yemeni beans used to stand in the highest regard; they were transported overland, and therefore called *barriyyah* (from CA *barr*, "land, open country").

477 *Dīwān*, 18. A saying, *hōlih w-jōrih*, that mocks a self-important attitude, in this case the pretensions of a *muṭawwaʿ*, a semi-educated man of religion (al-Juhaymān, *Amthāl*, 8, 75).

478 It is said that Abū Zēd was a man from ʿUtaybah tribe. Ḥnēf ibn Sʿēdān was a poet of the Muṭayr tribe with whom Ibn Sbayyil was in jocular correspondence (of which I found no trace) and who was a regular visitor to Nifī. It seems the poetry of Ḥnēf and Muṭawwaʿ Nifī, Sʿēdān ibn Msāʿid, was often confused, also because the similarity of their name, al-Masridī (*Muṭawwaʿ Nifī*, 54). In addition, Abu Zēd and Ḥnēf is an expression meaning "anyone, men without special distinction."

479 *Dīwān*, 19. Al-Masridī mentions that he preferred not to include this piece for reasons of discretion (*Muṭawwaʿ Nifī*, 54).

480 "Fast-shooting" *tiṭārīf* are "burnished copper tubes in which gunpowder is carried" (Musil, *Rwala*, 131). Hence, *milḥiǵt at-tiṭārīf* "men who continuously reach for these tubes," i.e., "fast shooters" (CA *alḥaqa*). Here the fighters *yḥattitūn* "pepper (the enemy with bullets)."

481 The word *zaʿānīf* (CA *zaʿnafah pl. zaʿānif*) means "pieces of leather; anything base and useless." Here the expression *ya-māl al-zaʿānīf*, lit. "may it, or you, go the way of useless rubbish," is a derisive expletive. The first part of the hemistich is not clear, but probably has some sexual connotation. According to Ibn ʿAqīl it is a reference to menstruation (*Ḥadīth al-shahr*, 177).

482 It is not known to which incident this piece refers. The tribe of al-Fuḍūl may have robbed some families in Nifī, like the raid on the town's sheep that inspired Poem 5, and Ibn Sbayyil could have done more to help the victims, in the opinion of al-Muṭawwaʿ. The last line seems to refer to a pilgrimage to Mecca, where the mosque of al-Khayf is situated in Mina. The translation of some of this piece's wording represents a best guess.

483 This exchange is found in al-Masridī, *Muṭawwaʿ Nifī*, 56.

484 A Bedouin made an unannounced visit to Ibn Sbayyil, while he was in the company of Muṭawwaʿ Nifī. They had never seen him before. When he had left, they joked that they should have locked the door before he came (al-Masridī, *Muṭawwaʿ Nifī*, 56). The doors were made from the wood of palm trees and tamarisks. The huge wooden locks were opened with a big wooden key made to fit in notches inside the lock.

485 During a prolonged absence of his wife, Nūrah, on a visit to her family in the region of al-Sirr, Muṭawwaʿ Nifī led his congregation in evening prayers. When he said, "Now make

a straight line!" (*i'tidilū*), he noticed that the sky had clouded over and he saw a flicker of lightning in the direction of al-Sirr (there is a double meaning: the light, *nūrih*, of the lightning, is similar to his wife's name). Then he raised his hands and said this verse. Ibn Sbayyil responded at once with his verse and then called: "Pray!" and the prayer was performed as if nothing had happened. Al-Masridī, *Muṭawwaʿ Nifī*, 55–56.

486 The MS of al-Rabīʿī, 149–50. The mountain is Jabal Ajā, the granite formations that dominate the city of Ḥāʾil. The only source for this piece, the manuscript of al-Rabīʿī, attributes these verses to a poet by the name of Smēr, without further detail except that he belongs to the tribal confederation of ʿUtaybah. The occasion is said to be the death of Muḥammad ibn Rashīd, the ruler of Ḥāʾil, in 1897.

487 "The East" is a rather grandiose designation for the princely fiefdom of Ḥāʾil. Perhaps the poet considers that Ibn Rashīd formally paid allegiance to the Ottoman sultan.

488 A piece of tribal boasting: the riding camels of enemy tribes, usually their best animals, were taken as booty by Ibn Rashīd and distributed among allied tribesmen, who used them for themselves or may have sold them to oasis farmers for the most demeaning labor imaginable for a pedigree racer: as a beast used for well traction. See nn. 26, 359, and 397.

489 The sedentary population was kept on a short leash, but the Bedouin had more affinity with the tribal-based Ibn Rashīd dynasty.

490 In Arabic, the diminutive *ḥaḍēr* is used for *ḥaḍar*, "villagers, settled persons." Traditionally, a man's honor resides in his facial hair, so to be pulled along by the beard, or to have his mustache shaved, is utterly humiliating.

491 In the final line, the Bedouin versifier jokingly makes an exception for Ibn Sbayyil because of his reputation for hospitality. This is a backhanded, condescending version of the compliments traditionally paid to the addressee. In his reply, Ibn Sbayyil does not take this lying down and pays back in kind and then some.

492 The MS of al-Rabīʿī, 150.

493 Al-Ḍayāghim is an honorific designation of the ʿAbdah division of Shammar. They are said to have descended from the ʿAbīdah division of Qaḥṭān in Wādī Tathlīth, beyond the southern borders of Najd. Abū Mitʿib is ʿAbd al-ʿAzīz ibn Mutʿib (r. 1897–1906), the successor of Muḥammad ibn Rashīd. Obviously, this piece of fulsome praise for the House of Rashīd is a later composition than Ibn Sbayyil's ode in praise of Muḥammad ibn Rashīd, see n. 249 and introduction, n. 8.

494 That is, horses and camels.

495 Lit. "salubrious with regard to her finely chiseled teeth" (*'adhiy ar-rahāfi*). It refers to the tribe's women who were left defenseless out in the open when their men were defeated by Ibn Rashīd.

496 Minī' al-Gi'ūd of al-Dawādimī (Ibn 'Aqīl, *al-Shi'r al-nabaṭī*, adds: *al-ṣāni'*, "the blacksmith, " p. 223–24; the lines are also found in Ibn Khamīs, *Man al-qā'il*, 2, 378–79).

497 This piece is in the *hazaj* meter. Ibn Hindī: Muḥammad ibn Hindī ibn Ḥmēd, the shaykh of the al-Mgiṭah tribe and the entire Bargā division of 'Utaybah. The poet's town of al-Dawādimī lies in the general area of this tribal group. His taunts are aimed at tribes that belong to the al-Rūgah division, the other half of 'Utaybah.

498 The Ḥawrān region in southern Syria is often mentioned for its excellent falcons.

499 A *jōbah* is a wide, open, featureless, waterless expanse of land through which people travel without making a halt (*mjawwib*). Wḍākh is the classical Uḍākh, mentioned by the pre-Islamic poet Imru' al-Qays, situated in the land of Banū Numayr. Now it is a village twenty-eight kilometers northwest of Nifī and seven kilometers south of al-Athlah, and about hundred kilometers north of al-Dawādimī. It is situated in a flat expanse of land, which is probably the reason it is called Jōbat Wḍākh.

500 A war cry of Shammar is "[tribesmen] swollen with fury" (*aṭ-ṭanāyā*).

501 Ṭalḥah is a divison of al-Rūgah of 'Utaybah.

502 "Swollen with fury," see n. 261.

503 Abū Mit'ib, see n. 493. Ibn 'Aqīl's substitution of *ḥukm*, rule, for "under his foot" in §44.6, is an example of the Saudi editors' tendency to upgrade the political and cultural correctness of earlier Najdī poetry or even purposely omit words or verses.

504 Ibn Sbayyil is mentioned derisively, as Little 'Abdallah, 'Bēlah, at the end of the piece. There is no known reply by Ibn Sbayyil. The piece gives a rare insight into the town's situation a few years after the previous poem, with tribal and dynastic conflicts washing up to its gates. The story of this poem is told in the manuscript of al-'Ubayyid: "'Abd al-'Aziz ibn Mit'ib al-Rashīd raided incessantly but men no longer stood in awe of him, though he killed and was merciless with those he subjugated. In 1902, he set out with a small army from Buraydah with the intention of raiding the camels of Ibn Mḥayya [shaykh of al-Ḥanātīsh and all of the Ṭalḥah division of 'Utaybah] that were pasturing far from the camp at al-Ridāmā, a place between al-Athlah and Dakhnah. Their tents were pitched at Nifī, where they stayed at the town's wells. As soon as he had rounded up their camels, he decided to head for their camp at Nifī. But Sarrāy ibn Zwēmil, one of the chiefs of Shammar, said, 'May God grant you a long life, at Nifī's wells we will find only pieces of tent and other cloth. We have captured their camels and despoiled them of all their property. Let's turn back to Buraydah.' 'Abd al-'Azīz said, 'I am the brother

of Nūrah! Do you think I am the leader of the Ṣilīlāt tribesmen [one of the second-class tribes, called "crooked smoke," *ʿawaj dikhkhān*, because in the same camp the aristocratic tribes would not allow them the prestige of their own reception area, and they had to do their cooking stealthily]? I will not change my course. By God, I will drive these camels toward their tents.' When the herds overran the tents, a fierce battle ensued until he broke their resistance and took their tents, together with the camels. These events inspired the poet Minīʿ al-Giʿūd from the town of al-Dawādimī, who received regular gifts from Ibn Rashīd and spent time with him for the ruler's entertainment. Each year he went to pay his respects and receive his reward from the prince." *Al-Najm al-lāmiʿ*, 3, 225; Ibn ʿAqīl, *al-Shiʿr al-nabaṭī*, 223–24.

505 The women have been robbed of their outer garments, *mifāṣikh* and *fiṣīkh* (CA *fasakha*, *infasakha* "to be knocked out of place, torn").

506 This line, and Ibn Sbayyil's reply, are in the *hazaj* meter; the lines are found in the Ibn Yahyā MS, 672. Rbayyiʿ al-ʿAbd is from the town of Ḍiriyyah, not far from Riyadh. In his manuscript, Ibn Yaḥyā writes that the girl is also from Ḍiriyyah and that the poem was well-known, but I have not found further information on the poet.

507 The blacksmith and his class are traditionally assigned a low rank in Arab tribal society, e.g., the mocking verse of Jarīr: "You, son of a slave girl, O Farazdaq, amuse yourself at your smithy's fire, the bellows befit a slave" (*wa-anta bnu qaynin yā-Farazdaqu fa-zdahir / bi-kīrika inna l-kīra li-l-qayni nāfiʿū*) (*Sharḥ dīwān Jarīr*, 370). "O Tamīm, is it possible that the honor of Qays is impaired by a slave, a blacksmith whose beard is burnt by sparks?" (*a-qaynun yā-Tamīmu yaʿību Qaysan / yaṭīru ʿalā lahāzimihi al-sharāru*) (Bakhouch, *La rivalité de l'honneur*, 508). An associated species is *al-ṣalab*, the pariah tribe, famous for the beauty of its white-skinned women, who used to accompany the Bedouin and do menial work for them, see Kurpershoek, *Oral Poetry*, 2, 45–46; 3, 259. As explained by an informant, the girl whose beauty is vaunted by the poet Rbayyiʿ al-ʿAbd is compared not to a young and sprightly she-camel, a *ḥāshī*, but to an old she-camel whose calf was slaughtered at birth and that was then made to suckle another camel's calf; such a camel is called a *ḍīr*. She is then compared to a promiscuous she-ass. Therefore, according to this informant, she is a *qaḥbāʾ mafḍūḥah*, "a whore, and known as such to all and sundry."

508 For the *ḍabb*, the Arabian spiny-tailed lizard, also called dabb lizard, see Kurpershoek, *Arabian Satire*, xxiv. The *mikūn* is a female lizard (CA *al-ḍabbah al-makūn* "egg-bearing female dabb lizard").

509 This is reminiscent of the many descriptions in ancient Arabic poetry about the male wild ass biting the female, e.g., the male wild ass who severely bites the female in her rump in a poem of Kaʿb ibn Zuhayr. Bauer, *Altarabische Dichtkunst*, 2, 132–35.

510 Nāmī ibn Thaʿlī of al-ʿIḍyān, an ʿUtaybah tribe led by the al-Ḍīṭ family (see n. 60), took protection money, *akhāwah* or *khuwwah* (lit. "brotherhood"), or *khafārah*, "money paid to a watchman," from Ibn Sbayyil, with the promise to return any possessions from inhabitants of Nifī robbed by members of the ʿUtaybah confederation of tribes. At some point members of al-ʿIḍyān had settled in Nifī, and later left again. Because of these old relations, they were the most obvious choice for Nifī's people to turn to in case property was stolen from them by ʿUtaybah Bedouin in the area surrounding Nifī. Therefore, the verses are probably part of a jocular exchange. Nevertheless, they point to a practice that was condemned and suppressed wherever the Wahhābī movement and the House of Saud imposed their rule. During the first decades of Ibn Sbayyil's life, however, Saudi political power was at its lowest ebb. Poem 5 exemplifies the circumstances in which this "brotherhood" is invoked and how difficult it often was for villagers to make the Bedouin party comply with its obligations. These verses are also quoted by al-ʿUbayyid, who explains Ibn Sbayyil's words as follows: "You have no reason to boast. My payment is in exchange for your barking on the town's outskirts to protect us from any of your kinsmen who violate our property" (*al-Najm al-lāmiʿ*, 273). They are also quoted in al-Fahad, "The ʿImama vs. the ʿIqal," 63, as an example of the practice of paying protection money to the Bedouin. In another version, these lines are exchanged between two anonymous poets, one a Bedouin who says, "I have no fear and it is not out of kindness when you pay us protection money," i.e., it is your own best interest to do so (*mā adrī dhill w-lā tṣafṭūn, antum yōm tiʿṭūn al-akhāwah*), to which the sedentary poet replies: "We give it to you as food for the dog, so that he will protect us, / like cheap makeup women smear on their faces, and let you bark behind our houses" (*niʿṭīhā nabīhā lik ḍarāwah, ḥattākum warānā tanbaḥūni / ṣābightin bi-wajhik ṣibgh jāwah, tanbaḥ min warā al-dīrah w-dūnī*) (al-ʿUbūdī, *Muʿjam al-kalimāt al-dakhīlah*, 1, 198; *Muʿjam al-malābis*, 87). See also n. 430.

511 "Bleary-eyed," *ghmēṣān*, an epithet for "lazy, sleepy," because *ghamaṣ* (from CA *ghamṣ*, "a foam-like effusion from the eye that congeals in a corner of the eye"; *ghamāṣah*, "a little clot in the corner of the eye," Ibn Manẓūr, *Lisān*, 3298) collects in the eye when sleeping. It also denotes the contracted skin under the eyes of someone who just woke up and is still drowsy.

512 Cows are only kept by people of the settled areas and are despised by the Bedouin, and even by a sedentary poet like Ḥmēdān al-Shwēʿir (see Kurpershoek, *Arabian Satire*, 45,

§42–43). When the Bedouin poet al-Dindān asked me about camels in the Netherlands, and I told him that Dutch animal husbandry was mainly about cows, he groaned and said, *yā-gōm*, lit. "the enemy," (CA *qawm*, "people, armed men"), meaning "that's too bad," and the less said about it the better. In this line, it is a slur addressed to sedentary folks with the innuendo that they lack the lofty ambition, far vision, daring, and taste for adventure that characterize the Bedouin and for which the camel is the irreplaceable vehicle.

513 "Gnawed-off bone," *shiluw*, from CA *shilw* pl. *ashlā'*, "remains of skin and tissue of meat that has been skinned and eaten; last remains," as in Zuhayr ibn Abī Sulmā's line: "Shreds of meat where birds of prey hop around" (*daman 'inda shilwin taḥjulu l-ṭayru ḥawlahū*). *Sharḥ dīwān*, 227.

Glossary

The principal source for the names of places in this volume is the geographical dictionary by Saʿd al-Junaydil (1924–2006) that covers the area of High Najd (ʿĀliyat Najd).

Abānāt a famous landmark, visible from a great distance, at the confines of the region of al-Qaṣīm, described by Doughty as two mountains, one behind the other.

ʿAbdallah ibn ʿWēwīd a poet and contemporary of Ibn Sbayyil. One of the members of the "romantic school" of poets in High Najd that counts Ibn Sbayyil as its most prominent representative. His ancestors, who belonged to Ibn Sbayyil's tribe of Bāhilah (pl. Bawāhil), left the town of al-Midhnab for the village of al-Athlah, together with their kinfolk of al-ʿWēwīd (Āl ʿUwaywīd), and built a fortress in the settlement. ʿAbdallah married his uncle's daughter, Ḥisnā, much to the chagrin of Fhēd al-Mijmāj, another poet of this group, whose mother was the sister of Ḥisnā's father. Only a few of his poems have survived–delicate and melodious ghazals that lend themselves to being sung.

Abū Thintēn, al-Gassāmī a family of shaykhs of the al-Gsāsimah tribe of the Dhuwī ʿAṭiyyah section of al-Rūgah of the ʿUtaybah confederation.

ʿAkkāsh an old well, mentioned by the classical geographers as a well of Banū Numayr in Baṭn al-Sirr. There is also a mountain by this name, next to Mt. Ṭimiyyah and near ʿUqlat al-Ṣuqūr, to the west of al-Qaṣīm and northwest of Nifī.

ʿĀliyat Najd (High Najd) the western part of Najd, locally called *al-dīrah al-ʿluwwah*, "the higher district," because of its greater altitude. To go upcountry to the High Najd in a westerly direction is *sannad*, "to go up the elevation"; the eastern districts are called *al-dīrah al-ḥadriyyah*, "the lower regions," and to go in an easterly direction is *ḥaddar*, "to go down to lower country." Lower Najd is the area of Nafūd al-Sirr and Nafūd al-Khabrā, and the lands to their south and west; the High Najd stretches from there westward to the borders of the Hijaz.

al-Anjal a well with brackish water, but fit for camels to drink, in the southern part of the dunes of al-Sirr, about halfway between Tibrāk and al-Quwayʿiyyah.

ʿArjā also called ʿArjah, a well and village thirty kilometers north of al-Dawādimī in Wādī al-Rishā'. It is frequently mentioned in poetry. Yāqūt, writing in the thirteenth century, mentions that the al-ʿArijah well belonged to Banū Numayr. In the nineteenth century it was the location of a famous tribal battle between Ḥarb, Muṭayr, and Qaḥṭān on one side, and on the other ʿUtaybah led by Muḥammad ibn Hindī, who triumphed after a long fight.

al-Athlah a village about eighteen kilometers northeast of Nifī, where the clan of Ibn Sbayyil first settled. It was closely connected with Nifī through family ties. Together with Nifī, it was the center of "the romantic school" (*al-madrasah al-wijdāniyyah*), of which Ibn Sbayyil is considered the foremost representative. Among its poets are Fhēd ibn ʿAbdallah al-Mijmāj, whose work shows many similarities with that of Ibn Sbayyil, and ʿAbdallah ibn ʿAbd al-Hādī ibn ʿWēwīd.

Bargā (Barqā) a major division of the ʿUtaybah tribe, the other half being al-Rūgah. The tribal ranges of Bargā are to the south of al-Rūgah. The two divisions were often on different sides of political and other conflicts. For instance, the chief of Bargā, Ibn Ḥmēd, was one of the leaders of the *ikhwān* who rose in rebellion against ʿAbd al-ʿAzīz ibn Saʿūd, whereas the chief of al-Rūgah played an important part in supporting the later king. Earlier, Bargā was blamed by al-Rūgah for not coming to their aid when they were attacked by the ruler of Ḥā'il, Muḥammad ibn Rashīd.

ʿBēd ibn Hwēdī al-Dōsirī a poet who belonged to the class of *mawālī*, emancipated black slaves, and lived in the small oasis town of al-Shaʿrā'. His imagery is derived from both Bedouin and sedentary life. He is one of the poets of the "romantic school" of High Najd, together with his son Ibrāhīm ibn ʿBēd ibn Hwēdī.

Bjād one of the robbers mentioned in Poem 5. He is known as Bjād al-Kharrāṣ, a member of the al-Kharārīṣ tribe of ʿUtaybah.

blacksmith (ṣāniʿ) the blacksmith and craftsman was held in particular contempt by the Bedouin. The term is often used of the social class associated with the profession. This prejudice has a long history and is shared by Najdī sedentary classes with tribal roots, and is based on the view that, unlike the tribal population, members of this class are from "unknown roots" and therefore of suspect "purity."

Brēh one of the three divisions of the tribe of Mṭēr (Muṭayr). Unlike the ʿIlwā and their shaykhs of al-Duwīsh, there are many shaykhs of Brēh. One of their famous shaykhs and knights was Nāyif ibn Bṣayyiṣ of the al-Ṣiʿrān tribe, who took a prominent role in the nineteenth-century tribal wars against ʿUtaybah.

al-Daʿājīn one of the tribes of the Bargā division of ʿUtaybah. Its members achieved notoriety throughout Najd as raiders. The Bedouin would acknowledge their skill as camel rustlers with grudging respect. Its chief, Nāṣir ibn ʿGayyil, refused to join the movement of the *ikhwān* under the leadership of Ibn Ḥmēd, at that time the paramount shaykh of ʿUtaybah.

David (Dāwūd) the David of the Bible, mentioned several times in the Qurʾan, sometimes together with his son and successor Sulaymān, as in Ibn Sbayyil's poem. In Najdī poetry he is often associated with metalwork and coats of chain mail.

Dhuwī ʿAṭiyyah a major section of the al-Rūgah division of ʿUtaybah.

al-Dimāsīn a subtribe of the al-ʿIḍyān, a tribe of the al-Mzāḥmah section of the al-Rūgah of the ʿUtaybah confederation.

al-Ḍīṭ the family of shaykhs of the al-ʿIḍyān tribe of the al-Rūgah division of ʿUtaybah. Members of the al-ʿIḍyān had settled in Nifī for some time, before leaving again, and the town maintained friendly relations with these shaykhs in the hope that they would protect them against marauding Bedouin of ʿUtaybah.

al-Duwīsh the name of the family of shaykhs of ʿIlwā and of all Mṭēr tribesmen in general (plural al-Dūshān). Ḥsēn al-Duwīsh became a follower of Wahhabism before 1790, but the tribe always kept its Bedouin character.

al-Gāḍī (al-Qāḍī), Muḥammad al-ʿAbd Allāh (1809–68) a learned and wealthy Nabaṭī poet from the town of ʿUnayzah who was famous for his hospitality. He engaged in poetic correspondence with Muḥammad al-ʿAlī al-ʿArfaj, the poet-prince of the neighboring town of Buraydah, and Aḥmad ibn Muḥammad al-Sudayrī, a prominent figure in the Saudi regime of that time. His poem on the subject of coffee making as a prelude to his musings on the woman with whom he was in love, but whose faithfulness he doubted, was translated by Alois Musil.

al-Grayyāt (al-Qurayyāt) a location in northern Arabia, north of al-Jawf oasis, on the way to Jordan.

al-Hazzānī, Miḥsin (d. 1796 or 1805) an important poet from al-Ḥarīq in southern Najd, whose style has been said to resemble that of ʿUmar ibn Abī Rabīʿah. He introduced the *ramal* meter into Nabaṭī poetry. He was also the first of the Nabaṭī poets to introduce strophic rhyme. He was on friendly terms with the family of shaykhs of the Muṭayr tribe, al-Duwīsh.

al-Ḥēd (al-Ḥayd) an agricultural village southwest of Nifī, where a group of Āl Mḥayyā of the al-Ḥanātīsh of ʿUtaybah settled with the sedentary population. There is also Ḥēd al-Ridāmā, a big rocky protrusion in the higher part of Wādī al-Arṭāwī, north of Nifī, about a hundred kilometers north of al-Dawādimī. Both places occur in Najdī poetry.

al-Hēḏal family of chiefs of al-Daʿājīn of the Bargā division of ʿUtaybah.

al-Htēmī, Mashʿān a poet associated in particular with a love poem that opens with the poet's name. Practically nothing is known about his life. His tribe, Htēm, was regarded as being of lower status than the "true Bedouin." From his poetry, one can deduce that as a nomad he wandered from Ḥaḏn, the district of the Bgūm tribe, at Najd's western gate to Mecca, to the area of the Muṭayr tribe in the east. Like other poets in High Najd at that time, he may also have worked as a seasonal laborer in oasis villages.

Ḥwēd ibn Ṭihmāj al-Wāziʿī a poet of the al-ʿIḏyān tribe of the ʿUtaybah confederation who settled with other groups of al-ʿIḏyān, led by shaykhs of the family of al-Ḏīṭ, in Nifī. After ten years they left Nifī for the new settlement (*hijrah*) of Kabshān. But twelve years later he and his kinsmen resumed their nomadic life until he died at the age of sixty-seven in the Rumḥah sands in 1941. One of his sons, Marzūg, became a famous transmitter of his father's and his tribe's poetry and lore, and Marzūg's sons were also transmitters.

al-Hyiyshah see Wādī al-Hyiyshah.

Ibn Liʿbūn, Mḥammad (1790–1831) left Najd for al-Zubayr in southern Iraq, where he engaged in poetic duels with the poet ʿAbdallah ibn Rabīʿah (d. 1856). Following al-Hazzānī, he used the *ramal* meter in love lyrics. His tunes, called *al-alḥān al-liʿbūniyyah*, or *al-sāmirī*, became widely popular and are sung in the Gulf area.

Ibn Rashīd, ʿAbd al-ʿAzīz ibn Mitʿib (r. 1897–1906) the successor of Muḥammad ibn Rashīd. He was an active and warlike emir, but did not command the respect his famous predecessor did. During his rule, the influence of the Ibn Rashīd waned, while the fortunes of the House of Saud were on the rise again. He died in a battle against ʿAbd al-ʿAzīz al-Saʿūd in 1906.

Ibn Rashīd, Muḥammad (r. 1869–97) the ruthless and powerful emir of Ḥā'il and the surrounding area, called the Mountain of Shammar (Jabal Shammar), after the dominant tribe to which the House of Rashīd also belonged. He came to power by killing most of the family members who could have disputed his position, but then showed himself to be a shrewd and competent ruler. He figures in countless stories of European travelers who visited his court and in those of the Bedouin and sedentary people of Najd. His rule is probably the apogee of Arabian Bedouin culture, also because it coincided with a low tide in Wahhābī power connected with the House of Saud. His court was frequented by many poets, especially those from the northern areas and the northern part of Central Arabia. Unlike other members of the Ibn Rashīd family, he was not known for being a poet himself.

Ibn Zirībān, Fayḥān ibn Ǵāʿid (Qāʿid) a knight in the desert tradition of chivalry (*muruwwah*), whose battle cry (*nakhwah*) was "brother of Nūrah" (*akhū Nūrah*), and a shaykh of al-Rikhmān tribe of the ʿIlwā division of Mṭēr (Muṭayr). He was also a well-known poet who celebrated his exploits in verse and exchanged poems with Ibn Sbayyil as part of a poetic correspondence (*murāsalah shiʿriyyah*) in a bantering tone, featuring the conceit of assistance in the shaykh's search for a certain Bedouin beauty. He became one of the legendary figures of the nineteenth-century "Battle Days of the Arabs" (*ayyām al-ʿarab*), so called after the lore connected with the pre-Islamic tribal wars, when the tribes in Central Arabia were very much a law unto themselves. He distinguished himself in famous episodes, such as the string of skirmishes that preceded the battle of al-Ḥarmaliyyah (1891/2), in which ʿUtaybah suffered a rare defeat against Muṭayr. Later he joined the campaigns of the future king ʿAbd al-ʿAzīz and took part in the conquest of Buraydah. He was killed in the campaign for the eastern province of al-Aḥsāʾ in 1905 by a warrior of the al-ʿIjmān tribe.

Ibrāhīm ibn ʿBēd ibn Hwēdī son of ʿBēd ibn Hwēdī al-Dōsirī, who continued his father's work as a poet and prodigious transmitter (*rāwī*). He was born in al-Gwēʿ, near al-Gwēʿiyyah (al-Quwayʿiyyah), and later moved to al-Ḥāyir, south of Riyadh. As an agricultural laborer, he lived a life of penury, like the poets with whom he was in "poetic correspondence" (*murāsalah shiʿriyyah*), Hwēshil ibn ʿAbdallah and ʿAlī al-ʿWēshnī. Later in life, he became part of the circle of companions at the court of Prince ʿAbd Allāh ibn Fayṣal in al-Ṭāʾif.

al-ʿIḍyān (al-ʿUḍyān) see al-Ḍīṭ.

ʿIlwā a section of Mṭēr (Muṭayr) to which belonged the redoubtable chiefs of the tribe as a whole, al-Duwīsh (pl. al-Dūshān), see above.

Jacob (Yaʿqūb) the Jacob of the Bible; son of Isaac, son of Abraham. He is mentioned in the Qur'an sixteen times in ten surahs. Ibn Sbayyil presents him as an example of patience and trust in God in the face of suffering, following the Qur'an and the Hadith literature that expands on it.

Jarīr (d. 728–29) a poet especially famous for his exchanges of invective poetry (*hijāʾ*) with his rival al-Farazdaq. Their clashes in meter and rhyme (*naqāʾiḍ*), over a period of forty years, are considered a literary monument of classical Arabic poetry. He died in his eighties in the little town of Uthayfiyah in al-Yamāmah province of Najd, where in the eighteenth century another feared *hijāʾ* poet, Ḥmēdān al-Shwēʿir, had found refuge from his enemies in his hometown of al-Qaṣab.

Jimrān an old well, and a sharp-pointed black mountain (*madhrūb Jimrān*) of the same name, north of al-Dawādimī and ʿArjah village, in the tribal territory of al-Rūgah of ʿUtaybah, frequently mentioned in poetry on account of its good pastures.

Job (Ayyūb) the Job of the Bible, mentioned only twice in the Qur'an, but whose story was greatly amplified in later literature. His piety and generosity made him the target of the devil (Iblīs) who challenged God to test him. Obviously, this is Ibn Sbayyil's model for the trials he must undergo as an adherent of the cult of love (*ahl al-hawā*) and explains his use of the word *imtiḥān*, "test, trial," in several poems.

Jonah (Yūnus) the prophet Jonah of the Bible, mentioned four times in the Qur'an as Yūnus, once as Dhū l-Nūn ("He of the Nūn"), and once as "the whale man" (*ṣāḥib al-ḥūṭ*), i.e., a prophet who is swallowed by a whale. If he had not praised God, he would have remained in the whale's belly until the resurrection.

Joseph (Yūsuf) the Joseph of the Hebrew Bible. The Surah of Yūsuf in the Qur'an is completely devoted to the telling of the Joseph story.

Kabshān an old well in the province of al-Dawādimī that is often praised in poetry for its sweet water. Its village is inhabited by members of the al-Marāshdah tribe and the al-ʿIḍyān tribe of ʿUtaybah, but after some time the latter tribe left again. It is mentioned by Doughty as a landmark in the High Najd on his way from al-Qaṣīm to Jeddah, as a basalt mountain and water source.

al-Kharrāṣ the singular of al-Kharārīṣ, a tribe of the Dhuwī ʿAṭiyyah section of al-Rūgah of the ʿUtaybah confederation.

al-Kirzān a subdivision (with the nisbah Krēzī) of the al-Mgiṭah tribe—itself one of the eight divisions of Bargā, the division that together with al-Rūgah constitutes the ʿUtaybah confederation. Its importance resides in the fact that al-Ḥmidah, the sons of Ḥmēd, Ibn Ḥmēd, who are the house of paramount chiefs of Bargā, constitute one of the sections of al-Kirzān.

al-Majmaʿah a regional center founded in 1427 by ʿAbd Allāh al-Shammarī with permission from Ibn Mudlij al-Wāʾilī from nearby al-Ḥarmah, a town that was subsequently eclipsed by the new settlement. The ʿUthmān family, whose ancestor is mentioned by the poet Ḥmēdān al-Shwēʿir, are his descendants.

al-Marāshdah a tribe of the al-Mzāḥmah section of al-Rūgah of the ʿUtaybah confederation.

al-Midhnab a town on the southern edge of the al-Qaṣīm region on the way to the al-Sirr region.

al-Mijmāj al-Tamīmī, Fhēd ibn ʿAbdallah ibn Fhēd a poet whose grandfather, like Ibn Sbayyil's forefathers, moved from al-Midhnab to al-Athlah, where he married the sister of Ḥmūd and ʿAlī al-ʿWēwīd. A contemporary of ʿAbdallah ibn Sbayyil, he eked out a living in agricultural labor. Like Ibn Sbayyil, al-Mijmāj excels at painting stirring scenes about the Bedouin who spent the hot season at the wells of al-Athlah.

Moses (Mūsā) the Moses of the Bible, in the Qurʾan a prophet who is a precursor of Muḥammad and the nemesis of Pharaoh, his unbelieving enemy. He baffles Pharaoh's magicians when his rod devours their rods, and performs other miracles. Najdī poetry also refers to al-Sāmirī who fashions the lowing golden calf.

Mrēṭbah (Murayṭibah) a wide plain from which the water runs into Wādī al-Rishā, at a distance of between fifty and one hundred kilometers to the northeast of al-Dawādimī, in the tribal land of al-Rūgah of ʿUtaybah. It is frequently mentioned in poetry because of its good pasture, especially the salty plants (*ḥamḍ*) on which the camels thrive.

Mṭēr (Muṭayr) one of the major tribal confederations of Central Arabia. When Ibn Sbayyil flourished as a poet, it was in warlike competition with many of its peers: the confederations of Shammar, Qaḥṭān, ʿUtaybah, ʿNizah (ʿAnizah), Ḥarb, al-ʿIjmān, and others. Its territories are on the eastern side of al-Yamāmah and al-Qaṣīm, adjoining the al-Dahnā' sands. Its legendary leader Fayṣal al-Duwīsh played a prominent role in the Saudi conquests. In 1912 he and his tribe founded al-Arṭawiyyah, the first settled colony (*hijrah*) of Bedouin, who joined the fiercely Wahhābī cohorts of the *ikhwān*. They did not consider themselves "subjects." Fayṣal became the ringleader of the *ikhwān* who rebelled against the later king ʿAbd al-ʿAzīz, who defeated them in the battle of al-Sbilah, not far from al-Arṭawiyyah. The confederation consists of three major tribal groups: Binī ʿAbdillah, Brēh, and ʿIlwā. Fayṣal al-Duwīsh, and his family of al-Dūshān, belong to the ʿIlwā, as does Ibn Sbayyil's poetic correspondent, Fayḥān ibn Zirībān, who is the shaykh of another group of the ʿIlwā.

al-Muʿallaqāt "the suspended poems," a pre-Islamic collection of poems which in the early centuries of Islam were among the most admired long poems of the qasida type. They are apparently so called because the poems, written on cloth in letters of gold, were said to have been hung on the walls of the Meccan Kaaba, but other explanations are also given.

Najd generally understood as the central part of the Arabian peninsula—the plateau area roughly situated to the east of the mountain ranges of the Hijāz, south of the Nafūd desert, west of the al-Dahnā' sands, and including Wādī al-Dawāsir in the south but not beyond it. This large region is subdivided into areas that differ greatly in character. Historically and environmentally, its society has been characterized by contrast between sedentary and Bedouin groups. Nabaṭī poetry is essentially a Najdī phenomenon with roots in classical Arabian culture, a pedigree shared by many of the sedentary and Bedouin tribes in Najd.

Nifī a town known in ancient Arabia as Nafy, and a well mentioned by the pre-Islamic poet Imru' al-Qays. The small town is situated ninety kilometers to the north of al-Dawādimī. The Ibn Sbayyil family moved to Nifī from al-Midhnab, together with families of the Htēm tribe. They dug wells and started to work in agriculture. It was settled for some time by the al-Ḍīṭ family of shaykhs of the al-ʿIḍyān tribe of ʿUtaybah, who later left again. In the first half of the twentieth century it was settled by ʿUmar ibn Rbēʿān (Rubayʿān) of Dhuwī Thbēt (Thubayt), the shaykhs of al-Rūgah division of ʿUtaybah, who had fought as close allies of King ʿAbd al-ʿAzīz. In the town, the Ibn Sbayyil family kept the mayoralty of the original sedentary population. The current mayor is Muḥammad ibn ʿAbd al-ʿAzīz ibn ʿAbdallah, a grandson of the poet, who has published a diwan of his grandfather's poetry and makes television programs about poetry.

al-Nijaj a big black mountain and a famous landmark between the lower end of Wādī al-Shubrum and Wādī al-Jarīr, opposite the Ashmāṭ Mountains. Wādī al-Jarīr runs between it and the Gāʿān and ʿAblān mountains. It lies in an area inhabited by Ḥarb and the Binī ʿAbdillah division of the Mṭēr.

Nimr ibn ʿAdwān (1745–1823) a poet of the ʿAdwān tribe in the al-Balqāʾ district of Jordan, who became famous for the poetry in which he mourned the loss of his wife Waḍhā, a member of the Binī Ṣakhr tribe who died at a young age from cholera.

al-Nīr a big black mountain, intersected by many wadis and rich in waterholes, on the road between al-Dawādimī and ʿAfif. It is one of Najd's most famous landmarks and is mentioned in numerous poems. Its northwestern part is in the territory of al-Rūgah of ʿUtaybah and its southeastern part in that of al-Nfaʿah of the Bargā division of ʿUtaybah.

Noah (Nūḥ) the Noah of the Bible, a figure frequently mentioned in the Qur'an and popular in legend. He appears as prophet and admonisher, is laughed at by his people, and saves two of every kind of living creature by taking them into the ark.

Qaḥṭān traditionally tribes of South Arabian descent, as opposed to ʿAdnān, the northern Arabian tribes. For centuries it has denoted a large tribal group in areas southwest of Najd, like Wādī Tathlīth and Bīshah, and the desert lands known as Ḥaṣāt Qaḥṭān, "Qaḥṭān Rocks," where they frequently clashed with the Bargā divison of ʿUtaybah. They also migrated farther north and settled in many towns. They are mentioned in chronicles for the first time in the second half of the sixteenth century, as an ally of the Dawāsir tribe.

al-Qaṣīm a prosperous agricultural region approximately four hundred kilometers northwest of Riyadh.

al-Ridāmā see al-Ḥēd.

al-Rifīʿah a small village about fifty kilometers north of al-Dawādimī, inhabited by members of the al-Maghāyrah tribe of the al-Rūgah of ʿUtaybah.

al-Rikhmān one of the tribes of the ʿIlwā division of the Mṭēr (Muṭayr). Von Oppenheim mentions that Fayḥān ibn Zirībān (miswritten as "Djreibān") is named as the shaykh of this tribe.

al-Rūgah (al-Rūqah) the northern division of the ʿUtaybah confederation (see also Bargā), whose tribal lands straddle the road from Riyadh to Mecca. The division's paramount shaykh is Ibn Rbēʿān (Ibn Rubayʿān), whose headquarters are now in Nifī, the town of the poet Ibn Sbayyil.

Ṣalab singular *ṣlubī,* a member of the pariah tribe of handicraftsmen who used to accompany the Bedouin tribes on their migrations. Renowned as skilled hunters, they dressed in the hide of the game they killed and rode donkeys, not camels. They shod the Bedouin's horses, repaired their metalwork, and performed other manual jobs, but otherwise lived a life completely separate from them. When a Bedouin camp was raided and plundered, the *ṣalab* would go on with whatever they were doing, knowing that they would not be touched. If one of their possessions was accidentally included in the booty, it would be returned as soon as the mistake was discovered. As a species of the *ṣāniʿ*, the blacksmith, a social class which was held in particular contempt by the Bedouin, no *ṣlubī* would be allowed to marry a Bedouin's daughter. The daughters of the *ṣalab* were reputed for their white skin, beauty, and supposedly looser morals, and for that reason feature in many young Bedouin's erotic daydreams.

al-Sarḥā there are many torrent beds with this name, which is derived from *sarḥ*, a great tree with spreading branches of the *Cotoneaster nummularia.* There is one likely candidate at Damkh mountain in the land of Bargā of ʿUtaybah; one west of the town of ʿAfīf, with a good well, in the land of Dhuwī ʿAṭiyyah of ʿUtaybah; one about fifty kilometers west of ʿAfīf, also in the land of ʿUtaybah; and one north of al-Khāl mountain, west of al-Difīnah in Mecca province, in the land of ʿUtaybah.

Ṣayʿar a tribe of Qaḥṭān origin whose area extends from the northern Hadramawt in Yemen to the southern part of the Empty Quarter desert in Saudi Arabia. Like the al-Sharārāt tribe in the north, it is famous for its breed of fast and hardy camel mounts. The tribe is frequently mentioned in Wilfred Thesiger's *Arabian Sands*, where its name is rendered Saar.

Shaddād ibn ʿĀd a legendary figure, the king of the people of ʿĀd and the lost city of Iram of the Pillars, mentioned in the Qurʾan, destroyed for its defiance of the warnings given by the prophet Hūd. Shaddād is said to have conquered Arabia and Iraq and is mentioned in narratives as a ferocious fighter. He is the subject of the 277th to 279th nights of *The Thousand and One Nights*, where he is presented as the mightiest king of the earth and the owner of untold riches, and is eventually destroyed, together with his armies of unbelievers.

Shaqrāʾ a town in al-Washm region that served as a trading post for the Bedouin of the High Najd. Its inhabitants belong to Banū Zayd (Binī Zēd), a group that traces its descent from Qaḥṭān.

al-Shaʿrāʾ an old town at the foot of the Thahlān mountain, thirty-five kilometers east of al-Dawādimī, on the pilgrim and caravan road to Mecca and the Hijaz, surrounded by good pasturelands and with plentiful water sources. It was an important market and commercial center for the Bedouin.

al-Sharārāt a tribe in northern Arabia that in Bedouin opinion belonged to the lower-status tribal group of Htēm (Hutaym) because they paid protection money to other tribes and to the Ibn Rashīd princes in Ḥāʾil. They enjoyed renown as hunters and were skilled breeders of excellent riding camels. After the establishment of Saudi rule, their status improved and many of them attained positions of privilege.

al-Shiʿb many places are called after a *shiʿb*, "a minor dry watercourse." Perhaps it refers to what is known as Shiʿb al-ʿAsībiyyāt between Wādī al-Jarīr and Wādī al-Shubrum to the west of ʿAfīf in the tribal area of al-ʿIḍyān of ʿUtaybah.

al-Sirr a famous wadi, long known by this name, east of al-Dawādimī, that on its eastern side runs into the sands of Nafūd al-Sirr. It is an agricultural area, rich in water, that supplies the markets of Riyadh and is intersected by the old road from Riyadh to al-Qaṣīm in a south–north direction.

Sudayr a populous agricultural region about 180 kilometers north of Riyadh. It encompasses most of Wādī al-Faqī. Among its many towns are Julājil, al-Majmaʿah, al-Ghāṭ, al-Rawḍah, al-Tuwaym, al-Ḥawṭah, and al-Ḥuṣūn.

al-Ṣummān a large tract of rugged, stony uplands in eastern Arabia, east of the sands of al-Dahnāʾ. It is excellent pastureland after rains, and mentioned already by early poets, notably Dhū l-Rummah. In more recent times it was a grazing area for the Bedouin of the Mṭēr (Muṭayr), al-ʿIjmān (al-ʿUjmān), Gḥaṭān (Qaḥṭān), Sbēʿ (Subayʿ), and Binī Khālid.

Ṭāmi the name of a member of the Abū Thintēn family of the al-Gsāsimah tribe of ʿUtaybah.

al-Thanādī also in the singular, al-Thanduwah, a hilly and rocky desert where the camels walk with difficulty. It runs in a north–south direction to the northeast of al-Dawādimī.

Thirb (Tharib) the first of four wells on the way from Najd to Medina, in the tribal area of Binī ʿAbdillah of Mṭēr. According to Yāqūt's thirteenth-century geographical dictionary, Tharib is a well in the tribal land of Muḥārib.

al-Ṭwāl deep wells on the caravan road from Najd to Kuwait, among them al-Lahābah and al-Laṣāfah.

ʿUmar ibn Abī Rabīʿah (644–712 or 721) the most prominent representative of the Hijazi school of the ghazal (love poetry); he was a member of the Meccan aristocracy.

ʿUtaybah a confederation in Central Arabia whose tribal ranges stretch over a vast expanse of high desert between the Saudi capital, Riyadh, and the Hijaz province and Mecca. Ibn Sbayyil's town, Nifī, is situated in this territory.

Wādi al-Hyiyshah a torrent bed north of Nifī that runs east, parallel to Wādī Nifī, toward Wadī al-Rishā. It is known as one of the best pasturelands and after rains the Bedouin jockey for space on its meadows. It is situated about one hundred kilometers north of al-Dawādimī in the tribal lands of al-Rūgah of ʿUtaybah.

Zēd a generic name given to the beloved whose identity should not be revealed. In Najdī poetry, the beloved is generally referred to by the male pronoun.

Bibliography

Abū Dhu'ayb al-Hudhalī. *Dīwān Abī Dhu'ayb al-Hudhalī*. Edited by Sūhām al-Miṣrī. Beirut: al-Maktab al-Islāmī, 1998.

Abū Tammām. *Naqā'iḍ Jarīr wa-l-Akhṭal: 'Uniya bi-ṭab'ihā li-awwal marrah 'an nuskhat al-Astānah al-waḥīdah wa-'allaqa ḥawāshīhā Anṭūn Ṣāliḥānī al-Yasū'ī*. Beirut: al-Maṭb'ah al-Kāthūlīkiyyah al-Ābā' al-Yasū'iyyīn, 1922.

Ahlwardt, W. *The Divans of the Six Ancient Arabic Poets Ennābiga, 'Antara, Tharafa, Zuhair, 'Alqama and Imruulqais*. London: Trübner, 1870.

Bakhouch, Mohamed. *La rivalité d'honneur ou la fabrique de l'altérité: Les joutes satiriques [Naqā'iḍ] entre Ǧarīr et al-Aḫṭal*. Marseille: Presses Universitaires de Provence, 2018.

Bauer, Thomas. *Altarabische Dichtkunst. Eine Untersuchung ihrer Struktur und Entwicklung am Beispeil der Onagerepisode*. Wiesbaden: Harrassowitz, 1992.

———. "The Arabic Ghazal: Formal and Thematic Aspects of a Problematic Genre." In *Ghazal as World Literature II: From a Literary Genre to a Great Tradition*. Edited by Angelika Neuwirth, Michael Hess, Judith Pfeiffer, and Börte Sagaster, 3–13. Orient-Institut Istanbul 4. Istanbul: Orient Institut Istanbul and Ergon Verlag, 2006.

———. *Liebe und Liebesdichtung in der arabischen Welt des 9. und 10. Jahrhunderts. Eine literatur und mentalitätsgeschichtliche Studie des arabischen Ġazal*. Diskurse der Arabistik 2. Wiesbaden: Harrassowitz Verlag, 1998.

Behmardi, Vahid. "The Wajdiyyāt of 'Ayn al-Quḍāt al-Hamadānī: Youthful Passions of a Ṣufi in the Making." In *Ghazal as World Literature II: From a Literary Genre to a Great Tradition*. Edited by Angelika Neuwirth, Michael Hess, Judith Pfeiffer, and Börte Sagaster, 39–46. Orient-Institut Istanbul 4. Istanbul: Orient Institut Istanbul and Ergon Verlag, 2006.

Bloch, A. "Qaṣīda," *Asiatische Studien* 2 (1948): 106–32.

Bräunlich, E. "The Well in Ancient Arabia." *Islamica* 1(1925): 41–76, 288–343.

Al-Bulayhid, Muḥammad ibn 'Abd Allāh ibn. *Ṣaḥīḥ al-akhbār 'ammā fī bilād al-'Arab min al-āthār*. 5 vols. Cairo: Maṭba'at al-Sunnah al-Muḥammadiyyah, 1972.

Burckhardt, John Lewis. *Notes on the Bedouins and Wahabys*. London: H. Colburn and R. Bentley, 1830. Reprint, Cambridge: Cambridge University Press, 2010.

Bürgel, Johann Christoph. "The Mighty Beloved. Images and Structures of Power in the Ghazal from Arabic to Urdu." In *Ghazal as World Literature I: Transformations of a Literary Genre*. Edited by Thomas Bauer and Angelika Neuwirth, 283–309. Beiruter Texte und Studien 89. Beirut: Orient Institut Beirut and Ergon Verlag, 2005.

Burton, Richard F. *Personal Narrative of a Pilgrimage to al-Madinah and Mecca*. 2 vols. London: Tylston and Edwards, 1893. Reprint, New York: Dover Publications, 1964.

Dhū al-Rummah, Ghaylān ibn ʿUqbah al-ʿAdawiy. *Diwān Dhī al-Rummah*. Edited by ʿAbd al-Quddūs Abū Ṣāliḥ. 3 vols. Beirut: Mu'assasat al-Īmān, 1982.

Dmitriev, Kirill. "Hudhayl, Banū." In *Encyclopedia of Islam, Three*. Edited by Kate Fleet, Gudrun Krämer, Denis Matringe, John Nawas, and Everett Rowson. Brill Publishers, 2017. Online edition.

———. *Das poetische Werk des Abū Ṣakhr al-Hudhalī: Eine literaturanthropologische Studie*. Diskurse der Arabistik 15. Wiesbaden: Harrassowitz Verlag, 2008.

Doughty, Charles M. *Travels in Arabia Deserta*. 2 vols. London: Jonathan Cape, 1936. Reprint of the third edition, New York: Dover, 1979.

Euting, Julius. *Tagebuch einer Reise in Inner-Arabien*. 2 vols. Leiden: E. J. Brill, 1896–1914.

Al-Fahad, Abdulaziz H. "The ʿImama vs. the ʿIqal: Hadari-Bedouin Conflict and the Formation of the Saudi State," in *Counter-narratives: History, Contemporary Society, and Politics in Saudi Arabia and Yemen*. Edited by Madawi Al-Rasheed and Robert Vitalis, 35–76. New York: Palgrave Macmillan, 2004.

Al-Faraj, Khālid. *Dīwān al-Nabaṭ, majmūʿah min al-shiʿr al-ʿāmmī fī Najd*. Vol. 1. Damascus: Maṭbaʿa al-Taraqqī, 1952.

Farrāj, ʿAbd al-Sattār Aḥmad. *Dīwān Majnūn Laylā*. Cairo: Maktabat Miṣr, n.d.

Al-Fuhayd, Mandīl ibn Muḥammad ibn Mandīl. *Min ādābinā al-shaʿbiyyah fī l-jazīra al-ʿarabiyyah, qiṣaṣ wa-ashʿār*. 4 vols. Riyadh: n.p., 1981–84.

Geiger, Bernhard. "Die Muʿallaqa des Ṭarafa." *Wiener Zeitschrift für die Kunde des Morgenlandes* 19 (1905): 323–70.

Habib, John S. *Ibn Sa'ud's Warriors of Islam. The Ikhwan of Najd and Their Role in the Creation of the Sa'udi Kingdom, 1910–1930*. Leiden: E. J. Brill, 1978.

Al-Haftā', Khālid ibn Hajāj, and Manṣūr ibn Murwī al-Shāṭirī. *Ta'rīkh qabīlat Muṭayr. Markaz Qabīlat Muṭayr li-l-Dirāsāt wa-l-Buḥūth al-Ta'rīkhiyyah bi-l-Mamlakah al-Muttaḥidah*. 2010. www.mtcshr.com.

Al-Ḥātam, ʿAbd Allāh ibn Khālid. *Min al-shiʿr al-Najdī, dīwān al-shāʿir ʿAbd Allāh ibn Ḥmūd ibn Sbayyil*. Dhāt al-Salāsil, 1984.

———. *Khiyār mā yulṭaqat min al-shiʿr al-nabaṭ*. Vol. 2. 1st ed., al-Maṭbaʿah al-ʿUmūmiyyah: Damascus, 1968. 3rd ed, Kuwait: Dhāt al-Salāsil, 1981.

Al-Haṭlānī, Muḥammad ibn Ibrāhīm. *Dīwān ashʿār nabaṭiyyah min al-jazīrah al-ʿarabiyyah.* Riyadh: n.p., 2009.

Hess, J. J. "Beduinennamen aus Zentralarabien." *Sitzungsberichte der Heidelberger Akademie der Wissenschaften*, 19. Heidelberg: Carl Winter's Universitätsbuchhandlung, 1912.

———. *Von den Beduinen des Innern Arabiens.* Zurich: Max Niehaus Verlag, 1938.

Ḥmēdān al-Shwēʿir. *See* Kurpershoek.

Holes, Clive. *Dialect, Culture, and Society in Eastern Arabia.* Vol. 1, *Glossary*; vol. 2, *Ethnographic Texts*; vol. 3, *Phonology, Morphology, Syntax, Style.* Leiden: E. J. Brill, 2001–16.

———. "The Language of Nabaṭi Poetry." In *Encyclopaedia of Arabic Language and Linguistics On-Line Edition.* Edited by R. De Jong and L. Edzard. Leiden: E. J. Brill, 2012.

Homerin, Th. Emil. "Mystical Improvisations: Ibn al-Fāriḍ plays al-Mutanabbī." In *Ghazal as World Literature I: Transformations of a Literary Genre.* Edited by Thomas Bauer and Angelika Neuwirth, 107–29. Beiruter Texte und Studien 89. Beirut: Orient Institut Beirut and Ergon Verlag, 2005.

———. "Preaching Poetry: The Forgotten Verse of Ibn al-Shahrazūrī," *Arabica* 38 (1991): 87–101.

Huber, Charles. *Journal d'un voyage en Arabie (1883–1884).* Paris: Société Asiatique et la Société de Géographie, 1891.

Ibn Abī Rabīʿah, ʿUmar. *Diwān ʿUmar ibn Abī Rabīʿah.* Beirut: Dār Ṣādir, 1966.

Ibn ʿAqīl, Abū ʿAbd al-Raḥmān al-Ẓāhirī. *Ḥadīth al-Shahr. Min Shiʿr Muṭawwaʿ Nifī* 7. Riyadh: Maktabat Ibn Ḥazm, 2010.

———. *Al-ʿIjmān wa-zaʿīmuhum Rākān ibn Ḥithlēn.* Kuwait: Dār al-Salāsil, 1995.

———. *Kayfa yamūt al-ʿushshāq.* Riyadh: Dār ibn Ḥazm, 1997.

———. *Al-Shiʿr al-nabaṭī, awzān al-shiʿr al-ʿāmmī bi-lahjat ahl Najd wa-l-ishārah ilā baʿḍ alḥānih.* Riyadh: self-published, 1992.

Ibn Duwayrij, ʿAbdallah. *Dīwān ʿAbdallah ibn Duwayrij (Dwērij).* Edited by Bandar ibn Nāṣir al-Dūkhī. Riyadh: Iṣdārāt al-Nakhīl, 1990.

Ibn Hadhlūl, Suʿūd. *Ta'rīkh mulūk Āl Suʿūd.* 2 vols. 2nd ed, Riyadh: Maṭābiʿ al-Farazdaq, 1982.

Ibn Juʿaythin (Jʿēthin), Ibrāhīm. *Dīwān min al-shiʿr al-shaʿbī li-shāʿir Sudayr.* Edited by ʿAbd al-ʿAzīz Muḥammad al-Uḥaydib. Riyadh: Maṭābiʿ al-Ishāʿ, 1982.

Ibn Junaydil, Saʿd ibn ʿAbd Allāh. *Khawāṭir wa-nawādir turāthiyyah.* Riyadh: al-Maktabah al-Suʿūdiyyah, al-Jamʿiyyah al-Suʿūdiyyah li-l-Thaqāfah wa-l-Funūn, 1987.

———. *Man al-qā'il, As'ilah wa-ajwibah fī l-shiʿr wa-l-ḥikam wa-l-amthāl.* 2 vols. 1st ed., Riyadh: n.p., 1985. 2nd ed., Riyadh: n.p., 1993.

———. *Min aʿlām al-adab al-shaʿbī, shuʿarāʾ al-ʿĀliyah.* Riyadh: al-Maktabah al-Suʿūdiyyah, al-Jamʿiyyah al-Suʿūdiyyah li-l-Thaqāfah wa-l-Funūn, Maṭābiʿ al-Farazdaq, 1980–81.

———. *Al-Muʿjam al-jūghrāfī li-l-bilād al-ʿarabiyyah al-suʿūdiyyah ʿĀliyat Najd.* 3 vols. Riyadh: n.p., 1978.

———. *Al-Sānī wa-l-sāniyah.* Riyadh: Maṭābiʿ Jāmiʿat al-Imām Muḥammad ibn Suʿūd, 1988.

Ibn Khamīs, ʿAbd Allāh ibn Muḥammad. *Al-Adab al-shaʿbī fī al-jazīrat al-ʿarabiyyah.* 2nd ed, Riyadh: n.p., 1982.

———. *Taʾrīkh al-Yamāmah, maghānī al-diyār wa-mā lahā min akhbār wa-āthār.* 7 vols. Riyadh: Maṭābiʿ al-Farazdaq, 1987.

Ibn Manẓūr. *Lisān al-ʿArab.* Cairo: Dār al-Maʿārif, n.d.

Ibn Raddās, ʿAbdallah ibn Muḥammad. *Shāʿirāt min al-bādiyah,* 2 vols. 6th and 4th ed. Riyadh: Maṭābiʿ al-Bādiyah, 1984/5.

———. *Shuʿarāʾ min al-bādiyah,* 4th ed. Riyadh: Maṭābiʿ al-Bādiyah, 1984/5.

Ibn Sbayyil, Muḥammad ibn ʿAbd al-ʿAzīz. *Dīwān Ibn Sbayyil: shiʿr al-shāʿir al-mashhūr ʿAbd Allāh ibn Ḥmūd ibn Sbayyil.* Riyadh: n.p., 1988. References are to the second expanded edition of 2004.

Ibn Shuraym (Ibn Shrēm), Sulaymān. *Dīwān Sulaymān ibn Shuraym.* Edited by Bandar al-Dūkhī. Riyadh: Muʾassasat al-Nakhīl li-l-Nashr, 1989.

Al-Iṣfahānī, Abū l-Faraj. *Kitāb al-Aghānī.* Cairo: Maṭbaʿat Dār al-Kutub al-Miṣriyyah, 1928.

Jacobi, Renate. "Die Anfänge der arabischen Ghazalpoesie: Abū Dhuʿaib al-Hudhalī." *Der Islam* 61 (1984): 218–50.

———. "Nasīb," in *Encyclopedia of Islam,* Edited by P. Bearman, Th. Bianquis, C. E. Bosworth, E. van Donzel, and W. P. Heinrichs. 2nd ed. E. J. Brill, 2012. doi:10.1163/1573-3912_islam_COM_0849

———. *Studien zur Poetik der altarabischen Qaṣide. Wiesbaden*: Franz Steiner Verlag, 1971.

———. "Time and Reality in Nasīb and Ghazal." *Journal of Arabic Literature* 16 (1985): 1–17.

———. "ʿUmar ibn Abī Rabīʿa," in *Encyclopaedia of Arabic Literature.* Vol. 2, Edited by Julie Scott Meisami and Paul Starkey, 791–92. London and New York: Routledge, 1998.

———. "Al-Walīd Ibn Yazīd, the Last Ghazal Poet of the Umayyad Period." In *Ghazal as World Literature I. Transformations of a Literary Genre.* Edited by Thomas Bauer and Angelika Neuwirth, 131–55. Beiruter Texte und Studien 89. Beirut: Orient Institut Beirut and Ergon Verlag, 2005.

Jarīr. *Sharḥ dīwān Jarīr.* Edited by Muḥammad Ismāʿīl ʿAbd Allāh al-Ṣāwī. Cairo: Maṭbaʿah al-Ṣāwī, n.d.

Juʿaythin, Ibrāhīm ibn. *Dīwān al-shāʿir al-shaʿbī li-shaʿir Sudayr Ibrāhīm ibn Juʿaythin.* Edited by ʿAbd al-ʿAzīz ibn Muḥammad al-Uḥaydab. Riyadh: Maṭābiʿ al-Ishāʿ, 1982.

Al-Juhaymān, ʿAbd al-Karīm. *Al-Amthāl al-shaʿbiyyah fī qalb al-jazīrah al-ʿarabiyyah.* 10 vols. Riyadh: n.p., 1982.

Kamāl, Muḥammad Saʿīd. *Al-Azhār al-nādiyah min ashʿār al-bādiyah.* 17 vols. Al-Ṭāʾif: Maktabat al-Maʿārif, 1960–81.

Kuntze, Simon. "Love and God. The Influence of Ghazal on Mystic Poetry." In *Ghazal as World Literature I: Transformations of a Literary Genre.* Edited by Thomas Bauer and Angelika Neuwirth, 157–79. Beiruter Texte und Studien 89. Beirut: Orient Institut Beirut and Ergon Verlag, 2005.

Kurpershoek, P. Marcel. "Free and/or Noble? The Hunting Falcon and Class in Arabian Nabaṭi Poetry." In *Falconry in the Mediterranean Context during the Pre-Modern Era.* Edited by Charles Burnett and Baudouin Van den Abeele. Geneva: Droz (Bibliotheca Cynegetica 9), 2018.

———. "Heartbeat: Conventionality and Originality in Najdi Poetry." *Asian Folklore Studies* 52 (1993): 33–74.

———. *Oral Poetry and Narratives from Central Arabia.* 5 vols. Leiden: E. J. Brill, 1994–2005.

———. "Praying Mantis in the Desert." *Arabian Humanities* 5 (2015). https://journals.openedition.org/cy/2962.

———. "Two Manuscripts of Bedouin Poetry in Strasbourg National and University Library and the Travels of Charles Huber in Arabia." *La Revue de la BNU (Bibliothèque Nationale Universitaire de Strasbourg)* 17 (2018): 92–103.

Kurpershoek, P. Marcel, ed. and tr.. *Arabian Satire. Poetry from 18th Century Najd.* Ḥmēdān al-Shwēʿir. New York: New York University Press, 2017.

Layish, Aharon. *Legal Documents from the Judean Desert: The Impact of the Shariʿa on Bedouin Customary Law.* Leiden: E. J. Brill, 2011.

Al-Luwayḥān, ʿAbd Allāh. *Rawāʾiʿ min al-shiʿr al-nabaṭī.* Cairo: n.d.

Al-Masridī, Masʿūd ibn Fahd. *Saʿd al-Junaydil. ʿĀliyat Najd wa-Najd al-ʿĀliyah.* Beirut: Jadawel, 2014.

———. *Suʿaydān ibn Musāʿid (Sʿēdān ibn Msāʿid), Muṭawwaʿ Nifī, ḥayātuh wa-shiʿruh.* Beirut: Jadawel, 2016.

Al-Maydānī, Abū Faḍl. *Majmaʿ al-amthāl.* 2 vols. Edited by Naʿīm Ḥusayn Zarzūr. Beirut: Dār al-Kutub al-ʿIlmiyyah, 1988.

Meisami, Julie S. "Courtly Love," in *Encyclopedia of Arabic Literature.* Vol. 1. Edited by Julie Scott Meisami and Paul Starkey, 176–77. London: Routledge, 1998.

Montgomery, J. E., "'Umar (b. 'Abd Allāh) b. Abī Rabī'a," in *Encyclopaedia of Islam*, Edited by P. Bearman, Th. Bianquis, C. E. Bosworth, E. van Donzel, and W. P. Heinrichs. 2nd ed. 2012. Online edition.

Al-Mufaḍḍal, Abū 'Abbās ibn Muḥammad aḍ-Ḍabbī. *Dīwān al-Mufaḍḍaliyyāt.* Edited by Charles James Lyall: vol. 1, Arabic text (1921); vol. 2, Translation and notes. Oxford: Clarendon Press, 1918–21.

Al-Mutanabbī, Abū l-Ṭayyib. *Dīwān Abī l-Ṭayyib al-Mutanabbī bi-sharḥ Abī l-Baqā' al-'Ukbarī.* 4 vols. 2nd ed. Cairo: Maṭba'at Muṣṭafā al-Bābī al-Ḥalabī, 1956.

Musil, Alois. *The Manners and Customs of the Rwala Bedouins.* Oriental Explorations and Studies 6. New York: American Geographical Society, 1928.

Al-Nābighah al-Dhubyānī. *Dīwān.* Edited by Karam al-Bustānī. Beirut: Dār Bayrūt, 1986.

Nöldeke, Th. "Dhurumma." *Zeitschrift für Assyriologie und verwandte Gebiete* 33 (1921): 169–97.

Schippers, Arie. "Nasīb and Ghazal in 11th and 12th Century Arabic and Hebrew Andalusian Poetry." In *Ghazal as World Literature I: Transformations of a Literary Genre.* Edited by Thomas Bauer and Angelika Neuwirth, 311–24. Beiruter Texte und Studien 89. Beirut-Würzburg: Orient Institut Beirut and Ergon Verlag, 2005.

Sowayan, Saad Abdullah. *The Arabian Oral Historical Narrative. An Ethnographic and Linguistic Analysis.* Wiesbaden: Otto Harrassowitz, 1992.

———. *Ayyām al-'arab al-awākhir: asāṭīr wa-marwiyyāt shafahiyyah fī l-ta'rīkh wa-l-adab min shamāl al-jazīrah al-'arabiyyah ma'a shadharāt mukhtārah min qabīlat Āl Murrah wa-Subay'.* Beirut: Arab Network for Research and Publishing, 2010.

———. *Fihrist al-shi'r al-nabaṭī.* Riyadh: self-published, 2001.

———. *Nabaṭī Poetry. The Oral Poetry of Arabia.* Berkeley, CA: University of California Press, 1985.

———. "A Poem and Its Narrative by Riḍa ibn Ṭārif al-Shammarī," *Zeitschrift für arabische Linguistik* 7 (1982): 48–73.

———. *Al-Ṣaḥrā' al-'arabiyyah, thaqāfatuhā wa-shi'ruhā 'abra al-'uṣūr, qirā'ah anthrūbūlūjiyyah.* Beirut: Arab Network for Research and Publishing, 2010.

———. *Al-Shi'r al-nabaṭī: dhā'iqat al-sha'b wa-sulṭat al-naṣṣ.* Beirut: Dār al-Sāqī, 2000.

Sowayan, Saad Abdullah, ed. *Al-Thaqāfah al-taqlīdiyyah fī al-mamlakah al-'arabiyyah al-su'ūdiyyah.* Riyadh: The Circle for Publishing and Documentation, 1999.

Al-Suhalī, Suwaylim al-'Alī. *Dīwān Suwaylim al-'Alī al-Suhalī.* Edited by Sa'ūd ibn Sa'd ibn Muḥammad al-Quraynī. Riyadh: n.p., 1980.

Al-Suwaydā', 'Abd al-Raḥmān ibn Zayd. *Faṣīḥ al-'āmmī fī shamāl Najd.* 2 vols. Riyadh: Dār al-Suwaydā', 1987.

Al-Tibrīzī, Abū Zakariyā Yaḥyā ibn ʿAlī. *Kitāb sharḥ al-qaṣāʾid al-ʿashr*. Edited by Charles J. Lyall. Calcutta: Asiatic Society of Bengal, 1894. Reprint, Farnborough: Gregg Press, 1965. Commentary on ten ancient Arabic poems.

Trench, Richard, ed. *Gazetteer of Arabian Tribes*. Farnham Common, UK: Archive Editions, 1996.

Al-ʿUbayyid, Muḥammad al-ʿAlī. *Al-Najm al-lāmiʿ li-l-nawādir jāmiʿ*. MS on the website of Dr. Saad Sowayan.

Al-ʿUbūdī, Muḥammad ibn Nāṣir. *Al-Amthāl al-ʿāmmiyyah fī Najd*. 5 vols. Riyadh: n.p., 1979.

———. *Muʿjam alfāẓ al-maraḍ wa-l-ṣiḥḥah fī al-mawrūth al-shaʿbī*. Riyadh: Dār al-Thalūthiyyah, 2015.

———. *Muʿjam al-anwāʾ wa-l-fuṣūl*. Riyadh: n.p., 2011.

———. *Muʿjam al-azwāj fī al-turāth*. Riyadh: Dār al-Thalūthiyyah, 2017.

———. *Muʿjam al-ḥayawān ʿind al-ʿāmmah*. 2 vols. Riyadh: Maktabat al-Malik Fahd al-Waṭaniyyah, 2011.

——— . *Muʿjam al-kalimāt al-dakhīlah fī lughatinā al-dārijah*, 2 vols. Riyadh: Maktabat al-Malik ʿAbd Al-ʿAzīz al-ʿĀmmah, 2005.

———. *Muʿjam al-malābis fī al-maʾthūr al-shaʿbī fī al-manṭiqat al-wusṭāʾ min al-Mamlakah al-ʿArabiyyah al-Suʿūdiyyah*. Riyadh: Dār al-Thalūthiyyah, 2013.

———. *Muʿjam al-tijārah wa-l-māl wa-l-faqr wa-l-ghinā*. Riyadh: Dār al-Thalūthiyyah, 2012.

———. *Muʿjam al-uṣūl al-faṣīḥah li-l-alfāẓ al-dārijah*. 13 vols. Riyadh: n.p. 2008.

Al-ʿUmarī, Muḥammad al-Ḥamad. *Dīwān Suʿaydān ibn Musāʿid Muṭawwaʿ Nifī*. MS owned by King Saud University in Riyadh. Its index lists twenty-six poems, mostly short pieces, and the longest of which counts thirteen verses.

Wallin, Georg August. *Travels in Arabia*. Cambridge, New York: The Oleander Press, 1979.

Webster, Roger. "Notes on the Dialect and the Way of Life of the Āl Wahība Bedouin of Oman." *Bulletin of the School of Oriental and African Studies* 54, no. 3,(1991): 473–85.

Yāqūt al-Ḥamawī, Shihāb al-Dīn Abī ʿAbd Allāh. *Muʿjam al-buldān*. 5 vols. Beirut: Dār Ṣādir, 1984.

Al-Zawzanī, Abū ʿAbd Allāh al-Ḥusayn ibn Aḥmad ibn al-Ḥusayn. *Sharḥ al-muʿallaqāt al-sabʿ*. Beirut: Dār Bayrūt, 1982.

Al-Ziriklī, Khayr al-Dīn. *Shibh al-jazīrat fī ʿahd al-malik ʿAbd al-ʿAzīz*. 2 vols. 3rd ed. Beirut: Dār al-ʿIlm li-l-Malāyin, 1985.

Zuhayr ibn Abī Sulmā. *Sharḥ dīwān Zuhayr ibn Abī Sulmā*. Edited by al-ʿAbbās Aḥmad ibn Yaḥyā ibn Zayd al-Shaybānī Thaʿlab. Cairo: Dār al-Qawmiyyah, 1964.

Index of Poems, Editions, and Manuscripts Used for this Edition

This edition is based on published collections and manuscripts, specifically the ones listed below. The poems have been ordered by rhyme according to the position of the rhyming consonant in the Arabic alphabet, as is customary in editions of classical Arabic poetry. Unless otherwise indicated, the meter of the poems is a variant of the classical Arabic *ṭawīl* meter called *mashūb* in Nabaṭī poetry.

The shorthand references in bold at the start of each source listed below indicate where a particular poem can be found. These references are followed by page numbers and the relevant number of verses of the poem in that edition or manuscript. The versions in a published edition are listed first, followed by the manuscript versions on a separate line.

As for Ibn Sbayyil's poetic exchanges with other poets, these have been divided into three separate categories: his jocular exchanges with his neighbor, Muṭawwaʿ Nifī; invective verse exchanged with other poets; and verses in which he is addressed. When Ibn Sbayyil's poem is a response to another poet as part of a poetic correspondence, the verses of the other poet come first, followed by Ibn Sbayyil's reply in which he elaborates on points made by the poet who addressed his verses to him. Putting Ibn Sbayyil's poem first would have made some of these points less easy to understand.

Sources of the exchanges with Muṭawwaʿ Nifī and the invective pieces are given in notes to these pieces and not in this Index.

Printed Editions

FK refers to Khālid al-Faraj's *Dīwān al-Nabaṭ, majmūʿah min al-shiʿr al-ʿāmmī fī Najd*, vol. 1, published in Damascus in 1952.

IS refers to the second edition of the dīwān collected by the poet's grandson, a poet and expert in Nabaṭī poetry in his own right, Muḥammad ibn ʿAbd al-ʿAzīz ibn Sbayyil, *Dīwān Ibn Sbayyil, shiʿr al-shāʿir al-mashhūr*

ʿAbd Allāh ibn Ḥmūd ibn Sbayyil, published in Riyadh in 2004. The first edition was published in 1988.

Manuscripts

The best available description of manuscripts containing Nabaṭī poetry, and the challenges they pose to researchers, is the chapter on this subject in Sowayan, *al-Shiʿr al-nabaṭī*, 196–206.

The Manṣūr al-Ḥusayn al-ʿAssāf [**Assaf**] manuscript can be found on the website www.saadsowayan.com.

The al-Dāwud [**Dawud**] manuscript is also on the Sowayan website.

The ʿAbd al-Raḥmān Ibrāhīm al-Rābīʿī manuscript [**Rabii**] is on the Sowayan website. I also received a printed copy from Muḥammad al-Ḥamdān, who published an annotated edition of Ḥmēdān al-Shwēʿir's diwan and is the learned proprietor of the Qays Library in Riyadh. In ʿUnayzah I copied some of al-Rābīʿī's collection of notebooks in the Ibn Ṣāliḥ Library.

The Sulaymān al-Sikkīt manuscript [**Sikkit**] is also on the Sowayan website. On the first page it states that he was a man of religion, shaykh, and *muṭawwaʿ* from the town of al-Bukayriyyah in al-Qaṣīm province.

The voluminous Muḥammad ibn ʿAbd al-Raḥmān ibn Yaḥyā manuscript [**Yahya**] is on the Sowayan website; a copy, including the section on Ibn Sbayyil, was given to me by the writer and book collector Muḥammad al-Ḥamdān.

يالله ياكاشف عن ايّوب ما بِه   من الضرّ يا قابل مِطاليب يَعقوب

Poem 1, p. 2
KF 208, 10 vv.; IS, 152, 10 vv.
Rabii 132, 11 vv.; Yahya 661, 9 vv.

وِشّ خانة المِقْطان لو قيل ما احلاه   صَيّور ما جا بالليالي غَدَتْ بِه

Poem 2, p. 4
KF 205, 22 vv; IS 157, 22 vv.
Dawud 176, 11 vv.; Rabii 127, 22 vv.; Yahya 639, 24 vv.

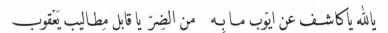

يا عَين وَين احبابك اللي تودّين   اللي الى جَوا منزلٍ ربّعوا به

Poem 3, p. 8
KF 188, 23 vv.; IS 60, 23 vv.
Dawud 170, 23 vv.; Rabii 115, 26 vv.; Yahya 666, 29 vv.

يا زَيد اشوفِك عِقْب الاقبال صَدَّيت   بعينك وقلبك ما اذْري وَيش غَيبه

Poem 4, p. 12
IS p. 163, 16 vv.
Rabii 150, 16 vv.

قِم يا نديبي قَرِّبها   حَمْرا بِيضٍ مَحاقِبها

Poem 5, p. 14
Meter: long syllables.
IS 178, 54 vv.
Rabii 147, 62 vv.; Yahya 661, 62 vv.

لا تَمْحَنون القَلْب يا عاذلينه   الامر لله والحَكي ما يِشيب

Poem 6, p. 22
KF 204, 14 vv.; IS 74, 14 vv.
Rabii 126, 14 vv.; Yahya 649, 14 vv.

البارحه وَنّيت ونّة يتيمِ   ما له جِدا كود البكا والتَّنهّات

Poem 7, p. 24
Rabii 131, 22 vv.; Sikkit 156, 22 vv.; Yahya 646, 24 vv.

يا صاحبي دونِك عَدُوٍّ الى جِيت   يَلْبَس عَليّ الجِلْد لِبْسِه عَباتِه

Poem 8, p. 28
KF 190, 18 vv.; IS 137, 18 vv.
Rabii 117, 18 vv.; Yahya 664, 20 vv.

يا لله يا اللي تَسْجِد الخلق لرْضاه   يا وامِرٍ عَبده على حَجّ بيتِه

Poem 9, p. 32

KF 181, 18 vv.; IS 86, 18 vv.

Dawud 178, 10 vv.; Rabii 111, 19 vv.; Yahya, 656, 19 vv.

يالله يا اللي ما لغَيرِك تَرَجَّيت   يا واحدٍ ما غيره احْدٍ رِجَيتِه

Poem 10, p. 36

IS 161, 13 vv.

Dawud ms p. 173 14 vv.; Rabii ms p. 142 17 vv.; Yahya 657, 14 vv.

اجَل عَنْك ما الدِنيا بتُوخَذ بحِيلاتِ   وانا شاطِرٍ باحْوال نَفْسي وحالاتِ

Poem 11, p. 40

IS 35, 13 vv.

Rabii ms p. 144 18 vv.; Yahya 644, 13 vv.

يا لله تَجْعَل كِل دَرْبي سِماحِ   بِهْداك تامِرني على اللي به اصلاح

Poem 12, p. 44

KF 197, 15 vv.; IS 111, 15 vv.

Dawud 171, 15 vv.; Rabii 121, 16 vv.; Yahya 654, 15 vv.

ما لَومِ يا نفسٍ عن الزاد مِعْطاه   والماي ما يِبْرِد لَهَبها بروده

Poem 13, p. 46

KF 167, 37 vv.; IS 144, 37 vv.

Assaf 168, 32 vv.; Dawud 169, 33 vv.; Rabii 102, 40 vv.; Yahya 665, 41 vv.

يا راكبٍ من عنْدنا صَيعريات   من ساس عَيراتٍ عرابٍ تلادِ

Poem 14, p. 54, in reply to a poem by Ibn Zirībān.

KF 173, 55 vv.; IS 117, 56 vv.

Assaf ms p. 166 54 vv.; Dawud 167, 43 vv.; Rabii 106, 59 vv.; Yahya 670, 60 vv.

تَرى حَلات الكَيف يا مِشْرِبٍ لِه   لا فارِقوك اهل الحَسَد والِنجاسِه

Poem 15, p. 62
IS p. 33 9 vv.
Rabii 143, 12 vv.; Yahya 667, 11 vv.

تَرى المِطَر باوّل سَحابه رِشاشٍ   وتاليه وِدْيانٍ يِشيلنّ الادباش

Poem 16, p. 64, in reply to verses by Ibn Zirībān.
IS 31, 11 vv.
Yahya 673, 4 vv.

يا راكبٍ من فوق سَلْسات الاقران   ما قَرَّبوهِن للسرا والمَغابيش

Poem 17, p. 68, in reply to verses by Masʿūd Āl Masʿūd from al-Shaʿrāʾ.
IS p. 53, 13 vv.

الله لَحَد يا تَلّ قَلْبي من اقْصاه   تَلّ القِطيع اللي شَعَوه الطِماميع

Poem 18, p. 72
IS 90, 19 vv.
Rabii 130, 19 vv.; Yahya 654, 20 vv.

حَلّ الفراق وحَنّ رايم لمَرْيوم   وقَوَى الفراق اللي كبارٍ دفوفِه

Poem 19, p. 76
KF 194, 20 vv.; IS 107, 20 vv.
Dawud 178, 9 vv.; Rabii 119, 21 vv.; Yahya 640, 20 vv.

الله من عينٍ تهِلّه عَبارِ   يِشْبِه هَماليل السَحاب اندِفاقِه

Poem 20, p. 80
KF 212, 10 vv.; IS 150, 10 vv.
Dawud ms p. 174 8 vv.; Rabii 138, 15 vv.; Yahya 656, 12 vv.

يا العَبْد قَيِّس ما طَرا لِك على البال   دِنْياك لا تِلهيك عن تَبْع دِينِك

Poem 21, p. 82
KF 214, 24 vv.; IS 166, 24 vv.
Rabii 145, 24 vv.; Yahya 645, 25 vv.

يا تَلّ قَلْبي تَلّ رَكْبٍ لشِمْشول   رَبْعٍ مِشاكِيلٍ على كِنَّسٍ حِيل

Poem 22, p. 86
KF 198, 24 vv.; IS 132, 24 vv.
Dawud 172, 13 vv.; Rabii 122, 29 vv.; Yahya 641, 24 vv.

بِدَيت بذِكْر الله على كِلّ ما طَرا   مجيب الدّعا مِعْطى العَطايا الجِزايل

Poem 23, p. 90
KF 215, 51 vv.
Assaf 180, 53 vv.; Rabii, 133, 55 vv.; Yahya 637, 54 vv.

يا ذعار انا قَلْبي من العام حَوِله   لليوم يَنْقِص ما بِقى الّا قِليِله

Poem 24, p. 98
KF 178, 25 vv.; IS 80, 25 vv.
Assaf 167, 24 vv.; Dawud 175, 8 vv.; Rabii 110, 25 vv.; Yahya 647, 27 vv.

قال مِن غَنّى وغَرْهَد على رُوس العدام   واوْنَس البارد بكَبْده عِقِب لَفْح السموم

Poem 25, p. 102
Meter: *madīd*. In Najd the tune is called *ʿarḍah*, which is used for sword dances and warlike chants, Sowayan, *al-Shiʿr al-nabaṭī*, 167, 175.
IS 27, 9 vv.

يا مِن لقَلْبٍ طار عنه اليِقينِ   من يوم قَفَّنّ الظَعاين زَهازيم

Poem 26, p. 104
KF 202, 17 vv.; IS 154, 16 vv.
Rabii ms 125, 17 vv.; Yahya 655, 18 vv.

يا راكبٍ عَشْرٍ من الهاربات   ما وَقّفوهِن بالمِبايع للاثمان

Poem 27, p. 112, in reply to a poem by Ibn Zirībān.
KF 170, 39 vv.; IS 42, 39 vv.
Rabii 104, 40 vv.; Yahya 651, 41 vv.

اسباب ما فاجَى الحَشا وابْتِلاني   غِرْوٍ طَغى بالغَيّ طَلْقٍ لسانِه

Poem 28, p. 118
IS 65, 21 vv.
Dawud 172, 26 vv.; Rabii ms p. 140 16 vv.; Yahya 659, 25 vv.

يا جرّ قَلْبي جَرّة القَوس حانِيه   ظَرْفٍ مِطاوِعْتِه يِدِه بِلْعَبانِه

Poem 29, p. 122
KF 192, 27 vv.; IS 69, 27 vv.
Dawud 175, 16 vv.; Rabii 118, 28 vv.; Yahya 649, 29 vv.

سِنْعوس وِش عِلمِك بِمَشْيِك تَرَدَّيت   ما ذا بعِنْدِك يومِ انا اقول بالهُون

Poem 30, p. 126

يا طالبين الغَيّ خَلّوه خَلّوه   خَلّوه يومِ انّه سِجٍ لا تِبُونِه

Poem 31, p. 128
IS 193, 6 vv.
Dawud 174, 6 vv.; Rabii 143, 6 vv.

اللهلا يِسْقي لِيالٍ شِفاشيف   ايامِ راعى السَمِن يِخْلِص ديونِه

Poem 32, p. 130
KF 184, 23 vv.; IS 102, 23 vv.
Rabii 113, 23 vv.; Yahya 660, 23 vv.

يا تَلّ قَلْبي تَلّ رَكْبٍ لِشِرْشوح   ذَودٍ عَلى تالى الدِبَش خاطفينه

Poem 33, p. 134
KF 213, 16 vv.; IS 99, 16 vv.
Dawud 171, 12 vv.; Rabii 139, 18 vv.; Yahya 648, 17 vv.

يا تَلّ قَلْبي تَلّ رَكْبٍ لسَرّاق   مع دَعاجينٍ سَروا حايفينه

Poem 34, p. 138
Rabii 141, 11 vv.; Yahya 658, 8 vv.

يا عيني اللي بالهَوى عَذِّبَتْني   تبَكي واشُوف الدَمْع حَرّق وجَنها

Poem 35, p. 140
KF 196, 11 vv.; IS 50, 11 vv.
Dawud 174 8 vv.; Rabii 120, 13 vv.; Sikkit 154, 13 vv.; Yahya 659, 12 vv.

يا الله يا عالِمٍ خَفِيات الاسرار   يا عالِمٍ ما يَطْرِق المُودِمانِ

Poem 36, p. 142
KF 200, 29 vv.; IS 93, 29 vv.
Assaf 168, 19 vv.; 187 29 vv.; Dawud 176, 14 vv.; Rabii 124, 29 vv.; Sikkit 155, 29 vv.; Yahya 640, 27 vv.

عَدَّيْت مِرْقابٍ براسه رجومِ   مِرْقاب طَلّاب الهَوى يوم عَدّاه

Poem 37, p. 146
KF 210, 19 vv.; IS 128, 19 vv.
Dawud 176, 14 vv.; Rabii 137, 19 vv.; Yahya 658, 17 vv.

هنيّ من قَلْبِه دِلوهٍ ومَمْنوح   حاله كما حال البَغَل من غْذاها

Poem 38, p. 150
KF 209, 16 vv.; IS 77, 16 vv.
Rabii 136, 17 vv.; Yahya 653, 17 vv.

يا وَنّتي وَنّـة طِـعـين الشِـطـيرِه   في ساعـةٍ يُوخَـذ طِمَعها عْشـاوِه

Poem 39, p. 154
KF 182, 18 vv.; IS 56, 18 vv.
Rabii 112, 18 vv.; Yahya 643, 19 vv.

يوم الرِكايب عَـقّبَن خشْـم ابانات   ذِكَرْت مَـلْهوف الحَشا من عَـنايَـه

Poem 40, p. 158
KF 186, 19 vv.; IS 171, 19 vv.
Dawud 177, 11 vv.; Rabii 114, 19 vv.; Yahya 642, 17 vv.

ياهَنّ مِمّا ينْعِش الروح شِفْ ـيلي   ما دِمْت انا مـاجود والنَفْس حَيّه

Poem 41, p. 162
KF 207, 16 vv.; IS 141, 16 vv.
Dawud 178, 12 vv.; Rabii 128, 16 vv.; Yahya 651, 17 vv.

Index

Majnūn Laylā, xlvi n59, 195n71, 246n441
market, xi, xiii, xviii, §18.5, §24.1, §24.25, §27.1.25, 187n22, 191n46, 216n224, 225n287; marriage market, 245n436
al-Marrār ibn Munqidh, xliii n33, 195n71, 199n89, 207n143, 211n174, 231n341
marriage, xii, xv, xxxviii n4, xxxix n14, xl n22, xliv n35, xlv n42, xlv n48, §9.10, §23.30, §27.2.20, §§35.5–10, §39.5, §42.2.1, 202n108, 229n326, 245n436, 249n463; divorce, xliv n35, §23.30, 229n326; husband, xlv n42, §27.2.20, 221n263, 229n326; wife, xliv n35, xlv n42, §42.7.1, 186n16, 203n108, 206n134, 236n379, 250n474, 250n475, 251n485. *See also* family
maxims. *See* proverbs
measure, xix, xxvii, §23.10, §26.5, §37.15, 197n82, 218n239, 234n368
meat, xxiv, §3.10, §5.20, §5.30, §7.10, §8.15, §14.2.15, §19.15, §23.45, §29.15, 201n102, 256n513
Mecca, xlvii n62, §14.1.10, §18.15, §22.30, §23.5, §27.1.25, 189n39, 208n156, 209n157, 214n203, 216n224, 250n472, 251n482
medicine. *See* cure
memorize, xli n26, li n85
memory, xxiii–xxiv, xxxiv, §5.50, §8.1, §8.10, §26.1, §40.5, 196n80. *See also* forgetting
men, xi, xiii, xix, xxxi, xxxiv, xliii n35, xlvii n62, §3.20, §4.5, §5.5, §5.10, §5.45, §5.55, §11.15, §§13.15–20, §14.2.30, §14.2.50, §16.2.1, §17.2.5, §18.15, §22.1, §22.10, §22.15, §23.15, §24.5, §24.15, §24.25, §23.1, §25.5, §26.15, §27.1.5, §27.2.20, §27.2.35, §29.25, §32.10, §38.10, §§42.1.1–5, §§42.6.1–5, §42.6.5, §43.2.1,
men(cont.), §43.2.5, §45.2.1, 194n64, 206n134, 213n201, 220n249, 220n251, 227n312, 229n326, 231n249, 240n405, 252n490; male, masculine, xv, §45.2.5, 184n9, 192n52, 195n72, 215n213, 255n509
mercy, xvii, xxii–xxiii, xlvii n62, §6.5, §27.1.25, 183n1, 195n75, 230n339, 243n418, 244n427; merciless, §6.5, 253n504
message. *See* communication
messenger. *See* communication
meter, xii, xxx, xlvi n54, l n79, 193n59, 239n397, 253n497, 254n506, 276; *hazaj*, 253n497, 254n506; long meter (*ṭawīl*), l n79, 276
al-Midhnab, xii, xv, xxxiii
al-Mijmāj, Fhēd ibn ʿWēwīd, xiv–xv, xxxvii n1, xl n20, xl n22, xlii n31, 184n11, 185n12, 185n13, 189n38, 201n104, 212n186, 212n192, 218n245, 226n294, 229n328, 234n367, 236n378, 236n379
milk, §§3.10–15, §5.20, §5.30, §§5.40–50, §7.15, §8.5, §13.10, §22.30, §23.45, §24.20, §26.10, §32.5, 190n41, 193n60, 207n135, 210n169, 211n174, 212n191, 216n225, 226n296, 234n365, 234n369; camel milk, §3.15, §7.15, §22.30, §23.45, §26.10, 190n41, 207n135, 210n169, 211n174, 212n191, 226n296; cow milk, 216n225; goat and sheep milk, §5.20, §5.30, §§5.40–50, §13.10, 193n60, 234n365; milk skins, §24.20, §32.5, 234n369
miser, §§11.10–15, §29.20. *See also* hospitality

pre-Islamic, xxvii, xlvi n61, 183n6, 185n14, 190n41, 191n47, 204n123, 210n174, 216n221, 227n307, 237n388, 240n404, 242n411, 253n499. *See also* Islam

pride, xvii, xxii, xxiv, xxv, §34.5, 198n89, 215n218

prophet: Muḥammad, §18.20, §23.55, §27.1.25, §28.25, §41.5, 184n9, 201n101, 247n448; other prophets, 183n4, 183n5

protection, xxi, xxii, §3.15, §5.55, §14.2.25, §17.2.5, §22.30, §27.2.1, §27.2.20, §46.2.1, 193n60, 200n95, 206n132, 212n191, 228n322, 236n379. *See also* protection money

protection money, xxvi, §46.1.1, 193n60, 250n472, 255n510; tithe, 228n317; tribute, §26.15, 250n472

proverbs and sayings, xxiv–xxv, xxviii–xxx, xxxii, xxxviii n3, xlvi n56, xl n19, xlv n48, xlviii n67, xlviii n68, xlviii n69, §6.10, §8.1, §9.15, §12.10, §13.5, §13.30, §13.35, §14.2.30, §14.2.55, §19.1, §20.5, §24.15, §27.2.30, §29.10, §29.15, §29.20, §32.20, §33.10, §36.10, §38.1, §38.5, §§39.10–15, §40.15, 183n1, 184n9, 186n17, 187n20, 187n25, 188n31, 190n43, 194n71, 195n76, 196n78, 197n81, 198n87, 200n95, 200n96, 200n98, 202n106, 202n108, 203n110, 203n111, 205n128, 206n132, 206n133, 207n140, 207n143, 207n144, 210n172, 211n176, 211n183, 211n185, 213n194, 213n196, 213n198, 213n199, 213n200, 213n202, 217n228, 217n229, 217n233, 217n234, 217n237, 218n240, 220n253, 223n281, 223n282, 224n283, 230n333, 230n336, 231n342, 231n345,

proverbs and sayings (cont.), 231n347, 231n349, 232n350, 232n351, 232n353, 232n354, 232n355, 232n356, 235n370, 235n372, 235n373, 235n374, 236n376, 236n389, 237n385, 237n387, 237n388, 237n389, 237n390, 240n404, 241n408, 243n419, 243n420, 244n421, 244n429, 244n430, 244n432, 247n442, 247n443, 247n444, 247n449, 247n450, 249n460, 249n463, 249n466, 251n477. *See also* wisdom

pulley wheel. *See* well

qasida, xiv, xxxi, 204n123, 245n434

al-Qāḍī (al-Gāḍī), Muḥammad al-ʿAbdallah, xli n24, xlvi n59, 183n5, 245n435

al-Qaṣīm, xii, xiv, xx, xxxviii n8, §7.5, §23.15, 220n255, 225n290, 225n292, 241n408

Qurʾan, xx–xxi, xxiv, xxxiv, li n86, §10.1, §27.1.1, §28.15, §28.25, 183n1, 183n4, 184n7, 195n73

rabies, §12.10, 205n128

al-Rabīʿī, ʿAbd al-Raḥmān Ibrāhīm, xxxiv, l n82, 208n148, 227n301, 238n396, 252n486, 252n492, 277

raid, xii, xxxvii n1, xxxviii n8, xli n25, §3.15, §§5.15–30, §23.30, §24.20, §32.20, §42.1.5, §42.2.1, 190n41, 191n49, 191n50, 192n51, 215n218, 218n242, 219n246, 220n257, 223n279, 224n286, 232n357, 236n381, 236n383, 238n396, 242n417, 244n426, 248n460, 251n482, 253n504. *See also* battle, war

rain, xi, xviii, xlix n75, §1.5, §3.5, §14.2.5, §16.2.1, §17.2.5, §20.1, §23.45, §23.55, §27.1.25, §32.1, §32.10, §32.20, §34.5,

About the NYU Abu Dhabi Institute

The Library of Arabic Literature is supported by a grant from the NYU Abu Dhabi Institute, a major hub of intellectual and creative activity and advanced research. The Institute hosts academic conferences, workshops, lectures, film series, performances, and other public programs directed both to audiences within the UAE and to the worldwide academic and research community. It is a center of the scholarly community for Abu Dhabi, bringing together faculty and researchers from institutions of higher learning throughout the region.

NYU Abu Dhabi, through the NYU Abu Dhabi Institute, is a world-class center of cutting-edge research, scholarship, and cultural activity. The Institute creates singular opportunities for leading researchers from across the arts, humanities, social sciences, sciences, engineering, and the professions to carry out creative scholarship and conduct research on issues of major disciplinary, multidisciplinary, and global significance.

About the Typefaces

The Arabic body text is set in DecoType Naskh, designed by Thomas Milo and Mirjam Somers, based on an analysis of five centuries of Ottoman manuscript practice. The exceptionally legible result is the first and only typeface in a style that fully implements the principles of script grammar (*qawāʿid al-khaṭṭ*).

The Arabic footnote text is set in DecoType Emiri, drawn by Mirjam Somers, based on the metal typeface in the naskh style that was cut for the 1924 Cairo edition of the Qur'an.

Both Arabic typefaces in this series are controlled by a dedicated font layout engine. ACE, the Arabic Calligraphic Engine, invented by Peter Somers, Thomas Milo, and Mirjam Somers of DecoType, first operational in 1985, pioneered the principle followed by later smart font layout technologies such as OpenType, which is used for all other typefaces in this series.

The Arabic text was set with WinSoft Tasmeem, a sophisticated user interface for DecoType ACE inside Adobe InDesign. Tasmeem was conceived and created by Thomas Milo (DecoType) and Pascal Rubini (WinSoft) in 2005.

The English text is set in Adobe Text, a new and versatile text typeface family designed by Robert Slimbach for Western (Latin, Greek, Cyrillic) typesetting. Its workhorse qualities make it perfect for a wide variety of applications, especially for longer passages of text where legibility and economy are important. Adobe Text bridges the gap between calligraphic Renaissance types of the 15th and 16th centuries and high-contrast Modern styles of the 18th century, taking many of its design cues from early post-Renaissance Baroque transitional types cut by designers such as Christoffel van Dijck, Nicolaus Kis, and William Caslon. While grounded in classical form, Adobe Text is also a statement of contemporary utilitarian design, well suited to a wide variety of print and on-screen applications.

Titles Published by the Library of Arabic Literature

For more details on individual titles, visit www.libraryofarabicliterature.org

Classical Arabic Literature: A Library of Arabic Literature Anthology
Selected and translated by Geert Jan van Gelder (2012)

A Treasury of Virtues: Sayings, Sermons, and Teachings of ʿAlī, by al-Qāḍī al-Quḍāʿī, with the **One Hundred Proverbs** attributed to al-Jāḥiẓ
Edited and translated by Tahera Qutbuddin (2013)

The Epistle on Legal Theory, by al-Shāfiʿī
Edited and translated by Joseph E. Lowry (2013)

Leg over Leg, by Aḥmad Fāris al-Shidyāq
Edited and translated by Humphrey Davies (**4 volumes; 2013–14**)

Virtues of the Imām Aḥmad ibn Ḥanbal, by Ibn al-Jawzī
Edited and translated by Michael Cooperson (**2 volumes; 2013–15**)

The Epistle of Forgiveness, by Abū l-ʿAlāʾ al-Maʿarrī
Edited and translated by Geert Jan van Gelder and Gregor Schoeler (**2 volumes; 2013–14**)

The Principles of Sufism, by ʿĀʾishah al-Bāʿūniyyah
Edited and translated by Th. Emil Homerin (2014)

The Expeditions: An Early Biography of Muḥammad, by Maʿmar ibn Rāshid
Edited and translated by Sean W. Anthony (2014)

Two Arabic Travel Books

Accounts of China and India, by Abū Zayd al-Sīrāfī
Edited and translated by Tim Mackintosh-Smith (2014)

Mission to the Volga, by Aḥmad ibn Faḍlān
Edited and translated by James Montgomery (2014)

Disagreements of the Jurists: A Manual of Islamic Legal Theory, by al-Qāḍī al-Nuʿmān
Edited and translated by Devin J. Stewart (2015)

Consorts of the Caliphs: Women and the Court of Baghdad, by Ibn al-Sāʿī
Edited by Shawkat M. Toorawa and translated by the Editors of the Library of Arabic Literature (2015)

What ʿĪsā ibn Hishām Told Us, by Muḥammad al-Muwayliḥī
Edited and translated by Roger Allen (**2 volumes; 2015**)

The Life and Times of Abū Tammām, by Abū Bakr Muḥammad ibn Yaḥyā al-Ṣūlī
Edited and translated by Beatrice Gruendler (2015)

The Sword of Ambition: Bureaucratic Rivalry in Medieval Egypt, by ʿUthmān ibn Ibrāhīm al-Nābulusī
Edited and translated by Luke Yarbrough (2016)

Brains Confounded by the Ode of Abū Shādūf Expounded, by Yūsuf al-Shirbīnī
Edited and translated by Humphrey Davies (**2 volumes; 2016**)

Light in the Heavens: Sayings of the Prophet Muḥammad, by al-Qāḍī al-Quḍāʿī
Edited and translated by Tahera Qutbuddin (2016)

Risible Rhymes, by Muḥammad ibn Maḥfūẓ al-Sanhūrī
Edited and translated by Humphrey Davies (2016)

A Hundred and One Nights
Edited and translated by Bruce Fudge (2016)

The Excellence of the Arabs, by Ibn Qutaybah
Edited by James E. Montgomery and Peter Webb
Translated by Sarah Bowen Savant and Peter Webb (2017)

Scents and Flavors: A Syrian Cookbook
Edited and translated by Charles Perry (2017)

Arabian Satire: Poetry from 18th-Century Najd, by Ḥmēdān al-Shwēʿir
Edited and translated by Marcel Kurpershoek (2017)

In Darfur: An Account of the Sultanate and Its People, by Muḥammad ibn ʿUmar al-Tūnisī
Edited and translated by Humphrey Davies **(2 volumes; 2018)**

War Songs, by ʿAntarah ibn Shaddād
Edited by James E. Montgomery
Translated by James E. Montgomery with Richard Sieburth **(2018)**

Arabian Romantic: Poems on Bedouin Life and Love, by ʿAbdallah ibn Sbayyil
Edited and translated by Marcel Kurpershoek **(2018)**

Dīwān ʿAntarah ibn Shaddād: A Literary-Historical Study
By James E. Montgomery **(2018)**

English-only Paperbacks

Leg over Leg, by Aḥmad Fāris al-Shidyāq **(2 volumes; 2015)**
The Expeditions: An Early Biography of Muḥammad, by Maʿmar ibn Rāshid **(2015)**
The Epistle on Legal Theory: A Translation of al-Shāfiʿī's *Risālah*, by al-Shāfiʿī **(2015)**
The Epistle of Forgiveness, by Abū l-ʿAlāʾ al-Maʿarrī **(2016)**
The Principles of Sufism, by ʿĀʾishah al-Bāʿūniyyah **(2016)**
A Treasury of Virtues: Sayings, Sermons, and Teachings of ʿAlī, by al-Qāḍī al-Quḍāʿī with the **One Hundred Proverbs**, attributed to al-Jāḥiẓ **(2016)**
The Life of Ibn Ḥanbal, by Ibn al-Jawzī **(2016)**
Mission to the Volga, by Ibn Faḍlān **(2017)**
Accounts of China and India, by Abū Zayd al-Sīrāfī **(2017)**
A Hundred and One Nights (2017)
Disagreements of the Jurists: A Manual of Islamic Legal Theory, by al-Qāḍī al-Nuʿmān **(2017)**
What ʿĪsā ibn Hishām Told Us, by Muḥammad al-Muwayliḥī **(2018)**
War Songs, by ʿAntarah ibn Shaddād **(2018)**
The Life and Times of Abū Tammām, by Abū Bakr Muḥammad ibn Yaḥyā al-Ṣūlī **(2018)**

About the Editor–Translator

Marcel Kurpershoek is a senior research fellow at New York University Abu Dhabi and a specialist in the oral traditions and poetry of Arabia. He obtained his PhD in modern Arabic literature at the University of Leiden. He has written a number of books on historical, cultural, and contemporary topics in the Middle East, including the five-volume *Oral Poetry and Narratives from Central Arabia* (1994–2005), which draws on his recordings of Bedouin tribes. In 2016, Al Arabiya television broadcast an eight-part documentary series based on the travelogue of fieldwork he had undertaken in the Nafūd desert of northern Arabia for his book *Arabia of the Bedouins* (in Arabic translation *The Last Bedouin*). In 2018, Al Arabiya broadcast his five-part documentary on Najdī poetry, including one episode on Ḥmēdān al-Shwēʿir, based on the Library of Arabic Literature's edition of his work in *Arabian Satire*. He spent his career as a diplomat for the Netherlands, having served as ambassador to Pakistan, Afghanistan, Turkey, Poland, and special envoy for Syria until 2015. From 1996 to 2002, he held a chair as professor of literature and politics in the Arab world at the University of Leiden.